Writing and Vulnerability in the Late Renaissance

Writing and Vulnerability in the Late Renaissance

Jane Tylus

Stanford University Press, Stanford, California, 1993

Stanford University Press
Stanford, California

Printed in the United States of America

CIP data are at the end of the book

To my parents

Acknowledgments

This book is the product of many conversations over the past few years, and it is a pleasure and privilege to bring to mind those exchanges here. For their ongoing encouragement and advice from start to finish, I want to thank William Klein, Laura Levine, and Helen Tartar. Karen-edis Barzman, Catherine Connor (Swietlicki), Elyse Crystall, Jonathan Crewe, Frances Dolan, Jonathan Goldberg, Theresa Krier, Ullrich Langer, Fannie LeMoine, Joseph Loewenstein, Mary Quinlan-McGrath, Marjorie Rhine, Mary Beth Rose, Pauline Scott, Steven Suppan, Peter Wiggins, Mary Ann Frese Witt, Ronald Witt, and the readers for Stanford University Press provided often invaluable suggestions regarding individual chapters. I am also indebted to the University of Wisconsin Graduate School, the Institute for Research in the Humanities, and the Newberry Library / National Endowment for the Humanities for funding various stages of this project. There was something ironic about completing a study on the threatening shade of early modern institutions while in residence at the Newberry Library. I cannot imagine a more congenial and supportive environment in which to work and write. I am profoundly grateful for the Newberry's generosity and for the community I encountered there, particularly Fran Dolan, Peggy McCracken, Julie Solomon, and Eli Zaretsky.

I have also been fortunate to have had rigorous and supportive mentors over the years. At the College of William and Mary, Peter

Wiggins first introduced me to the English and Italian Renaissances. Little did he know that his willingness to take on my senior honors thesis on Spenser would launch a long-term academic relationship that, as Alison Lurie has commented, is the only thing on earth not subject to the law of entropy. At Johns Hopkins, Stephen Orgel and Nancy Struever were both inspiring pedagogues and intellectual models, and I continue to learn from their work and their example. In the midst of their busy and productive lives, they have been more generous with their time and suggestions than any ex-student has the right to expect. My indebtedness extends to colleagues past and present who have provided unfailing moral support, particularly Clare Cavanagh, Catherine Connor, Mary Layoun, Leah Marcus, and John Tedeschi, and to my own graduate and undergraduate students at the University of Wisconsin. Without their comments, their inquiries, and—especially during the later stages of the preparation of this manuscript—their understanding, this book simply would not exist. In almost every case, my readings of Renaissance texts have emerged in the classroom and from my students' willingness to share with me their refreshing and often brilliant insights. I am also most grateful to Lynn Stewart, Associate Editor at Stanford University Press for the patience and care with which she guided this book through publication.

Finally, I want to thank my parents, Joseph and Doris Tylus, to whose generosity, inspiration, and humor this book is dedicated; my father-in-law, Ned Klein, for the timely gift of an IBM computer; my son Alex, whose wonderful vulnerabilities have been a source of much joy as I've finished writing; and especially Bill, who sacrificed countless hours so that this book could come into being. His intellect and unstinting criticism are manifest on every page. In many ways, this book is as much his as it is mine.

Several portions of *Writing and Vulnerability in the Late Renaissance* have appeared elsewhere. Sections of Chapter 2 were published as "Resisting the Marketplace," in a special issue of *Bucknell Review* entitled *Reconfiguring the Renaissance*, ed. Jonathan Crewe (vol. 35, no. 2 [1992], pp. 34–50). The first section of Chapter 4 appeared as "Veiling the Stage" in *Theatre Journal* 41 (1989) 16–29. Chapter 5 on Spenser is an extensively revised version of "Spenser, Virgil, and the Politics of Poetic Labor," *English Literary History* 55 (1988) 53–77. My thanks to Bucknell University Press and The Johns Hopkins University Press for permission to reprint.

J. T.
Madison, Wisc.

Contents

Writing and Vulnerability in the Late Renaissance

1 ·

Introduction: Renaissance Vulnerabilities

The word *invulnerabilis* was first used during the Silver Age of Roman writing by the philosopher and teacher Seneca. Derived from the Latin *vulnus*—a wound, an injury, a rent—*invulnerabilis* and its opposite, *vulnerabilis*, occur in Seneca most frequently in a military context. Hence we find Seneca speaking of the legendary African serpent who could be wounded by neither the simple Roman bow nor the most elaborate machinery of war.[1] On several occasions, however, Seneca uses *invulnerabilis* to refer not to physical invulnerability but to moral and psychological impregnability to hostile others. When he sets out to define the true Stoic and wise man in his dialogue *De constantia*, he goes about it in this fashion:

> I assuredly did not intend to deck up the wise man with the fanciful honour of words, but to place him in the position where no injury may reach him. "What then?" you say; "will there be no one to assail him, no one to attempt it?" Nothing in the world is so sacred that it will not find some one to profane it. . . . The invulnerable thing is not that which is not struck, but that which is not hurt (invulnerabile est non quod non feritur, sed quod non laeditur); by this mark I will show you the wise man. Is there any doubt that the strength that cannot be overcome is a truer sort than that which is unassailed, seeing that untested powers are dubious, whereas the stability that repels all assaults is rightly deemed most genuine? . . . Consequently I will assert this—that the wise man is not subject to any injury. It does not matter, therefore, how many darts are hurled against him, since none can pierce him.[2]

Once again we encounter the use of *invulnerabilis* in a military context, but now that context has become largely metaphorical. The multitude of darts hurled against the Stoic sage are the angry and derisive words of others, the wise man's armor the quality of *apatheian* or sublime indifference that Seneca discusses in one of his epistles. "Our [Roman] wise man feels his troubles but overcomes them; their [Greek] sage does not even feel them. But we and they alike hold this idea—that the wise man is self-sufficient," a self-sufficiency rooted in his conviction of moral and intellectual superiority.[3]

Such a novel preoccupation with invulnerability and the state of contingency and exposure against which it defends was hardly an idle one for Nero's tutor. Struggling first to impress his ideals on Rome's future ruler, then to maintain his integrity in a corrupt empire, Seneca finally committed suicide in a desperate attempt to render himself impregnable once and for all to his erstwhile student. It is probably not incidental that the first recorded use of "invulnerability" in English refers to a dead man slain by corrupt powers. When, on the ramparts of Elsinore Castle in the first scene of *Hamlet*, the sentinels attempt to strike the frightening, armored apparition of Hamlet's father's ghost with their pikes, they must confess, "We do it wrong, being so majestical, / To offer it the show of violence, / For it is as the air invulnerable, / And our vain blows malicious mockery" (1.1.143–46).[4] In Shakespeare's tragedy, informed as it is by Seneca's Stoic preoccupations, no one is invulnerable to the slings and arrows of fortune except the dead, as the young Hamlet recognizes in his famous soliloquy. By the same token, the act of suicide with which Hamlet briefly flirts may not offer the same consolation it offered to the Roman Stoic. "To sleep—perchance to dream: ay, there's the rub, / For in that sleep of death what dreams may come / When we have shuffled off this mortal coil, / Must give us pause" (3.1.64–67).

Hamlet is not the only Shakespearean character who returns to Seneca, albeit with a difference informed by a Christian horror of suicide. The later tragedies also stage a desire for invulnerability, as Macbeth goads on his nemesis Macduff with the deluded cry, "Let fall thy blade on vulnerable crests, / I bear a charmèd life" (5.8.11–12).[5] Here too Shakespeare is using the word in the context of a battle; like the dead King Hamlet, Macbeth is secured in armor. But Macbeth's preoccupation throughout the play is with an invulnerability that, though a far cry from the solaces of Stoicism, nonetheless has much to do with his psychological and moral inviolability before the dark forces of his universe. Similarly, we have another Shakespearean figure, equally concerned with inviolability, addressing his wife toward the end of *Coriolanus*: "The god of soldiers, / With the consent of supreme Jove, inform / Thy thoughts with nobleness, that thou mayst prove / To shame unvulnerable" (5.3.70–73). In neither of these cases will the hero's desires be fulfilled. Macbeth is killed and decapitated by Macduff, who exposes his head on a pike to all of Scotland; Coriolanus, having disdainfully refused to display his wounds to the Roman crowd, is carried onstage after his death and paraded before the very plebeians he once spurned.

This book suggests that this concern with invulnerability was by no means limited to the English playwright. It maintains instead that the Senecan preoccupations of Shakespeare's tragic heroes were rather characteristic of the era from roughly 1550 through 1660. These dates are not incidental; they embrace what some historians have called a time of "crisis in Europe" and others a period of transition from the medieval to the early modern state.[6] It was precisely this liminal period, more fully elucidated later in this chapter, that prompted Shakespeare's concern and that of a number of his contemporaries—such as Benvenuto Cellini, Teresa of Avila, Torquato Tasso, Edmund Spenser, and Pierre Corneille—with staging conditions of invulnerability for themselves and for their characters. All these writers were dependent for recognition and livelihood on the various institutions of power that they served. Their intensely individual responses to this dependency produced a complicated array of textual performances designed to protect themselves and their writing from the *vulnus* that late Renaissance authorities increasingly had the power to inflict. Unlike Seneca, of course, they did not have Nero to contend with. But neither were they able simply to embrace the (however delusory) solaces of Stoicism in an era during which the pressures exerted on them by ecclesiastical and secular authorities forced them to return to Seneca's concern with invulnerability.[7]

In fact, in many ways, this book charts the failure of the myth of invulnerable selfhood shared by Coriolanus, Macbeth, and Seneca. This is a myth that has often been associated with the Renaissance in toto, most notoriously by Jacob Burckhardt, who enthusiastically announced over a century ago that the Italian Renaissance witnessed the emergence of modern subjectivity and the autonomous, willful Renaissance man.[8] The present generation of Renaissance scholars now conceives of an era strikingly different from that which the nineteenth century imagined, and this study owes a great deal to the recent work of Thomas Greene, Stephen Greenblatt, Margaret Ferguson, Natalie Davis, Jonathan Crewe, and others.[9] Their work has not only reinvigorated Renaissance studies in recent years, it has also had important ramifications for literary and cultural studies in general. Perhaps their most far-reaching contribution is the suggestion that the Senecan—as well as essentially modern—concept of the heroic ego impervious to assault was hardly imaginable in a period in which self-definition was habitually articulated in reference to others.[10] But as the works of Shakespeare and his contemporaries attest, that concept was *easily* imaginable. What was not imaginable was its actualization. In the works of late Renaissance writers one witnesses again and again the *failure* of that imagined model so vividly depicted in Seneca's writings.

That failure, I believe, occurred for several reasons. First of all, the posture of economic dependency on powerful others—and thus of vulnerability to those superiors—was at best ambiguous in the Renaissance. Recent work, in fact, suggests that dependency was relatively unstigmatized before the industrial period.[11] This is not to say, however, that no one tried to define conditions of vulnerability as ignominious during the late Renaissance. The goldsmith Benvenuto Cellini provides a particularly instructive example along these lines. As Cellini recounts in his *Vita*, written after he left Paris for the less hospitable atmosphere of Florence, the unconditional generosity of princes was a thing of the past, and the *Vita* tries unsuccessfully to offset Cellini's uncomfortable vulnerability vis-à-vis the tyrannical Duke Cosimo de'Medici with a myth of masculine independence. Cellini was to discover only late in life the antidote to the failed dynamics of princely generosity and abortive selfhood when he characterized himself as the dependent member of a community: the community of artisans, who provided him with an audience and legitimation for his last works.

But as the *Vita* also reflects, often the institutional "shadow" beneath which a writer worked offered protection from equally (if not more) hostile situations beyond it—not only the threat of indigence, but what an artist such as Cellini perceived as the impersonal forces of a marketplace, or in Saint Teresa's case, the world beyond the convent walls, which had little to offer an ambitious and talented woman.[12] The conditions of economic security that the institution had power to grant thus shaded, often imperceptibly, into conditions of moral and psychological security as well. The writers I discuss were, not surprisingly, as ambivalent about the desirability of dependency as they were about the requests made of them in exchange for protection.

Nonetheless, because of the instability of sixteenth-century Europe, institutions themselves were far from invulnerable during the late Renaissance. Certainly they were interested in attaining such a posture, and arguably by the time of Corneille, with which this book closes, this status was less elusive than it had been before. It is no accident that Macbeth is a *king*, albeit an illegitimate one. Forced to a defensive stance by religious wars, a rising bourgeoisie, and a restless aristocracy, church and state alike were aware of their own vulnerability amid historical change and disruption. They therefore turned to those intellectuals who worked for them to articulate the myth—and increasingly the reality—of monolithic status. But this very reliance on figures such as Cellini, Tasso, and Spenser illustrates a mutual dependency of which these writers themselves were hardly unaware.

Moreover, Cellini's turn to a social group distinct from Florence's political institutions reflects a movement apparent in the careers of most of the writers I will be discussing. For if historical conditions in late Renaissance Europe tended to enhance writers' vulnerability to secular and ecclesiastical powers, such vulnerability was considerably mediated by the existence of various communities and collective experiences. While the work of Stephen Greenblatt in particular has offered a welcome corrective to Burckhardt's Renaissance man who willed himself into existence, it nonetheless goes too far toward the other extreme by arguing, after Michel Foucault, that the Renaissance subject was isolated and defenseless before powerful authorities.[13] As the following chapters illustrate, late Renaissance writers were not vulnerable solitaries inhabiting the margins of power. Far from enacting ad nauseam a drama of individual opposition to a faceless and monolithic authority, the late Renaissance witnesses the emergence and validation of numerous communities and forms of collective experience. The convent, the artisanal community, the intellectual circles surrounding but not synonymous with the court, the acting company, the theatrical audience: in almost every case, the authors to be discussed were able to depend on and to derive identities from collectivities that were not identical to the institutions they served.

But although these communities offered writers audience and identity, they could also serve as sites of contestation, and they should hardly be seen as refuges. Indeed, just as writers were ambivalent about the shade proffered by late Renaissance authorities, so were they often ambivalent about subscribing to alternate modes of communal authority. Teresa, Shakespeare, and to a certain extent Spenser afford striking examples of writers who professed their allegiance to communities distinctly different from the church and the court. But the personae crafted by Cellini, Tasso, and Corneille stage a resistance to incorporation, attempting for as long as possible to speak with the voices of individual and invulnerable subjects.

Each of these writers, however, ultimately, if at times belatedly, recognizes the bankruptcy of the invulnerability for which Seneca yearned. One might even suggest that the very means of generating personae who stage their authors' respective conditions within their texts is itself a sign of such bankruptcy. Informing all of these texts is the awareness that any act of identification makes its author vulnerable to interpretative violence. For the writers discussed in this study, the ongoing work of literary creation hinges on an emergent dialectic between creator and character, both of whom are dependent on and hence vulnerable to one another for their own formulation. Insofar as this process of identification is discernible in the works discussed, one can argue that late Renaissance writers are aware not only of their own historical vulnerability, but of ways in which they might use their vulnerability and that of others to their advantage. Such awareness, in turn, leads to the production of the author, whose emergence this book charts. Yet as will become apparent, the phenomenon of authorship is expressed in often paradoxical and unexpected ways.[14] We are still far from a notion of authorship tied exclusively to literary property or individual genius. A process rather than a designation, authorship instead depends in large part on identification with those communities peripheral and often antagonistic to the more centralized powers of church and state.

This book appropriately begins with two examples of the genre that most deliberately establishes an identification between author and subject matter: autobiography. It then addresses genres in which this relationship is more attenuated: pastoral and tragicomedy. The fact that all three are minor literary genres and as such pose questions about the political function of the so-called major genres such as tragedy and epic—which generally are concerned with important "others" and not a common and dependent author—has considerable bearing on the analyses presented in the next six chapters. Even in their ancient configurations, autobiography, pastoral poetry, and tragicomedy are characterized by a guarded relationship to the powerful figures and traditions that inform and at times sustain them. As recast by Cellini, Teresa, Tasso, Spenser, Shakespeare, and Corneille, these minor genres directly engage issues of vulnerability involving both the developing personae within the works and the authors beyond them.

But if these remarks begin to answer how the dialectics of vulnerability were expressed, it is not yet clear why that expression was limited to the period that spans the century between the Council of Trent and the ascendancy of Louis XIV and the consummate bureaucrat Colbert. By way of illustrating the integrity of the late Renaissance—the century between Cellini's symptomatically unfinished autobiography and Corneille's revised *Cid*—the next pages will argue that there were not one but several Renaissances, and that the late Renaissance radically departed from the epochs that preceded it. First we find the moment of initial excitement of trecento and quattrocento humanists such as Petrarch, Boccaccio, and Bruni; then a transitional moment in the early sixteenth century when Erasmus, More, Castiglione, Vives, and Rabelais became aware of the potential *dangers* of an "open" humanist discourse; and finally, a moment that witnessed a powerful defense against the intervention of church and state by writers as diverse as Teresa and Shakespeare.

The texts produced by this vulnerable consciousness of the late sixteenth and early seventeenth centuries resisted both the deliberately exposed individuality of Petrarch and the ambiguous parlance of Erasmus. If humanists such as Petrarch rejected a conception of the act of writing as insular and totalizing, if Erasmus and the early sixteenth century believed that writing could provide a necessary space of immunity, late-sixteenth-century figures abjured both notions of textual openness and textual closure in defending against an "outside" that increasingly wanted to control the process through which culture was created. With the writers discussed in Chapters 2–7, one encounters a new and at times desperate interest in the protective shadows an early and more optimistic humanism rejected. Yet one also witnesses the emergence of communities far more tangible and concrete than the fictional community sought by Petrarch in his letters to dead poets and the abstract international community of scholars to whom Erasmus addressed his works.

This historical trajectory differs significantly from those posited by two other literary historians of the Renaissance, Thomas Greene and Mikhail Bakhtin, and the rest of this chapter elaborates on this trajectory by engaging their work. In particular, it offers readings of two figures crucial to Greene's and Bakhtin's discussions of Renaissance vulnerability: respectively, Petrarch and Erasmus. Greene derives his model of vulnerability from Petrarch, who is depicted as painfully aware of his inferiority before the integral world of antiquity in general and the inimitable works of Virgil in particular. Bakhtin's much less baneful formulation of Renaissance vulnerability hinges on his readings of Rabelais and Erasmus, who defied their inferiority by invoking the irreverent vehicle of popular culture. Both Greene and Bakhtin have offered extremely convincing interpretations of the European Renaissance; and yet the following assessment suggests that their readings work best when confined to specific moments *of* the Renaissance. To be sure, the figures Greene and Bakhtin set forth as Renaissance models were influential in and characteristic of their respective eras. But as the final section of this chapter argues, Petrarch and Erasmus defined responses to the phenomenon of vulnerability that later writers were both unable and unwilling to imitate.

In *The Light in Troy* and his collection of essays, *The Vulnerable Text*, Thomas Greene suggests that Renaissance writers had to defend themselves not against contemporary authorities, but against a poignant sense of their vulnerability before the looming specter of antiquity. In Greene's impressive reading, humanists from Petrarch to Jonson are profoundly and often eloquently troubled by their belatedness. Virgil in particular emerges in Greene's work as emblematic of a cultural integrity impossible for the Renaissance to recapture. In a telling page from *The Light in Troy*, Greene chooses the final moment of Virgil's first Eclogue to illustrate the lost unity of classical culture. This poem closes with lengthening shadows falling about both Tityrus, a shepherd newly secure in the lands granted to him by the benevolent emperor Octavian, and Meliboeus, exiled by the same emperor from his own farmland and destined to wander "shores unknown." "Et iam summa procul villarum culmina fumant / maioresque cadunt altis de montibus umbrae" (Even now the housetops yonder are smoking and lengthening shadows fall from the mountain heights),[15] observes the hospitable Tityrus in the last lines of the poem. Thus is Meliboeus urged to suspend his wanderings, as the "umbra" that had earlier represented the imperial shade in which Tityrus reveled becomes the "umbrae" of night and, less directly, of a poem that has obliquely challenged the mores of empire. Piecing together Petrarch's interpretation of the poem's quiet close from various lines in Petrarch's *Secretum* and sonnets, Greene writes:

> The shadow that lengthens about Tityrus and Meliboeus gathers them into a unity with the Arcadian landscape about them, and if Meliboeus will be required to leave it, his exile will only heighten our perception of its beautiful integrity. His darkening shadow is as yet unfallen; it is innocent of psychologistic or theological or rhetorical perplexities. It lies on the far side of a gulf whose near side is marked by the Psalmist's withered grass and declining days, Dante's stony chill. . . . Petrarch's intertextual proliferation avoids anachronistic chaos by organizing its subtexts on either side of this gulf, and by dramatizing the slide across it as an entry into division and into anxieties of adumbration.[16]

Yet this eloquent passage about a Petrarch saddled with a Christian consciousness of the Fall and desirous of the comforting shadows of Roman empire and Virgilian text disregards Petrarch's most explicit reading of the first Eclogue. This reading finds in the lengthening shadow neither the solaces of community nor the integrity of paganism. Petrarch's interlinear gloss on the eclogue (which Greene dismisses as offhandedly as he dismisses Petrarch's own attempt at pastoral, his *Bucolicum carmen*) [17] closes with a melancholy reflection on the brevity of *all* cultural moments, specifically Roman ones. Petrarch glosses the line "Maioresque cadunt altis de montibus umbrae" with "Aucte temporis cursu vel ducibus vel poetis ut differat obliviones" (How, by the bountiful march of time, oblivion scatters both emperors and poets).[18] The shadows that descend on Tityrus's little valley are, in fact, the shadows of forgetfulness, as Petrarch invokes the trope of scattering so frequent in his verses to designate what happens to the "integral" moment of pagan antiquity.

One may, as Greene does, cite the gloss as an example of Petrarch's residual medievalism. Is his retreat to allegory not simply one more attempt to read classical texts within the framework of Christian belief? (Virgil's fourth Eclogue, with its annunciation of a messiah, was clearly one of the first victims of such a hermeneutic, and an immensely significant one.) But regardless of its source, Petrarch's invocation of scattering performs a function that Greene's theory of Renaissance vulnerability will not allow. That invocation denies to antiquity in general—and to Virgil in specific—the very "integrity" it was supposed to possess, as the descending shade of the first Eclogue is said to figure not a lost and simple unity but the forgetfulness that overtakes those writings and actions thought to be most inviolable to change.

In medieval and early Renaissance Europe, the work of Virgil *had* been presumed to possess such inviolability. The consummate model of classical and poetic integrity, Virgil had long been identified with the secure Tityrus of Eclogue I. But Petrarch both qualifies this integrity—as when he almost childishly points to the unfinished nature of the *Aeneid* in his "letter" to Virgil ("With much effort you strove to raise [Aeneas] to the stars, but death, envious of such solid foundations, opposed your attempt") [19]—and ultimately finds it undesirable.

Elsewhere in his letter (from the final book of the *Rerum familiarium libri*), Petrarch addresses Virgil *as* the shade that he has become, asking plaintively, "Which circle of Avernus keeps you from us?" and wondering,

> How far from the truth were your dreams, and how far has wandering Aeneas emerged from the ivory portal? Or rather does a peaceful region of the heavens contain the blessed spirits, and do the stars smile upon the peaceful shades of the illustrious, following the conquest of the Stygian abodes, and the plundering of the Tartarean regions by the coming of the Highest King who, victorious in the great struggle, crossed the ungodly threshold with pierced feet, and in His power crushed the eternal bars of hell . . . and tore the gates asunder from their horrid-sounding hinges? All this I should like to know. (Bernardo, 3: 340)

This passage must seem to someone like Greene an example of medieval "misreading," as Petrarch pointedly contrasts the ignorance of paganism and the "lumina" of the present. But such distance and isolation are not merely the result of Virgil's paganism. Horace, too, was a pagan; yet Petrarch's letter to Horace conveys an immediacy and accessibility that the epistle to Virgil lacks. Virgil cannot be located in the afterlife ("Which circle of Avernus keeps you from us?"); but Horace serves as Petrarch's guide through "the purple hills, the green meadows, the cool lakes and dewy grottoes" (ibid., p. 336). In contrast, Virgil is a poet of shadows, of a Roman empire of which Petrarch now "considers it better not to know," of a famous but unfinished epic ("death, envious of such solid foundations, opposed your attempt") (ibid., p. 341).

Indeed, the differences between the letters to Horace and Virgil may be highly revealing. When Petrarch calls to the errant Horace, "Wherever you may proceed, whatever you may do, pleases me," he creates a powerful bond of identification between himself and the epistolarist and satirist who dared to "assail vices with deserved sniping" and "condemn the guilty city" (ibid., p. 337). Financed like Virgil by the wealthy Maecenas, Horace nonetheless may well have seemed to Petrarch more skeptical about his sinecure than was Virgil, and Petrarch's own poetic output of letters, lyric fragments, and diatribes against the corrupt church in Avignon more closely resembles the scattered writings of Horace than the monumental opus of Virgil. Petrarch's own generic innovativeness suggests that for him, the text created in protective isolation (the security of a Virgil) was less compelling, ultimately less truthful, than the text produced through exposure and *exchange*[20]—precisely those qualities that Petrarch claims to have found in Horace, who "precede[s Petrarch] in [his] anxiety" (ibid., p. 337).

Even and especially in those poems in which Petrarch did attempt to emulate the Virgilian career, namely, his *Africa* and *Bucolicum carmen*,[21] there is a clear, and arguably intentional, disparity between what Petrarch perceived as Virgil's career of "shadows" and his own historical situation as exile and wanderer.[22] In the first Eclogue of the *Bucolicum carmen*, the shepherd Silvius (Petrarch himself) *rejects* the hospitality proffered him by the Tityrus-like character named Monicus. Silvius is a wanderer of sun-drenched deserts, of mountain peaks and mossy crags exposed to thunder. Monicus, protected ("conditus") within his tranquil cave, asks his brother why he refuses a life of "squalid huts" and "safe leisure" ("turpesque casas et tuta pavescis / Otia?").[23] Silvius's pursuit of fame drives him away from the condition of "safety"—a safety associated, perhaps, with the historical blindness Petrarch would again and again link to the mentality of the Middle Ages. In the closing lines, Silvius decides against the respite offered by his brother, far from the tumult and "chance" ("casus") of the highways.

Unlike Meliboeus, Silvius is not the victim of exile and a harsh emperor. Rather, he knowingly and willfully refuses the condition of shadows. Such a refusal is also intimated in the second Eclogue, often interpreted as an elegy to King Robert of Naples, Petrarch's sometime patron and the monarch who crowned him poet laureate in 1341. In his most explicit reference to the protective "umbra" of a patron in his *Bucolicum carmen*, the poet describes the fall of the cypress beneath which he and other shepherds once peacefully sang. The eclogue modulates into an elegy, modeled on that for Julius Caesar in Virgil's fifth Eclogue and sung by two shepherds, Pythias and Silvius—the same Silvius of the first poem. Annabel Patterson has called attention to the deep pessimism that runs throughout the poem,[24] an interpretation that looks to Greene's own generally elegiac treatment of Petrarch (and indeed, of Renaissance literature in general). Yet as the two songs performed by Pythias and Petrarch's persona, Silvius, demonstrate, it is the *former* shepherd who is much more affected by the patron's death. Pythias bewails the loss of protection and of a stable community, plaintively asking, "Who . . . will succor the wretched?" (II.88) and "What, without you, will become of the hills, the caves and the thickets? / Who would survive—if he could—your passing?" (II.89–90). However, in a much briefer song, Silvius responds with platitudes—"Even so, fortune / Alternates cruelly our joys and sorrows"—and suggests that their patron yet lives, on a "peak high above us," from which he both "observes our cares and our troubles" and marks "how small the woodland now seems that once he reigned over" (II. 116–19).

This steady demystification of the need for shade is apparent even in the tenth Eclogue, in which Silvius mourns—mistakenly, as it turns out—the destruction of his "private" laurel tree (readers of the *Canzoniere* will recognize an allusion to Laura of the lyric poetry). This destruction of shade demystifies the *idea* of enclosure, of the imagined integrity of Virgil, whom Petrarch imagines in the *Familiares* as haunting "arboris umbras" and "curvi secreti lacus" (shady groves and a recess in the curving banks of the lake). Isolated in such dark recesses, Virgil becomes emblematic of the cave-loving Monicus who craves "otium," or of the Pythias who infers from the death of the cypress the death of an entire pastoral community. It is, rather, the lyricist and civic satirist Horace whom Silvius emulates in his *un*protected pursuit of fame: "Lead me, if you will, over the oar-furrowed sea, or to the cloud-enshrouded mountain summits" (Bernardo, 3: 336). Silvius's reckless path exposes him to the "casus" from which Virgil, enclosed within the shadow of patronage, of empire, of his careful pattern of a poetic career, is immune.

Petrarch's treatment of Virgil suggests that he embraces what might be called an ethos of vulnerability rather than the closure and incommunicability of the Virgilian model. What Greene perceived as Petrarch's pathetic *failure* to restore Virgil's model—his "unsatisfying" eclogues, his incomplete *Africa*—might be more fairly construed as his refusal to find in the protected and monumentally unified Virgil a model fully compatible with his own resilient writings.[25] One might then ask why Greene's striking observation that a work's vulnerability inheres in its very desire for, and inevitably fallacious assertions of, totality cannot be said to have been Petrarch's as well—and one that Petrarch might have made regarding the figure who most fully represented the ancient culture he and other humanists longed to recover.[26] Shaped by several centuries of medieval commentary and allegorization into the formidable originator of the poetic career and the prophet of the Christian era, Virgil may well have been seen by Petrarch as a writer ultimately deluded by the totality of his work and his historical vision.

This interpretation, needless to say, takes issue more with the tradition of medieval exegesis than it does with the Virgilian texts per se, and Petrarch's failure to distinguish between commentary and text may indeed be symptomatic of his larger shortcomings as an "allegorical reader," to which Greene has called attention. But despite or because of this tendency to conflate exegesis and poetry, Petrarch is guardedly suspicious of the various "umbrae" within which the Virgilian poet worked—the shade of imperial protection, the shade of a self-protective and obfuscatory poetic—preferring instead a poetry of vulnerability that counsels active engagement in reading and, ideally, in the social and political spheres.[27] Rather than decrying his own distance from the integrity of ancient culture and a Virgilian career spent beneath the emperor's shadow, Petrarch may in fact have derided Virgil's invulnerable life and texts for their inaccessibility and ultimately tragic silences.

Petrarch's desire to emerge from the "shade" of Virgilian poetics suggests that Petrarch's humanism, rather than being anxiously conscious of its own belatedness and obsessed with creating a poetics of defense against the monolithic presence of antiquity, may in fact articulate its willingness to embrace a condition of vulnerability.[28] That is, Petrarch's "allegorical" reading of Virgil does not point to his limitations as an interpreter of antiquity. Given Virgil's dwelling place within the shadow of empire, given what Petrarch and Dante alike understood to be Virgil's tragic ignorance of his historical limitations (for Virgil is also a "shade" in Dante's text),[29] Petrarch's reading must be understood as a willful choice. Rather than desiring to resurrect Virgil and the imperial shadow beneath which he wrote, Petrarch was central in identifying the undesirability of the Virgilian model in his quest for an immediacy and vulnerability that the *rota Virgilianae* foreclosed.

Yet the paradigm of vulnerability embraced by this so-called first humanist would not, in fact, be that of his many descendants, and Petrarch's humanist ethos of vulnerability did not survive the early sixteenth century. As Greene turns to the late fifteenth and sixteenth centuries and to writers such as Angelo Poliziano, Castiglione, Maurice Scève, and Ben Jonson, the arguments he makes for the presence of a more than metaphysical anxiety become more persuasive. This may well be because of the nature of the historical moment on which the second critic mentioned above, the Soviet writer Mikhail Bakhtin, has elaborated in important and fascinating ways.

Bakhtin presents a version of the Renaissance antithetical to that offered by Greene; for him it is a renaissance that only fully emerges in the early sixteenth century. If Greene's humanists are cautious figures obsessed with literature's vulnerability vis-à-vis its relationship to ancient culture and the more certain "sciences" of logic and syllogistic reasoning,[30] Bakhtin's humanists—Erasmus, Rabelais, Shakespeare, Lope de Vega, and Grimmelshausen—*defy* vulnerability through laughter and festivity.[31] If Greene, moreover, charts the Renaissance as a primarily intellectual movement initiated by an elite class's recovery of antiquity, Bakhtin sees the Renaissance originating in a popular reaction against church and state, an overturning of the early hierarchies that had dominated the Middle Ages.[32] Greene's alienated intellectuals, struggling to produce "invulnerable" texts against all odds, are starkly opposed to the humanists who primarily interest Bakhtin: a generation of writers who situate their texts in the marketplace, a public forum for the "people" that enlists the competitive exchange of words and ideas.[33]

These strikingly different interpretations are, of course, in large part the result of opposed critical orientations. Bakhtin's concern with societal intervention and opposition sharply distinguishes his work from Greene's largely formalist criticism, devoted to the analysis of textual boundaries. But the different interpretations are also a function of the different originating moments on which the respective critics focus. Greene's Petrarch wrote when institutional opposition to the writer as writer was largely nonexistent, in part because the institution itself did not exist as such.[34] But the increasing consolidation of religious and secular institutions in the face of schism and attack led, among other things, to the censuring of Rabelais's writings and the death of his friend and erstwhile publisher, Etienne Dolet, at the stake. Despite such growing repressiveness—or perhaps because of it—Rabelais's "language of the marketplace" boldly proclaimed its hostility to official doctrine. Paradoxically, Bakhtin's consummate humanist, writing in a century when "official institutions" sought increasingly to control cultural production, emerges as the model writer capable of cutting "the umbilical cord" between self and work, as his words "tumble out on the water," unprotected by their parent.[35] In Greene's analysis the metaphysical angst of Petrarch calls forth a complex and subtle process of negotiation between vulnerable texts and an alterity that the writer can never definitively grasp.[36] In Bakhtin's reading, however, the very real threats posed by the historical environment of a writer such as Rabelais invite the condition of exposed words set free from their loving parent.[37]

Yet this condition of vulnerability is not as straightforward as it might appear. Nor is it to be equated with the ethos of vulnerability willingly embraced by Petrarch. Rather, Bakhtin both recognizes and mediates this paradox between exposure and repression by calling attention to Rabelais's spirit of "play." Rabelais's "popular-festive system of images with its charter of freedoms consecrated by many centuries" is "a merry play and therefore immune"; "Rabelais' friend Etienne Dolet perished at the stake because of his statements, which although less damning had been seriously made. He did not use Rabelais' methods," the methods, in short, of laughter.[38] But Bakhtin's privileging of laughter as a force that is free to criticize and yet immune from criticism—Rabelais's only critics, Bakhtin claims, were those "who granted no special rights to laughter"[39]—disingenuously ignores the real methodology that Rabelais used.

For Rabelais's refusal to locate his *own* voice within his text is a strategy of self-protection. The masks of the clown, the giant, and the drunkard, masks that "grant the right *not* to understand, the right to confuse, to tease, to hyperbolize life; the right to parody others while talking, the right to not be taken literally, not 'to be oneself,' "[40] dislocate the authorial voice from its context in a way that prevents any direct criticism of that voice. They therefore render the author impervious to challenge by creating a new kind of textual integrity very different from that which Petrarch saw in Virgil. In the marketplace celebrated by Bakhtin as the legacy of the Rabelaisian novel, everything is public and exposed except for the author, whose methods of control are unavailable for questioning. Thus one has the vertiginous preface to the *Gargantua* in which Rabelais attacks his readers as "boozers" and Baudelaireian *hypocrites, frères*. Like the Socratic Silenus also invoked in Rabelais's preface, the evasive voice of "Rabelais" obscures the relationship between textual "outside" and intentional "inside." Like the gadfly that is never still, the narrative voice refuses to occupy a stable place in which it might reside. Far from renouncing a desire for invulnerability, the Rabelaisian novelist attempts to take on a posture of immunity: a posture, as Bakhtin notes, that is altogether new in Renaissance writing.

Or almost new. By way of elaborating on the above remarks, I would like to address briefly the writer of the Renaissance text that Bakhtin sees as "most in tune [albeit anachronistically] with the Rabelaisian world": Erasmus, author of the mad oration *The Praise of Folly*.[41] In many ways, *The Praise of Folly* is the Bakhtinian text *par excellence*. Its juxtaposition of popular proverbs and "festive images" with the language of the elite, its scatological references, its clever and vertiginous use of masks: such are the features of the "Rabelaisian world" before that world ever existed. As Erasmus observed to one of his critics, Martin Dorp of the faculty of Louvain, some six years after *The Praise of Folly* was composed, to isolate a single statement or viewpoint in this product of the "ideally pluralistic consciousness" of the orator Folly is brazenly to misrepresent the whole.[42] As any reader of *The Praise of Folly* well knows, Erasmus's monologue defies the imposition of unity because Folly herself possesses no unifying voice.[43] Folly's praise of "natural folly" in the first section of the encomium is difficult to reconcile with her praise of Christian folly in the work's final section. Similarly, her distaste in the book's first 34 chapters for those who profess to take themselves "out of the world" and feign objectivity seems forgotten soon thereafter when she lambastes the various professions in a section reminiscent of satires of the medieval estates. Erasmus's witty diatribe is a textual labyrinth in which the voice of an author is impossible to locate. As the final palinode of the work discloses—"If anything I've said seems rather impudent or garrulous, you must remember it's Folly and a woman who's been speaking"[44]—*The Praise of Folly* is a textual orphan, abandoned by its begetter.

As such, Erasmus's work provides an excellent example of the daring playfulness of sixteenth-century humanism as Bakhtin has described it. And yet, between the composition of the oration in 1509 and that of the above-mentioned letter to Martin Dorp in 1515, the rationale for Erasmus's purported "playfulness" might be said to have completely changed. Clearly hostile not only to Folly's attack on clerics but to Erasmus's forthcoming edition of the New Testament in Greek, the conservative Dorp protested Erasmus's bantering treatment of theological issues, anticipating the more sustained attack on Erasmus's work to come from a defensive church. Erasmus's response recasts his "little book" as a work aimed at protecting itself against the very criticisms Dorp was raising; he protests that those who complain about his mock encomium have taken statements made by Folly completely out of context. "You can see that everywhere I've always been careful to avoid anything which could be at all offensive. But those whose ears are open only to propositions, conclusions and corollaries pay no heed to that. What was the point of arming my little book with a preface which I hoped would forestall misrepresentations?" (pp. 236–37). Erasmus complains because Dorp removed Folly's lines from their *source*, the complicated and circuitous oration of a fool. Hypotheses were turned into corollaries and propositions associated not with Folly but with Erasmus himself—precisely the move Erasmus claims to have been defending himself against, as he impatiently repeats Folly's foolish palinode.

To wrench a single statement of Folly's out of context and to ascribe it to Erasmus is to confuse author and fictive character. It is also to destroy the work as a totality: to splinter a part from the whole and to misrepresent the work itself. In retrospect, *The Praise of Folly* becomes a work that resists *any* act of interpretation, a resistance that Erasmus most explicitly formulates when he calls attention to the vehicle that Bakhtin associates with openness and vulnerability: laughter. "Who ever heard of a humorous essay (ludicrum argumentum) being subjected to a theologian's scrutiny? If this is approved practice, why don't they equally apply this rule to all the writings and witticisms of the poets today?" (p. 237). Although, a few lines later, Erasmus protests that he "wouldn't want to seek shelter beneath an example like this" (neque tamen postulem istorum exemplum mihi patrocinari),[45] it is clear that he is intent upon locating his text within a poetic "genre" that resists scrutiny. Folly may recite a palinode after her oration is completed—in her closing lines she cites a newly coined proverb to the effect that "she hates an audience that won't forget"—but Erasmus, in responding to Dorp's suggestion that *he* recant in order to calm his critics, ardently refuses. Why should he "pacify the theologians' hostility and recover their former good will by producing a *palinodon* in praise of Wisdom to counter [his] praise of Folly" (p. 240)? "Any hostility which may have arisen amongst a handful of prejudiced, uneducated people certainly wouldn't be removed but would be still more inflamed" (p. 241) by such an act of rewriting. Folly may ask that her audience forget all that she has said, but Erasmus, who claims no single statement that Folly has uttered as his own, need produce no such recantation.

Implicit in Erasmus's biting remarks to Dorp may well be his growing sense that the potential danger for a Petrarchan humanism that prided itself on its vulnerability was censorship. On the one hand, Erasmus, like Petrarch, manifests a distaste for the "protectiveness" furnished by institutional security and textual closure. His *Antibarbarians* chastises those who sought the comforting retreats of monasteries or universities; Saint Bernard, for example, greatly erred in "betaking himself to trees rather than to men."[46] And in his noted commentary on the adage "Herculei Labores," he calls attention to the open-endedness of his project of collecting proverbs when he asks why he should spend years rewriting, scrutinizing, and even *finishing* such "endless" work: "Since the job is endless, and contributes to the general good, what is to prevent our sharing out the labour and finishing our work by our joint efforts? I have done my stint and I am handing on the torch. Let someone else take up the succession."[47] On the other hand, however, Erasmus's apparent disdain for authorship—"It does not matter under what name my works are read, I shall not trouble myself about who gets the glory as long as we have given students the opportunity to possess a thing of such value" (pp. 29–30)—may look toward the phenomenon apparent in a work such as the *Encomium moriae* and accentuated in the letter to Dorp: the tendency to obscure the location of the voice that writes. If Petrarch revels in the errancy of a Silvius who refuses to reside even briefly in the protected cavern of Monicus, he nonetheless enables his reader to locate that voice in its errancy. Yet Erasmus refuses to disclose even a provisional connection between his authorial voice and his fictive characters.[48]

This new and admittedly sporadic pursuit of immunity is particularly evident if one turns to the trope of shade that Petrarch mistrusted. *The Antibarbarians*, briefly mentioned above as a critique of the reclusiveness of monastic communities and, by extension, of the medieval university, is a dialogue among several of Erasmus's friends in a "rural corner" of Brabant during an attack of the plague.[49] In this supposed retreat, Erasmus, who tellingly absents himself from the discussion that ensues by taking on the role of scribe rather than participant, invites his cohorts to set up an academy on the model of Plato's:

> No matter if we have not a plane tree like the Platonic or Ciceronian ones, which were planted and grew by favor of the writings of the most eloquent of philosophers and the wisest of orators, rather than being watered in the ordinary way. I am offering you real trees instead of imaginary ones, and in the place of one poor tree a whole orchard. . . . What if we water this place too with our discussions, so that it will never dry up at any future time? And under that great pear tree, practically in the middle of the garden, there are some very comfortable seats, and I will order cushions to be brought. . . . (p. 39)

Several lines later, Erasmus specifically alludes to Plato's *Phaedrus*: "If so weighty a philosopher as Socrates could be allured (as in the *Phaedrus*) by the pleasantness of the place to lie down on the grass and converse beside the little spring, why should we not be tempted to sit down here?" Yet whereas Socrates had only a "little fountain of ice-cold water," Erasmus and his friends have "a murmuring stream which flows round the garden and irrigates them." Whereas Socrates had only a plane tree, Erasmus and his companions have an entire orchard. The pastoral locale of Socrates' countryside, with the dry, harsh sound of the cicadas and the penetrating noonday sun, has been replaced by a landscape that is georgic in character while also resplendent and lush; the pear tree not only furnishes protection from the sun, but "gladdens [their] eyes with blossom and refresh[es their] nostrils with the sweetest scent" (p. 40).

Not only does this setting amplify and exaggerate that of Socrates, it also amplifies that of Petrarch: the cave of Monicus from which Silvius departs, the single laurel tree beneath which the lyric poet lamented and which will finally be transplanted in heaven. Moreover, this verdant orchard furnishes the site not for a dialectical sifting of truth from "fiction" but for the exchange and accommodation of various perspectives. Even the saint attacked for engaging with trees rather than men is rehabilitated within the dialogue, his pursuit of the woods transformed from what Erasmus called in the letter to Dorp a "fear of exposure" (p. 248) into the precondition for creativity.[50] Saint Bernard is "saved" in Erasmus's humanist text, as the shade that had furnished a wholly negative example emerges as a positive locus for poetic production and safety ("secessum") from an unarticulated threat.

Such subtle accommodation is imaged in the shaded locus bearing the signs of both man's work (the irrigating stream) and nature's abundance ("these gardens which Epicurus himself might praise") (p. 40). It symbolizes *in nuce* the pattern established by Erasmus in his early writings and exploited throughout his long and prolific career as teacher, writer, and philologist. Accommodation is at the very heart of Erasmus's work, dedicated as so much of it is to the unification of antiquity and modernity. But accommodation is also a strategy, as the letter to Dorp confirms, that evolved into a defense against an environment that grew increasingly suspicious of any direct attacks on ecclesiastical or secular authorities. Erasmus's professed playfulness, which examines an argument or proposition *in utramque partem* and is evident in the dialogism of most of his major works, may have served initially as a method of humanist expression. Certainly it derived from Erasmus's own experiences within a university environment rather than from any real or perceived kinship with the "folk."[51] But as a defense against criticism and misinterpretation, such playfulness became increasingly necessary. Particularly with the debates over Erasmus's translation of the New Testament into Greek, the writer's initially playful confusion of dogmas evolved into a strategy of evasion. This strategy is evoked in the letter to Dorp as well as in the revisions Erasmus made to his youthful *Antibarbarians* after 1516.[52] His growing distrust of direct statement is nowhere more apparent than in his (albeit assertive) claim to Luther from his discourse on free will: "So great is my dislike of assertions that I prefer the views of the sceptics wherever the inviolable authority of Scripture and the decision of the Church permit."[53] That distrust, like his apparent willingness to publish a text such as the *Adages*—imperfect, unpolished, and putatively disowned—lends itself to a refusal to be pinned down, a resistance to appropriation by a potentially hostile reader. The real shade that the pear tree furnishes Erasmus, elusive writer of *The Antibarbarians*, is the shade of dialogue and a copious discourse that renders any one single voice invulnerable to attack.

One may thus speak of a relatively new interest in textual immunity in the sixteenth century. The earlier part of this chapter suggested that Thomas Greene's account of Petrarch's virtually self-imposed concern with vulnerability overlooks Petrarch's own resistance to Virgil's "protected" texts. Yet Bakhtin's championing of a festive laughter that openly transgressed official boundaries while remaining blissfully immune from official jurisdiction also overlooks something: the manipulative aspects of such "festivity."[54] Far from being passionately involved with "folk" culture, writers such as Rabelais and Erasmus chose the shadow not of one mask but of many masks. Of necessity, Erasmus used the strategies of laughter in more manipulative fashion than Bakhtin would allow, and not in order to celebrate popular culture but to obscure the voice of a defensive author and prevent its identification. The apparent indecisiveness of the authors Bakhtin celebrates obscures their at times corrosive critiques. Moreover, Bakhtin's focus on the novel and his search for the presence of the popular voice unmediated by the contaminations of the elite humanist overlooks the resistance to a "marketplace" mentality among many writers eager to transcend their nonelite origins and find acceptance in the less visibly materialist domain of the court. Finally, rather than representing the Renaissance in toto,

Bakhtin's carnival with its heady and dialectical movement between openness and concealment is better understood as the product of a particular moment in Renaissance history, albeit a profoundly transitional one. Positioned on the cusp between the vital humanism of the quattrocento and the Counter-Reformation of the sixteenth century, Erasmus and Rabelais were both painfully aware of the dangers of self-exposure.

Yet the posture of indeterminacy adopted by both writers became increasingly suspect and, indeed, impossible to sustain. It is a historical irony that the space Erasmus chose for his nondogmatic voicings would in years to come be appropriated by the authorities he mistrusted. The *Index* of the mid-sixteenth century banned Erasmus's *oeuvre* from Catholic Europe: not for its supposedly heretical statements, but, as Silvana Seidel Menchi has argued, because it represented the creative inquiry of an intellectual who had invoked "poetic fictions" (to cite a Pisan Inquisitor's report from 1564) as a manner of preserving and protecting his work.[55] Such anxiety over Erasmus's covert fictions is a sign that church and state were attempting to control cultural production itself, to appropriate the spaces of immunity that Petrarch spurned and Erasmus so delicately fashioned.

The process of centralizing modern institutions—a process that accelerated in mid-sixteenth-century Europe with the crystallization of the nation-state and the reorganization of the Catholic church—might even be called the history of the refusal to grant license to anyone but the authorizing institution itself. The centralization of pardons in the French monarchy and a new emphasis on recantation within the Catholic church are two of the most blatant examples of this refusal.[56] But there were other, more gradual signs of a transition as well, such as the progressive takeover of ecclesiastical and civil sanctuaries by the English crown from the late fifteenth through the seventeenth centuries;[57] the breakup of the immunities characteristic of the feudal system;[58] and, most importantly for the following chapters, a new emphasis on censorship; the harnessing of popular festivities and rituals to church and state celebrations; and increased control of marginal groups as diverse as religious women and acting companies.[59] The emerging "absolutist" state, both secular and religious, gradually embraced what Frederic Lane has seen as one of the central functions of the modern institution: the production of a particular service, that of protection,[60] often in the interests of suppressing and controlling the production of knowledge.

Numerous writers seeking their *own* immunity—Machiavelli, Jean Bodin, and Giraldi Cinzio, as well as apologists for the Counter-Reformation church, such as Loyola, Suarez, and Justus Lipsius[61]—supported these various attempts at centralization. They thereby enhanced sovereign claims to immunity and to "invulnerability." While the errant Erasmus might well have spurned these public servants in search of sinecures, he may also have been conscious of a possible tension between authors' and authorities' desires for immunity. In this regard, one final Erasmian tag clearly relevant to Bakhtin, "Aut fatuum aut regem nasci opportere" (One must be born either a king or a fool) becomes telling. Erasmus explains in his 1515 edition of the *Adages* that the proverb originated "among the [early] Romans, who hated the name of king as barbaric and tyrannous, and contrary to political freedom, of which they at that time were the most enthusiastic supporters."[62] But soon after the republic ended, the negative association of king and fool was replaced by a more positive one. Kings began to believe that, *like* fools, "they [were] free to do just what they like[d]" (*Erasmus on His Times*, p. 38), and they therefore arrogated to themselves the license normally reserved for fools: "For everything is permitted to fools, because of the weakness of their minds. And everything in the way of praise is awarded to kings, because of their power" (ibid., p. 43). Thus if the proverb originated in Rome's hatred of tyranny, during the empire it developed into a maxim. Deployed by the likes of Julius, Nero, Tiberius, Caligula, Commodus, and Domitian, all of whom provide trenchant examples of the abuse of power, the proverb licensed a prince's claim to an immunity far exceeding that of the fool, since a prince's foolishness can lead to "the immense detriment of the whole world" (ibid., p. 37).

Erasmus's concern about kings seizing for themselves the "immunity" traditionally given to fools was dazzlingly prescient of the situation that would soon become a reality in Europe. It also suggests an interesting commentary on the foolish writer hoping to obtain a sinecure—the kind of writer Erasmus and the six figures discussed at length in later chapters strove not to become. For the intellectual unwilling to commit suicide—and thus unwilling to follow in the footsteps of Seneca, whose own preoccupations with invulnerability opened this chapter—there is the danger that "safety" and political complacency, even compromise, become necessary trade-offs; the "autonomous" intellectual is granted his protection by the political fiat he has encouraged. For the monarch responsive to the flattery of his would-be advisors, there is the danger that immunity, with its etymological roots in a freedom from the burdens (*munis*) of public service, will manifest itself as abuse of law and the public good. Invoking invulnerability allows the monarch not only to escape from history, but to control history. Erasmus's proverb exposes the potential neutralization of the intellectual class, which should furnish a prince's most effective and articulate critics. Too often, that class sanctions the removal of the prince to a realm beyond accountability and blame, the realm that Erasmus's writings inhabit, and the realm that Bakhtin maintains is invulnerable to "official" culture.

As the history of his writings attests, Erasmus's refusal to locate his voice and to identify the perspectives that were his own ceased functioning as a successful strategy of evasion in the course of the church's debates about his work. Nor was his relative independence from religious and secular institutions possible to maintain. Like his good friend Thomas More's punning refusal to situate his fantastic realm, Utopia, on the great globe, Erasmus's refusal became inimitable in the period following *The Praise of Folly*.[63] Like More's Utopian dialogue, Erasmus's copious but disunified *Praise of Folly* resists the "scrutiny of theologians" because it asks its reader to grasp it as a totality that it does not create. Hence it is ever elusive, ever within its own counterinterpretative shade.

But as Thomas More was forced to realize, political sea changes in mid-sixteenth-century Europe compelled those who attempted to be "no place" to arrive at *some* place. For his own, belated placement of voice, More was ultimately executed. Erasmus's work was also "placed" within the category of a poetic fiction that could no longer defend itself against the scrutiny of theologians impatient with and distrustful of a "ludicrum argumentum." Finally, Erasmus's utopian vision for his work increasingly served as the model for a political agenda that likewise sought immunity for its pronouncements.[64] It is to this disturbing agenda—and to those who had no choice but to work within the protection it offered rather than without—that the remainder of this chapter turns.

The preceding pages argued that Greene's and Bakhtin's eloquent formulations of Renaissance vulnerability are suggestive but finally inadequate. In fact, it is the consideration of their critical blindnesses that has allowed a historical narrative to emerge. This narrative insists on the presence of three distinct phases in the period often simplistically designated as "the Renaissance," the period of several hundred years between the so-called death of medievalism and the birth of a neoclassicism that attempted to regulate and to challenge the strategies discussed in this work. The first phase is that of the active humanism of Petrarch, who defies the protective medium of shade as well as the totalizing formulas of Virgil's empire and career. The second is that of the more cautious humanism of Erasmus, in which Petrarch's notorious physical errancy is replaced with a textual errancy that refuses to disclose its originating voice and relies on a self-protective shadow of its own tenuous formulation. It is on the third "Renaissance," a post-humanist moment during which the free play of Erasmus is neither possible nor desirable, and during which writers no longer conceive of neutrality as a viable option and ground their voices in real rather than manufactured communities, that the remainder of this study focuses.[65]

Those writing during such a moment could hardly fail to recognize the centrality of the institutional shadow, the space within which Virgil's Tityrus sang the first Eclogue, the space that grants him protection and requires his loyalty in return. For those unwilling to succumb to the shadow cast by monarch or church in the years following Erasmus's death in 1536, the posture of independence became increasingly difficult to sustain.[66] For Cellini, Teresa of Avila, Tasso, Spenser, Shakespeare, and Corneille, the role of the so-called "traditional intellectual" (to cite Antonio Gramsci's term for the "literary men, philosophers, [and] artists" who "see themselves as autonomous and independent of the ruling social group")[67] was largely unavailable. All flourishing after Erasmus's death, these six writers were intimately connected with the very ruling powers from which

Erasmus, however tenuously, had been able to remain aloof. All, moreover, depended for their livelihoods on the early modern institution in some form, whether in the guise of the absolutist state of a Cosimo de'Medici, Alfonso II d'Este, or King James, or in that of the Counter-Reformation church. No longer able to remain aloof from centers of power, they had to reconceptualize their relationship to authority in order to prevent themselves from occupying the margins of power as solitary and vulnerable figures.

The following analysis departs from Greene insofar as it argues that vulnerability is a historically contingent phenomenon in the Renaissance, the function of social, political, and economic pressures rather than of the literary text or the project of rebirth per se. It also departs from Bakhtin in suggesting that the means of so-called festive resistance to official culture might ultimately be preempted by that culture itself, and that resistance rested not with an amorphous popular culture but with groups whose distinctive identities were challenged and even enabled by the growth of the early modern institution. Finally, it suggests that the writers to be studied do much more than simply defend their work from co-optation from above.[68] All of them strive, in one way or another, to refuse to fulfill the request for immunity of those in power. They thus invert the flattering mirror that Seneca (reluctantly) held up for his patron and student Nero, or Virgil's Tityrus for Octavian; for example, Cellini depicts Cosimo de'Medici as a monstrous Medusa, and Shakespeare prevents James from inhabiting the idealized space of the masque.[69] Far from being mere accomplices of the social and political orders, the writers to be considered attempt to manipulate those orders while seeking legitimation for their voices through different and, in their own eyes, higher authorities. In so doing, they refuse to permit their own creative strategies of immunity to be appropriated by those for whom, ostensibly, they write. And in so doing, they furnish for their writing, sometimes at great cost, a separate space within a larger, ominous shadow.

The following pages thus stage the tense dialogue that emerges not only between writers and institutions, but between writers and their communities—the convent, the cultural circles surrounding but not synonymous with the Renaissance court, the artisanal community, the acting company, the theater-going public. They also demonstrate the existence of a historical trajectory that might be best characterized as increasing skepticism regarding the need and desire for "shade."

The first three figures encountered in this study, Cellini, Saint Teresa, and Tasso, never wholly dismiss the topos of a benevolent, paternal figure who will grant their vulnerable voices both authority and repose. Thus, despite his powerful critique of Cosimo de'Medici's failures as patron, Cellini still believes in monarchs' abilities to fashion themselves in the image of a protective father who will shield his faithful subjects from the social, legal, and economic realities of the world beyond the palace gates.[70] Teresa and Tasso likewise invest a heavenly father (and in Tasso's case, that father's embodiment in the church) with properties of nurturance and protection. But with Spenser, who aggressively counters England's imperial father-mother Elizabeth with a community of male "heroes," one begins to sense a cynical and revisionary attitude toward the possibility of benevolent shade. Shakespeare continues to dismantle the fantasy of the benign parent in his late plays, opposing the dramatic form that all-powerful monarchs produced by and for themselves—the court masque—to the more capacious romance. Finally, Corneille, resentful of the paternalistic French Academy that was intent on protecting the theater-going public from Corneille himself, does away with protective shadows altogether. Only through the resistance of subjects like Corneille to the Academy and to the performative authority of a dazzlingly theatrical Louis XIV could the fantasies associated with the proffering and welcoming of shade be undone.

It is here that a second trajectory begins to emerge in this study, one that has to do with the dynamics of gender. As noted earlier, Cellini engages in an abortive attempt at masculine self-definition by identifying his patron with the powerful—but ultimately conquerable—Medusa. Similarly, Spenser struggles to create a narrative in which Elizabeth is contained and defined by a masculine community of poets and readers, an attempt that is not entirely successful. Tasso and Corneille likewise try at various stages in their careers to "engender" vulnerability by associating it with the feminine—and thus to stigmatize and displace the posture of vulnerability that they experience all too well. Yet Teresa's writings suggest a manner in which the vulnerable female might herself be construed as capable of resisting the Counter-Reformation church, given the very nature of her dependency on a much more authoritative deity. And Shakespeare recognizes the potential challenge to authority represented by the maligned figure of the unruly wife, who serves as a potential double for the unruly actor. Even Tasso and Corneille are unable to maintain the finally artificial divide between female creatures of vulnerability and themselves. In the revised versions of the *Gerusalemme Liberata* and *Le Cid*, respectively, they equate their subordination with that of a principal female character; Corneille even finds in this equation a new formula for protest. Thus, within the careers of the individual authors discussed in this study, one encounters an initial attempt to "engender" vulnerability as female, followed by the gradual eclipse of that attempt as the authors find it impossible to conceal their own experiences of vulnerability in their work. In fact, gender increasingly becomes a vehicle for examining alternate voices within a hierarchy that is revealed to be far from absolute.

In part, these changes of attitude vis-à-vis protection are results of the gradual transformation of local court into extensive bureaucracy. In part, they are functions of the writer's new attitudes toward his or her relationship to a bourgeois economy that existed largely outside the grasp of an early modern state attempting, as Perry Anderson has convincingly argued, to retain the vestiges of feudalism against all odds.[71] But it is equally important to insist that these trajectories hardly culminate in the glorified apotheosis of a "self" named Corneille. Nor can one claim to recover fully and unproblematically an authorial voice, a voice that, like all fictional constructs, is the product of a mimetic process and is thereby distorted by the act of representation itself. Rather, the deliberately shaped personae encountered in the works to come must be seen as the products of strategies that had a resounding influence on the writing of early modern Europe as long as intellectuals remained subordinate to the claims of patronage, principate, and church.

Arguably, such subordination persists to some degree even today, and Corneille might be said to function as merely an arbitrary end point. Yet in at least one way the period between 1550 and 1660 was particularly distinctive. Later figures such as Racine and Rousseau, on the one hand, and Pope and Richardson, on the other, conceive of themselves in their battles against institutions as the alienated individuals more familiar to our own era, and their works as their own "property" through which they acquire meaning and a place in their complicated worlds. But for writers such as the six figures discussed in this book, who are exemplary of their period rather than unique, the consolation of literary property is not an option, although Corneille's collected works, published in 1660, foreshadow what is to come. Nor do they formulate their struggles against authority as struggles of alienation, although once again, Corneille emerges as a partial exception. Rather, they define themselves as members of a social or communal body that buttresses them against their respective institutions. In so doing, they sharply distinguish themselves not only from those who come after them but from those who came before, such as Petrarch and Erasmus, whose own communities of readers were much more remote and contrived.[72] It is to the complexities and risks of these vulnerable writings of several generations of authors that the following chapters turn.

2 ·

The Merchant of Florence: Benvenuto Cellini, Cosimo de'Medici, and the *Vita*

> Essendo in alloggiati a un certo luogo, il quale è di qua da Chioggia in su la man manca venendo inverso Ferrara, l'oste volse essere pagato a suo modo innanzi che noi andassimo a dormire; e dicendogli che innegli altri luoghi si usava di pagare la mattina, ci disse: "Io voglio esser pagato la sera, e a mio modo." Dissi a quelle parole che gli uomini che volevan fare a lor modo, bisogniava che si facessino un mondo a lor modo, perché in questo non si usava così. —Cellini, *Vita*
>
> (We happened to stay at a place on this side of Chioggia, on the left as you go towards Ferrara. The innkeeper wanted to be paid in his own way before we went to bed, and when I said that in other places it was usual to pay in the morning, he answered, "But I want to be paid this evening, and in my own way." In reply to this I said that men who wanted to be paid to suit themselves had better make a world to suit themselves, since it was done differently in this world.)[1]

So begins one of Benvenuto Cellini's remarkable exploits, with an innkeeper's innocuous request that his guests pay him before they retire for the evening and Cellini's response that the innkeeper should design a different world for himself to live in, because the real world doesn't work in such fashion. Partly because of the frightened companion, Tribolo, with whom Cellini is traveling en route from Ferrara to a Florence recently taken over by the tyrant Alessandro de'Medici, Cellini gives in to the innkeeper's demand and pays him, but he will not let the incident go unremembered. Before departing the next morning, he takes care to slash the four beds upstairs to shreds, "in modo che io cogniobbi aver fatto un danno di più di cinquanta scudi" (in such fashion that I knew I had done damage worth more than fifty scudi) (I.lxxix; Bull, p. 144)—far more than the innkeeper had been paid the night before. So does Cellini awaken his host to the "real world" in which he, perforce, must play a part.

The slashing of four beds is clearly less heinous than the various thefts, rapes, and murders that fill Cellini's autobiography, but this particular action, like so many of the others, attests less to the refusal of Cellini's "enemies" to conduct their lives as others insist than to *Cellini's* refusal to do so. What is especially relevant about the incident recounted above is the fact that it is occasioned by a request for money, a request made by the representative of a world of commerce and exchange from which Cellini, like a later Don Quixote, would prefer to keep himself aloof. But Cellini's act of violence, uncannily echoed in Cervantes's text when Quixote assaults the innkeeper's bedclothes believing them to be demonically inspired monsters, also reveals the extent to which Cellini is unable to avoid the claims made on him by that world. This entrapment prompts a relentless cycle of insult and revenge as dizzying as Quixote's windmills, and of which an admiring Goethe, praising the forcefulness of the Italian character, would remark, "The offended one, unless he takes his revenge instantly, falls into a kind of fever that plagues him like a physical disease until he has healed himself through the blood of his opponent."[2]

It was precisely Cellini's intensely individual response, nourished by a suspicion of the claims exacted by insidious agents of greed such as the innkeeper in Chioggia, that struck the first readers of Cellini's autobiography. But these readers were the contemporaries of Goethe rather than of Cellini himself. After languishing unpublished for almost two centuries, the incomplete manuscript of the artist's life was printed only in 1728. It quickly achieved a notoriety apparent in the imitations and/or translations of Casanova, Goethe, and Stendhal.[3] Cellini's account of his artistic, sexual, and military exploits went on to become one of the key texts for European romanticism as well as for one central nineteenth-century study of the Italian Renaissance, Jacob Burckhardt's *Civilization of the Renaissance in Italy*.[4] Both Cellini's literary style—daring, incautious, forceful, vigorous—and his life were admired in the nineteenth century, as narrative "manner" came together with autobiographical matter in the estimation or even overestimation of the Florentine's place in literary history. Such a superb union of form and content, it was felt, had not been achieved in the sinuous overformality of Cellini's famous saltcellar for Francis I, or in the Perseus poised over the writhing, decapitated body of Medusa, which Cellini had designed for Cosimo de'Medici's "mannerist" outdoor museum in the loggia of the Piazza della Signoria. In the view of the romantics, the *Vita* rose above not only the oppressions of a society increasingly authoritarian in nature—thus Goethe's praise for Cellini's ability to cure his fever by taking things into his own hands—but above the useless decadences of mannerist art.[5]

The belatedness of the autobiography's publication thus clinched its status as a masterpiece in an era that saw or wanted to see itself in the text, and it confirmed Cellini's status as the last great Renaissance man and the first great romantic, born two centuries too soon. Yet this still pervasive assessment of Cellini's romanticism must be understood within the context of Cellini's endless hagglings with dukes, popes, and messengers for financial compensation, as detailed not only in the *Vita* but in the account books, now in the Laurenziana, that Cellini assiduously kept during his Florentine stay from 1545 until his death in 1571.[6] Unlike a Casanova or Goethe, a Cellini, who was dependent upon financial compensation from the wealthy, could only be a man of talent or *virtù* when a figure in power conferred that status upon him. Tellingly, the *Vita* was written only when the approval of powerful patrons, specifically that of Cosimo de'Medici, had been withdrawn. In the vacuum of commissions and official "sanction," it became an attempt to constitute, belatedly for the artist, a self-defined sphere of genius. In this light, the process of artistic creation that Cellini so carefully delineates—the making of the saltcellar, of the *Perseus*, of the doorway at Fontainebleau—is hardly the mere effect of "stylish mannerism," but is intricately linked to the problem of self-validation as Cellini quantifies the very labor that he invests in his art.

This retrospective attempt at self-definition is a defense not only against the often cruelly unpredictable whims of what John

Pope-Henessy has described as the "rigid, penny-pinching world of Medicean patronage,"[7] but against a perhaps even more hostile world from which Cosimo had failed to protect Cellini: the marketplace, of which the innkeeper who demanded payment in advance became symptomatic. Sensitive to the depersonalized nature of an increasingly abstract market that paid a man for the material object of his work rather than for his labor, Cellini sought throughout his career to remove his work from the competitive marketplace. According to the narrative of the *Vita*, he was frequently successful in finding beneficent monarchs who enabled him to do just that. While the autobiographer declares at one moment in his text, "Servo chi mi paga" (I work for whoever pays me), this professed indifference to the source of patronage masks a profound desire to be "paid" *only* by those who viewed themselves as priceless. Cellini's *Vita* recounts his search for those who would find in him a suitably flattering mirror, or, as Francis I supposedly claimed, "a man after my own heart." Once the monarch's narcissistic capacities fail him, however, the artist becomes vulnerable to the vagaries of the very system from which he desired to be immune.

As the following pages will recount, the *Vita* enacts a fall from a symbolic economy of nourishment and gift-giving, within which Cellini is protected by the shadows cast by Pope Clement VII and Francis I, into the *real* economy into which Cosimo's indifference and commercial heritage (for the Medici had once been a family of bankers) threatened to plunge the artist. The *Vita* is as much an attempt to valorize the divine shadows cast by monarchs who were willing to see in the valiant Cellini an image of themselves, as it is an effort to escape from the stifling shadow of a Cosimo de'Medici who paradoxically refused to protect the gifted artist. The result is a narrative that, like Cellini's destruction of the innkeeper's beds, has something of the prodigal in it, reminiscent of Stephen Greenblatt's suggestion that images of individualism in early modern Europe tended to be preceded by their representation in the realm of the perverse: "As the voluminous accounts of monsters . . . physical deformities, and so forth affirm, by means of these marvels people achieve a sense of the differences . . . that make possible the dynamic order of individuation."[8] If we are to believe Cellini, the monster is always the inveterate and obstinate other who refuses to grant him his wishes, the resistant innkeeper or, to look toward his most famous statue, the Medusa who is conquered by the proud, serenely defiant Perseus.[9] To this extent, one might note in Cellini's autobiography precisely that "spirit of anarchism" to which Louis Renza has called attention, the virtually suicidal break with a "metafather figure" that leads to the repetitive claim for self-identity.[10] Yet this concept of individual immunity and anarchy cannot sustain itself, as is revealed not only by the unfinished nature of the *Vita* but by the treatises on goldsmithing and sculpture to which Cellini turned after failing to complete the autobiography. It is first to his fascination with the monstrous and to the "mondo" that he attempted to create, belatedly and "a suo modo," that the following pages turn.

I

"With Jupiter's protection and with a pledge of future grace, I go happily into exile" ("Tuta Jove / ac tanto pignore / laeta fugor").[11] Such is the saying carved into the original base of Cellini's most famous statue, commissioned by Cosimo de'Medici shortly after Cellini arrived in Florence in 1545: his *Perseus*, a bronze copy of which still stands in Florence's Piazza della Signoria, displaying the head of Medusa, as one of Cellini's admiring contemporaries wrote, for all the world to see. The words are supposedly uttered by Danae, the mother of Perseus, as she flees from her cruel father after being impregnated by a Jupiter who came to earth in the form of a golden shower. Following this plenteous rainfall and the promise of immunity from harm—Jupiter is no mere lover but Danae's powerful tutor ("tuta Jove") in its fullest Latin sense of guardian and protector—Danae goes forth to a distant country with the promise of return and her future son's vengeance ringing in her ears, a testament not only to the tyranny of earthly fathers but to the generosity and solicitude of heavenly fathers.

The political rationale for such a saying, originally displayed beneath the writhing body of Medusa on which Perseus casually stands, was the desire of Cellini's final patron, Duke Cosimo de'Medici, to have a statue representing his Perseus-like heroism in rescuing Florence from the Medusa of past tyrants. Cosimo is thus the "pledge," exiled from the city and returned to become one of Florence's most powerful leaders. This program is implicit in Cosimo's desire to have a statue that would offset Donatello's statue of Judith carrying the head of Holofernes, next to which Cellini's *Perseus* would be placed. Sculpted in the early quattrocento and thus during Florence's final days as a republic, Donatello's statue attested to the vitality of popular revolt against tyrants, a program that the *Perseus*, symbolic of ducal order, would ideally decenter.[12] But if Cosimo can be seen as the "seed" Danae is carrying as she flies from the city, he is also the lover and guardian Jupiter who protected Florence from afar in the years when she was figuratively exiled from herself, suffering under the likes of Cosimo's despotic relative Alessandro. Finally, there may well be another—although an ultimately failed—allegory at work in the panel as well. Hardly an artist who carried out the desires of his patrons to the letter (he made his *Perseus* a good third higher than it was supposed to have been, and the body of Medusa is mentioned nowhere in the original commission),[13] Cellini may well have meant the panel to serve as a gloss on the patronage and protection of his ideal prince: a patronage that manifests itself in a shower of gold, unasked for but deserved, providing protection and immunity from indigence and the numerous civil and criminal charges that Cellini avidly recounts in the pages of his autobiography. "Impregnated" by the priceless value of Cosimo's gold, Cellini, like Danae, will give birth to priceless sons.[14]

Or, to cite Cellini's paraphrase (in the *Vita*) of Francis I's words to him after a friendly disagreement between monarch and favorite artist, "E poi aggiunse che mi affogherebbe nell'oro" (The king added that he would drown me in gold) (II.xlvi). And in Cellini's *Vita*, if not in this fanciful recasting of Danae's flight from her father, the tale of wealth and immunity is told again and again. As a personal tale, however, it is essentially over by the time Cellini begins his *Vita* in 1558, almost ten years after casting the *Perseus*. Writing in Cosimo's Florence while under house arrest on charges of sodomy, complaining that the duke was no longer granting him commissions, the goldsmith mourns the loss of a patronage system that sought a mirror for its immunity and generosity in the artists it supported.[15] More precisely, Cellini exposes the failings of a Cosimo who refuses to guarantee Cellini's immunity at the risk of undermining his own. In so doing, he removes the duke from his pinnacle of power and reveals the larger institutional forces already at work in mid-sixteenth-century Italy that would indeed, in time, compromise the politics of petty tyrants such as the Medici.[16]

Such an exposure occurs through a narrative that progresses from an ideal "golden" age of patronage to a corrupt modern one; if the *Vita* is a tale of three cities, Rome, Paris, and Florence,[17] it is also a tale of three styles of Renaissance patronage. In Rome, to which he travels after political turmoil in his native Florence, Cellini encounters the frequent hostilities—but just as frequent generosities—of popes such as Clement VII and Paul III. Clement VII magnanimously forgives Cellini not only of a homicide he committed while "serving the Church" in his heroic defense of the Castel Sant'Angelo, but of "all the homicides I had ever committed and all those I ever would commit in the service of the Apostolic Church" (I.xxxvii; Bull, p. 76). In a memorable phrase, Clement's successor, Paul III, places Cellini above the law after he is called in for committing yet another murder in the holy city: "Sappiate che gli uomini come Benvenuto, unici nella lor professione, non hanno da essere ubrigati alla legge" (You should know that men like Benvenuto, unique in their profession, are not to be subject to the law) (I.lxxiv). Such extensions of papal protection not surprisingly breed the envy of others in Rome—envy that only legitimizes Cellini's value in the eyes of the pope, himself not "subject to the law."

At the same time, although the Roman popes are generous in terms of pardoning the artist's violent crimes, they are not always capable of understanding his needs to take longer on commissions than they want him to. Thus Cellini's failure to produce a much-desired chalice by the time that Clement expects it results in numerous altercations between the artist and Clement's messenger, culminating in the pope's order that Cellini be arrested if he doesn't hand over the chalice immediately. The artist's response—"My lords, if I gave his Holiness the chalice I'd be giving what belongs to me and not to him. And I don't intend to let him have it, because having taken so much trouble to bring it near completion I don't intend it to fall into the hands of some ignorant beast who would find it only too easy to ruin it" (I.lxi; Bull, p. 115)—does, indeed, land him in jail; but it also reveals Cellini's desire to claim that on which he has labored as his own, if only through the convenient hindsight afforded him after some 30 years have elapsed.

Such a claim, as shall shortly be seen, threatens to replace the patron as the true *genetrix* of the work, the guarantor of a commission's ontological status, with the artist himself.[18] But this replacement becomes necessary only *after* the patron fails to provide the "nourishment" necessary to the laboring artist. If Clement VII and Paul III only partially provide such nourishment, as the first third of the *Vita* recounts, Cellini finds a much more generous patron in King Francis I of France. For although Cellini finds a (necessary) immunity for his person at the once-generous hands of Paul III, only in Paris, where he stays with Francis I for several years, is he granted immunity for his artistic labors as well as lordship and amnesty for his person. After creating a statue of Jupiter for the generous king, Cellini remarks that Francis claims, "Pero è da fare un gran conto di Benvenuto, che non tanto che l'opere sue restino al paragone dell'antiche, ancora quelle suparano" (We must rate Benvenuto very highly indeed: his work not only rivals, it surpasses the ancients) (II.xli; Bull, p. 298).[19] After completing a design for a fountain for Francis's residence at Fontainebleau, Cellini is addressed by the king as "mon ami" and told, " 'Io non so qual s'è maggior piacere, o quello d'un principe l'aver trovato un uomo sicondo il suo cuore, o quello di quel virtuoso l'aver trovato un principe che gli dia tanta comodità, che lui possa esprimere i sua gran virtuosi concetti' " (I don't know which is the greater, the pleasure of a prince at having found a man after his own heart, or the pleasure of an artist at having found a prince ready to provide him with all he needs to express his great creative ideas) (II.xxii; Bull, p. 271). Cellini's uncharacteristically modest response is that his own fortune is necessarily the greater, to which Francis answers with a laugh: " 'Diciamo che la sia eguale' " (Let's say that it's equal). Such "equality" between artist and king, in a city which Cellini in the *Trattato dell'Oreficeria* remarks that the Parisians call "*Paris simparì*, che vuol dire 'Parigi senza pari' " (a Paris without peers) (*Opere*, p. 644), places the former goldsmith and maker of coins on a level that is also without "peers": "There are a few great princes [like Francis] who have given to men the opportunity to rekindle those artistic gifts which were almost extinguished [in our day]" (*Opere*, pp. 713–14). If the monarchs of Rome shield Cellini temporarily from the weight of the law, Francis removes Cellini from the realm occupied by other "vulgar" artists, placing him beyond all possible rivals, including those of antiquity. Thanks to his own invaluable status, the king is capable of conferring upon his equal Cellini a similarly immeasurable value.[20]

The patronage Cellini enjoys in Rome and France until he arrives in Florence consists largely of withholding the artist from the marketplace and displacing him into an almost feudal relationship in which the patron is the "lord" or protector of his talented "vassal" (and it is as "divoto ed amorevole vassallo e servo" that Cellini continually addresses Cosimo in the course of his relentless pleas for compensation).[21] Only within this relationship do the artist's labors have value. But in Cellini's case, this value comes to be as inestimable as that of the patron himself.

Within this symbolic economy,[22] which resists the commodification of the work of art, the patron or would-be patron is frequently addressed not only by Cellini but by others throughout the sixteenth century as the natural participant in a natural process of a work's ripening and coming to fruition. Thus in an obvious and perhaps ironic allusion to the rhetoric of the many dedications that circulated in Renaissance England, Shakespeare writes to the Earl of Southampton, a generous patron of the arts, at the beginning of his first narrative poem, *Venus and Adonis*, "If the first heir of my invention prove deformed, I shall be sorry it had so noble a godfather, and never after ear so barren a land, for fear it yield me still so bad a harvest." Familial and agricultural relationships come together in these lines. Moreover, at least one powerful patron in the early seventeenth century, King James I, often uses the rhetoric of maternal bounty when speaking of his role as patron and king. In *The Trew Law of Free Monarchies*, he writes that his first "fatherly duty" is that of "nourishing" his subjects, and in the *Basilikon Doron*, he claims that he is a "loving nourish-father" to his people.[23] As Coppélia Kahn has noted, with James I, the *pater patriae* attempted to encompass the "generative" power of women; the magical power to give conferred upon the royal patron greater majesty while often playing upon his subjects' logically heightened dependency.[24] Such "bountifulness" was not incidentally mythologized in one of Ben Jonson's masques for James—*The Masque of Queens*—in the figure of "Heroic Vertue" or Perseus, a parent figure who is claimed by Jonson to give birth to none other than Fame: "Sing then *good Fame*, that's out of *Vertue* borne, / For, Who doth fame neglect, doth vertue scorn."[25]

Cellini too engages in the creation of a mythic "nourish-father," not only in the course of fashioning his *Perseus* with its mythology of Cosimo's supposedly generous patronage, but in the course of writing his autobiography.[26] But if Francis becomes the ideal parent through whom Cellini is raised to noble status, Cosimo de'Medici fails to fulfill the narcissistic role Cellini has come to expect of royalty. Arriving in Florence in 1545 after being alienated from Francis I by his mistress Madame d'Etampes, Cellini assumes that he will receive similar nourishment from his maternal city, the "natural" place of bounty to which he returns after a long sojourn in alien countries. It is also in Florence that Cellini announces he will finally show the Italians that he is no "mere" goldsmith—"for it was as such that they until now knew me"—but a *sculptor*, an artist rather than a mere craftsman, and thus worthy of a duke's patronage. Yet to a noticeably large extent, this is a status that Cosimo fails to confer upon Cellini, even though at their first meeting, the Florentine leader promises to outdo Francis himself: " 'Benvenuto mio,' " Cosimo solemnly declares, " 'se tu mi volessi fare qualche cosa a me, io ti pagherei bene altrimenti che non ha fatto quel tuo Re, di chi per tua buona natura tanto ti lodi' " (if you were to do something for me I would reward you in a way very different from the way that King, whom your good nature makes you praise so much, has done) (II.lii; Bull, p. 312).

Cellini blames himself for not having recognized Cosimo's failings at once, as he notes that he mistakenly treated Cosimo as a duke *rather* than as a merchant—two roles that are mutually exclusive in the *Vita*.[27] When Cosimo offers to write a careful contract itemizing the supplies that Cellini will need to cast his commissioned *Perseus*, Cellini refuses to draw up such a document, writing instead, "Singularissimo mio patrone, le vere suppliche e i veri nostri patti non consistono in queste parole ne' in questi scritti, ma sì bene il tutto consiste che io riesca con l'opere mie a quanto io l'ho promesse; e riuscendo, allora io mi prometto che vostra Eccellenzia illustrissima benissimo si ricorderà di quanto la promette a me" (Most rare patron, the real petition and the real agreement do not consist in these words or in these documents, they depend on how far I succeed in doing the work as I promised; and if I do succeed, then I am certain that your Most Illustrious Excellency will remember only too well all that you promised me (II.liii; Bull, p. 314). The duke's response is delight with "del mio fare e del mio dire" (both my actions and words), a response consonant, Cellini feels at the time, with his lordship (II.liii).

But the next few years are plagued with examples of the duke's parsimony and his failure to reimburse Cellini even for the money he has already spent on bronze, wood for the furnace, and other materials; with Cosimo's major-domo's jealousy over the manner in which Cellini seems, despite all of the artist's haggling, to be treated as one of the duke's favorites; and the envy of others, preeminently Cosimo's former sculptor Bandinelli. In the reconstructed narrative of his life that reinterprets and rewrites his past, Cellini calls attention to his failure to realize "that this lord behaved more like a merchant than a duke" as the source of his many problems in Florence ("non conoscendo io che questo Signiore aveva più modo di mercatante che di duca, liberalissimamente procedevo con sua Eccellenzia come duca e non come mercatante") (II.liii; Bull, p. 314).

With this judgment, Cellini condemns Cosimo by relegating him to a position within rather than above an explicitly monetary system of exchange, and thus within a system in which "any possession is alienable and its worth unstable, a reflex of how many other people happen to want it that day."[28] But by so displacing Cosimo from his role as duke and insisting on his bourgeois origins, Cellini also risks placing *himself* within a real economy rather than within the symbolic economy he so carefully fostered throughout his previous dealings with patrons. Cellini's insistence on Cosimo's merchant-like behavior thus not only denigrates the duke but also raises the dangerous possibility of exposing himself.

These effects are nowhere more explicit than in the lengthy narrative surrounding the *Perseus*—for the materials of which Cellini has not yet been reimbursed when he begins the autobiography. When, upon the statue's completion, Cosimo sends his secretary to ask Cellini how much he wants for it, Cellini is at first rendered (uncharacteristically) speechless. He is then informed that unless he names a price he will be in pain of falling into complete disgrace with his Excellency—a response that provokes Cellini's heated retort that not even ten thousand crowns would be enough. Valuing the *Perseus* at a fixed price takes away from Cellini's "own" price—and obviously from that of Cosimo, who becomes little more than a merchant or middleman rather than a *maker* of value. Cellini's question for the duke when the two finally confront each other over the issue of the artist's compensation is, " 'O come è egli possibile che la mia opera mi sia stimata il suo prezzo, non essendo oggi uomo in Firenze che la sapessi fare?' " (Oh, how is it possible that anyone can estimate the price of my work, when there's not a single man in Florence who knows how to make it?) (II.xcvii). The artist's uniqueness *should* find its mirror in the duke's uniqueness; but the duke's response to Cellini's insubordination is that he will simply name another, quite competent, sculptor—Cellini's enemy Bandinelli—to fix a price (a "giusto prezzo") that the artist will be paid.

If on the one hand, Cellini's autobiography demystifies the myths of Jupiter's golden rain and the shared immunity of patron and artist from the "real" world beyond the palace gates, it also must function in the *absence* of those myths to resist Cellini's absorption into the marketplace by valorizing his labors as the new standard of value. Prevented from working, he must give himself over to writing; or, to cite the end of the vastly truncated autobiography that he inserts into the *Trattato dell'Oreficeria*, "Da poi che m'è impedito il fare, così io mi son messo a dire" (*Opere*, p. 718). And what Cellini proceeds to narrate, although still constricted by the protective shadow of a duke who has revealed himself to be no protector at all, is the apparent eclipsing of a golden age by an iron age and Cosimo's subsequent attempt to place a vulgar, monetary value on both Cellini's labors and his work.

Thus the *Vita* exposes the saying on the *Perseus*'s base as a fiction and virtually creates a new myth of the artist as one of the gods. The god whom Cellini selects as his model, however, is one whose very identity might be said to challenge the extent to which Cellini *can* separate himself from a vulgar ethics of commodification: Vulcan, god of the forge, the cuckold of Venus whose frustrated desire for his absent wife is channeled into the making of beautiful things. Yet it is hardly the beauty of the priceless "object" that concerns Cellini—although he savors the first moment of its unveiling in the piazza—but the process of laboring over that object. And it is primarily in emphasizing the labor value of his work, meticulously conveyed in the pages of the *Vita*, that Cellini attempts to rescue his own esteem from the shadow of a mercantile and unworthy patron, who would ask others such as the despised Bandinelli to determine for the *Perseus* a "giusto prezzo" (II.xcvii) of which he himself refused to be the judge.[29]

II

Cellini's insistence on the laborious nature of his work and his life—"la vita travagliata," as he describes it in the sonnet that prefaces the *Vita*—is everywhere present in the autobiography. As such, he painstakingly describes his "fatiche" or labors as a partial justification for his narrative enterprise (his second chapter opens with a reference to "quegli uomini che si sono affaticati . . . hanno dato cognizione di loro al mondo"—those men who have worked hard and have made their mark on the world; he too is one of these men). This description forms a striking contrast to other sixteenth-century narratives that seek to displace or to annul the role of generally disparaged physical labors. Castiglione's *Book of the Courtier*, with its ethic of *sprezzatura* or elitist disdain for visible effort, is one tremendously influential example of the cinquecento. The courtier must rather labor to disguise his efforts to secure the good graces of a prince; and the *Book of the Courtier* ultimately glorifies the aesthetic object as an artwork that bears no traces of its work.

These concerns of the "good courtier," the bureaucrat anxious to be absorbed without a trace into the ennobling atmosphere of the Urbino court, found their way into the numerous writings of Italian artists shortly thereafter. They were equally anxious to proclaim the ennobling status of their art in an era in which it finally seemed possible to escape the reduction of the fine arts to merely mechanical praxis.[30] In the ongoing debate as to whether painting or sculpture was the most "noble" art, the painter Bronzino, who fared much more successfully with Cosimo de'Medici than did Cellini, wrote to Benedetto Varchi, "Dico . . . cerca lo scarpellare, che questo non fa l'arte più nobile, anzi più presto gli toglie dignità, perché quanto l'arti si fanno con più esercizio di braccia e di corpo, tanto più hanno del meccanico, e per conseguenza sono manco nobili"[31] (Regarding sculpture, I say that this is hardly a noble art; rather, it is an art that lacks dignity, because the more one exercises the body and the hands, the more one smacks of a mere mechanic, and consequentially the less of nobility). Tellingly, while Giorgio Vasari, who was charged with organizing and presiding over the significantly named Accademia del Disegno in Florence in 1563, praised Michelangelo's labors as a sculptor in his *Vite*, he did so in a manner that relegated the labor of the body below that of the "ingegno" or wit. Nature is incapable of imagining anything "sì strana e tanto difficile, ch'egli con la virtù del divinissimo ingegno suo . . . di gran lunga non la trapassi" (so strange and so difficult that he, by the virtue of his most divine *ingegno* . . . could not surpass it by far).[32] Moreover, Vasari reserved his highest praises in the *Vite* for the high-minded artist such as Raphael, who lived above the concerns of the flesh and who caused no trouble for his patrons—and who thus emerges as strikingly different from Cellini, who, Vasari observed in his 1568 edition of the *Vite*, was a man in all things "fiero, vivace, prontissimo e terribilissimo," ignorant of when to be diplomatic and silent.[33] Finally, Cellini's arch-rival, the Florentine Baccio Bandinelli (made, unlike Cellini, a *cavaliere* by the pope for his role in defending Rome), defended the contemplative role of the writer and the intellectual life of the painter. His own autobiography, which preceded Cellini's by several years, boldly asserted that the pen was far nobler than the chisel.[34]

Cellini's tactic is much different. Rather than reverse Bronzino's hierarchy and declare that sculpture is above painting because it requires less physical effort (a claim that would have been patently untrue), Cellini deliberately insists on the tremendous amount of time and energy he has invested in each of his projects, from the first works he fashioned as an apprentice to the life-size crucifix with which he closes his *Vita* and of which he says to the Duchess of Florence, "Una cotale opera nissuno uomo mai non s'è messo a una cotale estrema fatica" (No man has ever engaged in so much labor for such a work) (II.c). In one of his poems, he defends sculpture against painting's supposed supremacy by declaring, "Quell / opre che si fanno agevolmente / son poco degne perché presto han fine, / l'altre han gran lode più meritamente" (Those works that are easily done are of little worth because they are soon completed; thus other works are worthy of greater praise) (*Opere*, pp. 881–82). The difficulty and arduousness of the task define its worth; that which is done easily and quickly is not to be trusted, since labor has become the new standard of value. In a letter to Varchi that formed part of a lively debate during the 1540's among leading Florentine artists regarding the relative virtues of sculpture and painting[35] and that employs phrases which echo throughout his sonnets, Cellini declares:

> Vi ricordo e dico, come di sopra, che la scultura è madre di tutte l'arte dove s'interviene disegno; e quello che sarà valente scultore e di buona maniera, gli sarà facilissimo l'esser buon prospettivo e architetto e maggior pittor che quelli che bene non posseggono la scultura. La pittura non è altro che o arbero o uomo o altra cosa, che si specchi in un fonte. La differenza che è dalla scultura alla pittura è tanta, quanto è dalla ombra e la cosa che fa l'ombra. ("Lettera a Benedetto Varchi," *Opere*, pp. 1004–5)
>
> (I remind you that I said above that sculpture is the mother of all the other arts where *disegno* plays a part; and he who is a worthy and accomplished sculptor will find it much easier to be a good designer and architect and a better painter than those who do not possess the art of sculpture. Painting is nothing other than a tree or man or anything else that views itself in a fountain. The difference between sculpture and painting is such, that the one is merely a shadow; the other is that which casts the shadow.)

The supreme sculptor—and thus the supreme laborer—is God; "Che fecie i cieli e 'l mondo, e noi fé degni / delle sue mani, senza far disegni" (He made the heavens and the earth, and made us worthy of his hands, without first designing them) (Sonnet 13; *Opere*, p. 893); the supreme painter is the infernal Lucifer, who, unable to be God, "con tal ombre ha l'anime ingannate" (with such shadows has fooled souls).[36] *Disegno* is mere illusion, the reflection of a surface, the delusive "ombra" that deceives those such as Narcissus who gaze into it and imagine depth and being where none exist. The product of pure "facilità," a mere sleight-of-hand, painting tricks its viewers into believing in "una sola veduta" (a single view), whereas sculpture emerges through the surmounting of difficulties brought on by the aggregation of multiple viewpoints: "così gli [al scultore] vien fatto questa grandissima fatica con cento vedute o più" (*Discorso di Messer Benvenuto Cellini sopra la differenza nata tra gli scultori e pittori*; *Opere*, p. 866). "Nostra immmortal sacra scultura" (Sonnet 13; *Opere*, p. 893), which takes primacy over all of the other arts as their "madre," had its origins in the creative actions of the father, "God holy and joyous," who without any preconceived design ("senza far disegni") fashioned with his hands that which will endure forever ("sol quella eterna dura") (Sonnet 7; *Opere*, p. 888). Thus does the sculptor become the true "nourish-father" on whom all the other lesser arts and artists depend.

The above remarks are scattered throughout Cellini's numerous sonnets written while in Florence[37] and the *Discorso di Messer Benvenuto Cellini sopra la differenza nata tra gli scultori e pittori* of 1546. It is the *Vita* that industriously undertakes to compose from these observations on sculpture's labored yet divine origins a coherent narrative that places Cellini himself in the role of the productive father-mother whose own labors produce far more than "ombre"—and ideally remove him from the "ombre" cast by patrons. Moreover, this narrative places Cellini beyond the more immediate realm of Florence, where a Neoplatonic influence on the arts had been especially strong since Lorenzo de'Medici and Marsilio Ficino,[38] and where *disegno* was rapidly becoming accepted as the "principio dell'arte," the true *origin* of the work of art. In the ensuing divorce of intellectual from manual labor, the artist would gradually become an entity apart from the artisan, whose own semiskilled labors would be exploited within the emergent market.[39] Cellini's defense of sculpture and of labor becomes a defense of the artisan and maker, who like God is capable of working "senza far disegni" when he begins.[40] Finally, the *Vita* emerges as a defense of Cellini's independence from and superiority to the duke who spurned him. For dukes might also theorize, and thus provide the ontological *disegno* or blueprint from which an artist might proceed, but they could not *make*: they had not been through the long period of practice, apprenticeship, and agon with their masters that occupies the first thirty-odd *capitoli* of the *Vita*.[41]

In light of Cellini's defense of labor and, by the time of the *Vita*, his hostility toward Cosimo, it is possible to turn to the most memorable section of the autobiography—the casting of the *Perseus*—and to find there yet another dimension of the statue unanticipated in the original program. For Perseus becomes Cellini, the laboring and heroic "parent," and Medusa the failed and dangerous patron whose gaze, far from conferring nourishment and bounty, engenders only a fatal sterility. The *Perseus*'s fantastic birth from the fiery and explosive furnace comes only after dozens of pages recounting the artist's careful and prolonged "fatiche" in designing the clay model, casting the decapitated Medusa, and building a furnace that could contain the large, twisted figure of Perseus. In the course of all of these labors, which take over seven years, Cosimo and his wife continually interrupt the artist to give him less important commissions and visit the bottega to interrogate him on his proceedings, exuding mistrust of Cellini's capacities to consummate such a great work. Finally, however, Cellini sets the stage of the dark backroom of the bottega on the day when the bronze statue of Perseus, holding Medusa's head aloft, is to be cast and the difficult, perhaps impossible, act of fusion performed. During this dramatic finale, the workshop catches fire and an exhausted and overworked Cellini is forced to take to his bed with a bout of fever. When all hope that the metal will melt inside the clay seems to be lost, the inspired (and still feverish) artist commands that two hundred pewter bowls be thrown energetically into the furnace to feed the flame. With an awesome "thunderbolt" ("un lampo di fuoco grandissimo, che parve proprio che una saetta si fussi creata quivi alla presenza nostra") (II.lxxvii) that suggests that the power of the divine is guiding Cellini's massive enterprise, the furnace erupts and ejaculates a long stream of fire, as Cellini's assistants rejoice over the imminent fusion of the statue and praise their master for having "brought a corpse back to life" ("Or veduto di avere risuscitato un morto, contro al credere di tutti quegli ignioranti, e' mi tornò tanto vigore che io non mi avvedevo se io avevo più febbre o più paura di morte") (II.lxxvii). The long, painstaking process of labor and the overcoming of tremendous *difficoltà* that climax in the threatened sterility of Cellini's greatest work enable the artist to turn from celebrating his own power to revive the dead to that of God: " 'O Dio, che con le tue immense virtù risuscitasti da e' morti, e glorioso te ne salisti al cielo!' " (Oh God, who with your great powers brought yourself back from the dead, and ascended in glory to heaven!) (II.lxxvii).

If the miraculous resuscitation of the *Perseus* is depicted as the deserved completion of Cellini's seven years of labor and his victory over cynics such as Cosimo, there is little that is "natural" about the gestation or rebirth itself. Rather, the narrative that describes Cellini's labors is marked with others' observations of Cellini's transgressiveness, from Cosimo's initially skeptical remark that the rules of art won't permit the statue's completion[42] to the exaggerated report of Cosimo's major-domo to his prince that Cellini was no human but "uno spresso gran diavolo, perché io avevo fatto quello che l'arte nollo poteva fare; con tante altre gran cose, le quali sarieno state troppe a un diavolo" (an authentic and powerful devil, since I had done that which art was unable to do; and I had done other great things which would have been too much even for a devil) (II.lxxvii). With these remarks, Cellini's fellow artists admiringly concurred, although without replicating the language of demonic force. One Latin couplet affixed to the *Perseus* when it was first unveiled remarks, "Once nature was the archetype of art. But since Cellini has cast the Perseus, now art has become the archetype of nature." Yet another writer commented that it was no longer Medusa's face but Cellini's *Perseus* that would turn onlookers to stone.[43] Thus Cellini had overtaken Medusa—the threatening powers that would deny his worth, the maternal principle of nourishment become a monstrosity in the hateful figure of Cosimo—and neutralized her, appropriating her powers as his own.[44]

To an extent, such transgressiveness, as Mircea Eliade has suggested, is part of the ritual of metallurgy itself—a rite that undertakes to penetrate the bowels of the earth and to appropriate the natural process of ripening ore. Cellini's masculinization of labor, his taking upon himself the role of the father-mother in the creation of his

Perseus, thus participates in what Eliade has described as "the feeling of venturing into a domain which by rights does not belong to man—the subterranean world with its mysteries of mineral gestation which has been slowly taking its course in the bowels of the Earth-Mother. . . . The artisan takes the place of the Earth-Mother, and it is his task to accelerate and perfect the growth of the ore. The furnaces are, as it were, a new matrix, an artifical uterus where the ore completes its gestation."[45] Since the patron's help has not been forthcoming, Cellini himself has to delve into the "source" of creation and appropriate it, through his infernal yet godlike labors, as his own.[46] But this act of violent appropriation is far from being self-contained. The section on the *Perseus* in the *Vita* is rather designed to force the reader—like Cosimo—to marvel over the account of the statue's making. Indeed, it is not so much the object itself as the story of Cellini's labors that prompts others to marvel. The majordomo's account of the final casting of the *Perseus* transforms the casting into more of a "marvelous" feat than it was; and when Cellini himself travels to Pisa to tell the duke and duchess the story of his last labors in his own words, "It seemed to their Excellencies far more of a stupendous and marvellous experience to hear me tell of it in person (più stupenda e più meravigliosa il sentirla contare a me in vocie). When I came to the foot of the Perseus which had not come out—just as I had predicted to his Excellency—he was filled with astonishment (io lo viddi empiere di meraviglia)" (II.lxxviii; Bull, p. 349). Marvel, the petrifying reaction that Descartes would describe in *Les passions de l'âme* a century later as "a sudden surprise of the soul which causes it to apply itself to consider with attention the objects which seem to it rare and extraordinary,"[47] is produced as the result of hearing the *narration* of Cellini's "extraordinary" labors, which have transgressed into the realm of an angry and violent god. It is a marvel to which Cosimo is momentarily forced to be submissive. But some time later, as he hides behind a curtain in his palace to watch the crowds gaze admiringly at the newly unveiled *Perseus*, he informs Cellini that he will make *him* the submissive subject of "meraviglia": he asks his *cameriere* Sforza Almeni to find Cellini and tell him "da ma parte che é m'ha contento molto più di quello che io mi aspettavo, e diglio che io contenterò lui di modo che io lo farò maravigliare" (that for my part I'm much more content than I'd expected; and tell him that I will content him in such a manner that I will astonish him) (II.xcii).

Thus at the heart of Cellini's narrative of labor and insistence on the arduous and often transgressive nature of making or *il fare* is a rhetoric of violence and subjugation designed to force the rich and the powerful into willing submission.[48] That such momentary subjugation might be overturned by the prince in a manner that would make Cellini himself marvel at his monarch's liberality suggests that the production of awe is hardly limited to the artist himself. Rather, its effect is created in order to be reversed, so that Cellini himself can finally become the submissive figure "subject" to a duke's or king's liberal gift of gold. Such a rhetoric of force in Cellini's descriptions of the reactions of potentates from Clement to Francis to his *opere* reveals that the symbolic economy of gift-giving within which social identity is mutually ascribed is hardly an innocent one for Cellini, as some of the glowing accounts of the beneficent French king might otherwise suggest.[49] That such a reversal never occurred, however, in the case of Cosimo, despite the latter's false promise as he stood overlooking the crowded Piazza della Signoria, suggests that the indifferent Cosimo is finally immune to the force of Cellini's labors and *virtù*, with its powerfully gendered etymology. It suggests too that the labors of individual creation, dependent as they are on violence and transgression not only into the realm of "Dio" but also into that of the eternal Earth-Mother, in Eliade's phrase, are also ultimately dependent on another's gaze, another's propensity to articulate the forceful rhetoric implicit in Cellini's acts of making, acts that have no value in and of themselves. As Jean Baudrillard has suggested in his analysis of a Marxian economics that would also privilege a labor theory of value, no labor can generate its own value in isolation. Only in the realm of the imaginary can labor as the mirror of production, to cite the title of Baudrillard's perhaps most influential study, assume a totalizing—but falsely totalizing—status.[50]

Thus the final labors mentioned in the *Vita*, the "fatiche" with which Cellini creates a massive crucifix, end virtually in sterility and the comic deflation of his insistence that the crucifix was designed only for his pleasure ("io mi sono preso per piacere di fare una delle più faticose opere che mai si sia fatte al mondo") (II.ci). When, in the last pages of the truncated *Vita*, the duchess asks Cellini if she might buy the life-size crucifix for a private chapel, he responds that not even for two thousand ducats would he sell his work, given its uniqueness and the labors invested in its creation. Cellini's extraordinary "fatiche" remove the work from a system of monetary evaluation in which it would be subject to the vulgar commodification Cellini consistently seeks to avoid. Yet it is also with this last and supposedly transcendent work made for Cellini's pleasure ("piacere") alone that the artist tries to make one final, even pathetic bargain with the Medici court. Interested in obtaining a fine piece of marble for future work, he informs the duchess that he will gladly present her the crucifix as a gift if she promises to aid him in his quest for the marble. Only momentarily both the liberal patron and the laborer who alone knows how to evaluate his *opera*, Cellini becomes despite himself the victim of a situation in which his works assume a relative status within the economy of another, more powerful, figure's making.

Cellini's attempt to validate the autonomy and inestimable worth of his labors produces, as it must in a society that would increasingly value the marketplace on the one hand and the superficial *sprezzatura* of the aristocracy on the other, a narrative doomed to incompletion and obscurity. Cellini's defiance of market value, coupled with his unrelenting insistence on the worth of his labor, makes the *Vita*, like the *Perseus*, a fantastic narrative, although the nature of Cellini's Perseus fantasy had changed considerably after his disappointment at the hands of the merchant of Florence.[51]

Yet while it is thus possible to read the *Vita* as an unsuccessful work of "compensatory narcissism" in which what Cellini claims as his "own" is never fully his,[52] it is important to add an epilogue. For Cellini goes on from the unfinished *Vita* to write a very different kind of text, the *Trattato dell'Oreficeria* and the *Trattato della Scultura*. These works are also generated for a different reader than that "ideal" one of the *Vita*, whom one critic has intriguingly hypothesized to be none other than Cosimo himself.[53] To be sure, the *Trattato dell'Oreficeria*, which describes the various arts of jewelry-making from the simplest to the most complex in a manner that dovetails with the trajectory of Cellini's own life as an artist, is dedicated to Cosimo's son Francesco, who became *principe-reggènte* in 1565 when Cosimo began to withdraw as Florence's leader. The praise that Cellini lavishes upon Cosimo's son is, in all likelihood, designed as an appeal to Francesco to release the artist from the shadows that had fallen upon his productive life in recent years; but Cellini's lack of success is evident from the revised 1568 preface, dedicated no longer to Francesco but to his brother, the cardinal Ferdinand.

Yet if the *Trattati* represent Cellini's last chance to impress upon Florence's princes the worth of his labors, they also reflect Cellini's attempt to locate himself within a much different community, and one which, if his own accounts in the *Vita* of his distaste for working with others are correct, he has often spurned: that of other artisans. If the *Vita* functions largely to place Cellini beyond the realm of his fellow artists—with the exception of a rare few, such as the great Michelangelo, from whom Cellini claims to have learned everything he knows—the *Trattati* make Cellini's life of learning, laboring and surmounting *difficoltà* an exemplary one from which others may also learn. There are still, to be sure, several moments in the *Trattati* in which monarchs alone are deemed worthy of responding to and acknowledging the value of Cellini's "fatiche." But while Cellini's labors are still dependent on recognition from others—as is evident in a poignant moment in which he expresses his hope that his readers will be moved to great disdain for his bad fortune and compassion for his life[54]—those others are less frequently monarchs or popes and more often the fellow artists who initiated Cellini into his trade. He speaks fondly of one elderly goldsmith with whom he worked in Rome and reprints the verses by Florentine artists affixed to the base of the *Perseus* in an appendix to the *Trattato della Scultura*, thereby placing himself more securely than before within a group of readers he is now undertaking to initiate, as one who has practiced not just one art but many. And while the *Trattati* obsessively return to (and retell) crucial events in Cellini's life, such as the making of the *Perseus*, they situate that life in the context of others' lives: thus the *Trattato dell'Oreficeria* opens with the brief biographies of 22 artists who "furno i primi che dessino principio a resucitare tutte quelle arti che sono sorelle carnali d['oreficeria]" (were the first that began to revive all those arts that are sisters of jewelry-making) (*Opere*, p. 624).

Published only a few years before Cellini's death in 1571, the *Trattati* develop a tension already in evidence in rare moments in the *Vita*, such as when Cosimo's reluctance to pay Cellini for the *Perseus* clashes with Florentine artists' judgments of the statue's pricelessness—excluding, of course, the judgment of the hated and unworthy Bandinelli. The treatises thus become an attempt to protect Cellini from the forces of the market he resisted throughout the *Vita* by making of the artists themselves a community capable of assessing its own worth.[55] This vision, perhaps no less than that incomplete and unsatisfying one of the autobiography, also tries to ignore the essential vulnerability of the finished work to the gaze of others. David Ricardo would write two centuries later that the value of artistic artifacts "is wholly independent of the quantity of labour originally necessary to produce them"; and that the economic value of works of art merely "varies with the varying wealth and inclinations of those who are desirous to possess them."[56] But the *Trattati* also, however tentatively—and uncharacteristically for the artist so frequently heralded as the supposedly modern "Renaissance man"—look back to the era of guilds and corporations. Cellini's last written works seek to define the artist, not as an alienated individual, but as the member of a community whose knowledge of *il fare* and ability to pass that knowledge on to others might make it, if not self-sufficient, at least the possessor of secret "wisdom." And as the possessors of such wisdom, which is only manifest in the process of making, Cellini's readers would insure their separateness from, and, at least in Cellini's eyes, their superiority to, those who depended on them for the creation of beautiful things.[57]

3 •

Between Two Fathers: Teresa of Avila and Mystical Autobiography

> ¡Oh desventurados tiempos y miserable vida en la que ahora vivimos, y dichosas a las que les ha cabido tan buena suerte, que estén fueren de él! Algunas veces me es particular gozo cuando, estando juntas, las veo a estas hermanas tenerle tan grande interior, que la que más puede, más alabanzas da a nuestro Señor de verse en el monesterio; porque se les ve muy claramente que salen aquellas alabanzas de lo interior del alma. —Teresa of Avila, *Las Moradas*
>
> (Oh, unhappy are the times and miserable is the life which we now live, and happy are those who have had the good fortune to be outside of it! Sometimes it makes me especially glad when we are together and I see these sisters of mine so full of inward joy that each vies with the rest in praising Our Lord for bringing her to the convent; it is very evident that those praises come from the inmost depths of the soul.)[1]

As the preceding chapter suggested, Cellini turned only belatedly to an artisanal community to find validation for his labors. His transgressive autobiography, reflecting his painful inability to break out of the cycle of aggression and dependence, languished incomplete and unpublished for two centuries, while his *Trattati*, written after the *Vita*, found an audience within his lifetime. In turning to Teresa of Avila, whose writings are roughly contemporary with those of Cellini, one might well expect a strikingly different scenario.[2] Hardly embroiled in the countless petty scandals that characterized Cellini's life and far removed from dazzling cultural centers such as Paris and Rome, Teresa indeed produced autobiographical writings that form a radical contrast to those of the Florentine artist. Yet like Cellini's autobiography, Teresa's writings were also unpublished during her lifetime thanks in part to their "scandalous" content; and like Cellini, Teresa forcefully defended the *trabajos* (labors) of soul and hand alike. But it is perhaps Teresa's plaint for her "desventurados tiempos" that links her most convincingly to Cellini.

Teresa's lament, like many of Cellini's complaints, stemmed from the author's difficult relationships with "fathers." In Teresa's case, these were the men who supervised her and who insisted that she respect the laws of silence and *clausura* (seclusion) when she was brought before the Inquisition in 1575.[3] Teresa's spiritual autobiography, *Las Moradas*, written immediately after her experience with the Inquisition when she believed that her active life as a founder of convents was over, subtly explores the oppressive relationship between ignorant confessors and women struggling to embrace a different father. In strikingly different ways, Cellini and Teresa both combated what they perceived as the false shade of their earthly superiors and attempted to seek validation elsewhere. Cellini finally located that validation in an artisanal community defined by shared *opere*; Teresa sought to find it in a community of women shaped by and within the writings of a New Testament that she was forbidden to read.

But for Teresa, as for Cellini, such an attempt at validation was beset with obvious pitfalls.[4] Particularly in Spain, the second half of the sixteenth century was marked by institutional attempts not only to establish but to control the very conditions for the mystical experiences crucial to Teresa's alternative source of validation.[5] With the circulation of the *Indice de libros prohibidos* in Spain in 1559 by Inquisitor-General Juan Valdés, all books of mystical orientation were banned. Twenty-one people suspected of heresy—some of them associated with the *alumbrados*, a movement that believed in illumination from within by the divinity—were burned publicly in Spain in that year alone.[6] Symptomatic of the immense changes taking place in Catholic Europe during the second half of the sixteenth century were the very different receptions given women prophets in the Friulian region of Italy in 1511 and in the mid-1560's. In the former year, as Ottavia Niccoli has documented, a woman who announced that she had seen the Blessed Virgin was greeted with open arms by the church and the people, and her claims that Mary had warned the Friulians to fast and to make Saturday a holy day were taken seriously by the authorities. In 1561, when a poor woman named Marguerita announced that Mary had appeared to her with a similar message, the bishop of Piacenza informed her that her vision was a diabolic illusion. Orders were sent from Rome to prevent the marking of the site where Marguerita had had her visions with a chapel or shrine.[7] Similarly, in Spain, the (in)famous Magdalena de la Cruz, known for her extreme asceticism and visions, was accused in 1546 of having slept with the devil—a charge to which she finally confessed—and was sentenced to imprisonment in a convent for the rest of her life.[8] Finally, following the Council of Trent's insistence on communal discipline and unity in its final meetings of 1562–63—an insistence that represented the church's retreat from earlier tactics of hopeful compromise with the leaders of the Reformation—mysticism and the visionaries who practiced it became even more suspect.

As Niccoli has also noted, one of the greatest changes ushered in by the Council of Trent was its exaltation of the saintly and perfect doctrine of obedience, which the community was to observe regarding its often unsympathetic and hostile priests. Indeed, one of the church's reactions to Protestant innovation was a new emphasis as of 1567 on confession, a sacrament that embodies the doctrine of obedience. Confession attempts to mimic, to control, and in some ways to replace private experience. Conversion, repentance, the admission of past error, and the plea for forgiveness were thus securely institutionalized by the church by the beginning of the seventeenth century. The emergent relationship of power can become particularly insidious when the confessant is a woman, as Rudolph Bell has pointed out: "Armed with the certainty that even the holiest of women might purify their minds and bodies only after years of complete solitude and hard punishment, leaders of the Church Militant confidently expanded their control over female religiosity, placing themselves squarely between the penitent and her God, jealously guarding the prerogatives of a male-only priesthood."[9] One in fact hears the concerns of Teresa regarding such "jealous" guardianship in a notable passage from *Las Moradas*. One of her confessors, she reports, thinks that people to whom God grants spiritual favors "han de ser ángeles . . . y es imposible mientras estuvieren en este cuerpo, luego es todo condenado a Demonio u melancolía" (must be angels; and as this is impossible while they are in the body, he attributes the whole thing to melancholy or to the devil) (122–23; 131). And as duly noted by one of the first Inquisitional documents of Europe, the *Malleus maleficarum* of 1487, women especially were subject to the influence of the devil.[10] It was the confessor—the mediator between God and the nuns of Teresa's convents of the Discalced Carmelites—who had the power not only to create the discourse of diabolic possession and melancholy within which the women might be trapped, but to assure doubting nuns that their mystical visions were *not* the products of demonic intervention.

That such power bears a suggestive resemblance to the authority of the therapist in the psychoanalytic situation has not gone unnoticed. In the words of Bertha Pappenheim—also known as Anna O., whose "hysteria" gave rise to the case histories of Breuer and later of Freud—"Psychoanalysis in the hands of the physician is what confession is in the hands of the Catholic priest. It depends on its user and its use, whether it becomes a beneficial tool or a two-edged sword."[11] Whereas Pappenheim was able to break out of the psychoanalytic situation and go on to become an early advocate of women's rights, Teresa (whom Breuer called "the patron saint of hysteria")[12] always lived and worked within a church that was at once tremendously enabling for educated women, who had no other forum in which to pursue their intellectual goals, and terribly judgmental and confining. Teresa's frequent comments on those mediators whose ignorance caused unnecessary torment for herself and her sisters nonetheless suggest that fatherly intervention in women's private experiences has carried equal weight for Renaissance and modern women. In this Carmelite community of silent women for whom conversation with a confessor constituted a rare opportunity for exchange and self-validation, an accusation of melancholy or demonic possession could have severe ramifications. In one case, a sister was driven, like Breuer's Anna O., to aphasia: "Pues si se quiere tomar un libro de romance, persona que le sabía bien leer, le acaecía no entender más de él que si no supiera letra" (Although she was quite able to read, she found that, if she took up a book written in the vernacular she could understand no more of it than if she had not known her alphabet) (124; 131).

On the surface, *Las Moradas* might appear to enforce patriarchal attitudes by separating the "melancholic" from the genuine mystic.[13] But Teresa's work hardly accuses her *hermanas* (sisters) of inventing fictions of possession for the sake of notoriety or self-importance, a charge to which Teresa had been subject. Rather, *Las Moradas* attempts to ascertain the signs ("señales") that God gives to those who believe.

Very much a movement from darkness to light, *Las Moradas* opens in the bleak "escuridad" (darkness) beyond the walls of the brilliant, shining castle that is the soul, "tan resplandeciente y hermoso" (12), and proceeds into the seven illuminated "dwelling places," or "mansions," at the center. With this radical transformation of the soul into a secure and insular fortress with crystal walls that dazzle its enemies and invite its inhabitants to see their own reflections within, Teresa turns her handbook on mysticism into a defense of her own mystical experiences. Throughout the text, Teresa continually turns to the tortoise, the hedgehog, and the palamito shrub, a plant with a soft and succulent kernel protected by thick layers of leaves, as examples of things that resist outside interference by shrinking or shriveling up ("encogimiento").[14] These imaginative metaphors of the soul suggest the writer's awareness of a need to defend herself against the doubts and challenges of the Counter-Reformation church. Indeed, it is the assurance of security ("siguridad," a word repeated many times in *Las Moradas*) that the book tries to give its readers, so that they, like Teresa, will be able to assert "eso no lo sé yo, mas sé que es verdad lo que digo" (that I do not know, but I know that what I say is true) (61; 78).

Moreover, a Christ portrayed as saying to Mary Magdalene and to his disciples, "No hayas miedo, que Yo soy" (Be not afraid, it is I) (185) gradually emerges as the protector of this fortress and the only real father in the text. Perhaps paradoxically, Christ defends Teresa against a much different paternal figure, the doubting confessor to whom she and her sisters are occasionally subject. Not surprisingly, then, he is also cast as the true source of sustenance for a soul that depends on him alone. Soon after characterizing the "alma" (soul) as a virtually impenetrable castle, Teresa turns to a much more organic metaphor: "El alma está como un árbol plantado en [esta fuenta de vida] que la frescura y fruto no tuviera, si no le procediere de allí, que esto le sustenta y hace no secarse, y que dé buen fruto" (The soul is like a tree planted in [the spring of life] that would give no shade and yield no fruit if it proceeded not thence, for the spring sustains it and prevents it from drying up and causes it to provide good fruit) (13; 34). But in characterizing the soul as that which furnishes "frescura" or shade, Teresa also anticipates the shade that her own work will provide to her sisters in need of protection and consolation.

I

It was precisely Teresa's profession of "siguridad" with which her own confessors—men such as Jerónimo Gracián, to whom she had taken a vow of obedience in 1575—may have felt most uneasy. Gracián was himself brought before the Inquisition numerous times during the 1570's and 1580's and was ultimately expelled from his position as the first Discalced Provincial in 1592. His own concerns regarding *Las Moradas*, which he commissioned and which he carefully revised in 1580, along with Dominican theologian Diego de Yanguas and Teresa herself, might thus come as no surprise. Obviously aware of the dangers involved for Teresa and himself if Teresa's prose should at any point challenge an already defensive Counter-Reformation church, Gracián was overly cautious regarding the manuscript.

Indeed, given the close and apparently mutually respectful relationship between the now elderly Teresa and the young Gracián, one might speculate that Teresa too was anxious for a productive collaboration lest Gracián be forced to pay for her outspoken comments. She even introduced *Las Moradas* by referring to Gracián's request that she write a treatise specifically for "the nuns of these convents of Our Lady of Carmel [since they] need someone to solve their difficulties concerning prayer[;] and as (or so it seemed to him) women best understand each other's language . . . anything I might say would be particularly useful to them" ("me mandó escribir, que como estas monjas de estos monesterios de Nuestra Señora del Carmen tienen necesidad de quien algunas dudas de oración las declare, y que le parecía, que mejor se entienden el lenguaje unas mujeres de otras . . . será de alguna importancia si se acierta a decir alguna cosa") (3; 24). Not only was *Las Moradas*, like her *Vida*, an act of obedience,[15] although one that would create an important space for "el lenguaje" of women, but it was also a text that Teresa allowed to be corrected by those who had requested it and who would be indirectly responsible for its contents. And as Gracián's and Yanguas's emendations of Teresa's manuscript attest, Teresa's absolute proclamations of certitude regarding divine discourse and intervention were the most challenging aspects of *Las Moradas* for worried priests anxious to replace signs of conviction with language of doubt and qualification.

Thus, in her discussion of one of the clear "señales" that God gives his worshiper to convince her that she is possessed by neither demons nor melancholy, Teresa originally wrote, "Turning now to the indication which I have described as a decisive one." Gracián amended "as a decisive one" to "as being, I think, a decisive one" (88; 101). Two sentences later, Teresa originally wrote, "God implants Himself in the interior of that soul in such a way that, when it returns to itself, it cannot possibly doubt that God has been in it." Gracián amended the beginning of the last clause to "it cannot, it thinks, possibly doubt" (88; 101).[16] Interjecting an expression of doubt qualifies Teresa's own certitude of divine presence and revalidates the necessary mediation of a confessor who will unequivocally affirm or deny the reality of her experiences.[17] If one of Teresa's projects was to confirm for her sisters a secure realm of mystical experience, Gracián's additions suggest that women are dependent on the institution to confirm or to reject what they *think* they have seen and heard.

But if Teresa concurred with the emendations of a priest to whom she was obviously close, a telling passage in *Las Moradas* left untouched by the revisions comments on what Teresa may have considered a more typical situation regarding nuns and their confessors. Once a woman has reached the sixth of the seven mansions, Teresa recounts, she often feels that she is capable of speaking with and feeling "gran siguridad" in "lo interior del alma" (164). She nonetheless may have that security shaken by none other than her confessor: "Por otra [parte] anda muy afligida . . . las mormuraciones tiene poca pena, sino es cuando el mesmo confesor la aprieta" (On the other hand, she is in great distress . . . she is not hurt by what people say about her except when her own confessor blames her) (165; 163). How to avoid being blamed by one's confessor, whose "mormuraciones" (slanderous comments) are inevitably more authoritative than those of one's sisters? The solution involves a resolute agon not between Teresa and her priest, but between two very different fathers: the earthly father confessor and the heavenly father, God. From this struggle for paternity, Teresa tellingly absents herself—less to deny her allegiance than to challenge the confessor's authority by allowing God to speak for her.

That this struggle had its origins in Teresa's youthful past can be seen in a memorable moment from Teresa's *Vida*, written in 1563. As the opening pages of the *Vida* vividly recount, Teresa conceived her youthful identity in response and resistance to the figure of an earthly father. In making her decision to remain in the convent in which she was taught and to become a nun, she encountered some very real resistance from her biological father. Early in the autobiography, she depicts a Don Alonso de Cepeda blinded by parental love and unable to understand his daughter. Although he suspects Teresa of her youthful flirtation with "sin"—her reading of the chivalric romances—he fails to grasp fully the scope of her transgression or its proper remedy. "So excessive was my father's love for me, and so complete was the deception that I practised on him, that he could never believe all the ill of me that I deserved and thus I never fell into disgrace with him."[18] Don Alonso's most forceful (and potentially most fateful) intervention into Teresa's life is his refusal to allow her to receive confession when she believes that she is dying:

> I hastened to go to confession, for I was always very fond of frequent confession. They thought that this was due to fear of death, and in order that I should not be distressed, my father forbade me to go. Oh, what an excess of human love! Though my father was so good a Catholic and so wise—for he was extremely wise and so was not acting through ignorance—he might have done me great harm. That night I had a fit, which left me unconscious for nearly four days. (*Life*, p. 30)

In this description of Teresa's near-death and her father's over-scrupulous love, one sees for the first time in the narrative Teresa's strategy of opposing one father against the other. At this stage, that opposition is formulated as one "earthly father" against another, the secular Don Alonso versus the spiritual confessor, conceived as God's surrogate. In articulating this dynamic, so critical to her decision to give her life to the church, Teresa enacts the strategy at work in one of the first "confessions" of a Christian woman and mystic, written, some two hundred years before Augustine's more notorious *Confessions*, by his fellow Carthaginian, Perpetua. Daughter of a wealthy Roman patrician, Perpetua was martyred in the early third century in Carthage. In her *Passio*, preserved and commented on by one of her followers, Perpetua recounted her conversion to Christianity and her struggles against her father, who desperately sought to make her pray to the Roman emperor and save herself from persecution. As Mary Lefkowitz has noted, Perpetua died, like other early Christian martyrs, "in noticeable isolation from [her] famil[y], in defiance of, rather than in loyalty to, [her] husband or father."[19] But the structure of the family was not effaced at the moment of Perpetua's conversion. Rather, her "ascent" to Christianity, depicted in a series of visions in which God revealed her fate, was an ascent to a *new* father, described as "a grey-haired man [who] sat in shepherd's garb; tall he was, and milking sheep" in a beautiful plain.[20] It was this elderly father noticeably engaged in the maternal act of providing nourishment whom Perpetua tacitly opposed to her earthly father, on whom she finally took pity for his "old, grey hairs."[21] Her very identity as a Christian was premised not on the negation of the paternal relationship, but on an agon between two fathers. This agon would end only when Perpetua and her Christian compatriots reached their heavenly destination and were told by the calm deity that at last they might cease their earthly struggles and play: "Ite et ludite."[22]

Teresa's *Vida* enacts a similar kind of displacement, as we shall see. But although Perpetua's visionary narrative staged a conflict between biological and heavenly fathers, it had no place for the other paternal figure with whom Teresa ultimately struggles, a figure quite distinct from either Don Alonso or God. Teresa may initially substitute for her father the confessor with whom she yearns to converse.

But the *Vida* goes on to anticipate *Las Moradas* by enacting a series of displacements of *spiritual* fathers, suggesting that by 1563 Teresa has already experienced impatience with the mediations of confessors, although she still asserts a need for their validation. Thus she calls the benevolent and unaggressive Saint Joseph her "true father and lord" (*Life*, p. 229) and often emphasizes her independence of any one person's direction and guidance. Yet she nonetheless affirms the value of earthly counselors, especially to "weak women" ("mujercillas"). But this acknowledgment includes a clear warning that women should be careful as to the *type* of confessor they seek, and much of the *Vida* dramatizes Teresa's own search for the perfect spiritual advisor. The numerous learned Jesuits whom Teresa warmly describes become exemplary "fathers" with whom she contrasts ignorant and dangerous priests. This gradually emerging opposition between good and bad confessors foreshadows the dynamic of the later *Moradas*, in which priests no longer function as Christ's unquestioned surrogates on earth. One confessor mentioned in the *Vida* who tells Teresa to "snap her fingers" at her visions to make them go away is chastised not by Teresa but by God himself, who "told me not to worry about it and said I was quite right to obey, but He would see that my confessor learned the truth. When they made me stop my prayer He seemed to me to have become angry, and He told me to tell them that this was tyranny" (*Life*, p. 189). In such a moment, the doctrine of obedience to which Teresa is subject comes into sharp conflict with her own certitude regarding her visions, and the conflict is resolved in Teresa's favor by God himself. In informing the priest that his actions are tyrannical, Teresa momentarily reverses the penitential roles of the confessor as the vehicle for Christ's word and the sinner as the recipient of that word.

The *Vida* nonetheless ends by attesting (albeit in muted fashion) to the importance of a woman's choice of a confessor: "I am sure that the relations of penitent and confessor, and the type of confessor to be chosen, are very important matters, especially to women" (*Life*, p. 293). This is a climax that the later *Las Moradas*, which says little that may be construed as unequivocally positive about the role of the confessor, refuses to provide. In many ways, *Las Moradas* is a much bolder work than the *Vida*, in that its central opposition is not between good and bad confessors but between God and the priests to whom Teresa is subject. It is particularly striking that Teresa launches the majority of her complaints about confessors in the sixth mansion, which is also where the mystic begins to hear God's "locutions" ("unas hablas con el alma"), and hence the language of a different father, for the first time (134).

One incident recounted within this mansion exemplifies not only Teresa's oppositional strategies but her attempt to encourage her sisters to serve as witnesses for each other. In a lengthy passage, Teresa notes that one of her "friends" in the convent was initially perturbed by her visions and went to discuss her self-doubts with a priest. When he asked her to tell him what God's face looks like, the woman responded that she "no sabía, ni vía rostro, ni podía decir más de lo dicho; que lo que sabía era que era Él el que la hablaba, y que no era antojo" (that she did not know, that she had seen no face, and that she could not tell him more than she had done already; what she did know is that it was He who was speaking to her, and that it was no fancy) (185; 180). Her inability to describe what she had seen aroused in "others," such as the confessor, "hartos timores" or "grievous misgivings" (185; 180). Reliant on words alone, particularly the phrase that her divine father repeated to her again and again, "Be not afraid, it is I," Teresa's friend was forced to acknowledge that her apprehension of divine truth could in no way be described in earthly fashion: "This consciousness arose, not from those senses which tell us that another person is near us, but in another and a subtler way which is indescribable" and produces a feeling of absolute certainty ("mas es tan cierto") (186; 180).

Yet there is more to Teresa's friend's story than the topos of inexpressibility to which Teresa frequently has access.[23] The very words that her friend hears are sufficiently forceful to counter the doubts of a suspicious confessor. Particularly in the sixth mansion, Teresa has ample recourse to the power of God's locutions, which her words can so inadequately convey: "Tenían tanta fuerza estas palabras" (Such forcefulness had these words) (185). In one of the more memorable passages from *Las Moradas*, one that Teresa herself seems to recognize must be revised for the authorities, the writer compares her soul, "struck by some word," to the phoenix that springs up anew from its own ashes:

Una manera hay, que estando el alma, anque no sea en oración, tocada con alguna palabra, que se acordó u oye de Dios, parece que su Majestad, desde lo interior del alma, hace crecer la centella que dijimos ya, movido de piedad de haberla visto padecer tanto tiempo por su deseo, que abrasada toda ella como un ave Fenis, queda renovada, y piadosamente, se puede creer, perdonadas sus culpas.

(One kind of rapture is this. The soul, though not actually engaged in prayer is struck by some word, which it either remembers or hears spoken by God. His Majesty is moved with compassion at having seen the soul suffering so long through its yearning for Him, and seems to be causing the spark of which we have already spoken to grow within it, so that, like the phoenix, it catches fire and springs into new life, its faults forgiven.) (147; 149)

Immediately following this passage, Teresa adds a marginal notation that anchors it in church doctrine: "Hase de entender con la dispusición y medios que esta alma habrá tenido, como la Iglesia lo enseña" (One must assume that this soul is in the proper disposition and has used the proper means, as the Church teaches). Despite the belated qualification, Teresa nonetheless makes of herself a lesser Paul—she is struck only by a "centella" or spark,[24] not a bolt of lightning—who does not need the mediating power of the priest to pardon her or enable her to rewrite the narrative of her life in a confessional more circumscribed than that which God offers her. Whereas Paul experienced the lightning only once in his blinding fall from his horse on the road to Damascus, Teresa's spark returns to renew her, like the ever-resurrecting phoenix, again and again, in an ongoing process over which she can exert no control.

Teresa's helplessness before the torrent of divine language constitutes one of the most common motifs in *Las Moradas*, and it paradoxically turns into a defense.[25] Note, for example, Teresa's exhortation to her sisters regarding the "signs" with which God impresses his language on them: "Pues veis aquí, hermanas, lo que nuestro Dios hace aquí para que esta alma ya se conozca por suya" (Here, then, sisters, you see what our God does to the soul in this state *so that it may know itself to be His*) (99; 109; my italics). Submission allows God not only to "strike" the soul with "some word" but to "inscribe" ("esculpire") his words on that soul. Since some confessors continually accuse women of having overactive imaginations and a propensity to hear voices that are merely products of their wishful thoughts, Teresa takes it upon herself to call attention to the necessity for her *hermanas* to become their *own* judges, conscious of themselves as texts already written rather than as texts that might be written by suspicious confessors. They should depend not merely on the external judgment of a doubting father, but on the inner faculty of understanding or "entendimiento" that they already possess.

The first few mansions in particular establish a series of oppositions between the useless "turmoil of thoughts" on which confessors prey and the more encompassing, more serene understanding: "Yo he andado en esto de esta baraúnda del pensamiento bien apretada algunas veces, y habrá poco más de cuatro años que vine a entender por espiriencia que el pensamiento, u imaginación, porque mejor se entienda, no es el entendimiento" (I have sometimes been terribly oppressed by this turmoil of thoughts and it is only just over four years ago that I came to understand by experience that thought (or, as it is better understood, the imagination) is not the same thing as understanding) (59; 76). The insistence on "*entender*" in the passage ("se entienda"; "entendimiento") suggests the extent to which Teresa has moved from confusion and uncertainty over the process of divine intervention in her life to the "siguridad" that it is the goal of *Las Moradas* to obtain for its readers. She cagily notes in a related passage that "a learned man" ("un letrado") verified her definition of the understanding as "una de las potencias del alma" (one of the faculties of the soul), thus locating her discussion within the shadow of authority. But this brief discourse and subsequent allusions to the process of "entendimiento" attribute to Teresa as well as to her readers the power of interpretation and thus of self-understanding. Although they may be assailed by "mil bestias fieras y ponzoñosas" (a thousand wild and venomous creatures) (60; 77), they can nonetheless become capable of arriving at a certainty not always available from—and as one knows from the emendations Teresa's own confessors made, not encouraged by—the representatives of the church.

The subtle dynamics of such self-analysis characterize one of the writer's most daring moves. For if the experience of mysticism as Teresa recounts it is largely a passive one, the memory and consciousness of that experience are in no way passive. Rather, as one critic has recently remarked, memory itself comes to validate Teresa's narrative project,[26] thus to some extent displacing the act of confession in which the father-priest analyzes and forgives (or condemns) the woman's discourse. Particularly in the final mansions, Teresa undertakes to write her *own* confession and subject it to her own interpretation, thus bypassing the mediator of the confessional and locating true authentication elsewhere. The nature of this self-analysis is perhaps most apparent in the telling passage described above in which Teresa claims to write the biography of a woman whom she "know[s] quite well"—a woman who goes to her confessor when she is first perturbed by her visions. But in fact Teresa is really composing autobiography. The woman to whom "God grants such favors" emerges gradually as a double for Teresa herself, as the following passage subtly reveals: "She and I were so intimate that nothing happened in her soul of which I was ignorant and thus I can be a good witness and you may be sure that everything I say about it is true" (186; 181).[27] It is just this intimacy, the product of Teresa's "entendimiento" regarding her own experiences, that enables the writer to become a "good witness" for the other women who might find themselves in her text. In authenticating the discourse of her "friend," Teresa secures for her sisters the certitude that, for her male authorities, borders on the heretical.[28] These writings posit Teresa's friend as existing elsewhere, outside of the text that offers itself up to the confessors' gaze and numerous corrections.

John Freccero has commented that Teresa's autobiographical writings, unlike those of Augustine, do not divide the authorial self who writes in the present from the subjective past self who is written. But it is clear that this lack of a narrative breakthrough in Teresa's text reveals more than what Freccero sees as the possible essentialism of woman's writing.[29] To be sure, Teresa may never experience the Augustinian epiphany that Freccero sees as the inaugural moment of true autobiography. Her reaction to first stumbling upon Augustine's *Confessions* is one of "distress and affliction" because "after the Lord had once called [him], [he] did not fall again, whereas I had fallen so often that I was distressed by it" (*Life*, p. 56). Whereas Augustine writes (at least until book 9) a linear narrative that sets a blind and unknowing self against a converted, knowing one, Teresa gives us a doubled self from the opening pages of her text, a self that is consciously watching, "witnessing," and finally reading the self on whom God writes. There is no one single moment of conversion in the *Vida*, just as, to the distress of many of Teresa's readers, there is no culminating moment in *Las Moradas* in which the mystical marriage between God and his spouse reaches its desired climax.

By subtly valorizing the process of individual understanding, Teresa disarms others' attempts to invade her with their own "restless thoughts" and thereby increasingly emerges as the true mediator between her mystical visions and her worldly account of them. Thus although the sacrament of penance is still the seal of approval of mystical narratives (provided that Teresa approves of the priest administering it), that sacrament is relegated to the more secular function of giving otherwise silent women a necessary space for those narratives. Teresa assumes that the *hermanas* to whom she writes will acknowledge their sins before their confessors. But she also urges them to use the confessional as a place in which to tell—"contar"—their visions: "Lo que es mucho menester, hermanas, es que andéis con gran llaneza y verdad con el confesor; no digo el decir los pecados, que eso claro está, sino en contar la oración" (The really essential thing, sisters, is that you should speak to your confessor very plainly and candidly—I do not mean here in confessing your sins, for of course you will do so then, but in describing your experiences in prayer) (197–98; 189). Confession becomes a model for the process that Teresa's readers must perform for themselves: that of "contar" or telling, the exploitation of a narrative space whereby the faculty of understanding may come into fruition and the nun may be given license to speak.

Yet however she might seem to disregard the confessor's attempted intervention in her discourse, the narrator does not interpret this experience of "contar" as creating a radical feminine domain in which all language of the father may be silenced. Like Perpetua's envisioning of a Christian identity during Roman rule, Teresa's articulation of mystical identity cannot exist outside of the structures of a paternal relationship. Like Perpetua's *Passio*, Teresa's mystical autobiography positions its writer *within* paternal language.[30] Nonetheless, within this acknowledged narrative "trap"—or as Alison Weber has usefully termed it, this "double bind"[31]—Teresa manages to fracture the monolithic discourse of Catholicism into two different languages, thereby questioning the validity of the institutional authority that threatens to silence her sisters. By suggesting in *Las Moradas* that such silencing would result in no less than the silencing of God's original language—namely, Scripture itself, the very Scripture God "speaks" when he utters, "Be not afraid, it is I"[32]—she challenges the piety of her confessors. Thus while Teresa hardly emerges as the "maker" of meaning, functioning rather as the "bearer" of God's meaning,[33] she nonetheless takes her place by the end of *Las Moradas* beside two exemplary and very different figures cited at the beginning of her text: Saint Paul and Mary Magdalene. Both Paul and Magdalene are blank texts on whom the father has written and through whom "God's greatness may be known" (8; 30), and both are responsible for challenging the patriarchal mores of their times.[34]

Although Teresa tries both to discredit and to exploit the period's stereotypes of the "mujercilla," she does not reject or transcend the issue of gender. Rather, she writes as the member of a community of women first addressed in the sacred text that she translates and interprets throughout. For *Las Moradas* does not merely fashion a specular relationship between Teresa and Christ, such as that intimated at the close of the *Vida*. There Teresa compares her soul to a mirror ("espejo") in which she gazes at Christ's reflection, much as in her poem "Alma, buscarte has en Mí" she imagines a Christ imploring the soul that "thou wilt see / Thyself engraven on My breast—An image vividly impressed."[35] *Las Moradas* takes up the more ambitious project of creating a mirror for its female readers as well, allowing them to see themselves as *already* inscribed by God and thereby impervious to the accusations of their skeptical male superiors. Toward the close of *Las Moradas*, Teresa moves from the singular into the collective, as she exhorts her sisters, "Pues las palabras de Jesucristo nuestro Rey y Señor no pueden faltar; mas como faltamos en no disponernos y desviarnos de todo lo que puede embarazar esta luz, no nos vemos en este espejo que contemplamos, adonde nuestra imagen está esculpida" (The words of Jesus Christ our King and Lord cannot fail; but, because we ourselves fail by not preparing ourselves and departing from all that can shut out this light, we do not see ourselves in this mirror into which we are gazing and in which our image is engraved) (230; 217). In its outward turn to the communities that Teresa has helped to found, *Las Moradas* functions as a synthesis of the *Vida* and *Las Fundaciones*, of Teresa's interior and exterior *trabajos*. But such a move outward was only possible if Teresa engaged in the prohibited acts of reading and writing the shared language of Scripture.

II

Despite Teresa's initial anguish regarding a more perfect, less sinful Augustine, her reaction to the *Confessions* is one that deserves to be considered more carefully. Of Augustine's climactic conversion in the garden, Teresa comments in her *Vida*: "When I began to read the *Confessions*, I thought I saw myself there described. . . . When I came to his conversion, and read how he heard that voice in the garden, it seemed to me nothing less than that our Lord had uttered it for me: I felt so in my heart, I remained for some time lost in tears, in great inward affliction and distress" (*Life*, p. 56). As Barrett J. Mandel has commented, "At such a moment, St. Teresa's language merges with that of St. Augustine who seems to be speaking not only *to* her but *in* her."[36] True, there is indeed an act of "merging." But more importantly, Teresa initiates an act of displacement. It is Teresa rather than Augustine for whom the Lord utters (in the voice of a child) the crucial phrase "tolle et legge": take and read the Scripture.[37] Just as Augustine seized the Bible and read a passage as though it were written for *him*, so does Teresa hear the godlike voice in the *Confessions* as though it speaks just to her, telling her to seize Scripture for herself and thereby discover that it was "written" for her.

It is striking that after Augustine's conversion in book 9, the *Confessions* departs from a linear narrative and embarks on a prolonged meditation on a passage in Genesis. Thus does Augustine replace what one critic has called the "dead-end" project of narration with the more inclusive act of integrating his life into an already written and validated text: Scripture itself.[38] Teresa's act of decentering Augustine and making herself the audience of the child's call in the secluded garden suggests that Scripture has sanctioned *her* mystical project all along. But it was precisely such an appropriation of Scripture that was prohibited to Teresa and her contemporary Spaniards in the mid-sixteenth century. The church was particularly influential in Spain in preventing potentially seditious writings such as the New Testament both from being published at all and from falling into the hands of those who might misuse them.[39] As Pierre Chanu has argued in his magisterial study of the Tridentine church, the Counter-Reformation opposed Protestantism's private appropriation of the Bible by insisting that "Scripture was not authentic without the authority of the Church,"[40] and it is telling that the first vernacular translation of the Bible in Spain was not published until the mid-eighteenth century. Fra Luis de León, who oversaw the first edition of Teresa's works in 1588, was imprisoned for four years after translating the Song of Songs into Spanish.[41] Teresa's works, in fact, were attacked when Luis de León published them because they were written in the vernacular and thereby were accessible to members of the literate classes who could not read Latin.[42]

It is perhaps because of the danger inherent in a vernacular Bible that so many of Teresa's quotations from and allusions to the New Testament are couched in an oral context. Teresa "hears" phrases from the Gospels, perhaps recollections from a sermon or communal prayer, just as she heard the voice of Augustine's God. This is a strategy Teresa earlier employed in the *Vida*, as when she referred to a passage from the Canticles: "Without seeing each other, we look at each other face to face as these two lovers do: the Spouse in the Songs, I believe, says this to the Bride: I have been told that it occurs there" ("Sin ver nosotros cómo de en hito en hito se miran estos dos amantes, como lo dice el Esposo a la Esposa en los Cantares, a lo que creo, *helo oído que es aquí*" (*Life*, p. 174; *Vida*, p. 329; my italics). When Teresa cites Scripture in *Las Moradas*, it is almost always because she has heard it spoken by God's voice.[43] This is true of two of Teresa's most blatant attacks on the authority of misguided confessors, both from the sixth mansion, and both examples of moments in which Teresa's description shades into helpful prescription: "Está [un alma] afligida por haberle dicho su confesor, y otros, que es espíritu del Demonio el que tiene, y toda llena de temor; y con una palabra que se le diga sólo:—'Yo soy, no hayas miedo'—, se le quita del todo, y queda consoladísima, y pareciéndole que ninguno bastará a hacerla creer otra cosa" (A soul is distressed because its confessors, and others, have told it that what it has is a spirit sent by the devil, and it is full of fear. Yet that single word which it hears: 'It is I, fear not' takes all its fear from it, and it is most marvellously comforted, and believes that no one will ever be able to make it feel otherwise) (136–37; 141). In the passage in which Teresa speaks obliquely of the woman with whom she "is quite intimate" and who has been so frightened by her confessors, she cites once again the words "No hayas miedo, que Yo soy" (Be not afraid, it is I), words so forceful that she "was greatly strengthened and gladdened by such good companionship" (185; 180). No imaginary locution, "No hayas miedo" is the phrase uttered by the two angels to Mary Magdalene and several other women on Easter morning as they made their way to Christ's empty tomb. Its repetition here transforms Teresa and her sisters into the few chosen women to have seen Christ after his death, a privilege from which the doubting confessor is excluded.

With such seemingly innocuous and selective translations, Teresa proceeds to move into and place herself within the biblical text itself, most explicitly in the passages speaking of Mary Magdalene, of whom the final chapter of the seventh mansion is a virtual celebration. Teresa never portrays Magdalene as the once-reckless prostitute whose conversion and penitence made her an intriguing emblem of the weak "feminine" for a variety of male writers during the sixteenth and seventeenth centuries.[44] Magdalene emerges instead as a strong and saintly apostle delivered of the tainted origins to which Teresa refuses to refer. Ignoring the licentious aspects of Magdalene's character, Teresa celebrates instead the woman who goes "por esas calles, y por ventura, sola, porque no llevaba hervor para entender cómo iba, y entrara donde nunca había entrado, y después sufrir la mormuración del Fariseo, y otras" (through those streets—perhaps alone, for her fervour was such that she cared nothing how she went—to enter a house that she had never entered before and then puts up with uncharitable talk from the Pharisees and from very many other people) (248–49; 231). A page later, Teresa comments, "Tengo para mí que el no haber recibido martirio fué por haberle pasado en ver morir al Señor" (I think myself that the reason she was not granted martyrdom was that she had already undergone it through witnessing the Lord's death) (249; 232).

In the final chapter of *Las Moradas*, Teresa conflates the contemplative Mary, who sits at her Lord's feet while her sister Martha busies herself with housework, with the "glorious Mary Magdalen" (247; 230) who changes her way of life and bathes Christ's feet with her tears.[45] The primary witness to Christ's resurrection in all four of the Gospels, Mary Magdalene thus also comes to symbolize the woman who is allowed to listen to Christ while her sister bustles about the household. This posture was interpreted throughout the medieval and Renaissance periods as that of the *vita contemplativa*. But it also suggests, in a moment unique to Luke's Gospel, the renunciation of woman's purely domestic function. Allowed to listen to and learn from Christ, whom in John's Gospel she will address as "Rabbi" or "teacher" when he emerges from the tomb (John 20: 16), Mary attains momentary equality with the young Jewish men who study Torah and acquires an apostolic authority traditionally denied women.[46]

Teresa's emphasis on Mary's apostolic status and centrality in the drama of the Resurrection permits Teresa to assert Magdalene's central place in Catholic tradition. But it also permits her to criticize obliquely those who would criticize her—and Mary Magdalene—in return. After Magdalene and the other women are met at the tomb by two angels dressed "in veste fulgenti" (in shining garments—the Vulgate makes clear that the garments possess the same visually striking power as the lightning that toppled Paul from his horse), they relay the message of the Resurrection to the eleven apostles: "And they remembered Christ's words, and returning from the tomb they told this to the eleven and to all the rest. Now it was Mary Magdalene and Joanna and Mary the mother of James and the other women who told this to the apostles" (Luke 24: 8–9). But the apostles react to the stunning news of the empty tomb by treating Mary's message as a fiction, a mere vision: "But these words seemed to [the apostles] to be the effect of delirium, and they did not believe them" (Et visa sunt ante illos sicut *deliramentum verba ista*, et non crediderunt illis) (Luke 24: 11; my italics). The woman who appears in the beginning of *Las*

Moradas along with Paul as a figure through whom God displays his greatness becomes by the end of Teresa's text someone who implicitly challenges authority. That authority is represented not only by the Pharisees who scorn her as she travels alone through the streets on her way to Christ, but also by the momentarily disbelieving apostles.

More importantly, the disciples' refusal to believe Mary's story, their hurried denigration of the Christian message as vacuous words relayed by mere women, acts as a covert allegory for the rejection of Teresa's own messages to her confessors. Teresa associates herself with Magdalene when she notes that her first vision of Christ was of a resurrected Christ dressed in garments as fiery as those of the angels who appeared to Magdalene at the tomb: "A esta de quien hablamos [Teresa] se le representó el Señor, acabando de comulgar, con forma de gran resplandor y hermosura y majestad, como después de resucitado, y le dijo que ya era tiempo de que sus cosas tomase ella por suyas" (To the person of whom we have been speaking the Lord revealed Himself one day, when she had just received communion, in great splendor and beauty and majesty, as he did after his resurrection, and told her that it was time she took upon her his affairs as if they were her own) (225; 212). The final chapter from the sixth mansion, moreover, closes with an allusion to Magdalene, tormented by "las persecuciones y mormuraciones" (persecution and slander) (215) and defended by Christ, who instructs her persecutors to examine first their own propensity for sin. Is this not a subtle condemnation of the confessors who assail Teresa's sisters? The phrase "persecuciones y mormuraciones" looks not only ahead to Teresa's description of a Magdalene who defies the stares and mutterings of the Pharisees, but back to a passage that defends the woman mystic from the "mormuraciones" of others, particularly confessors, who doubt the veracity of her raptures (165; 163). The identification is hardly limited, however, to one between Magdalene and Teresa herself. Rather, the allusions to Mary and the other women at the tomb place Teresa within a female community falsely accused of speaking "words of delirium." Just as Teresa is a "good witness" for her "friend," so are she and her sisters reliable witnesses of a Resurrection vividly experienced in their visions.

Unlike other sixteenth-century Spanish religious handbooks, such as Loyola's *Spiritual Exercises* and Francisco de Osuna's *Third Spiritual Alphabet*, which guide their reader through a carefully controlled process of initiation and seek to rationalize the irrational,[47] Teresa's last work refuses linearity. Despite its ostensible movement from the first to the seventh mansion, *Las Moradas* addresses itself to women who are already familiar with mystical practice. Again and again, Teresa appeals to a shared body of religious experience as she claims, "Hay cosas tan delicadas que ver y que entender, que el entendimiento no es capaz para poder dar traza cómo se diga siquiera algo que venga tan al justo que no quede bien escuro para los que no tienen espiriencia" (There are such exquisite things to be seen and appreciated in [these mansions] that the understanding is incapable of describing them in any way accurately without being completely obscure to those devoid of experience) (55–56; 72–73). Again and again, Teresa insists that the validity of mystical experience must be demonstrated through its *effects*—"señales," a feeling of "siguridad"—effects of which in many cases the reader can only become aware by reading Teresa's text. Instead of writing a guidebook that an initiate might follow step by step, Teresa composes a book that permits women to valorize the experience of mysticism that they have already had by providing for them a scriptural language of authentication.

The "moradas" or mansions become the new confessional in which the feminine mystic's language may be authenticated rather than disproved, the new mirror in which the feminine mystic may see herself without discovering there the gaze of her earthly father. In speaking of the mystical experiences of the sixth mansion, Teresa writes, "A quien nuestro Señor hiciere esta merced, que si se la ha hecho, *en leyendo esto lo entenderá*, déle muy muchas gracias, que no tiene que temer si es engaño" (Anyone to whom Our Lord has granted this favour *will understand on reading this*; and must give Him most heartfelt thanks and must not fear that it may be deception) (131; 137; my italics). "En leyendo esto lo entenderá": reading *Las Moradas* becomes the basis for understanding, for furnishing the "mirror" into which Teresa's feminine readers may gaze and see themselves "esculpida." Thus Teresa's text and the Scripture in which it is grounded provide the very "siguridad" of which she and her readers have been deprived. These are readers who, far from needing a confessor to lead them through the varieties of religious experience, can enter their own interior mansions once they have finished Teresa's text, "sin licencia de los superiores podéis entraros y pasearos por él a cualquier hora" (at any time without asking leave from [their] superiors) (252; 234).

From the *Vida* to *Las Moradas*, Teresa's writings constitute an attempt to understand and to defend her sisters' vulnerable "centro" (center) in a realm untainted by the language of the judgmental fathers. This defense is grounded in the language of a loving father as well as in an attempt to redefine melancholy as the product of an at times crippling environment rather than as a "natural" inclination of the "mujercilla."[48] In attempting, like the feminine analysand, to wrest free from the overbearing and cynical sway of the father-confessor who can "cure" all ills, Teresa calls attention to the limitations of a confessional process that insists on a linear, unbroken narrative. As Stephen Greenblatt has recently remarked apropos of the similar limitations of psychoanalysis, "Identity in Freud does not depend upon existential autonomy; it is far more often realized precisely at moments in which the executive agency of the will has been relinquished."[49] The question that Greenblatt does not pursue—and that Teresa, as it were, insists that we ask—is: relinquished by whom and to whom? Teresa's refusal to relinquish her will to the earthly father and her reliance on that "other" language of Scripture enables her to safeguard the tenuous communities of women for whom she has struggled to create a "fundamento" (foundation). She thus seeks to confirm a collective subjectivity that may find validation in an awareness of its unacknowledged historical role.

III

The discussion above might be summarized by one final gaze at the infamous Cornaro Chapel in Santa Maria della Vittoria in Rome, in which Bernini fashioned his statue of Teresa in ecstasy. Most critical attention to Bernini's creation has been limited to the statue of Teresa herself, enraptured and disarmed before the loving but seductive gaze of an angel suspended, with his arrow, above the saint's submissive and vulnerable body.[50] The sculpture crystallizes the moment in Teresa's *Vida* where she describes the act of transverberation and penetration by God: the angel appeared "to pierce my heart [with a long spear of gold] so that it penetrated to my entrails. When he drew it out, I thought he was drawing them out with it, and he left me completely afire with a great love of God" (*Life*, p. 193). But this moment of intense mystical union is not all that there is to Bernini's sculpture. Just as important as the statue itself is its placement within the chapel. On each side of Teresa and her angel, Bernini has depicted four men, members of the wealthy Cornaro family of Venice, representative of sacred and secular powers alike, looking out over and into the chapel as though they are at a performance. Bernini makes Teresa into a spectacle, confined within and by two groups of influential men. But the male spectators do not directly watch her. They look distractedly elsewhere: at missals in their hands, at parishioners in their pews. To the modern-day visitor, Teresa is isolated from the figures who canonized her even while surrounded by them and functioning as the reason for their gathering. Their physical presence contains her in a spatial sense, yet their misdirected gazes hardly find in her mystical experience a mirror in which they might discover themselves inscribed.

Despite Bernini's probable acquiescence to the dynamics of patronage, there is something remotely challenging even in this Teresa, who looks not to the legitimizing gaze of the earthly fathers but within to the kindly gaze of the heavenly father. One is reminded of Teresa's insistence in the final mansion that women who have reached the last stages of mystical union should no longer present themselves as—or at—public spectacles. The raptures of the final stages "son muy raras veces, y ésas casi siempre no en público como antes . . . ni le hacen al caso grandes ocasiones de devoción, que vea, como antes, que si ven una imagen devota u oyen un sermón, que casi no era oírle" (happen only rarely, and hardly ever in public. . . . Nor have they any connection, as they had before, with great occasions of devotion; if we see a devotional image or hear a sermon, it is almost as if we had heard nothing) (238; 223). Mystical experience becomes increasingly less dependent on the Mass, on sermons, on the worshiping of public images—all aspects of Catholicism emphasized by a Counter-Reformation church anxious to institutionalize communal forms of worship starkly opposed to a more austere and private Protestantism. Teresa removes her female mystic from this public, institutionalized space. Her failure to respond to the exterior word of the priest's sermon ("as if we had heard nothing") is replaced by a new conviction that the self is an inner text that must be read and enacted rather than written on and questioned.

Such a challenge to a public space dominated by the father is registered by recent commentators who describe Teresa's *ek-stasis* as orgasmic, partaking in an excess and otherness that the male observer or critic cannot share. This too seems to be one aspect of Bernini's intensely private statue—which is nonetheless framed within the domain of the church. But ultimately, Bernini's chapel omits the element that transforms such potentially threatening "excess" into a mirror of confirmation, and Teresa's apparently negative mysticism into the more productive and communicative process that it becomes both in her activities as a founder of convents and in her last writings, such as *Las Moradas*. This missing link, crucial for Teresa's spiritual formation and central to her *vida* in every sense, can only be supplied if one imagines the statue in another site than Santa Maria della Vittoria, whose ceiling and altarpieces give glowing testimony to the victorious battles of Catholic men against the forces of the Reformation. Absent from the Cornaro Chapel is any representation of or allusion to the community of women readers to whom Teresa writes. Absent, too, is any sign of the tradition of female apostolic authority within which Teresa inserts herself and her *hermanas* in the pages of *Las Moradas*.[51] And therefore strikingly absent is the communal shade within which her sensually displayed vulnerability is provisionally protected from the appropriative and judgmental gazes of Christ's contemporary apostles.

Despite Teresa's potentially dangerous refusal of institutional mediation—because of which the church had to reappropriate her as its own soon after her death and the posthumous publication of her works—Teresa never dispenses with the image of the nourish-father that Cellini demystifies in his *Vita*. The Christ who refuses to judge Mary Magdalene, who implores the nuns not to be afraid, who reassures Teresa's readers of an interior and integral world of which others would deprive them, redefines the "ombra" of the convent as consoling rather than threatening. Teresa's works ultimately remain within this shade, which neither the Counter-Reformation institution nor the sisters alone were empowered to provide. If Teresa's writings challenge one space of protection by refusing to accept fully the discourse of the confessor, they nonetheless do not and cannot challenge the other space that is God's. In replacing one nourish-father with another, Teresa does not really question the nature of the idealized family romance in which she is forever the child. Nor does she question the possibility that her own desires for invulnerability might derive to some extent from the Tridentine church's defensive efforts to create a Catholic community immune to the challenges of Protestants. For a more self-conscious awareness of the possible dangers and bad faith of the desire for invulnerability vis-à-vis the two institutional forces with which Cellini and Teresa had to contend, the next pages will turn to Torquato Tasso, who relentlessly questioned the paradigms of immunity he created for his powerful audiences of prince and church as well as for himself.

4 ·

Courting Innocence: Tasso's Resistant Poetics

The writings of Torquato Tasso during the 1570's function both as a panegyric to the two institutions within which Tasso tried to find refuge all his life, the Estense court of Ferrara and the Counter-Reformation church, and as a refusal to validate the very metaphors on which that panegyric is based. This Janus-like stance or *bifrontismo*[1] can be glimpsed in two very different works, both written largely between 1569 and 1575, during the poet's most creative decade: the *Aminta* and the *Gerusalemme Liberata*. If both the pastoral play and the epic celebrate the beneficence of the Este court and the unity of the church following the Council of Trent, they are also extremely ambivalent about that celebration. For in the one text, Tasso presents pastoral characters whose "innocent" lives fail to function as a mirror for a court seeking to naturalize its relationship to power.[2] In the other, he refuses to portray an image of a Christian "body" achieving integrity through its own machinations.

Such resistance was facilitated by Tasso's own mistrust of the literary genres in which he was writing, the epic romance and pastoral play—or to use Tasso's designation for the latter, the *favola boschereccia*, in which shepherds' lives are meant to signify those of prince and courtiers. To quote from Richard Cody's suggestive study of the affinity of Renaissance courts for what had become by the late sixteenth century the doctrine of pastoral innocence, "Both the courtly myth and the myth of the shepherd imply a communion of the pure."[3] Yet whereas later writers in the pastoral tradition, such as Giovan

Battista Guarini and Ben Jonson, created a theater that would assure presiding "deities" of their power as well as of their purity, Tasso deconstructed that gesture from the start by insisting on the bad faith of mimetic desire and the essential opacity of the theatrical medium.

The *Gerusalemme*, on the other hand, is an uneasy blend of epic and romance elements that attempts to reconcile and put to rest earlier narrative traditions in the name of an overarching, unified church. Its numerous revisions, assembled and finally published as the streamlined *Gerusalemme Conquistata* in 1593, bear the traces of Tasso's own discomfort with such a mixture of genres.[4] The instability of the *Gerusalemme* is particularly apparent when it lapses into pastoral, as Erminia, disguised as the "woman warrior" Clorinda, asks that a shepherd and his family take her in beneath the shadow of their little community ("Forse fia che 'l mio core infra quest'ombre / del suo peso mortal parte disgombre").[5] In both the *Aminta* and the *Gerusalemme*, the engagement with pastoral produces texts whose "celebratory" intentions are severely qualified.

Yet while refusing to grant an authority's desire to see itself depicted as it *should* be, Tasso simultaneously indicts his own desire to be immune. For most of his life, as dozens of letters to friends and compulsive confessions to spiritual advisors attest, Tasso was obsessed with recovering an original innocence that apparently could be attained only through the intercession of powerful others willing to shield him from himself. The *Aminta* in particular criticizes a Tasso who celebrates both the "ozio" (leisure) given him unconditionally by the "god" of Ferrara and the god himself. Whereas Erasmus did not consider the sheltered orchard and the obscurity of poetic fictions to be potentially problematic retreats, Tasso, situated within the domain of late-sixteenth-century authorities, recognizes the bad faith of his own desire for "ozio" as well as that of his prince. The *Gerusalemme Liberata*, on the other hand, holds out the possibility of permitting its narrative voice *and* the Christians to which it sings to reach the stance of purification that the *Aminta* rejects. But it can do so only by severing that authorial voice from the militant religious community of the poem as well as of the sixteenth century, and thus by severing poet and Counter-Reformation institution.

As will shortly be seen, the *Aminta* and *Gerusalemme* vacillate between Tasso's acknowledgment that his desires for purity and protection within sixteenth-century institutions are contaminated, and the possibility that he might be able to transcend the corruptions of his environment to become the invulnerable spokesperson not of an earthly institution but of a divine authority, God. This vacillation is produced largely through the resolutely antimetaphorical stance of the two poems. The one resists an association of the prince and his court with the innocent shepherds onstage. The other resists a connection between the "body" of the church and that of the sacred poem.

I

The *Aminta* is frequently said to have introduced not only Italy but all of Europe to a passion for pastoral. Indeed, the great number of pastoral dramas produced shortly after the performance of Tasso's slender work before the Este court in June 1573 suggests that this is the case. Certainly the publisher of the *Aminta*, Aldo Manuzio, wished to propagate the myth that Tasso's play ushered in what quickly became a tremendously popular genre. In the preface to the first edition of the *Aminta*, not published until 1583 when Tasso was already confined to St. Anne's Hospital by his "protector" Alfonso II, Manuzio deplored the current state of Ferrara's inspired young poet. Given Tasso's unfortunate absence, he took it upon himself to be the first "to awaken in readers' hearts the desire for this most virtuous subject and one that is worthy of great fortune."[6]

Tasso, however, was hardly the first to employ pastoral in the services of courtly celebration. At least since Virgil's first Eclogue, the pastoral setting had been frequently invoked for purposes of royal entertainment and panegyric. Throughout the late fifteenth and sixteenth centuries, as attested by Poliziano's *Orfeo*, Castiglione's *Tirsi*, and numerous plays produced in Ferrara for the Este family (such as Giraldi's *Egle*, Lollio's *Aretusa*, and Argento's *Sacrificio*),[7] the pastoral space was used to provide at least an occasional entertainment for northern Italian courts, particularly the d'Este court. But with the *Aminta*, performed for an admiring Alfonso II d'Este and his court on the island of Belvedere, and informed by the praises of a "dio" who granted Tirsi / Tasso the "ozio" in which he found himself, we have one of the most explicit attempts yet to furnish a "natural" setting that might mime the praised "naturalness" of the court.[8] "O Dafne," proclaims Tasso's "spokesperson" in the play's second act, "a me quest'ozio ha fatto dio: / colui che dio qui può stimarsi, a cui / si pascon gli ampi armenti e l'ampie greggie / da l'uno a l'altro mare, e per li lieti / colti di fecondissime campagne, / e per gli alpestri dossi d'Apennino" (Oh Dafne, a god has given me this peace: at least, one might call him a god, whose countless flocks and herds feed from one sea to another, in the beautiful fields of the most fertile countrysides, and on the wild cliffs of the Apennines) (act II, sc. ii, line 271). With these lines, Alfonso the *warrior*—who has done all he can to have himself entitled a grand duke like his rival Cosimo de'Medici—becomes Alfonso the *shepherd*. Moreover, the lines freely translate the praise of Tityrus of his "god" Octavian in Virgil's first Eclogue, as the scepter of the ruler becomes the staff of the rustic into whose "campagna" Alfonso and his predecessors have indeed wandered.[9] These lines effectively locate the courtly ethos in a pastoral sphere in order to naturalize and neutralize the ruling ideology and permit Alfonso's identity to become associated with "nature" itself.

As noted by the authority most often credited with the formulation of realpolitik, Niccolò Machiavelli, it was important to the Renaissance ruler that his subjects perceive and accept his acquisition of authority as benign. In his advice to would-be monarchs, Machiavelli advocated a full-scale embrace of the facade of an innocent prince:

> In actual fact, a prince may not have all the admirable qualities we listed [mercy, honesty, humanity, sincerity, and religious piety] but it is very important that he should *seem* to have them. . . . Hence a prince should take great care never to drop a word that does not *seem* imbued with the five good qualities noted above; to anyone who sees or hears him, he should *appear* all compassion, all honor, all humanity, all integrity, all religion.[10]

Playing a role of religious piety and integrity to conceal the base but essential qualities of political efficacy and self-interest divorces the people's knowledge from the ruler's power. The portrait of a benign ruler displaces and disguises his desires for domination.[11] The pastoral play performed for Alfonso and his court in a locale that subtly places the tokens of princely power within the "wilderness"[12] furnishes a means of concealing the desire to dominate of which Machiavelli spoke.

But the possibility that the *Aminta*, with its simple and passionate story of shepherds' loves and lives, might offer its privileged viewer an enhanced reflection of himself is subtly negated in the course of the play. By insisting on the unreliability of the mimetic process, Tasso exposes the duke's and his court's more appropriative desires. As a reading of the play and several of Tasso's early lyrics suggests, these are desires from which Tasso, as the authorized maker of such a mirror and as a character in his own play who counsels the "innocent" shepherd Aminta to no less violent an action than rape, is hardly free.[13]

At the heart of the *Aminta* and many of Tasso's early lyrics is a meditation on the impenetrability of the loved one: the regrettably chaste mistress for whom Tasso yearns, and Silvia, Diana's young devotee, who refuses to yield her body or her thoughts to her ardent lover, Aminta. In both cases, this resistance of the feminine is articulated through reference to a mirror, which serves as a tentative allusion to the woman's potential narcissism.[14] Thus in one poem to his chaste mistress, entitled "He returns to show the mirror to his lady and describes her beauty and the pleasure she has while gazing at herself," Tasso imagines "la sua donna" enraptured by the image that *he* takes such pleasure describing. As she gazes into the mirror, "parea fra sé dir:—Ben veggio aperta / l'alta mia gloria e di che dolci sguardi / questa rara bellezza accenda il foco!" (she seems to be saying to herself, how well now do I see my great glory and rare beauty that kindles the fire with such sweet glances!)[15] The Narcissus lured to his death in the dangerous *umbrosus locus* (shady place) becomes (or seems to become) the figure for the young girl who turns the narrator away. But the verb "parea" in the verse above challenges the association of a self-conscious narcissism with the possibly innocent *vergine* and suggests that the poem's capacity to ascertain, let alone undermine, the woman's "innocence" is questionable at best.

Similarly, in act II of the *Aminta*, a cynical Dafne who has been in and out of love countless times describes the chaste, wild Silvia as a young woman who (surprisingly) reflects the growing corruption of the age. Talking to Tirsi, another jaded figure who emerges in the play as a double not only for Tasso himself but for the Tityrus who sang plaintively beneath the shade in Virgil's first Eclogue, Dafne at first warmly defends Silvia's innocence. "She is," she initially claims, "without art." But Dafne immediately adds, "Yet I am no longer sure if Silvia is as innocent as her words and actions make her out to be. Yesterday I saw a sign that gave me some doubts" ("Ora, per dirti il ver, non mi risolvo / se Silvia è semplicetta, come pare / a le parole, a gli atti. Ier vidi un segno che me ne dette dubbio") (II.ii.128–30). Dafne then describes a recent incident in which she watched Silvia watch herself in a shaded pond, on the very "isoletta" on which Tasso's Ferrarese audience gathered to watch the *Aminta* performed al fresco. "She bent, and it appeared as though she was in love with herself, and sought counsel from the water as to how she should arrange her hair, and above her hair her veil, and above her veil her flowers" ("sovr'esso un lago limpido e tranquillo / tutta pendente, in atto che parea / vagheggiar se medesma e 'nsieme insieme / chieder consiglio a l'acque in qual maniera / dispor dovesse in su la fronte i crini, / e sovra i crini il velo e sovra 'l velo / i fior che tenea in grembo") (II.ii.134–40). This act of self-consciousness—the attempt to negotiate her appearance and thus deliberately (rather than unconsciously) tease and tempt her would-be lover—might seem to furnish convincing proof of Silvia's awareness of the manipulative effects her chaste words and gaze have on others. Yet the incident is related through the medium of the voyeuristic messenger on whom the play comes increasingly to depend—a messenger, moreover, who is none other than the "scaltra" (cunning) Dafne, hardened from her various romances and ends of romances. We cannot know whether Dafne's own intentions shade and even shape Silvia's poisoning act of self-consciousness, or whether the event "happened" exactly as it is recounted to us. If Dafne's intrusiveness, like that of the poet himself, makes objective knowledge of the lyric object impossible, we are nevertheless wary of Silvia when she next appears onstage. The possibility that Silvia's shadow is a narcissistic one casts a pall over her character for the remainder of the play.

Again and again in the *Aminta*, as in the poet's lyrics, the phenomenon of mirroring, and by extension of mimesis, is rendered suspect because of its narcissistic overtones.[16] But this suspicion in itself separates the reader or spectator from the putatively innocent character, whose own inner life is finally rendered inaccessible. This inaccessibility is highlighted in a series of lyrics in which Tasso plays on the feminine subject's emergence into self-consciousness. In one lyric written several years after the *Aminta*, Tasso, using his pastoral voice of Tirsi, invites his "ninfa selvaggia e fera" (wild and savage nymph) to use *him* as her mirror so that she may see her "true" self: "Spero fontana divenir di pianto: / allora in me vedrete / quanto voi bella e quanto cruda sete" (I hope to become a fountain from weeping; so that you will see in me how beautiful and cruel you really are).[17]

Similarly, in a madrigal addressed to one of Leonora d'Este's ladies-in-waiting, the poet asks Amore to reveal at last to the lady her lover's sorrows in the wounds she has perhaps unwittingly caused: "Oh beautiful and innocent murderess, it is time that love show you (si mostri) now in your wounds our great suffering."[18] But Tasso's "donna" can only achieve such anagnorisis if she believes what love shows her: if she believes, that is, in the mimetic value of the representations that Tasso has led his reader to mistrust. Such an innocent belief in surfaces and images, in turn, will only be disappointed and end in the demise of innocence—a demise that the poet nevertheless refuses to enact. The poem ends instead with the request that Amore show the woman the spectacle of others' misfortunes. Tasso leaves us in the lyric suspension that is so characteristic of his verse, a suspension that both allows the "donna" to remain in her putative innocence and leaves the reader doubting the authenticity of her purity. And it is precisely this doubt that distinguishes the reader as a cynical rather than an innocent one, a Dafne rather than a Silvia. Tasso's madrigal traps reader and poet, both mistrustful of the veracity of representation, within the hermeneutic circle, while banishing the "pargoletta" (little girl) herself to its outskirts. Such banishment also occurs in the *Aminta*, which similarly re-creates a subtle division between the voyeuristic spectator of the play and the pastoral innocent who finally retreats from the theatrical space, leaving the court with only the parodic representation of its desires.

Despite the complex dynamics of the *Aminta*, the plot is deceptively simple. The young shepherd Aminta is in love with Silvia, who flees from any thoughts of romance and reduces the shepherd to a melancholic potential suicide. Finally, Tirsi and Dafne, who have been to court and in love many times before, decide to intervene on Aminta's behalf and coax the unwilling shepherd to sojourn near a pond where Silvia usually bathes, nude, after hunting, "là dove a le dolci acque fa dolce ombra / quel platano ch'invita a 'l fresco seggio / le ninfe cacciatrici" (there where the platan casts its sweet shadows on the sweet waters, and thus invites to its fresh plot the huntress-nymphs) (II.ii.208–10). When the reluctant Aminta, tricked into believing that Silvia has asked that he meet her, follows Tirsi's advice, he discovers that Silvia has been abducted by a satyr (who previously forewarned the audience of his attack). Aminta finds his beloved nude, bound by her own hair to the tree that casts such sweet shade. After her gallant rescuer unties her, an ungrateful and understandably embarrassed Silvia rushes off to hunt. When she fails to return from the chase, however, a tearful messenger rushes onstage with a bloody handkerchief and a (false) account of Silvia's probable death at the jaws of a wolf. The Pyramus and Thisbe story emerges in full as Aminta hastens to his own death, throwing himself from a cliff into the valley below, and Silvia returns unharmed from her sojourn only to hear of Aminta's suicide and to be transformed, finally, from an enemy of Amore into its impassioned devotee. She hurries to Aminta's side to learn with relief that the shepherd is still alive, and the play ends with an account by the elderly Elpino of Aminta's miraculous "resurrection" and the lovers' pledge of marriage.

This moving climax is possible only if Silvia's journey to "self-consciousness" can be convincingly demonstrated, and as has already been suggested, Dafne's somber message of Silvia's narcissistic corruption leads the audience to suspect the intentions of the "ninfa selvaggia e fera" early on in the play. But just as suspicion operates in divisive fashion in Tasso's lyrics, so it operates here. For in entertaining doubts about Silvia's "innocence," the spectator automatically places her / himself outside of the realm of pastoral purity. The entire *Aminta*, in fact, might be said to unfold as an exposé of the noble audience's *distance* from Edenic innocence.[19]

This exposé relentlessly begins when the first character comes onstage. Cupid, who presents the prologue, is disguised as a shepherd and seeks the audience's complicity in hiding him from his domineering mother, Venus. But that complicity extends beyond a tacit agreement to acknowledge Cupid as a "dio nascosto" (hidden god). For Cupid announces that his real mission in the woods is to invade the hard heart of Diana's chastest follower by using the mechanisms of theater: he will wait for tragic pity to weaken her rigorous vow of "honesty and virginal abstinence," and "in that point which is made softest" he will hurl his poisonous dart, cleverly disguised as a shepherd's arrow (Prologue, lines 62–67). Having transformed his powerful torch into a rustic staff—a transformation anticipating that of Alfonso's symbols of power later in the play—Cupid pretends to mingle, unnoticed and unsuspected, among the rejoicing shepherds while they celebrate their feast days. By cloaking himself in such a "velo" (veil), by transforming his potent dart into a mere shepherd's staff, Cupid symbolizes the allure of a courtly theater that attempts to negate its own theatricality, of a force that disguises its invasive potential.

Yet, of course, Cupid does admit his intrusive stance, although only to an audience tacitly implicated in his furtive acts. The prologue unfolds a dichotomy that will resonate throughout the *Aminta*. On the one hand are those who can "read" and who mistrust the opaque signs of theater, such as Dafne and Tirsi, who are associated with the court. On the other hand are those who have never been taught to question the surface meaning of signs, such as Silvia and Aminta. Thus despite the fact that only the audience witnesses Cupid's intervention into the pastoral world, Tirsi and the members of the chorus, who close each act with an often cynical commentary on the events that have just taken place, reveal themselves to be fully cognizant of the means of dissimulation that Cupid practices. Moreover, in its famous lines following act I, the chorus recognizes these means as completely essential in a "fallen" world dominated by the tyrant "Onore" (Honor). In this passage, which precedes the disquieting observations of one more "fallen" reader, the Satyr, the chorus sings an elegy for a golden age when theatricality and its mediating signs were nonexistent. One crucial mediator introduced in the first chorus will become particularly central to the remainder of the play: the veil, a cursed obstruction that prevents modern shepherds from glimpsing the fruits of their desires: "Allor . . . la verginella ignude / scopria sue fresche rose / ch'or tien ne'l velo ascose" (Then [in the golden age], the nude, young virgin would display her fresh roses that now a veil conceals) (I.chorus.598–601).

The drama's resolution is effected and the dialectic between complicitous spectators and innocent protagonists developed largely through several encounters with two mediating objects that double as comments on the fallen nature of representation itself: Silvia's veil and the bit of torn cloth that Aminta leaves behind when he leaps from the cliff. By the end of act I, the audience has already been enlightened by the courtly members of the chorus as to the duplicitous, coquettish nature of a woman's veil. The modern tyrant "Onore" has managed to veil "la fonte de i diletti / . . . tu a'begli occhi insegnasti / di starne in sé ristretti / . . . tu raccogliesti in rete / le chiome a l'aura sparte" (fountains of delight . . . teaching beautiful eyes to gaze downward, and gathering in snares beautiful hair once tossed to the wind) (I.chorus.604–11). Yet if the cynical chorus expresses an impatience with garments that insinuate themselves between one's gaze and another's body, the play's innocent protagonists exhibit a fascination with the veil and all it suggests as a result of their failure to perceive its mediating status. When in act III the shepherdess Nerina brings onstage the torn veil of Silvia, whom she incorrectly believes has been devoured by wolves, the garment becomes for lovesick Aminta the convincing sign of Silvia's death, beyond which he has no desire to gaze. "Nymph," he cries, "give me, I beg you, this veil which is the only, pitiful remnant of her I have left, so that she may accompany me for this brief space of life that remains to me; so that its presence might increase my suffering" ("Ninfa, dammi, ti prego, / quel velo ch'è di lei / solo e misero avanzo, / sì ch'egli m'accompagne / per questo breve spazio / e di via e di vita che mi resta, / e con la sua presenza / accresca quel martire") (III.ii.263–70). Symbolic of a false message, the veil nonetheless convinces Aminta to end his *own* life.

More importantly, when another messenger arrives with news of Aminta's "death," he bears the torn belt that he grasped in an attempt to prevent Aminta's suicidal plunge. For the believing Silvia, overcome by a pity that the cynical chorus claims deceives only the "simple people," this torn cloth demonstrates her own innocent belief in theater's signs as absolute, or more precisely, as fetishistic: "Cinto infelice, cinto / di signor più infelice, / non ti spiaccia restare / in sì odioso albergo, / ché tu vi resti sol per instrumento / di vendetta e di pena" (Unhappy belt of an even more unhappy master, the only fate that remains to you now is to serve as an instrument of his revenge and my torment) (IV. ii. 287–92). Having realized her effect on another through what love has shown ("mostrato"), Silvia at once demonstrates her innocence as a reader and unknowingly precipitates her own fall into self-consciousness. Upon reaching Aminta's body, which only *seems* to be a corpse, Silvia reveals theater's complete power over her for, presumably, the last time, as she is said to weep like a "bacchante" (V. i. 102).

But for those already on the far side of a self-consciousness consistently described in Tasso's play in cynical terms, the spectacle can have no power, can effect no catharsis. Thus when the final, courtly messenger of the play, Elpino, modeled on the court propagandist Giovan Battista Pigna, reports in act V that he has watched a man hurl himself from a precipice, he describes Aminta's fall as only "una dolente imagine di morte," a painful *image* of death (V. i. 40). Halfway through his descent, Aminta was stopped by "quasi un tessuto, un fascio grande"—a cloth or bundle of leaves and branches that broke his plunge and prevented his death; "this restraint took so much impetus from his fall that it was not fatal" (V. i. 72–78). In recognizing the mediating role of the "tessuto" or cloth, Elpino locates himself firmly outside of a realm in which theater has the power to persuade and move the innocent: "We stood mute with pity and amazement from this improvised spectacle, but"—an important but—"knowing that he was not dead, and that he was not even about to die, we check our grief" ("Noi muti di pietate e di stupore / restammo a lo spettacolo improvviso, / riconoscendo lui: *ma* conoscendo / ch'egli morto non era e che non era / per morir forse, mitighiam l'affanno")

(V.i.81–85; my italics). Such foreknowledge and ability to mitigate pity and theater's potential invasiveness finally separate Elpino, and with him Dafne, the chorus, the courtly audience, and Tirsi (and thus Tasso himself) from a Silvia and an Aminta who are drawn together by their shared belief in the veil or protective covering.

This dichotomy is illustrated nowhere more clearly than in the scene in which Aminta rescues Silvia from the lecherous Satyr. The latter's flight creates what Tirsi, who gives an account of the near-rape and heroic rescue, calls a "spazio di mirare," a space in which to gaze freely at Silvia's nude body. Faced with the chance to view Silvia's body untouched by a veil and thus without the mediations required by society in an age of "onore," Aminta nonetheless "draws reverently aside, not raising his eyes to look at her, denying to himself his pleasure as though to save Silvia the trouble of denying it to him." Tirsi, meanwhile, carefully hidden behind a tree, "saw and heard all." ("Ei si trasse in disparte riverente, / non alzando pur gli occhi per mirarla, / negando a se medesmo il suo piacere / per torre a lei fatica di negarlo. / Io che m'era nascoso e vedea tutto / ed udia tutto, allor fui per gridare" (III.i.109–14). The invasive gaze of the courtier who earlier praised the Este family becomes the voyeurism of the court itself, gathered not to avert its glance, along with Aminta, but to penetrate a veil that it regards as a nuisance, a source of obfuscation and delay. Thus in act I, scene ii, in a passage added to the play only for its publication almost ten years after the court performance,[20] Tirsi gives an extended account of the splendors of the Estense court that includes this passage: "O che sentii? che vidi allora? I' vidi / celesti dee, ninfe leggiadre e belle, / nuovi Lini ed Orfei, ed altre ancora / senza vel, senza nube, e quale e quanta / a gl'immortali appar vergine Aurora, / sparger d'argento e d'or rugiade e raggi" (Oh, what did I hear then? what did I see? I saw celestial gods, graceful and beautiful nymphs, new Linuses and Orpheuses; and even more, I saw the virgin Dawn free of veils or clouds as she appears to the immortals, scattering rays and dew of silver and gold) (I.ii.534–39). The court becomes, retroactively, a realm without shadows. But it is also condemned by its very passion for the "light," for that which lies beneath the veil, and therefore beneath the obfuscating medium of fictions. The result of such desire is the audience's inability to become engaged in and by theater's opaque signs and the cathartic climaxes they effect.[21]

Rather than allowing an identification between courtiers and actors, between the space of the court and the space of pastoral innocence praised by Aldo Manuzio in his preface to the 1583 *Aminta*, Tasso challenges the prerogative of the court to invade the pastoral space and appropriate it as its own. His theater firmly and implicitly rejects an analogy between an innocent audience and innocent characters, between purity offstage and purity onstage. The final union of Silvia and Aminta takes place, like so much else in the play, behind the metaphorical curtain, for news of it is only brought to the stage by the messenger and elder statesman Elpino, the transparent persona for the Este chronicler and propagandist Pigna. Like Dafne watching Silvia watch herself, the audience is reduced to uncomfortable and, in this last case, frustrated voyeurism, for the only figure they *do* see on stage at play's end is an image of themselves. Far from being part of the only real drama that takes place—Silvia's gradual capitulation—the courtly spectator of Tasso's *Aminta* is barred from the central action, while being made acutely conscious of his or her distance from innocence and of the invasiveness associated with the desire to witness that innocence. This exposé is principally directed at Alfonso himself. Yet the inclusion in the play of various courtiers who assist Alfonso in neutralizing his relationship to the stage, such as Pigna and Tasso himself, suggests that Tasso is far from indicting merely his prince. Silvia in particular emerges as the character most unable to protect herself from a theatricality revealed to be as invasive as Cupid's penetration of Arcadia. On a certain level the play even reveals itself (or cagily refuses to reveal itself) as not so much a consummation as a rape.

Insensitive to Tasso's careful critique of the link between nobility and a hermeneutics of innocence, Pierre de Rayssiguier, writing for the French court in 1632, would restage the play and its critical dynamic by displaying everything onstage that Tasso consigns to the mediation of a messenger. Thus the Satyr's attempted rape of Silvia, Silvia's rescue by Aminta, Aminta's suicidal plunge from the cliff, and the final resolution in which the two lovers are brought together all happen before the eyes of the spectators. As Rayssiguier transforms Tasso's drama of veils and mediations into a theater of full disclosure, the charge of voyeurism once subtly leveled against the Estense court and its chief propagandists is silenced, and the uneasy coexistence of pastoral and courtly spaces is no longer challenged. The very pity that invaded the innocent Silvia now invades the hearts of Rayssiguier's "innocent" spectators, who become the privileged subjects of the *Aminta*.[22] Rayssiguier willfully ignores Tasso's insistence that within the ideology of power—an ideology that of necessity must include the prince, his court, and his poet—there is no such thing as an innocent gaze or an innocent play space.

For much to Rayssiguier's discomfort, Tasso emphatically insists on the appropriative nature of such a gaze and such a space. By staging Aminta's recovery and union with Silvia in a realm that the courtiers and ruling powers of Ferrara may not see, the playwright finally protects his fictive characters from the tainted domain of the court. Thus the ultimate gesture of protection becomes the prerogative of the poet, although it does not include him. If Tasso's own quest for immunity can only place him within a court that vainly pretends to live without the shadow of mediating fictions, "senza nube, senza vele" (without clouds, without veils), he can at least save his innocent characters by procuring for them another, different space of immunity and removing them from the court's gaze altogether. At the same time, Tasso's chorus, which closes the play with a few brief lines, glosses over this act of disappearance and evasion. Like the courtly audience, the cynical chorus is immune from the passionate extremes suffered by Silvia and Aminta, who live apart from and ignorant of the complex dynamics of courtly politics.

> Ma se più caro viene
> e più si gusta dopo 'l male il bene,
> io non ti chieggio, Amore,
> questa beatitudine maggiore.
> Bea pur gli altri in tal guisa:
> me la mia ninfa accoglia
> dopo brevi preghiere e servir breve:
> e siano i condimenti
> de le nostre dolcezze

non sì gravi tormenti,
ma soavi disdegni
e soavi repulse,
risse e guerre cui segua,
reintegrando i cori, o pace o tregua.
(V.chorus. 145–58)

(But if the good is more dear and more pleasing after the bad, I do not ask you, Love, for this greater blessing—bless others instead in such a manner! May my nymph yield herself to me after brief prayers and brief service, and let the condiments of our sweetness be not such grave torments as those he has suffered, but gentle disdain, gentle repulses, quarrels and wars; and may they be followed, our hearts once again in accord, with either peace or a truce.)

Relieved that the space of Silvia and Aminta is not contiguous with their own, the chorus reinterprets the gap that has opened in the course of the *Aminta* between innocent lovers and appropriative courtiers as a fortunate one. With this ending, which hearkens back to Elpino's interpretation of Aminta's fall as fortunate—"fu felice il precipizio" (V.i.38)—Tasso saves his *innocenti* from being compromised by the invasive voyeurism of his padrone and saves his play from being too openly corrosive. The sentiment of Alexander Pope over one hundred years later might justly express the effect that Tasso himself may have wished his audience to feel:

I shou'd certainly displease all those who are charm'd with *Guarini* and *Bonarelli*, and imitate *Tasso* not only in the Simplicity of his Thoughts, but in that of the *Fable* too. If surprising discoveries shou'd have place in the story of a Pastoral Comedy, I believe it wou'd be more aggreeable to Probability to make them the effects of *Chance* than of *Design*; Intrigue not being very consistent with that Innocence, which ought to constitute a Shepherd's Character. There is nothing in all the *Aminta* (as I remember) but happens by meer accident; unless it be the meeting of *Aminta* with *Silvia* at the *Fountain*, which is the contrivance of *Daphne*, and even that is the most simple in the world.[23]

II

As the preceding pages have suggested, the *Aminta* stages an elaborate dialectic between those infiltrators who want to claim the pastoral space as their own, such as Tasso/Tirsi, and those who resist such acts of appropriation, such as Aminta and Silvia, who flee from the stage and thus from the court's gaze before the play is over. "A dio, pastori; / piagge, a dio; a dio selve, e fiumi, a dio" (Farewell, shepherds; farewell, mountains; farewell, forests, and streams, farewell) (IV.ii.345–46), calls Silvia as she runs off the stage in act IV, the torn belt of Aminta in her hand. "E voi restate ancora, / ch'io vo' per non tornare" (And you remain here, because I no longer wish to return) (III.ii.280–81) are Aminta's final words as he bids his audience goodbye. Characters' flights from the roles others would have them perform marks the *Gerusalemme* as well, although the centrifugal movement that dominates much of Tasso's lengthy epic poem is arrested in the final cantos, as the formerly recalcitrant Christian warriors Rinaldo and Tancredi rejoin their cohorts in battle to take Jerusalem. Even the pagan woman Armida, whose flight from the Christian camp was responsible for the desertion of numerous *cavalieri*, returns to the poem's sacred center and submits to Rinaldo as her "signore" just outside Jerusalem's walls. And Erminia, princess of Antioch, who fled from the Christian camp in canto VII as though she were a "cervo" (stag) hunted by dogs, enters the city at twilight along with the wounded body of Tancredi.

Yet although the *Gerusalemme* closes with a gathering in the poem's sacred city, joyous reconciliation does not always accompany the return to a privileged center. Goffredo may greet the prodigal Rinaldo's return to the army after thirteen long cantos with the decree "Ogni trista memoria omai si taccia, / e pongansi in oblio l'andate cose" (Let all sad memories be silenced, and let things that are past cast themselves into forgetfulness) (XVIII.2). But the same *capitano*, modeled on the historical Godefroy de Bouillon, who was appointed by Pope Urban II to lead the First Crusade in the late eleventh century, also engages in less docile suppressions of flight. Consider the poem's finale, a violent, even superfluous stifling of a last, desperate retreat. In the *Gerusalemme*'s penultimate stanza, Goffredo's last act as supreme warrior is to prevent the pagan fugitives from fleeing a city that was once their own.

> [Goffredo] tace, . . . e segue il corso poi de' fuggitivi.
> Fuggon quegli a i ripari, ed intervallo

> da la morte trovar non ponno quivi.
> Preso è repente e pien di strage il vallo,
> corre di tenda in tenda il sangue in rivi,
> e vi macchia le prede e vi corrompe
> gli ornamenti barbarici e le pompe.
>
> (XX.143)

(Goffredo was silent, . . . and he followed the path of the fugitives. They fled to their shelters, but even here they were not to find a respite from death. The rampart was taken, and turned to a place of slaughter; from tent to tent, the blood flowed in rivers, and it stained the prey and soiled the barbarians' ornaments and their pomp.)

It is only following this vision of "rivers of blood" that the poet is able to declare, in the next and last stanza, "Così vince Goffredo," and to announce that the victors enter "la città già liberata" (Thus does Goffredo conquer [and enter] . . . the liberated city). Once within, they proceed to the great tomb of Christ, where Goffredo suspends the battle and, still dressed in his blood-stained garments, "qui devoto / il gran Sepolcro adora e scioglie il voto" (with devotion, worships at the great sepulcher and fulfills his vow) (XX.144). Victory is intimately linked to the pursuit of the "fuggitivi," whose panicked flight ends only in a bloodbath.

Such a vision of almost superfluous brutality is hardly unique to the poem's last canto. Rather, the moment of slaughter and arrested flight echoes an earlier departure, not of anonymous fugitives whose gender and identity remain undefined, but of innocent women and children. After recounting the fateful battle between Tancredi and the fierce African warrior Argante in canto XIX, the poet shifts to a much different, much broader scenario: that of the "espugnata terra" (subdued land) of embattled Jerusalem and of a flight which anticipates that of canto XX:

> Ogni cosa di strage era già pieno,
> vedeansi in mucchi e in monti i corpi avolti
> là i feriti su i morti, e qui giacieno
> sotto morti insepolti egri sepolti.
> Fuggian premendo i pargoletti al seno
> le meste madri co' capegli sciolti,
> e 'l predator, di spoglie e di rapine
> carco, stringea le vergini nel crine.
>
> (XIX.30)

(Everything was full of bloodshed, everywhere one sees mountains of bodies, the wounded piled onto the dead, and here there lie beneath the unburied dead the buried wounded. Pressing their children to their breasts, the sad mothers flee, their locks undone, while predators laden with booty and plunder drag the virgins to them by their hair.)

As in canto XX, this escape by women and children proves to be fruitless. It culminates in rape by Christian "predators"—a brutality Goffredo warns his troops not to commit only some twenty stanzas *after* the poet has duly reported it to his reader (XIX.51).

If in the *Aminta* the departure from the play's contaminated, ideological center is sanctioned by a poet complicitous in his protagonists' flight, in the *Gerusalemme* the attempt to flee the holy city and find shelter elsewhere is doomed from the start. Even those pagans who try to find sanctuary within the city in the Tower of David are captured and killed. In a pitiful echo of the pastoral vocabulary of the *Aminta*, the Sultan beckons to his flock "like a shepherd" as he attempts to protect his "charges" from the invading troops. The moment alters a simile from the tenth book of the *Aeneid*, in which Virgil compares Lausus's attack on Aeneas to a "storm-cloud" from which ploughmen, husbandmen, and hapless wayfarers seek shelter.[24] In changing the "arator" (ploughman) into a shepherd anxious for his flock, Tasso makes the Sultan a more caring and responsible figure than his anonymous Virgilian prototype. At the same time, the Sultan is ironically incapable of protecting the bodies of those with whom he is entrusted, as the Tower of David is invaded by the marauding Christians. Goffredo's mission is such that even the sanctuary that once furnished immunity to those who sought protection within it is no longer inviolable.

Indeed, much of the *Gerusalemme Liberata* seems designed to destroy former havens of invulnerability in order to establish a new locus of protection: the church. Yet as the above remarks have suggested, this construction of an invulnerable church capable of protecting its "own" is accompanied by what seems to be almost gratuitous bloodshed. One might conjecture that Tasso felt some unease in granting the church—or, for that matter, the secular Goffredo, ancestor of Alfonso, who fought in God's name—the status of a benevolent and nurturing protector. Moreover, one might reflect here on the obvious anachronisms of Tasso's poem. The conditions permitting the suppression of centrifugality that was the First Crusade no longer exist in Tasso's own day, a point of which Tasso reminds Alfonso d'Este in his epic peroration, even as he praises Alfonso as the "Emulo di Goffredo." At the close of the fourth stanza of canto I, Tasso expresses the hope that "un dì fia che la presaga penna / osi scriver di te quel'ch'or n'accenna" (one day, may my prophetic pen dare to write of you those things which now it only hints). But this expression of hope that Alfonso will soon be another Goffredo yields in stanza 5 to a vision of Europe's present disarray: "È ben ragion, s'egli averrà ch'in pace / il buon popol di Cristo unqua si veda / . . . ch'a te lo scettro in terra o, se ti piace, / l'alto imperio de' mari a te conceda" (There would be good reason, *if* ever the good people of Christ will find themselves at peace . . . that to you the scepter on land will fall, or if it pleases you, the exalted rule of the seas) (my italics). For one thing, Jerusalem had been quickly reoccupied before the twelfth century was over by none other than the phoenix whom Solimano promises he will become in canto IX. Like a Dido who threatens to rise again from the ashes, the Sultan predicts the capture of Jerusalem by a descendant:[25] Saladino, the Turkish general whose military successes prompted the abortive Second Crusade.[26] For another thing, of course, the Reformation had intervened since the period of the Crusades, and the years immediately following the Council of Trent marked a concerted effort by the church to emphasize its unity in the face of the tumultuous events of recent European history. That emphasis was less the result of Paul III's impulse toward peace and reconciliation, with which he had originally hoped to convene the Tridentine council, than of nervous defensiveness in light of Protestantism's alarming success. Initially, Paul had wanted to pacify the European powers and to fight against the Turk, the *real* infidel. Yet the result of the Council was *not* conciliation but counter-reformation;[27] and as Kenneth Setton has recently observed, concern with the Turk, foremost in the summons of the 1545 Council to "launch an expedition of the most sacred sign of the cross against the infidel," had markedly declined by the Council's final meetings.[28] The body of Catholicism by then had a more important enemy in the Protestant.

Tasso's choice of a genre, with its return to the material of the early French and Breton romances and the chronicles that elaborate the details of the Crusade, was thus in many ways anachronistic. Phrases such as "sanctum collegium," "Christianorum congregatio," and "sacra fidelium Dei societas" (sacred college, union of Christians, and devout society of the faithful to God) echo throughout the Crusade accounts of Baldric, Robert, and Guibert as allusions to the unified community of the "early Church."[29] Whereas even when Tasso's most immediate precursor, Ariosto, began his epic poem around 1509 it was still possible to speak of comradery among Europeans fighting the infidel, by 1532 and the final revision of the *Orlando Furioso* Christian militarism against Islam was distinctly belated. Erasmus had already appealed to the powers of Christendom to heal their internal divisiveness, and Luther had wryly suggested in one of his sermons that the Catholics were as idolatrous as the Turks.[30]

But if these concerns seem trivial in light of what has recently been described as Tasso's attempt to create a "sacramental theology" for the Tridentine church that would heal a fractured Europe, one need only turn to the *Gerusalemme*'s evasive narrator and the character with whom he has frequently been associated to discern an ambivalent relationship with secular and sacred institutions designed to protect the faithful and excoriate those who seek immunity elsewhere.[31] For if it can be argued that the *Gerusalemme Liberata* celebrates a new partnership between church and state—while observing, as in the *peroratio*, that such a partnership exists in an as yet unrealized future—it is equally the case that within the poem there exists what Marilyn Migiel has recently called another perspective that "resists being integrated into the epic enterprise"[32] and that is associated not only with the poem's narrator but with a pagan: the princess Erminia. This parallel has been noted at least since the work of Eugenio Donadoni, who in collapsing poet and female character remarks that "Erminia is the poet himself, in his preferred guise of the ignored, fantastic, and unhappy lover. . . . And she, of all the figures of the poem, is that in which the poet has most fully narrated himself: or better, most eloquently expressed the grieving and elegiac voices of his own soul."[33]

But one need not have recourse to Tasso's proverbial helplessness in order to elucidate the connections between a narrator who refers to himself as a "peregrino errante" (wandering pilgrim) and the pagan princess subject to interminable errancy because she has been torn from her family, her city, and the enemy soldier she is destined to love. Nor should one argue for an absolute congruency between narrator and character. Rather, as the following remarks will argue, while character and narrator alike seem to posit an alternative perspective in the poem that redeems historical errancy and furnishes a nonviolent means of protection, there are fundamental differences between them. These differences suggest that Tasso is, in fact, using Erminia as a character onto whom he may displace, and through whom he may disguise, his own vulnerability vis-à-vis the institutions he both praises and subtly criticizes. Thus while character and narrator alike provide a critique of the militant violence that unifies Christendom and wins Jerusalem for Goffredo, Erminia also represents the poet's attempt to "engender" vulnerability by distancing it from himself—an attempt that is ultimately unsuccessful, as the last part of this chapter will argue. In the meantime, however, it is important to reflect on just who Erminia "is" and in what ways she might be construed as representing an alternative to the poem's relentless violence.

At first glance, Erminia may remind us not so much of the *Gerusalemme*'s poetic "peregrino errante" as of an earlier "peregrina" and pagan princess who would have been familiar to Tasso's readers. In this poem laden with references to another Ferrarese epic, the *Orlando Furioso*, Erminia serves as a chaster Angelica, whose own flight opens Ariosto's poem and draws in its wake numerous pagan and Christian warriors[34] as she attempts to return to her native Cathay. Precisely this attempt to return to an origin and an identity that elude her in the Christian camp creates for Angelica in flight the condition of vulnerability. But it is a condition she is capable of deflecting, first when she uses the magic ring that renders her invisible and thus immune to the desires of undesirable men,[35] and then when she stumbles upon Medoro's bleeding body in the course of her pastoral sojourn at the center of the poem. This pastoral locus, inhabited by a kindly elderly couple, becomes the site in which Angelica heals Medoro's wounds and in which he proceeds to heal hers as the two fall in love. The flight to pastoral arguably furnishes for Angelica a more integral identity as she becomes an actively desiring protagonist rather than only an object of desire, and as her refusal to be valorized within the overwhelmingly male world of the battlefield is concretized as a removal from the *Orlando Furioso* itself. If the traces that she leaves behind of her amorous sojourn enrage Orlando, she is nonetheless immune from Orlando's madness, having withdrawn in a "lucido intervallo," like the narrator himself, "from the dance."[36]

Erminia too is a character in flight, whose various *fughe*—from the walled city, from the "tende latine" (latin tents), from the Egyptian camp—are all attempts to flee the definitions and roles others would impose on her. Or, as she declares to Vafrino in canto XIX when she unmasks him as a spy, she flees the imperious requests of others ("fuggo l'imperiose altrui richieste") (XIX.89). But unlike Angelica, Erminia has no point of origin to which she may return. Her native kingdom of Antioch has been taken by the Christians, just as her heart has been taken by the Christian Tancredi, and her homelessness makes her a figure of considerable pathos. One of her flights, in canto VII, is to the domain of a kind shepherd and his family, beneath whose "ombra" she lingers for much of the poem. This suggests the pastoral locus of Angelica's encounter with Medoro as well as the idyllic space of the *Aminta*. But whereas the pastoral space furnishes for Angelica an integrity that renders her immune to the epic project of the *Furioso*, Erminia finds there no such integrity, as she uselessly laments her love for Tancredi.

We next see her in the pagan camp, which she leaves with the Christian spy Vafrino for yet another "errant" journey that takes her in canto XIX to Tancredi's wounded body. Once again, Tasso seems interested in providing a parallel with the two earlier texts.[37] When she encounters Tancredi in a setting outside the city that was earlier described in terms reminiscent of the valley where Silvia finds Aminta's body,[38] Erminia throws herself over the seemingly lifeless warrior. After lamenting his wounds and his miserable "fortuna" (XIX.105), she commences to treat him; as we know from an earlier canto when she was called upon to tend to the wounded Argante, she, like Silvia and Angelica, is an expert in healing, having learned from her mother "the secret virtues of herbs" and the songs or "carmi" with which "to heal every wound" (VI.67). She proceeds to stanch the flow of blood with the only bandages she has, her veil and her hair, reviving Tancredi much as Silvia and Angelica revived their wounded lovers:

> Ma non ha fuor ch'un velo onde gli fasce
> le sue ferite, in sì solinghe parti.
> Amor le trova inusitate fasce,
> e di pietà le insegna insolite arti:
> l'asciugò con le chiome e rilegolle
> pur con le chiome che troncar si volle.
> (XIX. 112)

(But in such a deserted spot, she has nothing more than a veil with which to bind his wounds. Thus Love finds for her a most unusual bandage, and teaches her through pity unheard-of arts: with her hair, she dries the wounds and again with her hair that she had wished to cut, she binds them.)

The repetition of "fasce" as both a verb and a noun recalls us to the "fascia" grasped by the shepherd as Aminta plummeted from the cliff and given to Silvia, indirectly becoming the "cure" for Aminta's wound. Whereas in Tasso's pastoral play the garment or cloth serves as the delusory symbol of theater's corporeality, it functions here to close a wound, the gap that threatens to take Tancredi's life. But the connections between Erminia and Silvia—or between Erminia and Angelica, for that matter—end here. For Angelica and Silvia vanish from their respective texts, along with the men who reciprocate their love, but Erminia returns to the *Gerusalemme*'s center essentially alone, disappearing into a hostel while Vafrino takes the wounded Tancredi to Goffredo. More importantly, whereas Silvia and Angelica cure only the men with whom they fall in love, Erminia's powers of healing are truly generative insofar as they extend beyond the single warrior Tancredi. In saving Tancredi from death she enables him to protect yet another from death, the warrior Raimondo in canto XX. She also brings a Tancredi who wandered from the fold of the army back into the larger community of the city. In effect, she heals the wounds of a church that had temporarily lost its members to the allurement of a rhetoric of individuality exemplified in Tancredi's mad desire to end the war with a single combat, to have himself stand for the Christian body as a whole.

Most significantly, Erminia is responsible for saving Goffredo by revealing to Vafrino the plan whereby the Egyptians are going to disguise themselves as Goffredo's "custodi" (guardians) and plunge a sword soaked in poison into his valorous breast: "e 'l ferro armato di veneno avranno, / perché mortal sia d'ogni piaga il danno" (XIX.88). In becoming the character who prevents the poison from penetrating the captain's body, Erminia assumes the role of the true "custodo" and protector of the Christian body as a whole.

It is in this fashion that Erminia creates a potentially subversive alternative to the poem's violence, as she emerges toward the end of the *Gerusalemme Liberata* as a pagan woman on whom the Christian body paradoxically depends. She thus appears to function as an agent of the destiny prophesied by Ugone to Goffredo during the latter's celestial "vision": "Al fin tutti i tuoi compagni erranti / ridurrà il Ciel sotto i tuoi segni santi" (At the end, Heaven will bring back all of your errant warriors)(XIV.18). But far from effecting a striking reversal of the roles of the traditionally dependent female "ward" of the state and the state itself, Tasso radically undercuts the possibility of such a reversal from the start. Despite her salvational acts of healing and protecting others so that the Christian army may be reunited at the end of the poem—and thereby generating a bloodless alternative to the violence committed by the Christians—Erminia is never fully acknowledged by the communities she so peripherally enters. Indeed, perhaps the alternative she furnishes is too much at variance with that violence. It is telling that despite her acts of healing she is destined to almost complete anonymity. When pouring out her complaints in the *locus amoenus* where her precursor Angelica sealed her love with Medoro, Erminia is greeted only with "tronchi sordi"; when she writes on these "deaf trunks" the messages she hopes Tancredi will someday read—carvings that recall the messages Angelica and Medoro emblazoned on the trees in their pastoral retreat—the narrator intimates that Tancredi, trapped within a different "ombra" far from that of Erminia, will never encounter them.

This inability to be *known*, to have her words and deeds acknowledged by the ideal reader Tancredi, is enacted once again in canto XIX. When Tancredi is momentarily revived by Erminia's tender ministrations, he raises his head and addresses his only words to Erminia in the entire poem: "E tu chi sei, medica mia pietosa?"

(And who are you, my merciful doctor?) (XIX.114). Doomed to linger unknown and unread, Erminia merely asks Tancredi to rest and to be silent—"or (te 'l comando / come medica tua) taci e riposa." While the poem ends with Goffredo on his knees before his Savior, Erminia disappears in canto XIX into the *albergo* that Vafrino finds for her within the city, thus entering yet another only temporary locus. The *albergo* is within Jerusalem, but it is within its walls, in isolation—far from the bloody scenes of battle that fill the final canto—that Erminia remains, not to be heard from again. Thus the figure responsible for preserving the Christian body's integrity by returning Tancredi to Jerusalem and revealing the Egyptians' plot against Goffredo is unacknowledged by that body at poem's end.

Yet rather than suggest that Erminia is simply a victim, Tasso complicates her situation by making such anonymity in part a function of her character. For Erminia consistently articulates her desires for independence in ambivalent fashion. Her quests for agency, her flights from others' imperious demands, are ultimately misguided and short-lived. It is not, in fact, autonomy that Erminia can be said to pursue—the autonomy of the woman warrior, Clorinda, whose armor she so briefly and so incongruously dons—but inclusion within a larger community and virtual regression to a childlike posture of dependency. The numerous repetitions of the verb *raccogliersi* (to gather within) suggest the extent to which Erminia is conceived of, and conceives of herself, as dependent upon a community that will effortlessly absorb her. In her first appearance in the poem, Erminia is described as having been "raccolse in corte" (received in the court) by Aladino when the Christians defeated Antioch and her father was killed (III.12); standing outside of the Christian tents dressed in Clorinda's armor in canto VI, Erminia asks the "belle . . . tende latine" (beautiful latin tents) to "raccogliete me dunque" (gather [her] within [them]) (VI.104; VI.105). In the following canto, she asks the elderly shepherd and his wife, "Me teco raccogli in così grato / albergo ch'abitar teco mi giova" (Gather me with you in this sweet resting place, where it will please me to live with you) (VII.15). Later she asks that her eager soul be gathered into the community of the dead as she urges the supposedly dead Tancredi to take her where he is going: "Raccogli tu l'anima mia seguace, / drizzala tu dove la tua se 'n gio" (XIX. 109). The last reference to Erminia in the poem directs her to one final, albeit temporary, resting place within the city of Jerusalem, the inn to which Vafrino escorts her: "Vafrino a la donzella, e non discosto, / ritrova albergo assai chiuso e secreto" (Vafrino finds for the young woman a lodging not far off, although hidden and private) (XIX. 119). Erminia's last *riparo* is the same as that of Goffredo and the other Christian warriors, including Tancredi himself.[39] Yet despite her timely assistance to those warriors, she is absent from the poem's final canto of Christian victory and unification.

Thus does Tasso create a character who exemplifies the dangers of absorption. The protection for which Erminia asks throughout the poem, her incorporation into the larger body that she anonymously protects, results in her being unknown and unread. Erminia's name is never mentioned when Vafrino reveals to Goffredo the Egyptians' deception, and another meeting between her and her would-be lover Tancredi in which he might at last learn her name never takes place. The result of protection, illustrated perhaps most poignantly when Erminia recounts her request to Tancredi to save her "onore" when he entered her native city in victory, is the *loss* of one's "libertà." Erminia thus vacillates between fleeing from communities that make "imperious requests" and being absorbed into communities that would silence her; between pursuing liberty through an always dangerous flight and losing freedom in the desire for an absorption that grants her protection but never a voice. In the course of such vacillations, however, Erminia preserves and enables the invulnerability of the Christian "body," and she does so in a manner markedly different from that of the warriors themselves. She thereby illustrates the *Gerusalemme*'s paradox of the viator who can protect *others* but never herself.[40]

What are we to make of this paradox, and how does the poet's narrator, himself a "peregrino errante," figure into it? If, as Marilyn Migiel observes, Tasso's narrator shares with Erminia her "narrative powers" and ambiguity, it is even more important that he shares with her the role of "buon medico": a role that Tasso conceives of, in the passage describing Erminia's medical talents, in terms of "carmi" with which one "sani ogni piaga e 'l duol si disacerbe" (heals every wound and sweetens one's pain) (VI.67). In the poem's third stanza, the narrator casts himself in the role of the good doctor when he claims, "Così a l'egro fanciul porgiamo aspersi / di soavi licor gli orli del vaso" (Thus do we give the sick child a glass of sour medicine whose rim has been sprinkled with sweet liquids), defending his right to "adorn his pages" with delights other than those of the celestial Muse and announcing his complicity in administering to his readers a dose of pleasure.

In these lines, Tasso has recourse to a well-known simile from Lucretius that reappeared during the Renaissance in works such as Castiglione's *Book of the Courtier*, which compares the perfect courtier to the "shrewd doctor" who "spreads the edge of the cup with some sweet cordial when [he] wish[es] to give a bitter-tasting medicine to sick and over-delicate children."[41] This simile justifies not only the delights of poetry—as in Lucretius—but, as Daniel Javitch has argued, the necessity for courtiers to comport themselves "poetically" in order to be politically effective. Tasso's invocation of the shrewd physician may indeed attest to the poet's realization that Ferrara is no different than Urbino, and that like Guidabaldo, Alfonso is "susceptible to beautiful play" and hostile to direct attempts at pedagogy.[42] And yet Tasso's invocation, following as it does his plea that Urania pardon him if "with pleasures other than [her] own [he] ornament his pages," betrays some unease regarding the doctor's and parent's deceptiveness. It perhaps betrays unease, too, over turning the tables by making the "dependent" poet into the physician and father and his princely reader into a child. As though in penance for this transgression, Tasso turns around in the next stanza to implore the real father and good physician of the Estense state, Alfonso, to provide him with a safe sanctuary and receive his poem:

> Tu, magnanimo Alfonso, il qual ritogli
> al furor di fortuna e guidi in porto
> me peregrino errante, a fra gli scogli
> e fra l'onde agitato e quasi absorto,
> queste mie carte in lieta fronte accogli,
> che quasi in voto a te sacrate i' porto.
>
> (I.4)

(You, magnanimous Alfonso, who from the fury of Fortune snatch me and guide me into port, a wandering pilgrim almost drowned among the reefs and mad waves, receive these my pages with a happy countenance, for I carry them and consecrate them, almost as an offering, to you.)

Thus it would appear that Erminia's vacillations are the poet's own, and that the pagan princess's distance from the poem's genuine locus of spirituality is also the distance of the poet, divorced by his transgressive métier from Urania. Yet the invocation to Alfonso demands closer attention. Tasso's narrator requests a place of shelter only at the *end* of his "errant" journey, when he asks Alfonso, "Emulo di Goffredo," to welcome him into a court that "nourishes and encourages the arts." So does Goffredo welcome his errant heroes at the end of the poem. The belatedness of Tasso's "request" becomes especially apparent in comparison with the corresponding request in an earlier, and unfinished, epic, the *Stanze per la giostra* of Angelo Poliziano. Like the fourth stanza of the *Gerusalemme*, stanza 4 of Poliziano's poem is directed to a patron, Lorenzo de'Medici, and it associates Florence's ruler with the repose Tasso would associate with Alfonso:

> E tu, ben nato Laur, sotto il cui velo
> Fiorenza lieta in pace si riposa,
> né teme i venti o 'l minacciar del celo
> o Giove irato in vista più crucciosa,
> accogli all'ombra del tuo santo stelo
> la voce umil, tremante e paurosa;
> o causa o fin di tute le mie voglie,
> che sol vivon d'odor delle tuo foglie.[43]

(And you, well born Lorenzo (laurel), beneath whose veil happy Florence rests in peace, fearing neither the winds nor the threats from the sky nor an irate Jove most terrifying in countenance, beneath the shadow of your holy stalk receive this humble, trembling, and fearful voice: cause and culmination of all of my wishes, which live from the fragrance of your leaves alone.)

The "ombra" for Poliziano, long patronized by the Medici as poet and educator, is a place not merely of repose and protection but of elevation; the "humble voice" will someday, the poet hopes in a later stanza, become the trumpet of the swan, as Poliziano basks beneath the "foglie" not only of Lorenzo's laurel but of Lorenzo's writing.[44] Yet if the shade of the laurel furnishes the locus beneath which Poliziano may begin his verses and someday find his voice transformed into that of the swan, Alfonso's port becomes a place in which Tasso's already written pages are received and preserved from future destruction. If Lorenzo, as both poet and patron, is Poliziano's protective muse, Alfonso is to Tasso what his father Ercole was to Ariosto: a port to which the poet turns *only* when a poem that is the product of apparent errancy is complete. Tasso may locate his request for safe harbor in the same stanza of his poem as Poliziano does. But the language of his invocation as well as its rhymes declare that his real precursor is the author of the *Orlando Furioso*, who in his final canto announces that his frail boat is majestically steering *itself* into the gracious *riparo* of Ferrara only when the poem is virtually complete: "Or, se mi mostra la mia carta il vero, / non è lontano a discoprirsi il porto; / sì che nel lito i voti scioglier spero / a chi nel mar per tanta via m'ha scorto" (Now if my page shows me the truth, it will not be much longer before port is discovered: where I can hope to complete my vow to the one who has escorted me for so long through the sea) (XLVI.1).

Tasso's apparent reluctance to bring the *Gerusalemme*'s moment of production—if not its moment of reception—within Alfonso's benevolent shade reveals his affiliation with his irreverent precursor Ariosto rather than with the more obliging and politic Poliziano precisely at the point of the work's most blatant encomium of Alfonso (as well as its only reference to the poet's historical identity).[45] If, then, Erminia is trapped between her desire for autonomy and her wish for inclusion, this most self-conscious of allusions to the narrator's role suggests that he suffers from no such vacillation. This "peregrino errante" wanders purposefully throughout the poem and asks for protection only when such a request is strategically beneficial. Like Erminia, Tasso's narrator desires to become the mediator who heals, who plays the good physician and parent rather than the violent *cavaliere*. But he can only function in such a capacity while he remains beyond the very *ripari* that Erminia constantly seeks, resisting the absorption within shade that threatens a loss of potency and a silencing of the poetic voice anxious for fame.[46] Such absorption and dependency are ultimately the desirable goals of all good Christians, according to a church that saw itself as paternalistic in Tasso's era. But Tasso defends against this absorption even while allowing Erminia to succumb to it.

This claim is possible because of the documents Tasso himself has left us regarding his own stratagems vis-à-vis a very real and potentially threatening ecclesiastical authority. One such stratagem is the "Allegoria" Tasso composed in late 1575 after most of the *Gerusalemme* was finished, a brief "preface" to his poem designed to appease the Roman Inquisitor, Silvio Antoniano, whose official imprint was required before the poem could be published. Shortly before drafting the allegory, Tasso expressed his worries regarding the Inquisitor's anticipated criticisms of the "marvelous" episodes of the *Gerusalemme* in letters to various friends such as Scipione Gonzaga. The "good father of the German college will be likely to desire more history and less poetry," Tasso commented in a letter to Gonzaga in the fall of 1575.[47] He went on to declare that "il maraviglioso sarebbe tenuto più comportabile, che fosse giudicato s'ascondesse sotto alcuna buona e santa allegoria" (the marvelous will be more acceptable, if it is judged as hiding beneath it a good and holy allegory). With the help of several friends "more versed in Plato than [he]," Tasso went on to write an allegory that might serve as an expedient defense against an Inquisitor who he felt would prefer a historical chronicle or a psychomachia—a spiritual contest—to a "poetic" epic.[48]

And it is indeed a psychomachia that Tasso's "Allegoria" provides.[49] His summary of the *Gerusalemme* for Antoniano offers a penetrating glance at the struggle between the forces of good, led by Goffredo, who functions as the "intellectual faculty," and those of evil, consisting of the infernal ministers Armida and Ismago, the "two diabolical temptations" from which all sins proceed.[50] Thus is the Christian soul engaged in a timeless struggle against intellectual and concupiscent temptations alike. Jerusalem is no longer the earthly city of the First Crusade but the beatific vision toward which "the Christian man" can finally turn and where his intellect will "riposarsi ne le orazioni e ne le contemplazioni de'beni de l'altra vita beatissima e immortale" (rest itself in prayers and contemplation of the goods of that other most blessed and immortal life) ("Allegoria," p. 30).[51] Goffredo is not merely the temporal leader of an army during the First Crusade but the hidden and eternal essence that is the soul. In effect, Tasso disguises the historically specific aspects of his poem by rendering an image of a soul and a church ultimately "invulnerable" to historical change.[52]

At the same time, Tasso compliments the Inquisitor's elitism by suggesting that this *essere intrinseco* or hidden meaning is not available to all readers of the poem. Just as the "Allegoria" divides the aristocratic and inspired Goffredo and Rinaldo from the base and anonymous "common soldiers" of the Christian body, so does Tasso divide the readers of his poem. On the one hand are those who can only apprehend "bodily" presences through the senses; on the other are those who can look *beneath* those presences to a greater and more sublime meaning. Tasso indeed seems to cater to the doctrine of a sacramental theology, which, as the earlier chapter on Teresa has suggested, was an intense attempt to accommodate a people from whom greater theological mysteries had to be withheld.[53] Yet it is notable that elsewhere in the poem Tasso unveils the pretensions of privileged interpreters when Peter the Hermit, the poem's chief "spokesman for the Counter-Reformation,"[54] warns Tancredi against having loved "una fanciulla a Dio rubella" (a girl rebellious to God) (XII.87) twenty stanzas *after* her conversion to Christianity: "Se rubella / in vita fu, [Dio] la vuole in morte ancella" (If she was rebellious to God in life, God made her his handmaiden in death) (XII.65). This episode calls ironic attention to the blindness of those who profess to be the gifted mediators between the unseen and the seen.

In effect, the "Allegoria" appears to sanction what had been the invasive gaze of the court in the *Aminta*, as the *Gerusalemme*'s "right" reader is guided beneath the poem's superficial "ombre." But in fact, the "Allegoria" conceals the more troublesome aspects of Tasso's poem—such as the acknowledgment throughout it that "Christian man" was far from unified in the late sixteenth century. That another of these troublesome aspects involves Erminia herself is, perhaps, a sign that the poet perceives himself as a worthy protector of his poem's more vulnerable characters: Erminia is mentioned nowhere in the allegory's celebration of Christian unity. Tasso shields his "merciful doctor" not only from Antoniano but from the violence inflicted on the pagan "fuggitivi" by the Christian warriors at poem's end—much as he removes Silvia and Aminta from the stage of his pastoral play long before the play is finished.[55]

But if the "Allegoria" defended the vulnerability not only of Erminia but of a poem that undertakes to question the dynamics of Christian empire, this defense was short-lived. Besieged not only by Inquisitors but by the influential Accademia della Crusca of Florence, which undertook to "correct" Tasso's poem in the light of its departures from conventional epic and pure Tuscan, Tasso slowly yielded his roles as protector of his fictions and subversive "medico" alike.[56] In the final *Conquistata*, the product of over a decade of anxious revisions, the poet's voice is absorbed when the poem has hardly begun, and there is no Erminia who wanders from pastoral setting to Egyptian camp to the center of Jerusalem as Goffredo's anonymous savior. Rechristened Nicea, Erminia is last heard from in the *Conquistata*'s penultimate canto lamenting the death of the pagan Argante, whom she can never hope to heal again through her compassionate ministrations ("Non ti spero veder mai piú risorto, / per mia pietosa cura") (XXIII. 126). As her own cries mingle with those of the other "grief-stricken handmaidens" ("dolorose ancelle") (XXIII. 127), all weeping for a hero who was killed by the old Erminia's love, Tancredi, Erminia / Nicea is once again absorbed into a community in which she finally becomes anonymous. This time, however, there is no danger that she may continue to serve as the unacknowledged physician of the Christian cause or that she will be confused with the text's Christian narrator. The *Conquistata* attempts, in fact, to eliminate all such sources of confusion. With its lengthy dedication to Cintio Aldobrandini and his uncle Pope Clement VIII as patrons of the arts and defenders of the church,[57] it firmly locates the poem's center within the nourishing and invulnerable church and suppresses the powerful ambiguities of the *Liberata*.

In many ways, Tasso's "Allegoria" ironically becomes the blueprint for the *Conquistata*, as the poet's errancy along with that of his characters is silenced within the timelessness of a universal church. But the changes to the *Liberata* may also suggest that the attempt to "engender" dependency, to make it the product of the displaced female poet and physician, was only marginally successful. That all the warriors are more dependent on and more respectful of Goffredo in the revised poem argues that earlier expressions of independence have collapsed and that Tasso's attempt to "engender" dependency has failed. The narrator's regression to unconditional acceptance of the all-powerful parent thus becomes a sign of his submission to the church's vision of itself as a paternal figure on whom its many subjects are absolutely dependent.

Tasso's troubled history attests to the difficulties of survival without recourse to the communities spoken of thus far. Like those of Teresa, Tasso's identity and, finally, his poetry acquire meaning only within the context of a religious "family romance"; unlike Teresa, of course, Tasso did not have a tightly knit community to defend him against the institutional powers to which he ultimately succumbed. And yet, it is worth noting that Tasso died in 1595 in Rome in the monastery of the Eremiti—a religious order that was not only reclusive, but even willfully regressive in an era of militant conversion and bureaucratization. It is also worth noting that much as Tasso's plight marked the fate of the Italian writer who tried to presume upon his independence of and superiority to the forces around him—even while recognizing his complicity with those forces, as in the *Aminta*—so did the plight of late-sixteenth-century Ferrara mark the fate of the small Italian principate struggling to remain aloof from Europe's imperial powers. As the Venetian historian Nicolò Contarini prophetically noted in 1598, Ferrara was on its way to becoming a mere border town, part of the Papal States under the very Clement VIII to whom Tasso had directed stanzas in the *Conquistata* once dedicated to Alfonso. "Ferrara, when occupied by Dukes, was forever growing; but now that it has been abandoned to the dominion of the priests, who do not wish to spend money on their neighbours, it will become deserted and turn into a swamp."[58] Tasso did not live to see this abandonment of his city to the powers of the church. But Ferrara's fate is indicative of the very conditions of absorption against which Tasso tried to defend both his innocent shepherds and himself.

5 ·

Orpheus in the Shade: Spenser's Pastoral Communities

As the preceding pages have suggested, the pastoral community in Tasso's works is a tenuous one. Complete submergence within it can ultimately produce for Silvia and Aminta, as for Erminia and the narrator of the *Gerusalemme Liberata* himself, little more than silence. Pastoral shade functions ambiguously in Tasso's work as a place of consolation and suppression to which the poet turns only belatedly or not at all. That Tasso does finally allow himself to be absorbed within the "pastoral" community of the Counter-Reformation church may well be the message of his *Gerusalemme Conquistata*, now virtually unread. But the more challenging poetry of an earlier decade, when he oscillated between sacred and secular authorities while succumbing to neither, offers a trenchant critique of the desire for invulnerability harbored by institutions and poets alike.

Edmund Spenser's work offers a similar challenge to late Renaissance authorities. Like Tasso, Spenser engages the vocabulary of pastoral shade in order to make explicit the dynamics of vulnerability in the second half of the sixteenth century. But Spenser's return to the story of a wounded young knight and the woman who heals him involves significant revisions that attest to the English poet's differing conception of shade. In the third book of *The Faerie Queene*, Timias is the wounded knight left for dead, Belphoebe the beautiful maiden who stumbles upon his body and revives it using her expert knowledge of herbs. But Belphoebe's very name indicates how Spenser is departing from his Italian predecessor regarding paradigms of female vulnerability.[1] Unlike either Erminia or Silvia, Spenser's "beautiful Diana" remains untouched by love. Spenser leaves it to Timias instead to fall hopelessly and wrenchingly in love with the woman warrior, as "foolish Physick" "heales up one [wound] and makes another."[2] Spenser's revision gives us a masculinity that is wounded within the shade of what the poet specifically identifies as a "pastoral theatre." Although many female characters in *The Faerie Queene* are assaulted under cover of protection—Amoret and Florimell, to name two—the episode with Timias suggests that rather than displace vulnerability onto his female characters, Spenser associates it with those directly affiliated with the court (Timias is Prince Arthur's squire), an affiliation that he necessarily shares.[3]

Spenser's revision of Tasso's episode is of even more interest given that in the proem to book 3, Spenser half-suggests that Belphoebe might be seen as a double for Queen Elizabeth herself, who steadfastly remained a "virgin Queen" throughout her reign.[4] In this light, the "pastoral theatre" in which Timias lies doubly wounded and exposed becomes the stage on which Elizabeth may watch her male subjects languish before her pitying but powerful presence. Much has been made in recent years of Elizabeth's tendency to cultivate a number of courtiers as prospective favorites in order to diffuse attempts on their part to overmaster her. Necessarily fashioning herself as self-sufficient "mother-father" of her state,[5] Elizabeth may have done much to further a climate in which the male subject is alienated from social and political communities other than the court. If Elizabeth is the state—a metaphor that she actively encouraged, and that is apparent in such paintings as the famous Ditchley Portrait[6]—then any relationship that does not include her is necessarily superfluous. But while Timias's unrewarded love for the beautiful but cold Belphoebe suggests Elizabeth's potential to alienate her male subjects from prior allegiances, it also betokens a sterility that Elizabeth was in danger of inflicting on her nation. Addressing Elizabeth by way of the Belphoebe and Timias incident in *The Faerie Queene*, David Lee Miller points out that "the virginal self-enclosure of [Elizabeth's natural body] calls the reproduction of the body politic into question"[7]—a "question" that concerned numerous Englishmen during Elizabeth's lengthy reign.

In this light, it is not surprising to read the words of one elegist who shortly after Elizabeth's death invoked the mystique of royal chastity for what it really had meant to many—barrenness and the uncertainty of English succession. In announcing the apparent collapse of Elizabethan pastoral mythology, John Fenton moves abruptly and triumphantly from Elizabeth's funeral to James's coronation:

> Eliza died in Winter, left the Spring
> To entertaine (with greater ioy) a King.
> At whose arrivall, loe the trees do bud,
> Saying our fruites in harvest will proove good:
> The Nightingale doth sing, so chirps the Larke,
> The aged Oakes put on a fresher barke,
> The day growes longer-ag'd, the night growes old,
> Withering by flourishing is now contrould[8]—

a "control" impossible before a potent King James took the throne. Indeed, Fenton's opposition between Elizabeth and James, between the wintry sterility of England's chaste queen and the springlike potency of a married and fertile king, is critical for Spenser, who, in the absence of James, attempts to define *himself* as potent, controlling "withering by flourishing." But this attempt is hampered by numerous obstacles, as Spenser's first published work, *The Shepheardes Calender*, demonstrates. First printed in 1579, Spenser's twelve eclogues suggest that even at this early stage in his career, Spenser was struggling to overturn what he perceived as the potentially threatening sterility of Elizabeth's court.

This struggle was informed by two important biographical factors. First, Spenser, son of a London merchant, was forced to work and write within an often stingy and unpredictable patronage system all his life. A sizar or "poor scholar," Spenser attended Cambridge on scholarship; he was then sent to Ireland to serve as Lord Grey's secretary, and he remained a civil servant—albeit one who eventually rose quite high within the imperial bureaucracy—for the rest of his short life. Second, Spenser was perhaps more influenced than any other writer in this study by the formidable career of Virgil. Particularly in *The Shepheardes Calender*, which conflates two genres Virgil solicitously kept apart, Spenser calls attention to the difficulties of following the Virgilian model in his own day, difficulties that have much to do with his own marginality and Elizabeth's "monstrous" status as virgin queen. In this bold poetic debut, he both expresses his conviction that he is worthy of becoming Virgil's heir[9] and suggests that inheriting Virgil's mantle is virtually impossible given the conditions of modern-day England. Like Tasso, Spenser warns that pastoral shade can have the effect of stifling the poet—and, coincidentally or not, Spenser was "exiled" to Catholic Ireland shortly after publishing *The Shepheardes Calender* in 1579. But whereas Tasso ultimately yielded to the authorities who cast potentially threatening *ombre* by revising the *Gerusalemme*, Spenser sought throughout his life to maintain his separateness from England's most celebrated source of shade in a fashion that both returns to and overturns the strategies at work in the *opere* of Benvenuto Cellini.

I

The "hero" of Spenser's first major poem is a lovesick boy named Colin Clout, who midway through *The Shepheardes Calender* associates himself with the luckless Aeneas: "I unhappy man, whom cruell fate,/And angry Gods pursue from coste to coste" ("June," 14–15).[10] In many ways, however, Colin is more of an anti-hero, a shepherd and poet who opens the twelve eclogues of *The Shepheardes Calender* by announcing his failures: "And yet alas, but now my spring begonne,/And yet alas, yt is already donne" ("January," 29–30). Thus he petulantly and melodramatically begins the calendar, only to hastily close it down. Throughout the calendar, indeed, Colin is involved in many an example of what could be called premature closure—or in the somewhat more judgmental phrase of Harry Berger, the "folly of instant senescence."[11] "January" ends with Colin breaking his pipes and forswearing his song because Rosalind, "the Widdowes daughter of the glenne" ("Aprill," 26) and "hys love and mistresse" ("January," 119), will not love him in return. "Aprill" and "August" give us shepherds who can only report songs Colin once sang and will sing no more, "June" stages Colin's anguish that he no longer dwells in "Paradise," and "November" and "December" are conceived as elegies: the first to "Dido," the second to Colin himself.

Colin's morbid fascination with death and prematurity appears to alienate him from the bustling world displayed elsewhere in the *Cal-*

ender—the strife between youth and age in "February," the festivities of "August," the ecclesiastical satire of "September." Certainly it alienates him from the calm organic cycle of agrarian labor implicit in the calendar's framework and identified in several of the woodcuts. The elusive ploughman whom Immeritô invokes in the "Envoy," as well as the retreating husbandmen in the woodcuts for "June," "Julye," and "August," whose presence might have reminded the reader of the popular *Calendrier des Bergers*, in which laborer and shepherd were *one*: these figures of and allusions to work would seem to suggest that Spenser is creating a rigorous divorce between those like Colin who are alienated from an organic process and the anonymous farmers who work within and profit from it.[12]

This divorce has not gone unnoticed by Spenser critics. One may suggest, as Isabel MacCaffrey has done, that it reflects the poet's preoccupation with the maxim *ars longa, vita brevis*. One might also agree with Louis Montrose that the genre of courtly pastoral to which Spenser aspires—and which Colin despite himself exemplifies—necessarily marginalizes the husbandman in order to legitimize the "idle," gentlemanly shepherd.[13] Indeed, Montrose's distinction between aristocratic shepherds and lower-class husbandmen is fundamental to *The Shepheardes Calender* and to this chapter; and much of the calendar seems designed to obliterate the social differences between the poor poet and the gentlemen, such as Philip Sidney, by whom the poem was destined to be read. But that distinction needs to be reformulated, particularly given Colin's sentiments regarding his relationship to the calendar's cycle of labor and productivity. Far from sanctioning a pastoral "idleness" that would affiliate him with the aristocratic norm of *sprezzatura* discussed in the chapter on Cellini, Colin in fact mourns his alienation from a cycle of "continuall spring, and harvest"—Spenser's characterization of the productive Bower of Bliss in *The Faerie Queene*'s third book (3.6.42). Hence his December lament: "Thus is my sommer worne away and wasted, / Thus is my harvest hastened all to rathe" (97–98). Colin invokes the images of successful labor, everywhere apparent in the calendar, only to lament his distance from them, much as Wyatt's narrator complains in *Tottel's Miscellany*, "I sowe the sede, they reape the corne. / I waste, they winne, I draw, they drive."[14]

Wyatt's poet speaks as a lover "who lamenteth other to have the frutes of his service." But as a diplomat and courtier, he is also expressing the frustrations of unrewarded "service" in Tudor England.[15] It is striking, although not at all unusual, that he employs metaphors of husbandry to do so. In fact, from Wyatt's complaint to Shakespeare's ironic promise to Southampton that if *Venus and Adonis* "prove deformed," he will "never after ear so barren a land, for fear it yield me still so bad a harvest," the language of patronage regularly coincides with the language of agrarian labor and organic process.[16] This conflation is not original to the sixteenth century. Rather, it has its origins in an earlier text that explores the contrived affinity between agrarian and poetic labor, and that can therefore be seen as a tentative model for poets who aspire to the status of one who "laboured lands to yield the timely eare" ("October," 58). In this verse, spoken by the fledgling poet Cuddie, the "eare" of corn is also the ear of a patron, a Maecenas or Augustus; the laborer is Virgil, the creator of the literary hierarchy that casts its shadow over so much of Spenser's work. And the poem of labor that finds its ultimate fruits in a human nature as receptive as the husbandman's soil—and that is therefore both economically and sexually potent—is, of course, the *Georgics*.[17]

The georgic is an ideal model for Spenser to follow, because it naturalizes not only the process of poetic creation, but the process of an empire's creation.[18] Moreover, it validates the poet as a laborer on whom the state depends for its very survival. Yet although Spenser's engagement in the making of empire is especially apparent in "Aprill"—an eclogue to which I will return in some detail—an account of the poet as the benevolent father figure training his readers in the labors of English empire does not do justice to "that most self-conscious of poetic debuts."[19] *The Shepheardes Calender* raises more questions about the continuing relevance of Virgil's work than it answers, as Cuddie's marginality attests. For the moment in the *Georgics* that Spenser's early poetry dwells on at greatest length is a moment that itself questions the relationship between patronage and poetic labor: the story of Orpheus. While at least one Renaissance humanist, Juan Luis Vives, conceived of the *Georgies* as the "most fruitful" of literary forms,[20] Virgil's poem closes with an uneasy meditation on Orpheus, whose "wasted labors" contrast strikingly with the pattern of labor and growth that the *Georgics* not only depends upon but creates.

This is a tale of a poet who is outside the georgic cycle of which Virgil's own narrator is a crucial part. Orpheus's alienation is articulated in the only genre allotted to him and, it would appear, to Colin: the elegy, which collapses temporal process by interfering with more "organic" labors.[21] The embracing of elegy is ultimately a return to the pastoral, the genre Virgil claims to be leaving definitively behind in his autobiographical close of the fourth Georgic. Recapitulating the opening line of the first Eclogue, the poet claims, "In those days I, Virgil, was nursed of sweet Parthenope, and rejoiced in the arts of inglorious ease (ignobilis oti)—I who dallied with shepherds' songs, and, in youth's boldness, sang, Tityrus, of thee under thy spreading beech's covert."[22] But for Spenser, who also waxes elegiac at the end of the calendar, this is a return with a difference, as Colin defies "arts of inglorious ease" and emerges as the Orphic figure whose negative poetics redefines the nature of pastoral "shade" cast by England's Proserpine, Elizabeth.[23]

As will be seen, Colin's lamented divorce from georgic rhythms ultimately becomes a strategy embraced by the "creators" of *The Shepheardes Calender* as well—an interpretation encouraged by the mysterious commentator E.K., who informs us in the calendar's epistle that in Colin "the Author selfe is shadowed" (Epistle, 148). The opening remarks of the poem's anonymous composer, the so-called "Immeritô," make it clear that, like Colin, he is engaged in foreclosing an uncertain future by imagining that his book is already envied by its readers and protected by its would-be patron, Philip Sidney: "And if that Envie barke at thee,/As sure it will, for succoure flee/ . . . . And when his honor has thee redde,/Crave pardon for my hardyhedde" ("To His Booke," 5–6, 11–12). Regardless of the book's success (or lack thereof), Immeritô "will send more after thee," a claim that bypasses the verdict of a patron and collapses the temporal process of reception. And the massive gloss surrounding Immeritô's poem, selflessly furnished by "E.K.," seems designed to protect its author against misinterpretation and even, perhaps, to prevent the publication of the poem from appearing premature.[24] E.K.'s learned marginalia ensure both the monumentality and the impenetrability of a text that, like Virgil's *Eclogues* or Ovid's *Metamorphoses*, has necessarily generated a supplemental reading, creating a text that has already been read—and thus a text that, like Colin's spring, is not only "begonne" but "already donne." It thus gives us a poem "already" anchored in a community of knowledgeable readers, a world of learning synonymous with neither the queen nor the court: a world to which print alone, a *tekne* that leaves the organic metaphors of the poem's husbandmen quite literally in the dust, can provide access.[25]

II

In his now classic reading of Ben Jonson's "To Penshurst" and "To Sir Robert Wroth," Raymond Williams argues that the country house poem characteristically suppresses the glaring fact of lower-class labor in order to sanction the landowner—and thus the existing social order—as the guarantor of plenitude: "Jonson looks out over Penshurst and sees, not work, but a land yielding of itself."[26] Williams has been our most eloquent spokesman for a criticism sensitive to the mediations and mystifications of pastoral poetry, a poetry that he claims is little more than a selective extraction from the full working year portrayed in Hesiod's *Works and Days* and Virgil's *Georgics*. Indeed, the absence of meaningful labor in pastoral is what renders one vulnerable to the attractions of *otium*. And yet the beneficent overseer who ensures the plenitude of "fat aged carps," "orchard fruit," and "blushing apricot"[27] is definitely present in the georgic from Hesiod on, not simply a seventeenth-century innovation, as Williams suggests. Whereas Williams sees the peasants' land of the *Works and Days* as an extension of the laborers themselves, Hesiod clearly defines this land and its fruits in terms of the principle of *díke*, which has implications of both customary usage and legal right. It is *díke* that ensures that a man will reap exactly what he has sown *if* he honors the rules and taboos encoded within the *Works and Days*. If he does not transgress his boundaries, he will be rewarded, and not by the immediate landowner but by the ultimate landowner: the gods.[28]

This archaic economy, with its intricate link between work and ethics, finds a home in Virgil's *Georgics* as well, where the mysterious but just deities of the earth have become Maecenas and Augustus, invoked at the beginning of the first Georgic: "Yea, and thou, O Caesar, whom we know not what company of the gods shall claim ere long; whether thou choose to watch over cities and care for our lands, that so the mighty world may receive thee as the giver of increase and lord of the seasons" (*Georgics* I.24–28). But Virgil complicates the dynamics of Hesiod's poem by casting himself as a laborer. Far from lowering the poet's status, this innovation makes him part of the same cycle as Hesiod's and Italy's farmers. As long as he respects the boundaries separating him from the gods, he is to be rewarded with the fruits of his labor, which the presiding deity willingly provides so that justice is not violated. This cycle of labor and fruition is broken only when the deity to whom the earth belongs becomes the victim of a violent act of transgression, which is precisely what happens at the close of the first Georgic when Virgil vividly recounts Julius Caesar's assassination.

Thus does Virgil turn Hesiod's georgic into a poetics of patronage. Flattered by being addressed as a god, the patron provides the poet with the gifts of patronage to make himself worthy of his status as presiding deity.[29] Yet as is clear from the invocations to Augustus and Maecenas, the mythical horizons of Hesiod's poem were already vanishing, and for all his dependence on the Roman "gods," whether Octavian or Bacchus, the Italian farmer was ultimately a self-sufficient entity whose surplus supported the state. As John Heywood's Plowman argues to the Merchant and the Knight some fifteen hundred years after Virgil, "For I have nede of no maner thyng / That ye can do to help of my lyffyng, / For euery thyng whereby ye do lyf / I noryssh it and to you both do gyf."[30] Moreover, at the same time that he creates the inclusive cycle of georgic labor, Virgil is forced to contend with the obvious alienation of the poet from that cycle because of the *inorganic* medium in which he works and his dependence on another for economic sufficiency. Virgil must deny the laborer's autonomy by insisting on an archaic "good faith" economy rather than one based on self-interest.[31] But there is another form of autonomy that Virgil must deny as well, one that has a good deal to do with Spenser: the act of transgression that places the poet among the gods and therefore threatens to violate the very boundaries and taboos necessary to ensure and preserve archaic justice. The dynamics of

Virgil's poem insist that the patron-reader validate and legitimize the poet's labors. Should the poet acknowledge the source of validation as being solely within himself, he would also admit to the intrusive act of self-consciousness that distinguishes him from the husbandman. In striving to minimize the poet's "intrusion" into an organic cycle of labor that is finally not his own, Virgil must avoid emphasizing an act that challenges the relationship of interdependence he has been careful to create.

Such a challenge is hinted at in the midst of the famous passage beginning "O fortunatos nimium" in the second Georgic, when the narrator becomes uncharacteristically explicit about his poetic method. After praising the farmer for his pacifism and *lack* of self-consciousness, the speaker suddenly intrudes with:

> Me vero primum dulces ante omnia Musae,
> quarum sacra fero ingenti percussus amore,
> accipiant caelique vias et sidera monstrent,
> defectus solis varios lunaeque labores;
> unde tremor terris, qua vi maria alta tumescant
> obicibus ruptis rursusque in se ipsa residant,
> quid tantum Oceano properent se tinguere soles
> hiberni, vel quae tardis mora noctibus obstet.
>
> (II.475–82)

(But as for me—first above all, may the sweet Muses whose holy emblems, under the spell of a mighty love, I bear, take me to themselves, and show me heaven's pathways, the moon's many labours; whence come tremblings of the earth, the force to make deep seas swell and burst their barriers, then sink back upon themselves; why winter suns hasten so fast to dip in Ocean, or what delays clog the lingering nights.)

Yet in a move that Cuddie will also make in "October," this quest, which would take the speaker to the boundaries of the universe, is abruptly reversed:

> Sin; has ne possim naturae accedere partis,
> frigidus obstiterit circum praecordia sanguis,
> rura mihi et rigui placeant in vallibus amnes,
> flumina amem silvasque inglorius. o ubi campi
> Spercheosque et virginibus bacchata Lacaenis
> Taygeta! o qui me gelidis convallibus Haemi
> sistat et ingenti ramorum protegat umbra!
>
> (II.483–89)

(But if the chill blood about my heart bar me from reaching those realms of nature, let my delight be the country, and the running streams amid the dells—may I love the waters and woods, though fame be lost. O for those plains, and Spercheus, and Taygetus, where Spartan girls hold Bacchic rites! O for one to set me in the cool glens of Haemus, and shield me under the branches' mighty shade!)

As Michael Putnam has observed in his commentary on the *Georgics*, Virgil's initial quest for primacy becomes a withdrawal to the "safe enclosure on enclosure" provided by Greece and its consoling mythologies.[32] Thus the breathtaking ascent into the sublime becomes a rapid descent into the familiar and the "pleasing," an attempted but ultimately false bravura followed by self-effacement and doubt. Even in his desired pursuit of the *causus rerum* (origin of things), the narrator asks that he be led by the Muses: "May the . . . Muses . . . *take me* (Me . . . accipiant) to themselves." In not daring to claim too much for himself, he transforms his poetry into the product of another—either of the Muses or preferably (and less dangerously) of the unnamed patron who will shield him "under the branches' mighty shade." He therefore remains within the confines of umbrageous patronage.[33]

The narrator's interruption virtually erases itself by modulating from the intrusive, quasi-scientific tones of Lucretian epic to the language of an enclosure sheltered by mystery, mythology, and "easeful toil"; in resisting Lucretius's relentless process of demystification, Virgil also resists the demystification of his own poem.[34] This resistance is repeated in the next passage, in which Virgil contrasts the daring "figure" who gains knowledge of "the howls of hungry Acheron" with the "fortunatus" who safely "plucks the fruits which his boughs . . . of their own free will, have borne" (II. 492–501). Virgil is alluding here to the bold Lucretius, but at the end of the final Georgic he turns to another equally bold poet who not only heard the howls of Acheron but momentarily silenced them. He was, however, far from happy; and for a different paradigm of poetic labor than that entertained by Virgil's narrator, one must go to that episode at the close of the fourth Georgic, which tells of Aristaeus's journey to learn the reason for his bees' sickness and of Orpheus's failure to win his wife because of a fatal, interdicted backward glance.

Orpheus's turn to face his beloved on the threshold of Hades has been construed to mean many things, but Virgil is explicit about what it signifies: wasted labor and a broken agreement ("effusus labor . . . rupta tyranni / foedera") (IV. 492–93). This reading of Orpheus's backward glance as the betrayal of his labor and his contract with the infernal gods blatantly distinguishes the legendary singer from the poem's narrator as well as from the anonymous farmers whose labors constitute the body of the poem. If the Italian farmers are capable of harnessing or containing natural forces in order to produce, Orpheus's labor yields only exhaustion and dispersal. Not only will Eurydice disperse into the shadows ("She spake, and straightway from his sight, like smoke mingling with thin air, vanished afar") (IV. 499–500), but Orpheus's song will be dispersed into the region of the nightingale ("She weeps all night long, . . . filling the region round with sad laments") (IV. 514–15), and finally his own body will be dispersed by the frenzied worshipers of Bacchus, the very women in whom Virgil's narrator had earlier delighted.[35] The dispersal moreover extends to the rupture of the treaty or "leges" (IV. 487) that Proserpine herself, mistress of both Pluto and the change of seasons, had ordained, and therefore to a community that can prosper only if it is attentive to both the laws of deity and the laws governing the year.

Orpheus's "fault"—or as Eurydice describes it, his "furor"—is to interfere with, and thus to interrupt, the process of labor: to stop and then look back ("restitit . . . respixit") while on the threshold of Hades, a location that attests to Orpheus's own liminality in the poem. Between these two verbs signifying Orpheus's intrusive glance is a telling phrase suggesting that through this turn Eurydice becomes—briefly—her husband's: "He stopped, and on his Eurydice, now on the verge of light, ummindful—alas! and his heart conquered, he looked back" (IV. 490–91). "Eurydicenque suam" signifies an appropriation that will be promptly undone only seven lines later: as she fades from her husband into the shadows, Eurydice cries, "I am swept off . . . and stretching out to you these strengthless hands—alas!—not yours" (IV. 497–98). "Tibi" (to you) and "non tua" (not yours) characterize a larger disjunction between Orpheus's attempt to gain Eurydice as his own and his failure to do so. In the eternal "nowness" ("iam") of the interrupted movement, Eurydice is both

Orpheus's and not Orpheus's. In interrupting Eurydice's movement toward the light, and in thereby defying the command of Hades' queen that he *not* turn to face his wife, Orpheus kills Eurydice, and ultimately himself.

When the passage is more carefully considered, however, Orpheus's fatal glance becomes linked closely to his role in the poem as a singer. For the forbidden act of turning is a *tropos*, an act of song and thus of poetry, the very poetry Orpheus is able so confidently to announce as his own when he descends into Hades and makes the ghosts wonder. Proserpine's decree that Eurydice can be his if only he not turn to face his beloved is a decree that would force Orpheus to yield his powers as singer in exchange for his wife. Orpheus's *tropos* represents his attempt to have both Eurydice and his song, a possession Proserpine prohibits by declaring, in effect, that Orpheus must choose between poetry and love ("for th[e] condition [that Eurydice follow behind] had Proserpine ordained") (IV. 486–87).

Moreover, Orpheus's turn must be related to the larger action of the final Georgic, in which Aristaeus also is to blame. Far from being entirely innocent, the consummate husbandman Aristaeus[36] is in fact the catalyst of the tragic events, having chased the unsuspecting Eurydice through the deep grasses where a serpent bit her and sent her to her death. Aristaeus's thoughtless action provokes in the dead Orpheus a thoughtful, powerful one: it is Orpheus's curse that leads to the death of Aristaeus's bees and to Aristaeus's heroic quest to learn the source of their sickness. Orpheus is capable of momentarily restoring life *and* taking it away, a dual function that he performs not only in the outer, framing episode about Aristaeus's bees, but in his descent to Hades: his song restores Eurydice to life, his gaze deprives her of it. In traveling to Hades, Orpheus becomes a powerful deity in his own right, and there is the muted suggestion that Proserpine has been overly harsh in her dictum against him; hence Virgil states bluntly that the "ruthless tyrant's pact was broken." Thereby contained within a poem that marginalizes the elegiac singer is a subtle criticism of a tyrannical queen who prohibits Orpheus his act of possession in the inverted pastoral theater of shade. Once propitiated, Orpheus translates his curse into a blessing. Appeased by Aristaeus's offerings, Orpheus reverses the sterility he has caused. In a magical act of parthenogenesis that defies the predictable cycles of which Virgil's narrator has sung throughout, he brings a new swarm of bees to life. Upon revisiting the grove where he sacrificed four bulls and heifers to the dead poet, Aristaeus notices "a portent, sudden and wondrous to tell—throughout the paunch, amid the molten flesh of the oxen, bees buzzing and swarming forth from the ruptured sides, then trailing in vast crowds, till at last on a tree-top they stream together, and hang in clusters from the bending boughs" (IV. 554–58).

This final, resplendent image of fertility and plenitude closes the *Georgics* proper, transforming Orpheus, the gifted poet whose work defies georgic's comforting patterns and who is yet subject to a harsh ruler's law, into a watchful and numinous power who not only takes away life but restores it. The divorce of the poet from the georgic cycle places him in control of the very process that less daring poets can appeal to only by situating themselves beneath a monarch's nourishing shade. The singer of empire cannot afford Orpheus's powers or his alienation from the georgic cycle. Orpheus is supplanted by the image of a more quiescent poet in the last lines of the *Georgics*, in which the narrator declares that he has now sung "of the care of fields, of cattle, and of trees" (IV. 559). Content to remain within a patron's mighty shade, Virgil's narrator will not defy deities, and he will make sure to suppress the very real incongruity between poet and laborer. As a result, he must disown his own heroic pursuits and differentiate himself from the poet who can bring death as well as life. He seeks instead a stability generated by self-effacing labor, a labor that will bear fruit beneath the reassuring shadow of patronage.

But poets after Virgil would not be as successful in convincing others to place them beneath similarly reassuring shade. For Edmund Spenser, drawn to an Orphic poetic and yet conscious of his very real dependencies, the problem was much like that confronted by Cellini: how could he legitimize his work as work? And how could he reengage Virgil's *Georgics*, with their metaphors of fruition and harvest, in an era dominated by an "idle" pastoralism that Spenser's own poetry would have the ironic effect of encouraging?

III

Spenser's most extensive treatment of the Orpheus myth is in *Virgils Gnat*, written shortly after *The Shepheardes Calender*. A liberal translation of the pseudo-Virgilian *Culex*, *Virgils Gnat* is one of Spenser's most direct attempts to become the Roman poet's heir. Spenser in fact opens the poem by having "Virgil" assure his "patron" Augustus that "season more secure / Shall bring forth fruit" (9–10). He thereby includes himself within the georgic process by alluding to the gradual development and perfection of his own season. But the allusion also suggests that the present poem is the product of infertility, of a wasted season that can only look ahead to and hope for a time when Pales, goddess of husbandry, might be invoked.[37] Indeed, it is telling that the shepherd within the poem, praised as "lord of himself," is privy to the delights of "frutefull Pales." Yet rather than fulfill his obligations as a servant of Pales in a "pleasant bowre" with its "fresh shaddowes" (56), the shepherd-guardian falls asleep, and it takes a gnat to wake him so that he will arm himself against the serpent about to kill him and devastate his flock. The gnat's reward for his service, however, is death. The shepherd himself strikes the annoying insect with his hand, and the bulk of the poem consists of the gnat's account to the shepherd of his descent to the underworld—from which he is excluded because he has not yet been buried.

In a sense, we have returned to a version of the Orphic tale, albeit a muted one. A poet—for such is the gnat with his vivid description of the underworld—haunts his nemesis from beyond the grave and forces him to commemorate his "noble" death. Indeed, it is the gnat who is monumentalized in the poem rather than the would-be shepherd, who has evaded his duties by falling asleep: "To thee, small Gnat, in lieu of his life saved, / The Shepheard hath thy deaths record engraved" (687–88). Protector of this dozing shepherd, the gnat poses an interesting counterpart to the unnamed narrator of Virgil's *Georgics*. By the same token, Spenser's Orpheus—for he does appear in *Virgils Gnat*, as in the original *Culex*—serves as an intriguing contrast to the Orpheus of the *Georgics*. A description of Orpheus and of his fatal flaw occupies much of the gnat's account, culminating in the lines, "But cruell *Orpheus*, thou much crueller, /

Seeking to kisse her, brok'st the Gods decree, / And thereby mad'st her euer damn'd to be" (470–72). The interruption of Orpheus's labor by his selfish desire breaks the "decree" that gives meaning to the poet's labors, thereby incurring the apparent wrath of Spenser's narrator. So far little has changed from the *Culex* or, for that matter, from the fourth Georgic. But several lines later, Spenser includes a passage that is as new to the *Culex* as it is to the *Georgics*, as he abruptly reunites Orpheus and his wife. In one of his very few deliberate departures from the pseudo-Virgilian text, he writes, "Yet are ye both receiued into blis, / And to the seates of happie soules admitted. / And you, beside the honourable band / Of great Heroes, doo in order stand" (477–80).

In fact, the abrupt and unaccounted for "Yet" allows Virgil's transgressive Orpheus to become Ovid's Orpheus, who, unlike his prototype in the *Georgics*, is rewarded in the *Metamorphoses* with the bride he lost:

> . . . Already was the Ghost of *Orphye* gone
> To *Plutos* realme, and there he all the places eft behilld
> The which he heretofore had seene. And as he sought
> the feeld
> Of fayre *Elysion* (where the soules of godly folk do wonne,)
> He found his wyfe *Eurydicee*, to whom he one whyle walks
> Togither with hir cheeke hy cheeke: another whyle he stalks
> Before hir, and another whyle he followeth her.[38]

Not only does Ovid unite the lovers, he also introduces an irate Bacchus into the episode to punish the women who dared to assault the singer. Spenser's departure from Virgil suggests that he may be using Ovid against Virgil—and paradoxically so, in a poem that "translates" Virgil. It is also clear that this apparent subscription to Ovid has the effect of humanizing Orpheus, of making him less demonic and less powerful. In providing a Bacchus who persecutes Orpheus's murderers and in reuniting the singer with his wife in a coyly domestic scenario in Hades, Ovid strips Orpheus of the numinous powers Virgil granted him, powers derived from his very isolation and alienation from the soothing and rhythmical cycles of the georgic universe. By the same token, Ovid simply takes to its logical conclusion the dictum pronounced by Hades' queen: no longer the powerful singer whose word determines life and death, Orpheus is satisfied with Eurydice alone. Ovid may be suggesting that Proserpine is inclined to mercy, a quality she does not have in Virgil's poems. But it is also the case that Ovid's contented Orpheus is a silenced Orpheus, and that in exchanging his voice for Eurydice, he is complying still with a tyrant's ruthless decree. Like so much of the *Metamorphoses*, the tale of Orpheus offers a compensatory narrative; Orpheus is rewarded for ostensibly giving up his song.

One may then ask why Spenser concurs in this domestication of the powerful singer. Could it be that Spenser is offering the "gnat," who intervenes to protect the georgic universe along with its protector, as a replacement for Orpheus? Or does Spenser include Ovid's narrative to suggest that Virgil's more rigorous—and dangerous—poetic archetype must be reconceptualized for Spenser's own day? Here it is important to note that at the same time as Spenser domesticates Orpheus by reuniting him with Eurydice, he also enacts a peculiarly Spenserian move resulting from a perhaps deliberate mistranslation of the *Culex*. Whereas, following his chastisement of an unrestrained Orpheus, the pseudo-Virgil suggests that Eurydice is included within the realm of "heroines" and promptly forgets her spouse, Spenser continues to address Orpheus when he declares, "And you, beside the honourable band / Of great Heroes, doo in order stand" (479–80).[39] This inclusion of the figure whom he had earlier celebrated as "Orpheus bold" within a "band" of heroes—and thus within a world of epic feats—makes Spenser's Orpheus part of a masculine community that may be not so much subject to as defiant of Hades' "grim Persephone" who rules "th'Elisian plain" (421–22). This reading, in turn, may be borne out by situating the poem within Spenser's oblique prefatory remarks to Leicester, his former and now "late deceas'd" patron: "Wrong'd, yet not daring to expresse my paine, / To you (great Lord) the causer of my care, / In clowdie teares my case I thus complaine / Unto your selfe, that only privie are" (Dedication, 1–4).

The exact reasons for Spenser's "paine" are unknown, although most scholars have tended to see in the prefatory sonnet a complaint against Leicester, the negligent shepherd of the poem who mistreats his "saviour."[40] And yet is it not possible that Spenser is complaining not *about* Leicester, but *to* Leicester, who indeed took "care" of Spenser in the 1570's and early 1580's, and that Spenser is complaining about someone else entirely? That Elizabeth herself may well have been Spenser's ungrateful shepherd/ess seems possible, given Spenser's highly mediated satire, *Mother Hubberds Tale*, on the queen's plans in 1578 to marry the French duke Alençon, a Catholic against whom England's militant Protestant community, Leicester and Sidney included, protested vociferously. Spenser may also have deemed the queen ungrateful for failing to respond appropriately to his labors on *The Shepheardes Calender*—labors which, as will be seen, attempted to redeem England and its queen from their plight of sterility.

Indeed, given that elaborate detective work has failed to uncover any notable breach between Spenser and the patron whose death in 1588 he mourns in *The Ruines of Time*, there is a good possibility that Spenser is aligning himself and his (male) patron against the queen.[41] The preface to *Virgils Gnat* thus constructs far more than what one critic has called a relationship of reciprocity that curiously reverses "the roles conventionally assigned to poet and patron."[42] To be sure, the body of the poem does suggest that it is the poet and not the careless patron who protects. But Spenser may well be playing the shepherd's inability to protect him/herself off against the male patron's success in generating fruitful shade. Moreover, the very fact that Leicester is "late deceas'd" means that the poet has to deal with another dimension of "shade" altogether by descending, like the gnat, into Hades to address the dead. And like the gnat, he returns, his poetic voice intact, accomplishing a heroic feat that finally makes him equivalent to the transgressive Orpheus or the Aeneas battered "from coste to coste."

The preface thus may subtly align Orpheus and other "heroes" against "the Queene of hell," the "feend" whom Eurydice herself knows "to be too cruell and severe." Like *The Ruines of Time*, which describes hell as "the horrid house of sad Persephone," *Virgils Gnat* envisions Hades as the realm dominated by a cruel queen—a queen whose vicious decree against Orpheus is overturned by nothing less than the power of the Muses in Spenser's later poem: "And they, for pittie of the sad wayment, / Which *Orpheus* for *Eurydice* did make, / Her back againe to life sent for his sake" (*The Ruines of Time*, 390–92). One must indeed wonder if Elizabeth is not split into two characters in *Virgils Gnat*: the ungrateful but finally repentant shepherd who promises to commemorate the gnat, and the infernal queen whose authority is mysteriously overturned as Orpheus regains Eurydice and wanders in hell not only with his bride but with his fellow "heroes."

This recourse to a subdued language of transgressive heroics both opposes and reveals the tyranny of shepherd(ess) and queen alike, although it is an "evill plight" that only the dead Leicester and a discerning "Oedipus," whom Spenser warns to "rest pleased with his owne insight, / Ne further seeke to glose upon the text," can fully appreciate (Dedication, 9–10). Spenser's laboring readers may be said to constitute a future community by which his own dark meanings may be read and sympathized with, if not overtly: a "band of heroes," as it were, that offers itself as a bulwark surrounding Spenser's transgressive Orphic poetics. That such a dynamic is already present in *The Shepheardes Calender* is apparent from two eclogues in particular: "October," the dialogue between the despondent poet, Cuddie, and his fellow shepherd, Piers, and "Aprill," Colin's erstwhile celebration of royalty.

It is not surprising that it is in "October," dedicated to revealing the "perfect pattern of the poet," according to E.K., that Orpheus should appear, and in the guise, moreover, of a successful poet. Cuddie opens the eclogue in this month of harvest with the complaint, "*Piers*, I have pyped erst so long with payne, / That all mine Oten reedes bene rent and wore: / And my poore Muse hath spent her spared store, / Yet little good hath got, and much less gayne" (7–10). Insisting to the despairing Cuddie that "the prayse is better, then the price, / The glory eke much greater then the gayne," Piers proffers the example of Orpheus as a suitable model for his companion:

> Soone as though gynst to sette thy notes in frame,
> O how the rurall routes to thee doe cleaue:

> Seemeth thou doest their soule of sence bereaue,
> All as the shepheard, that did fetch his dame
> From *Plutoes* balefull bowre withouten leaue:
> His musicks might the hellish hound did tame.
>
> (25–30)

Several points are notable here, particularly given Spenser's somewhat later treatments of the Orpheus tale in *Virgils Gnat* and *The Ruines of Time*. First, it is not Proserpine but Pluto who rules the "balefull bowre" and is depicted as the "hellish hound" with whom Orpheus must reckon. Secondly, Piers omits any mention of Orpheus's failure, let alone his death at the hands of the frenzied women or his invocations of sterility and fruitfulness. At the same time, Piers's choice of words might be said to be undermined by a force beyond his control working within the poem. The phrase "withouten leave" can refer just as much to Eurydice (who never left "Plutoes balefull bowre") as to Orpheus's transgression, and the act of taming in the final line can belong either to the "musicks might" or to the "hellish hound." Even though Proserpine's name is not uttered in Piers's encouraging speech, the effects of her presence are felt as Orpheus's resounding success becomes, on a second reading, Orpheus's failure.

Moreover, Proserpine does enter Piers's poem, although the queen of the "Elysian fields," as Spenser describes her in *Virgils Gnat*, is here present as "Elisa." After failing to rouse Cuddie with his story of Orpheus—explicitly returning to the metaphors of dispersal noted in Virgil, Cuddie retorts, "Sike prayse is smoke, that sheddeth in the skye, / Sike words bene wynd, and wasten soone in vayne" (35–36)—Piers turns to praise of England's queen as an alternative to pastoral song: "There [in epic notes] may thy Muse display her fluttyring wing, / And stretch her selfe at large from East to West: / Whither thou list in fayre *Elisa* rest, / Or if thee please in bigger notes to sing, / Aduaunce the worthy whome shee loveth best, / That first the white beare to the stake did bring" (43–48). Elisa is, as E.K. notes, "our most gratious soueraign"; the "worthy" whom Elisa loves is "the most honorable and renowmed the Erle of Leycester" (181–87). But the idea of "resting" in Elisa is likewise greeted cynically by a Cuddie who argues that Augustus and Maecenas alike are dead, prompting

Piers to respond, "Then make thee winges of thine aspyring wit, / And, whence thou camst, flye backe to heaven apace" (83–84).

The alternative, then, to resting with queens and receiving no compensation for one's heroic endeavors is to launch a flight of one's own: to contain within oneself the possibilities of Orphism that defy dependence on others and to enact an intensely private version of sterility and fruitfulness; to replace, in short, Hades' and England's queens with *oneself*. But this, too, is a possibility Cuddie rejects, as he intriguingly returns to the very language of Virgil's narrator from the *Georgics*. Like that narrator, he flirts momentarily with Orphic possibilities, imagining himself a "hero" in the same fashion that Virgil's narrator does in the second Georgic:

> O if my temples were distaind with wine,
> And girt in girlonds of wild Yuie twine,
> How I could reare the Muse on stately stage,
> And teache her tread aloft in bus-kin fine,
> With queint *Bellona* in her equipage.
>
> (110–14)

The moment is of course imaginary, for it is only within the protection of the subjunctive "if" that Cuddie enters the world of labor and reward. Yet subjunctives aside, even E.K. registers some unease with a poetic "madness" provoked by a patron's gift of wine and by Bacchus himself, protector and avenger of Orpheus in Ovid's account. Nervously aware that Cuddie is breaking boundaries rather than laboring within them, E.K. comments that "he seemeth here to be ravished with a Poetical furie. For (if one rightly mark) the numbers rise so ful, and the verse groweth so big, that it seemeth he hath forgot the meanenesse of shepheards state and stile" (255–57). Cuddie will not be led by the Muse but will lead *her* onto the "stately stage" and teach her to "tread aloft in bus-kin fine." In desiring to have his labors rewarded before they are performed, Cuddie places his poet beyond the traditional parameters of Virgil's poem.

But this invasive moment in which Cuddie disrupts the georgic cycle is just as abruptly retracted, in a manner again reminiscent of Virgil's narrator at the close of the second Georgic:

> But ah my corage cooles ere it be warme,
> For thy, content us in thys hymble shade:

> Where no such troublous tydes han us assayde,
> Here we our slender pipes may safely charme.
> (115–18)

Like Virgil's narrator, Cuddie is a failed Orpheus, resigned to the fact that he lacks "corage" to trouble the "tydes"—a word E.K. glosses as "seasons"—beyond his pastoral bower. Unlike that narrator, however, Cuddie asks not for a patron's mighty shade to place himself beneath, but "hymble shade." And as though in response to that request, Piers offers Cuddie a future prize for the song he has just uttered: "And when my Gates shall han their bellies layd: / *Cuddie* shall have a Kidde to store his farme" (119–20).

What appears to happen in the course of "October" is the rejection of Orphic courage and requests for patronage from "mighty" patrons alike. In the place of such failed poetic options is the exchange of a "Kidde" for a song, and, perhaps more importantly, of sympathy for a complaint. No such exchange is proffered in Spenser's most direct source for the dialogue, Mantuan's fifth Eclogue, in which the poet's interlocutor reveals himself to be a stingy and ungrateful benefactor.[43] Spenser's substitution of the responsive Piers for Mantuan's ornery Silvanus, who demands a song from the poor Candidus but offers nothing in return—prompting Candidus's annoyed response ("Why do you seek my song and invade, Silvanus, the share of another?")[44]—is telling. For Spenser both dissolves the social hierarchy of poet and patron and asserts, however subtly, the existence of a more immediate and more sympathetic relationship than the one deemed possible between Cuddie and "fayre Elisa" in an age when "great *Augustus* . . . is dead" (62). The Ovidian tag that Cuddie takes as his emblem at the very end of the eclogue, moreover—"Agitante calescimus illo &c." or "There is a god that lurks within us: when he breathes, our bosom warms"[45]—situates "October" within a resolutely homosocial community, as an unprofitable Elisa and a dark Proserpine are left behind for a male deity who is at one with and empowers the poet. This is a poet who labors by cultivating the sacred seeds sown by an inner god; or to continue the passage from Ovid's *Fasti*, "Impetus hic sacrae semina mentis habet" ([The god's] impulse it is that sows sacred seeds in the mind) (VI. 6, trans. James Frazer).

Cuddie disappears from the calendar at this point, not to be heard from again. His dialogue with Piers has revealed a *modus operandi* by which the constraining circumstances within which poets labor might possibly be redressed. Cuddie's retreat to his "hymble shade," however, with Piers as his patron and an unnamed "deus" as his source of inspiration and legitimacy, fails to take on the deadly queen who cost Orpheus his wife, and for a more "heroic" version of English poetics one must turn finally to Colin, that shadow for the "Author['s] self." For if Cuddie lacks the "corage" to move beyond the shade that both restrains and defines him, Colin emerges as the battered Aeneas of the calendar. If, moreover, Cuddie's "paynes" are finally rewarded, albeit modestly and in an indefinite future, by his fellow shepherd, Colin makes a dazzling transition from sterility to plenitude all by himself, effecting a parthenogenesis as striking as the sudden generation of Aristaeus's bees.

Such an act of parthenogenesis is especially notable in "November," the calendar's elegy, which follows Cuddie's plaint and suddenly and unexpectedly shifts from the "heavie herse" and dismal realm of death to the "*Elisian* fields" where Dido "walke[s] . . . so free" (179). Certainly, this radical shift from a posture of mourning to one of joy bespeaks the dual function of elegy that Orpheus, and now Colin, embodies: the ability to compress and interrupt organic process and to replace it with one's *own* version of time and poetic labor.[46] But a more original and far-reaching example of this act of compression and interruption can be found in "Aprill," where even the fussy commentator E.K. speaks enthusiastically of Colin's labor in what is supposedly the most celebrative and fertile month of the calendar. Discussing the closing lines of Colin's paean to the shepherdess Elisa, alias for Elizabeth, E.K. writes, "For having so decked her [Elisa] with prayses and comparisons, he returneth all the thanck of hys laboure to the excellencie of her Maiestie" (324–26). Colin is not present in this fertile season; his song is only reported by Hobbinoll, saddened over Colin's refusal ever to sing again. E.K.'s annotation nonetheless characterizes Colin's spontaneous song (which E.K. does not confuse with Hobbinoll's repetition of that song) as "laboure": work, process. And indeed, following the preamble about Colin's failure to make poems, the entire song to Elisa focuses on the temporal process of poetic making: a process that involves what E.K. defines as "overlabour[ing]" and, as in the case of Orpheus, both taking away and restoring.[47]

And moreover, as in the case of Orpheus, this process has an extraordinary amount in common with the type of poem with which Orpheus is most blatantly associated: the elegy. As Celeste Schenck has most recently noted, there is considerable overlap between "Aprill" and the more conventional elegy, "November." The echoes between the two poems, as well as what Schenck notes as the generic contamination in each of them—"The elegy, paradoxically, begins with a request for 'songs of some iouisaunce' (2); the epithalamium begins with a recognition that things are awry"[48]—suggest that Spenser certainly conceived "Aprill" and "November," both sung by Colin, as companion pieces that fulfill and complete each other. Yet one need not look to "November" to find the elegiac strains that are only implicit in "Aprill," for "Aprill" furnishes, all by itself, an example of the poet's unsettling powers to disrupt temporal process. The invocation of dainty nymphs, the call to Calliope and the Graces to sing, the darkening of Phoebus, the reference to an ever-mournful Niobe turned to stone, the pregnant silence of the deceased in the midst of the speaker's almost garrulous loquacity: all of these elements find their way into Spenser's celebration of majesty, and their elegiac underpinnings give us a celebration curiously tainted with the touch of death.[49] Far from being the polar opposite of "November," "Aprill" is its mirror image, as Elisa is only another name for Dido. These elegiac formulations that echo throughout the poem remind us that it is the poet who makes, in the vacuum created by the silence of the "deceased."

On the one hand, Spenser may be using the formulas of elegy to suggest that Elizabeth can conquer even death. But a darker interpretation suggests that he is "killing" her to reinvest her with his own meaning, to call attention to the elegiac process whereby the dead person is displaced and reconstituted by the live poet. And moreover, what he reconstitutes her as, in a move that neatly reverses the tradition of the blazon as practiced by Petrarch, Sidney, and others, is of vital importance. A "blazing forth" or "publishing" of what Shakespeare describes as "sweet beauty's best" (*Sonnets*,

106), the blazon typically undresses and displays the woman's body to a voyeuristic male audience, supposedly in order to celebrate the woman.[50] But Spenser's poem to Elisa has the odd effect of working in reverse. We begin with an Elisa free of "spotte" and "mortall blemish" (50, 54) and end with a queen "decked . . . in royall aray," (155–56), having been symbolically clothed in bay branches, olive branches, columbine, carnations, cowslips, and much, much more by Muses and "shepheards daughters" (127) alike. In this breathtaking floral display, which anticipates the countless flowers placed on the gnat's grave by the careless shepherd, the virginal Elisa becomes a provocative fertility goddess. Thus the poet not only renders the chaste—and sterile—Elisa "fit" for "Aprill" but also neatly reverses the Virgilian subtext to which the closing emblems allude. Thenot, who has listened to Hobbinoll's reconstruction of Colin's song, has for his emblem "O quam te memorem virgo?"; Hobbinoll has "O dea certe" (Oh, what shall I call you, maiden? / Certainly, a goddess) (163, 165). Both lines are from Aeneas's encounter with his mother Venus in the woods of Carthage. But what is significant about that meeting is that when she greets her son, Venus is dressed as a "virgo": a huntress of Diana, an Amazon, garbed, she claims, in the fashion of all young Carthaginian women. Spenser's "encounter" with a goddess produces the opposite result: the Elisa who departs at the end of the eclogue is a Diana dressed like Venus, adorned with "Coronations, and Sops in wine, / worne of Paramoures" (138–39). Just as the resistant Syrinx is refashioned in the course of the poem into Pan's compliant consort, rejoicing in the birth of her daughter, so is Diana refashioned as a fitting consort for the spring.

Elisa/Elizabeth is thus reborn as a symbolic entity in the course of Spenser's poem, "clothed" by her poet for the calendar's most fertile season. If the presence in "Aprill" of England's 46-year-old monarch seems incongruous, Spenser redeems this incongruity by killing off England's chaste Diana and resurrecting her as Venus. Moreover, it is not only the spring that a reborn Elisa inhabits, but Spenser's version of Virgil's fourth Eclogue, which looks forward to the advent of a golden age that will remain unfulfilled unless Elisa is recast in terms other than those of fatal self-sufficiency. Indeed, in supplementing "chaste" Elisa with flowers and royal "aray," Colin is intimating that

Elisa alone is radically *in*sufficient, that she requires the additions of the poet so that she will be decorously dressed for the season. If, moreover, another name for Diana is Hecate, Colin has in effect traveled to the bower of death to dispose of the poem's fatal Proserpine, author of the decree that imposed silence on Orpheus. Thus while John Fenton sang "Withering by flourishing is now contrould" once James took the throne, Spenser's Colin sings it long before James's ascension, as he furnishes not only for himself but for all of England a shade far more nurturing than that provided by an unwedded queen.

Louis Montrose is therefore right in arguing that in "laboring" to produce Elisa, Colin takes away from Elizabeth's status as "cultural genetrix."[51] But Colin also calls attention to the difficulties of continuing to carry out these poetic labors on which England and its queen are dependent. While "Aprill" provides a fantastic solution to the problem of sterility, it also registers the dangers already caused by England's Proserpine, who has prohibited Colin/Orpheus either his reward or his *tropos*. For like the gnat who speaks from beyond the grave, Colin too has been silenced. Even without its frame, the poem serves as an unsettling example of the poet's perverse powers. But with its frame—the concerned dialogue between Hobbinoll and Thenot about Colin's refusal to sing and the interruption of his labors—the poem becomes an elegy to queen and poet alike, a testament to the waste of Colin's skill to "make so excellent." It serves as a subtle reminder that given Colin's present silence, he no longer acts as mediator between queen and public by investing her with symbolic meaning; he no longer salvages the queen's sterility by reproducing her as Venus. Nor is Colin the only one who is silent: so are those of whom he would write, if he could. For Colin's reticence may be symbolic of others' silences—silences more threatening than the poet's own in that they are explicitly the result of censorship and political exile. The poem is dedicated to a Sidney only recently chastened by Elizabeth for his protests over her marriage negotiations with Alençon. "Julye" hints at the figure of Algrind, alias for Archbishop Grindal, asked to leave his ecclesiastical post for disagreeing with Elizabeth over matters of religious prophesying. Finally, the "ploughman" whom Immeritô asks his calendar to follow in the "Envoy" may be Robert Crowley, a Puritan who published *Piers Plowman*, a trenchant satire of the Elizabethan Compromise, in 1550 and lost some of his benefices as a result.[52] To take note in the margins of the poem of such suppression—in this case, that of the decisively *non*-courtly community of militant Protestants who threatened Elizabeth's autonomy—is also to criticize, if in extremely subtle fashion, the very ideologies one is purportedly championing.

Like Virgil's *Georgics*, "Aprill" has been said to create a "natural" vision of empire within which and for which its poet labors. And yet this vision is constituted by a disruptive pattern of temporality, by the arbitrary act of a poet who takes away as easily as he gives and whose own silencing is registered throughout the *Calender*—a silencing that prevents him from being the "productive" member of the georgic economy to which he aspires, and which would redeem England from its plight. One is reminded that the majority of Spenser's "ideal" pastoral settings—the Garden of Adonis, the rustic community of *The Faerie Queene*'s sixth book, the future Ireland envisioned in his treatise *A Vewe of the Present State of Irelande*—are places of productivity, reciprocity, and work. Hence shortly after the unfortunate wounding of Timias, Spenser turns to Venus's garden paradise, where "there is continuall spring, and harvest . . . / Continuall," where "the heavy trees" "seeme to labour under their fruits lode," and where Venus herself "reape[s] sweet pleasure of the wanton boy" Adonis (3.6.42, 46).[53] Yet it is also true that in this georgic paradise, the boys are "wanton" and the women "reape"; the "heavy trees" are conceived as pregnant trees rather than as sturdy Atlases carrying the "lode" of the world on their shoulders. Belphoebe's antithesis, Venus nonetheless produces a curiously similar effect on her wanton boy: in reaping *him*, she is the active party, he the passive one; she is the laborer, he the idle gentleman. From the organic cycle of female productivity, man is inevitably alienated, as Cellini obviously recognized. And like Cellini, Spenser/Colin attempts to compensate for this alienation. That act of compensation is possible, paradoxically enough, because Elizabeth herself is a failed Venus.

Spenser needs Elizabeth to be "unfruitful" so that he can make his own pastoral poetry. But it is only by appealing to what Theresa

Krier has noted was the more traditional, public, male-to-male bond of patronage that he prevents himself from being trapped within the claustrophobic and *non*-conventional relationship between monarch and subject.[54] Krier and others have called attention to the extent to which Elizabeth's self-sufficient presence destabilizes the literary conventions through which patronage relationships have been expressed. The shade she offers was conceived of as much more absolute and more threatening than that provided by aristocrats such as Leicester. It is thus striking that on the "public" surfaces of his poems, where his own voice is most unmediated—the dedication of *The Shepheardes Calender* to "the noble and vertuous Gentleman . . . M. Philip Sidney," the first fourteen dedicatory sonnets to *The Faerie Queene*—Spenser turns to a different expression of patronage that depends on relationships of male homogeneity. These are, finally, communal relationships that supersede and take precedence over the potentially stifling relationship between the male poet and his queen, from whose infertility he has "saved" his nation. Thus while Thenot's and Hobbinoll's dialogue prefacing Colin's lay has the effect of emphasizing Colin's silence, it also provides the occasion for a male community to repeat and thereby to preserve Colin's song. In the resolutely homosocial universe of pastoral poetry—a universe that Elisa's presence in "Aprill" scarcely changes, given her silence and submission to Colin's reverse blazon—Colin has found a means of commemoration and a grateful audience. The ever-absent Rosalind functions as the calendar's most obvious representation of an *un*grateful audience, but her looming silence is eclipsed and overshadowed by the many male voices that labor in the poem and on its margins to create what Spenser calls in his envoy a monumental "Calender for every year" ("December," 235). From the dedication to Philip Sidney to the closing allusion to Horace and the "ploughman" who may well be Robert Crowley, Spenser's poem situates itself among a chorus of male voices who will preserve and legitimize Colin's Orphic labors.

But it is questionable whether Colin, and therefore Spenser, is able to continue situating such heroism within a supportive community of readers envisioned as equals. To this extent, the sixth book of *The Faerie Queene*, written over fifteen years after the publication of *The Shepheardes Calender*, offers itself as both a logical culmination of Spenser's desire to fashion productivity from sterility for an admiring male audience, and as a reflection on the poet's failure to preserve himself from the queen's emasculating shade. I have already noted the bower of book 3 in which Timias suffers his wound, and immediately after that episode, the Bower of Bliss where Venus "reapes" from her wanton Adonis. Book 6, however, would seem to reverse these paradigms of male vulnerability. After much "labor," Calidore wins his mistress Pastorella, so that "of his love he reapt the timely frute" (6.10.38). And on Mount Acidale, "Belphoebe" seems to be subject to the piping poet, as over a hundred "Ladies" dance nude within the shade Colin Clout so assiduously protects. In fact, from this favorite haunt of Venus, in which Colin plays the role of privileged votary and priest—not surprisingly, given his role in "Aprill"—Elizabeth herself is excluded, replaced by a fourth Grace of Colin's own election.[55] Colin begs "pardon" of "great *Gloriana*, greatest Maiesty" for this uncharacteristic omission and substitution. But in a way, that process of substitution hearkens back to the earlier moment in "Aprill" when Colin replaces Diana with Venus. The only difference now is that his Venus is resolutely private; moreover, he can sing to her and gaze upon her without fearing the dangerous intervention of Hades' queen.

And yet Colin, of course, does not gaze and sing forever. For missing from this intensely personal vision is the buffer of the pastoral community, omnipresent in Spenser's earlier poem. Colin's reverie is interrupted by Calidore, representative of Gloriana's court, but also a temporary truant from that court thanks to his love for Pastorella: he now labors not in pursuit of the Blatant Beast but in woods and on Melibee's farm. Drawn to the music echoing from Mount Acidale, Calidore climbs this hill sacred to Venus and watches with intense fascination "a troupe of Ladies dauncing" (6.10.10). At first unwilling to "enter into th'open greene," Calidore spies, not unlike Tasso's Tirsi, "in the covert of the wood . . . / Beholding all" (6.10.11). Yet curiosity as to whether "it were the traine of beauties Queene, / Or Nymphes, or Faeries, or enchaunted show" finally moves him to leave the wood, and, predictably, to disrupt the dance: "But soone as he appeared to their vew, / They vanisht all away out of his sight, / And cleane were gone" (6.10.18). It is not Colin's gaze but Calidore's that proves fatal in this fragile poetic economy of a song that lures young maidens into a circle on the "open greene." Breaking his bagpipe, Colin "made great mone for that unhappy turne"—the turn of Calidore, and thus a return to Virgil's Orpheus.

Whether Calidore is a fellow shepherd or a member of an invasive court is ultimately irrelevant to the significance of the maidens' vanishing.[56] In either case, Colin's vision is unprotected from and threatened by the very audience of sympathetic courtiers/shepherds who had once echoed and preserved his transgressive song. To be sure, following Calidore's intrusion, the knight and poet "discourse" of many things, as Colin gives his willing listener a lesson in "Civilitie" and dancing ladies, prompting Calidore's apologetic, "Now sure it yrketh mee, / That to thy blisse I made this luckelesse breach, / As now the author of thy bale to be, / Thus to bereaue thy loues deare sight from thee" (6.10.29). So does Spenser suggest a reconciliation of sorts between the singer and the curious Calidore. But by making Calidore the "author" of Colin's "bereauement," Spenser is also intimating Colin's very real vulnerability to interpretative violence. Unwilling to suspend disbelief, Calidore must question the veracity of what he suspects may be merely an "enchaunted show." Arguably, he learns in conversation with Colin the meaning and importance of that show; and arguably, Spenser is constructing a hierarchy, absent from *The Shepheardes Calender*, demonstrating the laboring poet's superiority to his "peers." But even the invocation of this hierarchy, product of the poet's removal to Mount Acidale—or, perhaps, to Ireland—appears both suspect and finally defensive.

Like Tasso in the *Aminta* and the *Gerusalemme*, Spenser may well be protecting his slender fictions from others' desirous gazes. But unlike Tasso, Spenser constructs a relationship of mutual dependency between his readers and his archetypal poet as a way of defending them all against a disenabling queen. Spenser's elevation of Colin to vatic heights is in many ways the English poet's most supreme hymn to the power of poetic labor. But it is at the same time a troubling hymn. The maidens' spontaneous act of vanishing "all away" occurs independently of Colin's powers,[57] and Colin's solitary posture decisively precludes the deep-rooted nostalgia of the other writers we have thus far considered—Cellini, Teresa, and Tasso—for the nourishing and benign protection of a paternal authority or a community of kindred readers.

6 ·

"Put yourself under his shroud, The universal landlord": Shakespeare and Resistance to Authorship

Shakespeare is notoriously difficult to locate in his plays. There is no autobiography in which one can chart his struggles with patrons and acting companies, no poetic persona as accessible as Colin Clout or Tasso's Tirsi who offers veiled commentary on the artist and his work. Nor do we have an abundance of extraliterary documentation with which to piece together Shakespeare's life. The apparent resistance of the playwright to exposure—perhaps purposeful in the case of the plays, accidental in the case of the scarcity of biographical material—has only been enhanced by over a century of Shakespeare scholarship glorifying the bard as a poet for "all time." It is only fairly recently, in fact, that a concerted effort has been made to provide us with a localized Shakespeare, one whose work was the product of his historical era as well as of a social class intent on securing for itself a distinctive position in Elizabethan society. Yet on the whole, the new interest in historicizing Shakespeare has tended to produce either the protean figure identified earlier with Erasmus, impossible to place within the political and socioeconomic framework of his day, or a conservative figure whose desire for success and social acceptance led him to create plays that contain and neutralize those who transgress their own societal places.

The following remarks can hardly account for the Shakespearean career in full, but they are offered in the hope of locating the poet and actor within the dynamics of vulnerability discussed in the opening chapter. Like the other writers thus far encountered in this study, the London playwright constantly had to negotiate his relationship to authority. Unlike them, he was relatively independent of his aristocratic and royal patrons because he was a member of London's most successful theatrical company. Shakespeare was thus reliant on what Werner Gundersheimer has dubbed a new and challenging patron: the paying public.[1] The huge success of the London theaters after their commercialization in 1576 often allowed for partial ownership of the acting companies by their members. In time, a player might be able to amass a private fortune that could be used to purchase an estate or a heraldry (Shakespeare purchased both). By attempting, moreover, to model their organization on that of the city's guilds, the players tried to ensure for themselves the status of citizenship within London's walls.[2]

Despite (and even because of) these efforts to become "good citizens," professional actors were regarded with considerable suspicion. As Christopher Hill has pointedly reminded us, "This quite new commercialization in the theater . . . led to the so-called 'Puritan' attack on the stage—which in origin was not Puritan at all and was restricted to an attack on the commercial stage."[3] Men whose business was playing could not be part of a productive economy and threatened the very concept not only of the work ethic but of society itself.[4] It was on ethical grounds that actors in early modern England, as elsewhere in Europe, were particularly vulnerable, and it was here that the second patron of the London theater companies came into play. Before 1603, leading aristocrats such as Warwick and Leicester provided what Muriel Bradbrook has called a "protective shield . . . sometimes little better than a legal fiction" to enable actors to escape charges of vagrancy.[5] James's monopolization of the acting companies soon after he became king in 1603 granted the players a degree of legal and ethical legitimacy they had only sporadically enjoyed before.[6] But this new extension of royal shade, which enabled a member of Shakespeare's company to become a King's Man and to wear the livery of the royal family, generated questions and uncertainties as well. Moreover, recent studies have called attention to the theater's stubborn resistance to appropriation and "monumentalization," due to its improvisatory nature and its carnivalesque refusal to acknowledge any fixed and final allocation of authorship.[7] That Shakespeare partakes in such resistance is, in part, the argument of this chapter. Yet the chapter will also argue that particularly in the romances, written several years after Shakespeare became a "King's Man," the playwright is doing more than celebrating the popular stage. Rather, he is attempting to relocate the ethical legitimacy for which he must depend on his prince in a source of authority over which the monarch has no control.

Thus while in his *Apology for Actors*, composed shortly after James took the throne, Thomas Heywood argues that the stage is a worthy institution because since time immemorial it has been protected by "Kings and Monarches [who] are by God placed and inthroaned *supra nos*" (sig. D), there is little indication that Shakespeare shares that opinion of royal protection. Most of the playwright's references to sovereign shade are cast in the rhetoric of cynicism or servitude.[8] Apemantus's taunts of "The Poet" seeking patronage in *Timon of Athens* make of the writer's praises of Timon a self-serving sham. And the Earl of Cambridge utters his paean to Henry V's "sweet shade of government," beneath which "there's not . . . a subject / That sits in heart-grief and uneasiness" (*Henry V*, 2.2.26–28), only moments before Henry exposes him as a traitor to England. Perhaps one of the more ominous allusions to shade is uttered by Octavius's lackey Thidias, who invites a soon-to-be-conquered Cleopatra to "put yourself under [the emperor's] shroud, / The universal landlord" (*Antony and Cleopatra*, 3.13.71–72). In this request haunted by evocations of death and burial,[9] Cleopatra is asked to become an actress, to display herself as a trophy in Octavius's "triumph" before the crowds of Rome (5.1.66).[10]

Cleopatra sabotages this performance with her death, producing an alternate triumph that Octavius had wanted to prevent. In becoming a shade who, "hand in hand" with Antony, will "make the ghosts gaze" (4.14.51–52), Cleopatra undermines the extension of sovereign shade, implementing a much different type of theater than the royal pageant imagined by Octavius. The tragicomedies that follow *Antony and Cleopatra* return to the queen's dilemma. But they end by procuring for their consummate actors a "liberty" available not in the afterlife but in *this* life. Particularly in *The Winter's Tale*, the play on which the majority of this chapter will focus, the actor's vulnerability to charges of ethical illegitimacy is turned on its head. It is rewritten as the vulnerability of the monarch to the dramatic forms of which he believes himself to be in control.[11] Far more extensively than either *Macbeth* or *Coriolanus*, the Shakespearean tragedies mentioned in Chapter 1, *The Winter's Tale* offers a careful reading of the dynamics of invulnerability as crafted by James's court. Engineered by an unruly woman whose ambivalent social status coincides with the player's own and who faces social prejudices echoing the antitheatrical criticism of the period, *The Winter's Tale* forces its monarch to recognize that the royal authority depicted onstage is grounded not in his body but *outside* his body, beyond the shadow he casts in the hope of bringing a universe beneath his shroud.

I

With James I's peaceful accession to the English throne in 1603, writers throughout the country celebrated the beginnings of a new golden age. The poem to which countless Englishmen, Shakespeare included, relentlessly returned during the first decade of the seventeenth century was perhaps the most glowing tribute ever written to an era of peace: Virgil's fourth Eclogue. This poem predicts a time of universal peace when Rome will be undisturbed by trade, war, or travelers. English writers supplemented this influential vision of a world at peace with a tag from another Virgilian eclogue, the first: "Divissos orbe Britannos" (Britain divided from the world). Within the poem, this phrase refers to Meliboeus's bitter exile, but out of context, it could signify England's insulation from religious wars and the corruptions of the Continent. Capitalizing on the *pax* that characterized his reign, James I made every effort to appropriate the legacy of the Roman Augustus.[12] At his coronation, he rode beneath arches inscribed with the phrase, "Britain divided from the world," and Ben Jonson and George Chapman wrote masques celebrating him as a peacemaker who ensured his nation's natural insularity.

There was, however, more to this concerted insistence on the full-blown splendors of a new golden age than the fortuitous congruency of James's accession and English peace. Like the Estense court's manipulative uses of pastoral, James's vision of his reign as a return to

Augustus's peaceful era concealed more than it exposed. James harbored reasons for wanting to announce an absolute rupture with the recent past—a desire also associated with Octavius in *Antony and Cleopatra* and with Octavius's historical contemporary Cymbeline in the play that bears his name. For one thing, as a foreign monarch coming to the English throne, James needed to insist on the unification of once disparate, even unfriendly kingdoms, and he did so by appealing to the unity Augustus brought to Rome after a lengthy period of civil war. But the effort to return to a more distant past may also have been specifically related to the two women to whom James owed his claims to the English throne: his "heretical" mother, Mary Queen of Scots, executed in 1587, and his foster mother, Elizabeth. Dependent as James was on two queens for his claims to the throne (although he also owed his crown to his English-born father, the Earl of Darnley),[13] his strategies to procure for himself a legacy of exclusively male parthenogenesis may be readily explained. His insistence on divine right linked him both to the legacy of the *pater patriae* Augustus, selected by Caesar to be his heir, and to the Hebrew kings, whose genesis originated in the selection of Saul by Samuel and, of course, God.[14]

James's recourse to the vocabulary of drama in formulating his doctrine of the *pater patriae* and the necessary rituals of purgation that accompanied his justification of divine right is most evident in a treatise he published anonymously shortly after the abortive Gunpowder Plot in 1605. Writing as a knowledgeable courtier in *A Discourse on the Maner of the Discoverie of the Powder Treason*, James summarizes the events of the foiled insurrection by ponderously concluding:

> So have we all that are faithfull and humble Subiects, great cause to pray earnestly to the Almighty, that it will please him who hath the hearts of all Princes in his hands, to put it in his Maiesties heart to make such a conclusion of this Tragedie to the Traitors, but Tragicomedie to the King and all his trew Subiects, as thereby the glory of God and his trew Religion may be advanced . . . and this horrible attempt . . . to be so iustly avenged.[15]

One paragraph later, he notes that this vengeance will culminate in the "execution of famous and honourable Iustice upon the offendors; and so the kingdome [will be] purged of them." Thus the tragic "actors" who wanted "to have effaced our memories" will themselves be effaced, while "wee (as I said in the beginning) shall with all thankfulnesse eternally preserve the memory of so great a benefit." Confident in his ability to "make . . . a conclusion" that will stun his subjects into seeing him as God's earthly vehicle for justice, James both fashions himself as an author of plays and obscures his authorial function by locating it in the "Almighty" who has all princes' hearts in his hands.

In turning to Shakespeare's own "tragicomedies," we will have occasion to examine the extent to which the playwright confirmed James's vision of the tragicomic as a testament to divine authorship.[16] But the cultural form that most blatantly enacted what James called the "purging" of "Traitors" from his kingdom and verified his divinely chosen role as England's ruler was the Jacobean masque. *The Masque of Queens*, performed in 1609, was the first fully developed masque of the long and prolific collaboration of Inigo Jones and Ben Jonson. It consists of both a disorderly antimasque, acted by professional actors, and an orderly masque proper, performed by aristocrats and members of royalty, including Queen Anne.[17] The central opposition of the masque is that between the witchlike "hags" from the demonic realm of "Two-facèd Falsehood" and the godly and heroic Perseus, who presides over the House of Fame. In the dark and confusing antimasque, one garrulous witch after another takes the stage to utter her "Charm" against kings and their infernal preoccupations with peace. Or to quote from Jonson's own notes, Ignorance "begets" Suspicion, Suspicion Credulity, Credulity Falsehood, and so on; a host of "infernal sisters" are spewed forth as though "one link produced another, and the Dame [who calls forth the various vices] were born out of them all."[18] Jonson's antimasque yields a frightening vision of female parthenogenesis. Self-proclaimed "opposites / To Fame and Glory," Virtue and Nature (120–21), the witches are conquered by those very forces when "a sound of loud music" invades their "magical dance full of preposterous change and gesticulation," and the hags and the "hell into which they ran quite vanished" (327–36). With this sudden vanishing, Perseus himself appears—a Perseus who represents for Jonson, much as for Cellini, "heroic and masculine virtue" (342). Slayer of Medusa whose gaze turned men to stone, and now the wielder of that very power against the witches, Perseus triumphantly banishes the region of falsehoods and dangerous women to usher in a new era of peace presided over by the monarch and "Rex Pacificus, scholar and poet."[19] The witches do return, but they are "bound" to the chariots on which the aristocratic masquers descend, their silent presence contributing to the "eternal . . . triumph" of which Cleopatra deprived Octavius.

Yet more than the witches are bound. The insistently female disorder that vanishes to reveal chaste and harmonious queens is also indicative of the theatrical medium, which, as Jonas Barish, Thomas Greene, and others have suggested, Jonson the masque-maker so implicitly mistrusted.[20] This is the realm both of the witches and of the professional actors, whose potentially uncontrollable qualities of doubling and impersonation have to be rendered impotent.[21] In its place, a much different representational form emerges, that of the exquisite courtly dance. As Jean-Christophe Agnew has remarked, the masque proper "expressed the court's contempt for the players and, by that same measure, the world the players represented."[22] The resulting elitism may well reflect Jonson's ambivalence toward the stage for which he wrote. But it may also represent a monarch's triumph over the potentially threatening doubleness of the theater. The true masque of queens, completed by the presence of a *real* queen, is far removed from the furious "begetting" of base hags and professional antimasquers alike.

Performed two years before *The Winter's Tale* was seen at the Globe Theater, *The Masque of Queens* conquers the dark past that protests against the retrieval of the "Age of Gold" (129); it also conquers the specter of theatrical uncontrollability. Staged without dramatic conflict, Perseus's descent attests to the benign and nonviolent nature of a deity who defies the threatening duplications practiced by professional theater and witchcraft alike. As both author and privileged spectator, the monarch collapses the eminently theatrical tension between playwright and audience, in the same way that the elegant dance at masque's end dissolves the boundary between masquers and audience. Yet while Jonson insists that the infernal sisters are sprung from "an ugly hell" from which "all evils are, morally, said to come" (21–23), the logic of the masque insists on a somewhat different source of generation. If the king is author and center of the masque, for whom and *by* whom the spectacle is created,[23] does he not also initiate the illusion of darkness that is magically dispelled? As the seen yet unseen center of the masque, the king authorizes evil so that he can control it in a manner so absolute that all struggle is preempted. (It is hardly incidental that the "contest" between the Amazonian queens and the hags takes place offstage). Thus does the masque procure the sovereign's immunity from what he has in fact created. Even more pertinently, it procures his immunity from the potential skepticism of spectators, whose posture as witnesses is ultimately negated in the closing phenomenon of the dance.[24]

This analysis offers a potentially dark reading of *The Masque of Queens*, with its ominous but ultimately harmless antimasque "be-gotten" by hell. It is, of course, a reading offset by the *actual* existence of traitors (hence James's almost compulsive mythologizing of the foiled Gunpowder Plot) and witches, to whom James devotes his *Daemonologie* of 1597.[25] The *Daemonologie*, in fact, provides a neat parallel to *A Discourse on . . . the Powder Treason* insofar as it hinges on the failure of witches to drown James and his bride in 1590.[26] Another parallel between the two failed attempts at regicide is that James plays a central role in both as the sole "discoverer" of the plots against him.[27] To be sure, as one editor of the *Daemonologie* suggests, "in destroying the Devil's ministers the King really thought that he was only carrying out his plain duty towards God" (vi). But it can hardly be denied that behind the demonological treatise and *A Discourse on . . . the Powder Treason*, there is the lurking possibility that James generates evil *in order* to enable others to recognize him as "Gods annointed," and thus to cleanse himself of his past, with its ambiguously gendered Elizabeth and its vile, unruly, Catholic Mary.

Yet whereas *The Masque of Queens*, like the royal treatises that precede it, makes the king immune to the potent excesses of evil in his role as the "discoverer" of evil's dark unfoldings, Shakespeare refuses to grant his monarchs such immunity.[28] Given what the following pages will explore as Shakespeare's critique of a Jacobean dynamic of purgation, it is not accidental that so many of the late plays explicitly comment on the masque form.[29] As numerous critics have suggested, Shakespeare's last plays often parody the masque as an emblem of courtly order by rendering it a spectacle out of control. Jonathan Goldberg even suggests that *Macbeth*, perhaps the first Shakespearean play to be influenced by the spectacular pageantry of the Jacobean court, eludes the control not only of the king who watches it, but of the playwright himself, anxious, like his doomed protagonist, to purge and thereby control the dangerous generativity of theater and woman alike.[30]

But might one not find in the dark inversions of royal spectacle a somewhat different relationship between what Goldberg calls "the menacing heterogeneity of uncontrolled duplication" and the playwright? Indeed, in *The Winter's Tale*, on which the remainder of this chapter focuses, the various means of resistance to a monarch's dark imaginings allow one to discern a more complex and, perhaps, controlled relationship of the playwright to duplication than Goldberg implies vis-à-vis *Macbeth*.[31] In this play about a diseased king whose rabid insistence on rituals of purgation and forgetting makes him both an ominous and a comic producer of masques and tragicomedies, Shakespeare challenges a king's desires to escape from what he has authorized. He rather insists on that king's dependency on the supposedly uncontrollable forces of blackness through which he purifies himself and purges his kingdom. As the following analysis will suggest, in *The Winter's Tale*, the anxieties the masque is intended to diffuse—anxieties about the existence of uncontrollable counterplots and unruly witnesses who might protest a monarch's means of legitimation—are instead powerfully registered and arguably triumphant, as the female community that the mad monarch has brutally consigned to oblivion is resurrected. In so staging the irrepressibility of the dead, and in turn, the irrepressibility of the re-presentational mode of theater, Shakespeare forbids what Jonson imagined as the vanishing not only of his fertile witches but of the "memory of such a thing" (337). Like Jonson's hags, the unruly women of *The Winter's Tale* return to the stage. Unlike the witches, they return to stage their own triumph.[32]

II

The Winter's Tale opens with Polixenes' courtier claiming that Leontes has been so generous to his king during his lengthy sojourn in Sicily that Polixenes will be forever in Leontes' debt. This overwhelming generosity of a sovereign host is not original with Shakespeare; we have already seen such munificence evoked by Cellini in regard to Francis I. Nor, for that matter, is the plot of *The Winter's Tale* original; Shakespeare drew extensively on Robert Greene's *Pandosto*. But the "rare sights," banqueting, "sumptious cheer," triumphs, and shows prepared for the visiting Egistus in Greene's popular 1588 novel are supplanted in Shakespeare by the more abstract language of a beneficence that leaves its recipient permanently indebted, even crippled—a metaphor of infirmity to which the first scene's closing lines allude ("If the king had no son, they would desire to live on crutches till he had one").[33] Greene's King Egistus saw Pandosto's "princely liberality" as the token of true friendship, a friendship that quickly came to an end with Pandosto's onslaught of jealousy. But in *The Winter's Tale*, this "liberality" carries different overtones. Polixenes' courtier protests that the entertainment Leontes will receive when he "pays" Bohemia a deserved "visitation" "shall shame" the Bohemians: "We cannot with such magnificence—in so rare—I know not what to say" (1.1.12–13). His confessed inadequacies in describing Leontes' hospitality betray more than a courtier's modesty. The insistent hyperboles rather set forth a posture of inferiority and subjugation, which Leontes' generosity has arguably been designed to exact. Similarly, in picking up the thread of his courtier's truncated discourse in the second scene, King Polixenes begins his farewell: "Time as long again / Would be fill'd up, my brother, with our thanks; / And yet we should, for perpetuity, / Go hence in debt" (1.2.3–6).

Shakespeare's play begins with the uncomfortable image of a king insistent on controlling the conditions of exchange in order to dominate his indebted recipient. Yet this image, presented by a pair of awed courtiers, hardly accords with the real Leontes when he appears onstage in the following scene. In a line that may be said to serve as the *primum mobile* of the play as a whole, Polixenes declares that he must leave Sicily after his lengthy nine months' stay and return to Bohemia: "I am question'd by my fears, of what may chance / Or breed upon our absence; that may blow / No sneaping winds at home, to make us say, / 'This is put forth too truly' " (1.2.11–14). Such fears of things that might "breed" in a king's absence are put to rest not by Leontes, who is unsuccessful in persuading his friend to stay longer, but by his wife. Badgered by Leontes into speaking—"Tongue-tied, our queen?"—Hermione begins by correcting the words Leontes spoke first ("You, sir, / Charge him too coldly") and argues that "a lady's Verily's / As potent as a lord's" (1.2.29–30, 50–51). Rather than repeat and imitate Leontes' rhetoric of request, Hermione reveals herself from her opening lines to be a wife and queen whose words are not controlled by, and do not duplicate, her husband's. Hermione suspiciously succeeds where Leontes has failed, persuading Polixenes to stay "one sev'n night longer." Having spoken only once before "to better purpose," when she told Leontes that she was his forever, Hermione now speaks to the purpose twice, thereby "earn[ing] a royal husband" and "friend" (1.2.89–90, 107–8).

In employing her potent speech in conversation with Polixenes, Hermione both makes her husband dependent on her "good deed" (1.2.97) and, in Leontes' defensive imagination, dangerously duplicates her wedding vow. But what makes this act of duplication especially pernicious is an obvious fact of which the audience has been cognizant since the beginning of the scene. Standing between Polixenes and Leontes is a very pregnant Hermione, to whose condition Polixenes abruptly calls attention in his first line: "Nine changes of the watery star hath been / The shepherd's note since we have left our throne / Without a burden" (1.2.1–3). If the first scene portrayed a king intent on controlling exchange and preempting others' attempts to pay him in kind, the pregnant Hermione appears onstage as the visual emblem of a productive cycle over which a king has only attenuated and uncertain control.[34]

The threat of female productivity—a productivity that neatly contrasts with the Elizabethan sterility protested by Spenser—leads Leontes to stage the antimasque that is the play's first three acts,[35] as he both transforms Hermione into a traitor and disowns the act of transformation itself. Leontes' immediate response to the words bred by Hermione is to develop a narrative that distends the innocent gestures of his queen and Polixenes into a courtship ritual of which he is the author. Speaking to his courtier Camillo, Leontes moves abruptly from the seen to the unseen, and thus from the posture of spectator to that of omniscient author, as he brutally invades the minds of his "characters."[36] Upon observing his wife and Polixenes "whispering" and "leaning cheek to cheek," Leontes imagines them "wishing clocks more swift" (1.2.284–89), thus using Hermione's and Polixenes' visible gestures to construct their inner and unvoiced wishes, the most spectacular of which is to be unseen: "all eyes / Blind with the pin and web, but theirs; theirs only" (290–91). Yet at the same time that he constructs his peculiar narrative, Leontes abruptly declares it obvious to all, thereby making it not the invention of a diseased "affection" whose "intention stabs the center" (138) but the objectifiable reality of his wife's adultery. "Ha' not you seen, Camillo?" (267); "Say it be, 'tis true" (298); "You, my lords, / Look on her, mark her well" (2.1.64–65). In a series of stage directions, Leontes effaces his part in the plot of adultery by insisting on its visibility to all who have eyes. He becomes merely the enlightened discoverer of their plot rather than its author ("I have drunk, and seen the spider") (2.1.45). Moreover, when Leontes' lords oppose his imaginings, he takes refuge in the royal "we" that transfers the act of authorship from himself to the plural and abstract corporate body of the monarch: "Why, what need we / Commune with you of this, but rather follow / Our forceful instigation? Our prerogative / Calls not your counsels, but our natural goodness / Imparts this" (2.1.161–65).

Yet if Leontes' manipulations betray what Jonathan Crewe has called the doomed attempt "to embody or possess the imagined power of sole authorship,"[37] they also betray a signal unease with that power. To be sure, on the one hand, Leontes aspires to an authorship that exercises absolute prerogative even as it disclaims it, that claims immunity from its productions, that appropriates all within its domain at the same time it preserves its independence from whatever it "owns." Like the Macbeth who utters, "I go, and it is done" (2.1.62), a line that expresses authorial intention and yet effaces intentionality with the passive phrase, Leontes seeks to escape from the acts of authorship he so brutally commits in the course of the play, which will culminate in a violent ritual of purgation: "Say that [Hermione] were gone, / Given to the fire, a moiety of my rest / Might come to me again" (2.3.7–9).

But Leontes is also like Macbeth in his initial unease with the "burdens" of authorship. To this extent, he is sharply differentiated from his fictive prototype, Greene's King Pandosto. Pandosto wears the mantle of authorship gracefully, ordering his servant to murder Egistus without considering the servant's response. Nor is he concerned with the only occasionally acknowledged presence of a potentially unruly commons that clearly believes in the innocence of its queen. But Leontes constantly and nervously seeks the complicity and consent of others, betraying his subjection to his spectators, whose presence he paradoxically cannot do without. He demands that his trusted courtier Camillo repeat his words regarding Hermione's infidelity: "Say it be, 'tis true" (1.2.298), and he instructs his lords to "look on" Hermione and "be but about / To say 'she is a goodly lady,' and / The justice of your hearts will thereto add / ' 'Tis pity she's not honest, honourable' " (2.1.65–68). Importantly, it is Leontes (rather than, as in *Pandosto*, his queen) who asks that the oracle be consulted as to the "truth" of his accusation of Hermione: not to verify his suspicions, but to silence the credulous (2.1.189–93). Whereas Pandosto is blithely unconcerned with the charges of tyranny leveled against him, Leontes insists to his lords that he is *not* the tyrant Antigonus's unruly wife, Paulina, accuses him of being: "Were I a tyrant, / Where were her life? [Paulina] durst not call me so, / If she did know me one" (2.3.121–23).

In fact, as this remark to Antigonus suggests, Leontes is plagued by the threatening potency of a woman's words, a potency that the king believes will precipitate a breakdown in the exercise of male parthenogenesis that seeks to assure a monarch of his independence. It is precisely his fear that this breakdown has already happened that prompts Leontes to co-opt something that may be "breeding" behind his back: the popular discourse of cuckoldry, which holds the husband accountable for the transgressions of his wife. In being the first to accuse Hermione in public, Leontes seeks to control the very rites that traditionally vilify not only the froward wife, but the cuckold himself.[38] He thus protects himself from becoming the object of popular representation, from being staged by the "lower messes" about whom he anxiously questions Camillo in the play's first act. "Contempt and clamour / Will be my knell," he tells Mamilius, fearing the "disgraced" part "whose issue / Will hiss me to my grave" (1.2.188–90). Refusing to perform a role in a play staged by others who will inevitably breed their own stories and hiss him to his grave in an unruly ritual of shaming, Leontes stages Hermione's guilt before anyone can stage his. In accusing his wife "i'th' open air" (3.2.105) of a mock court of law, Leontes preempts the usurping rituals of those subjects whom, as we know from Polixenes' opening lines, kings fear as dangerously uncontrollable, potential traitors who might threaten the exclusivity of monarchical reproduction.[39] "Lower messes / Perchance are to this business purblind? say!" (1.2.227–28) the king demands of an uncomprehending Camillo. But this is a Camillo whose own act of witnessing—"[Polixenes] would not stay at [Leontes'] petitions" but did stay "at the good queen's entreaty" (215–20)—provides potentially powerful testimony that Leontes must try to co-opt. Only by displacing the community and its watchful witnesses, ever ready to drive the cuckold and his transgressive wife from their midst, can Leontes reinstate the image of himself depicted by Polixenes' awed courtier in the first scene.

Thus from the very opening of the play, kings are seen harboring fears that their subjects and witnesses are ever ready to usurp their roles as patriarchs the moment they appear to abandon those roles: Polixenes left his throne "without a burden," and Leontes is obsessively sensitive to others' observations that the words of his queen are more potent than his own. Yet in preempting the community's right to enforce communal stability, Leontes is forced back upon the rituals of that community. As will become apparent in the third section of this chapter, Leontes is made subject to the very ritual he feared. "Beaten" and wounded by the husband-beater Paulina, whose first entrance onto the stage is marked in the First Folio with the dubious stage direction "Paulina, a Gentleman" (2.2), the king undergoes the ritual of shaming he had tried to avoid.

In addition to challenging the masque per se, *The Winter's Tale* questions both the exclusion and the transmutation of all that is not associated with the court in the Jacobean fashioning of culture. If the place of the ever-wary popular witnesses is subsumed by a Leontes anxious to redirect ritual energy in the first part of the play, the second half, beginning with the arrival of Leontes' faithful courtier Antigonus in Bohemia and his tragicomic pursuit by a bear, signals the "invasion" of the court *by* the realm of unruly subjects it seeks to displace and to preempt.[40] It seeks that preemption nowhere more blatantly than in the countryside, where the entire fourth act, with its rustic festivities presided over by a disguised King Polixenes, is staged. It is telling that Polixenes himself had lovingly created a fantastic version of the pastoral landscape much earlier in the play, when still sojourning in Sicily. In a brief exchange during which Leontes was notably silent, Polixenes imagined his boyhood as a timeless moment when he and his "double" Leontes "knew not / The doctrine of ill-doing, nor dream'd / That any did" (1.2.69–71). In a passage that nostalgically recaptures an ideal of balance and symmetry in both its syntax and its images, Polixenes articulated a comforting and consoling vision of a pastoral Eden in which he and young Leontes were once "twinn'd lambs that did frisk i'th' sun, / And bleat the one at th'other," exchanging "innocence for innocence" (1.2.68–69).

As the chapters on Spenser and Tasso and the brief remarks by Polixenes suggest, Renaissance pastoral at times enables those in power to efface their manipulative actions in an "innocent" landscape. In this scenario, disorder and evil always come from a vicious outsider—devilish queen, Tasso's unruly satyr—from whom royal princes, secure in their innocent imaginings, are meant to be immune. Polixenes' pompous assertion to the beautiful shepherdess Perdita in act 4 that art *is* nature effaces the intrusion of the royal author and spectator into the pastoral community. Ironically, however, it is Leontes' lost child Perdita who resists the efforts of the court to find in Bohemia's rural folk, and in Perdita herself, a mirror of innocence. To Polixenes' probing questions about the art "which does mend nature" by marrying "a gentler scion to the wildest stock" (4.4.93–96), a clever metaphor for the illusion created by pastoral, Perdita replies that she refuses to bastardize her flowers and "paint" herself so that the royal youth who stands by her side should "only therefore / Desire to breed by me" (102–3).[41] To Camillo's sigh that he "should leave grazing, were I of your flock, / And only live by gazing," Perdita provides an abrupt disclaimer that undoes the specular dynamic of pastoral and returns to the calendrical realism of Spenser: "Out, alas! / You'd be so lean that blasts of January / Would blow you through and through" (109–12). Resistant to the idealizations thrust upon her by a king and his "gentle" courtier, Perdita refuses to grant them the power to preempt the community in which she was raised. She thereby refuses to allow pastoral to serve as a mirror for a court nervously defending its innocence and male chastity.

But this policy of preemption becomes much more forced, and therefore more apparent, when Florizel announces that he wishes to marry Perdita before the guests. Long before the disguised Polixenes and Camillo make their entrance, the audience is already aware that the feast day is "the day / Of celebration of that nuptial" which Florizel and Perdita "have sworn shall come" (49–51). In the marriage ceremony that almost ensues, the Shepherd first makes sure that his daughter can repeat the earnestness of Florizel's triumphant promise—"But my daughter, / Say you the like to him?" (380–81)—and then uses the language of Autolycus to proclaim, "Take hands, a bargain! / And, friends unknown, you shall bear witness to't" (384–85). Florizel echoes the sentiment ("But come on, / Contract us 'fore these witnesses") (390–91) and is only then interrupted by Polixenes, who insists that a father "should hold some counsel / In such a business" (410–11). When the irate father removes his mask and instructs Florizel to "mark [his] divorce" (418), the king invades the communal ritual with the insistence that the groom's father and king has the right to override that community, to negate the consent of witnesses, and to banish as traitors those who fail to conform to his will. With his abrupt "discovery," Polixenes immediately resorts to the same vocabulary and accusations as had Leontes three acts and fifteen years earlier. The old, fatherly shepherd becomes, like Camillo, a traitor ripe for hanging; Florizel is banished from the succession; and Perdita, once a hapless and innocent babe, turns into a witch.

This sudden and ironic transformation of the pastoral domain into a threat to political and religious orthodoxy is, of course, more revealing of Polixenes than it is of Bohemia's countryside, particularly for an audience well aware of Perdita's royal heritage.[42] The pastoral scene that had for several decades served as a mirror for princes threatens here to undo the authorship of kings, positing an alternative system of representation: in this case, one that results in the breeding of a royal son with a base shepherdess. As such, it functions as an explicit affront to what Leah Marcus has suggested was the

Stuart court's attempt to "erase the mark of otherness" of the English countryside by imposing official regulations regarding volatile customs and festivities such as May Day celebrations.[43] By ostensibly approving the pastimes that Elizabeth had tried to banish, James extended royal power into what Marcus calls "an area of ambivalence and instability," thereby ensuring that festive license would paradoxically represent submission to the state. But during the brief period of late summer license in *The Winter's Tale*, royalty in the form of an officious Polixenes is rebuffed, his kingly and fatherly authority challenged by his son as well as by an old shepherd and his supposed daughter. Far from controlling and redirecting the ritual energies of the sheepshearing festivities, Polixenes is forced to interrupt those festivities, unmasking himself to reveal only the ugly and invasive satyr who had presented the play's "antimasque." Far from discovering in the rustic landscape a docile locale that echoes his idealized sentiments, Polixenes is faced with shepherdesses and sons who insist on generating their own scripts.[44]

But if Polixenes' authorship is undermined by his son and the base shepherdess who admits, when the king has vented his anger and departed, that she "was not much afeard" (4.4.443), it is another figure who links the exercise of authorship to the generation of uncontrollability in Leontes' court. This is Autolycus, who as thief, seller of ballads and trifles, and manipulator of theatrical stratagems may seem as far removed from the goings on at court as he does from the shepherds he swindles. As more than one critic of the play has realized, however, Autolycus provides a parodic double for a pair of kings,[45] particularly insofar as he shares their penchants for authorship. His staging of a biblical parable—that of the good Samaritan, a *pièce de théâtre* in which the Clown is forced to become an unknowing participant—mimics Leontes' own staging and overturning of a court procedure supposedly designed to bring justice to the innocent and to punish the unjust. In representing him as the innocent victim of robbers, courtiers, and a hostile world at large, Autolycus's manipulations save him from becoming the butt of others' taunts. Such manipulativeness repeats Leontes' efforts to divert rituals of shaming from himself. More significantly, Autolycus's engagement in the medium of print, and hence of authorship, is a sign of the power with which he readily abuses others—the rustics Dorcas and Mopsa who will buy his ballads only if they are convinced of their "authority." "I love a ballad in print, a life, for then we are sure they are true," claims Mopsa (4.4.261–62).[46] Foolishly susceptible to a code of authorship that Leontes, like the more blatantly materialistic Autolycus, attempts to dominate, such readers reveal the extent to which the medium of print was a power available for social control.[47]

Yet while the rustics' naiveté leads to a willingness to believe songs simply because they are printed—thus rendering them more loyal subjects than either Perdita or Florizel—Mopsa's expression of "love" for printed ballads is mediated by her insistence on knowing whether Autolycus can produce witnesses to verify his tales. The ballad-singer readily replies that he has the "midwife's name . . . one Mistress Taleporter, and five or six honest wives that were present" on a "very doleful tune, how a usurer's wife was brought to bed of twenty money-bags at a burden, and how she longed to eat adders' heads and toads carbonadoed" (4.4.263–72). In this light, it is not print and authorship that verify legitimacy, but the audience of the event, another source of verification entirely. However trumped-up Autolycus's response might be, the exchange suggests a concern with a kind of legitimacy that print in and of itself cannot confer. That this legitimacy, moreover, is conferred by women ("six honest wives") ironically returns us to Leontes' concern regarding the potency of women's words, words on which men anxious about ensuring the legitimacy of their heirs are forced to depend.[48] Most significantly, the community that calls on female witnesses to verify events—the "lower messes" about whom Leontes violently interrogated Camillo—does not share Leontes' fears about women's potent words. Polixenes' rustic subjects stage ballads such as "Two maids wooing a man" (290) and praise "old wives" who on feast days play both dames and servants, sing songs and dance their turns, "now here / At upper end o'th' table, now i'th' middle; / On his shoulder, and his" (57–60).

Indeed, the presence of "five or six" witnesses is crucial not only to the sheepshearing scene, with its festive songs and weddings, but to later developments in the play. When the gentlemen who inform the audience of Perdita's discovery in the play's penultimate scene repeatedly insist on news that is "like an old tale" (5.2.28, 62), they make the connection of the play's finale with Autolycus's ballads explicit. Like the spectacular events recounted in ballads, the events that take place on the royal stage in act 5, scene 2, and that are "worth the audience of kings and princes; for by such [are they] acted" (5.2.79–80), require witnesses for verification. But the scene in which Perdita's true identity is revealed and Leontes and Polixenes are reconciled is concealed from the audience. Thus does Shakespeare demarcate a sharp divide between the popular audience of the play and the royal participants in the masquelike scenario of unfoldings and revelations.

At the same time, the ending that the penultimate scene could easily have provided *is* no ending. Just as there is much in the play to suggest that royal goings on cannot be confined or contained within the claustrophobic world of a court over which Leontes must relinquish control, so is it fitting that the final scene is staged in the private space of Paulina's humble house, and before a "popular" audience that includes the rustics and ourselves. For this reason, Shakespeare does not end with the mediated nature of the gentlemen's earnest reports, the syntactical confusion of which returns us to the overblown language of Polixenes' courtier. Rather, *The Winter's Tale* closes with a scene that stages dead "hags" coming to life, a scene played to an audience whose presence is necessary to endorse not only the unbelievable fictions of the stage but the dicta of kings. To this extent, as the next section will suggest, *The Winter's Tale* insists that the "popular" theater, and not the elite and insular masque, is the only means of ensuring that kings are held accountable for the productions they create in their misguided quest for invulnerability. Thus does Shakespeare compose his own defense of the professional stage. But he does so in very different fashion than contemporaries such as Thomas Heywood, to whose *Apology for Actors* the next pages return.

III

Toward the end of his *Apology for Actors*, Thomas Heywood sets out to demonstrate the usefulness of the contemporary stage to the commonwealth by elaborating on several "strange accidents" that had lately happened at plays. Two of the three examples center on murderous wives. In the one case, the appearance onstage of the ghostly apparition of a husband forces a wife in the audience to exclaim that she sees "the ghost of her husband fiercely threatening and menacing [her]"; in the other, the enactment of the murder itself forces the act of self-betrayal. Although the representations of the crimes are quite different, the reactions of the murderous wives are identical. Upon witnessing their crimes onstage, both women find their "consciences" "extremely troubled" and cry out, "Oh my husband, my husband!" The two are ultimately arraigned, condemned, and burned. Thus does theater assist in the "discov[eries] of many notorious murders, long concealed from the eyes of the world" (sigs.G1–2).

In a recent study on murderous wives in early modern England, Frances Dolan asks why wives and not husbands are apprehended through the intervention of "fearefull image[s]" on Heywood's stage. She conjectures that one reason is the greater visibility given in Jacobean England to homicidal wives, whose crimes were categorized as petty treason. But Heywood's examples also play a crucial role in his defense of the theater "as a means of, rather than an obstacle to, social control."[49] Indeed, according to Heywood, what *is* the stage if not a means of ensuring the commoners' obedience to monarchy and making them docile subjects? "Playes are writ with the ayme, and carryed with this methode, to teach the subjects obedience to their King, to shew the people the untimely ends of such as have moved tumults, commotions, and insurrections, to present them with the flourishing estate of such as live in obedience, exhorting them to allegeance, dehorting them from all trayterous and fellonious stratagems" (sig.F3v).[50] By "proving" that the stage apprehends "wanton" and murderous wives, Heywood distances his livelihood from the insubordination and unruliness affiliated with the "soules of wanton" women who overthrow their subservient positions and provoke disorder in both marital relations and the state.

But Heywood also distances his livelihood from the very attacks leveled against it in the late sixteenth and early seventeenth centuries. If *The Masque of Queens* arraigns unruly hags and theatrical uncontrollability alike, Heywood's roughly contemporary defense is careful to purge theater's connections with unruliness. He thereby militates against a discourse that had long associated social disorder with the actor, the dangerous insubordinate who in the writings of Stephen Gosson and others threatens to "infect" the commonwealth with his wanton body and volatile tongue.[51] In subscribing to a widespread cultural discourse desirous of apprehending the insubordinate wife in the interests of communal and patriarchal stability—a discourse that seems to have become particularly shrill in the early seventeenth century—Heywood stresses the extent to which actors are loyal to "the Royall and Princely services, in which we now live" (sig. A3). The anxiety that propels this insistence on fidelity is arguably the playwright's recognition that *like* wives, actors are dependent on a husband/patron. Unlike the treasonous wives of Heywood's account, actors are loyal servants working in the best interests of the state that benevolently shields them.[52]

Heywood's defense constitutes one strategy of protecting the actor's vulnerability in early modern England, a strategy that is also invoked by other playwrights such as Thomas Lodge.[53] Shakespeare's formulations regarding theater and "unruly women" in his own theatrical defense, *The Winter's Tale*, are strikingly different. If Heywood is intent on apprehending the unruly wife, Shakespeare seems particularly interested in postulating her centrality for the always unruly stage. If Heywood defends theater as a communal ritual that might purge from its presence wanton women, Shakespeare redefines the nature of this communality, making it tolerant, even accepting, of an unruly wife to whom ultimately a king is indebted. *The Winter's Tale* is full of putatively "treasonous" wives who threaten insubordination to their husbands and, by extension, the kingdom: Paulina, Hermione, and, on a significantly smaller scale, the shepherdess Mopsa, instructed by the annoyed Clown to "clamor [her] tongue" when she "whistle[s]" his "secrets" before the guests at the festivities (4.4.247–49). Yet the ghost that walks in the play to rebuke guilty consciences is not the ghost of a murdered husband but that of a murdered wife, Hermione, who appears to Antigonus in a dream shortly before he is killed by a bear and whose part Paulina threatens to play in the inevitable tragedy that would ensue should Leontes remarry: "Were

I the ghost that walk'd, I'd bid you mark / Her eye, and tell me for what dull part in't / You chose her: then I'd shriek, that even your ears / Should rift to hear me; and the words that follow'd / Should be 'Remember mine'" (5.1.63–67).[54] Far from being executed for treasonous acts of resisting their husbands and for supposed "wantonness," unruly women are instrumental in forging a new and much different relationship of subordination than that with which the play begins.

In redefining theater's relationship to female insubordination, Shakespeare appropriates the figure of the would-be actress Paulina, whose role in *The Winter's Tale* contradicts Heywood's ghostly recountings. First as noble but uncontrollable wife and scold ("What, canst not rule her?" Leontes belligerently asks Antigonus when she bursts into the court carrying Perdita) and later as legally empowered widow, Paulina occupies an ambivalent place in Sicilian (and English) society. Supposed to be a submissive wife but clearly subordinate only when she chooses to be, self-cast in the role of "loyal servant" and "obedient counsellor" (2.3.54–55) but prepared to disobey the orders of her sovereign, Paulina is the play's most vivid example of a female unruliness that evades patriarchal control. Numerous critics of Shakespeare have argued that the plays themselves defend that control.[55] Yet despite the fact that Paulina may be "working in Leontes' best interests" and that she "accepts a second marriage" when Leontes informs her that he has found her an appropriate husband in Camillo,[56] it is impossible to ignore the domineering role she occupies throughout the majority of the play. She does, of course, contribute to the play's comic climax in which the king and his slandered queen are reconciled. But the nature of this reconciliation ensures a striking change from the tainted patriarchal economy described at the beginning.

From her very first appearance, her arrival at the prison where Hermione is confined and newly delivered of her daughter, Paulina is carefully disassociated from the creation of new lives and a new order that will ultimately displace the old one. When Paulina arrives at the prison, Hermione has already given birth, aided by the midwife Emilia, a character invented only for this particular scene. While Paulina associates herself with the role of a physician—she comes to court bearing "words as medicinal as true" (2.3.37), and a chastened Leontes speaks of the "affliction" he experiences from her "cordial" in the final scene (5.3.76–77)—Shakespeare is careful to imply that she does *not* possess the medical skills most frequently associated with Elizabethan women, those of midwifery.[57] Indeed, it is a quite different doctor who presides as midwife over the birth of a new generation on Sicily: Leontes' servant Camillo, addressed by Florizel as "the medicine of our house" (4.4.588) and central to transporting everyone from Bohemia to Sicily for the play's climax.

But if Camillo ensures the continuity of the body politic, thus serving as Heywood's good "actor" who guarantees the health of the state and the maintenance of patriarchy, Paulina's medicinal capabilities are directed to much different ends. Her ministrations of "physick" are as far from those of Camillo as they are from those of the anonymous and virtually silent Erminia in Tasso's *Gerusalemme Liberata*. She does not heal wounds but keeps them open; she does not render the body "whole" and invulnerable to disease, but insists on the vulnerability of the king's body.[58] While in act 5 Dion and the other lords invoke the language of ritual purgation as they urge Leontes to remarry ("for royalty's repair, / For present comfort, and for future good, / . . . bless the bed of majesty again") (5.1.31–33), Paulina refuses to privilege the abstract and deathless body politic over the body natural. She prohibits Leontes both procreation and recreation, forbidding him to look to "future good" and to erase his past.[59] If Dion sanctions the image of a virile king whose potent disseminations ensure the vitality of the state, Paulina threatens to unman the king in her constant ritual of wounding. "Thou strik'st me / Sorely, to say [I killed the queen]," Leontes tells Paulina after she insists that he is a murderer ("she you kill'd / [Is] unparallel'd") (5.1.15–18). The process culminates in the unveiling of Hermione's body, a stone that "pierc[es]" and "rebukes" Leontes' soul (5.3.34–37) and with which Paulina threatens to "afflict [the king] further" (5.3.75).

This unmanning, moreover, takes place through a seemingly endless process of representation and uncontrollable repetition. Paulina's own engagement in maddening repetitiveness is apparent in her first exchange with Leontes. "Good my liege, I come—, / . . . I say, I come / From your good queen"; in response to Leontes' ironic "Good queen!" she reiterates: "Good queen, my lord, good queen: I say good queen" (2.3.52–59). Reentering the court to inform a suddenly chastened Leontes of Hermione's death, Paulina insists on reading and thus repeating for the king the list of heinous crimes he has just committed: the betrayal of Polixenes, the poisoning of Camillo's honor, the "casting forth to crows" of his daughter, the death of Mamilius, and finally, the murder of Hermione: "the queen, the queen, / The sweet'st dear'st creature's dead" (3.2.191–200). Although she apologizes for having "made fault / I'th'boldness of [her] speech" (217–18), she nonetheless insists on rehearsing Leontes' transgressions even in the midst of her apology.[60] But her potent speech, not to be readily silenced, has already prompted Leontes to create for himself a salient textual reminder of the consequences of his mad fictions. He orders that Mamilius and the queen be buried in the same grave, and that upon their tombstone "shall / The causes of their death appear, unto / Our shame perpetual. Once a day I'll visit / The chapel where they lie, and tears shed there / Shall be my recreation" (3.2.236–40). Unable to appropriate the purgative language of religious ritual to which Cleomenes refers when he appeals to Leontes to find a new wife ("You have . . . perform'd / A saint-like sorrow . . . Do as the heavens have done, forget your evil; / With them, forgive yourself") (5.1.1–6), Leontes will find no recreation in his prayers. Because of Paulina's constant mediations, Leontes discovers only the re-creation of the very deeds he wishes to disown, and never more blatantly than when he is affronted by the representation of Hermione herself. In her staging of a play with a single character around whom she periodically threatens to draw the curtain, Paulina continues to wound a king's body, making it permeable to the reproductions to which it had once sought impermeability.

Unlike the soothing consolations of Leontes' courtiers, who "creep like shadows" by their monarch (2.3.34), Paulina's wounding representations violently separate the king from the corporeal body politic. In thus subjecting Leontes to the dynamics of representation, she assumes by and for herself the role of a communal witness who forces Leontes to gaze upon what he has produced: "Look down / And see what death is doing" (3.2.148–49). Thus does Paulina assume the part of the exhorting witness who is "played" by a much different character in Greene's *Pandosto*. After the death of his son and queen, it is Pandosto himself who initiates the "bitter speeches" that recapitulate his crimes: "My innocent babe I have drowned in the seas; my loving wife I have slain with slanderous suspicion; my trusty friend I have sought to betray." These self-inflicted barbs begin with the king's appeal to the supreme faculty that has been the heretofore silent spectator of his mad deeds: there is no "surer witness than conscience" (p. 198). Shakespeare's dramatization of Pandosto's impassioned speech transforms the soliloquy into a dialogue in which Paulina has become the "sure witness," the paradoxical alter ego of a king. The playwright's creation of a character wholly new to the play suggests that Leontes is unable to be his *own* witness, that he requires the presence of an other to make him accountable for his deeds.[61] That other is precisely the figure who has threatened from the very beginning of the play to undermine a king's efforts at legitimation: the woman of potent words.

But Paulina is also feared insofar as her true allegiance is not to the king but to "unruly hags" from the world of death, ominous witnesses from whom she draws her authority. On the one hand, Paulina claims that the statue that appears in the play's final scene is hers. As stage director and producer of the little play that takes place before the startled gazes of royalty, Paulina consistently suggests that she is in absolute control of the drama they are witnessing. On the other hand, however, when Hermione finally speaks in the last scene, she claims that she "preserv'd / [her]self to see the issue" of Apollo's oracle and her own body (5.3.727–28). Such self-preservation intimates freedom from Paulina's powers of reproduction. Indeed, in a line that appears little more than a formality, Paulina informs Emilia when Hermione is yet in prison, "Pray you, Emilia, / Commend my best obedience to the queen" (2.2.35–36). This declaration suggests that Paulina's impunity in the presence of a king originates from her allegiance to another monarch, the living queen in act 2, and the "dead" queen in acts 3 through 5.

It is not, however, only Hermione who refuses to die, who haunts a king throughout the play and returns as a ghost in act 5.[62] Rather, Hermione belongs to a community of ghostly witnesses who range from Time itself, seen by contemporary mythographers as a manifestation of Charon, the transporter of dead souls; to Proserpine, invoked by Perdita in an elegiac apostrophe to the queen of the dead who annually returns to earth for six months ("O Proserpina, / For the flowers now that, frighted, thou let'st fall / From Dis's waggon!") (4.4.116–18); to Mamilius, whose winter's tale about "a man— / . . . [who] Dwelt by a churchyard" returns in the play with its "sprites and goblins" awakened angrily from their graves (2.1.26–30).[63] Indeed, given that the young prince is one of two characters to die in the course of the play, it might even be conjectured that the winter's tale Shakespeare conjures for his audience is told from beyond the grave: a tale whispered by Mamilius into his mother's ear while Leontes accuses Hermione of her gross infidelities, and one that constitutes a powerful alternative to the story of Leontes' own enacting. The irrepressibility of these ghosts overwhelms the exclusivity of Leontes' masque and the power of monarchs not only to disseminate evil but to destroy it with a sleight of hand. The "gap" announced by Time in his cryptic prologue to act 3 is kept open[64] by none other than Paulina, so that the ghosts Leontes wishes buried can return.

The gap to which Time alludes is, of course, the space of sixteen years, and Time's announcement marks what for most critics of the play is the transition between the first three tragic acts and the final two comic ones. Or as the old Shepherd informs the Clown, fresh from watching the bear half-dine on Antigonus at the end of act 3, "Now bless thyself: thou met'st with things dying, I with things new-born" (3.3.112–13). But this is a transition that Paulina refuses to gloss over, disallowing the burial of the old that is enacted by the Clown and the Shepherd when they go off to bury Paulina's own husband, "if there be any of him left" (3.3.129). The "gap" to which the "grave and good" Paulina (5.3.1) is particularly attentive is the gap made *by* the grave, a grave that is never completely filled.

As the agent of remembrance who freely consorts with the dead by refusing to allow graves to be filled and things to be "new-born," Paulina frustrates not only the cathartic rituals of religion and tragedy but the purgative structure of the masque Leontes wanted to enact. She thus commands and is commanded by a much different ritual of repetition and representation in a society desperately attempting to bury the dead and to initiate, as Gonzalo's speech from *The Tempest* implies, a new golden age: the golden age over which James, like his prototype Octavian, wants to preside. If "forgetting" and "vanishing" are the cornerstones of the masque and James's "Tragicomedie" alike, the ghosts of *The Winter's Tale*, like the invulnerable ghosts elsewhere in Shakespeare, prohibit such forgetting. Wrinkled and aged when she reappears in act 5, the queen serves as a potent reminder to the monarch that he cannot go backward in time. Nor can Leontes be the author he once imagined himself. The Ovidian Pygmalion who creates a *simulacra suae puellae*, an ideal maiden fashioned in ivory, is replaced by a wounded king who is forced to contemplate the ghostly image Paulina describes as hers ("my poor image"; "the stone is mine") (5.3.57–58).[65] The "remember me" of the elder Hamlet becomes the "remember mine" of the ghost Paulina threatens to play, as she makes Leontes reflect obsessively on the community he has silenced and prevents him from taking part in the ritual of cleansing he so badly desires.[66] Teeming all around the wounded king are the issue of the wounds themselves: a cadre of unruly subjects who ensure that Leontes cannot purify himself of what he has produced.

IV

A brief caveat might be appropriate regarding the above pages, which have argued that Shakespeare effaces the pretensions of omniscient authorship in order to privilege "witnesses" ever ready to become actors in their own right. For there *is* an omniscient author in the play, one who enjoys absolute immunity from the representation he controls. This is Apollo, the all-seeing sun-god who supervises the play's events from far-off Delphos, and in whom Shakespeare may well be paying homage to his king. Both author and spectator, Apollo, who utters his oracle in a climate "delicate" and "sweet" (3.1.1), attests to the crimes of a blind Leontes and determines the play's resolution from afar. One critic has even seen the trip by Leontes' courtiers to Delphos as the play's *real* masque, albeit one too sacred to be seen.[67] The invisibility of Apollo appeals to both the ideally invisible monarch of the Jacobean court, whose distaste for appearing in his subjects' representations was well known, and to a concept of transcendent authorship, uncontaminated by the conditions of performance.

Yet Shakespeare is far from endorsing Apollo as the *only* author and physician in the play. Indeed, as we have already seen, Camillo and Paulina share the role of physician, and Mamilius and the shadowy figure of Time relate the "tale" embodied on the stage. But in addition to embedding authorship in multiple figures, Shakespeare also circumscribes the extent of Apollo's control. For one thing, Shakespeare's Apollo is almost perversely dependent for his lines on the Apollo of Robert Greene. It is intriguing to note that Greene had nothing but scorn for the young Shakespeare and blasted his junior and uneducated colleague as an "upstart crow"—and thus, as Samuel Schoenbaum has conjectured, as a mime and a plagiarist.[68] Whether or not there was substantial evidence for the charge of plagiarism, it is appropriate that some twenty years after Greene's death, Shakespeare should turn to one of the Elizabethans' most popular novels and "mime" substantial portions of it. Even more striking, given Apollo's supposedly supreme authorship, is that virtually the only passage that Shakespeare quotes verbatim from Greene is the oracle itself. "Bellaria is chaste: Egistus blameless: Franion a true subject: Pandosto treacherous: His babe an innocent; And the king shall live without an heir, if that which is lost be not found," reads the oracle in *Pandosto* (p. 196). With the appropriate name changes, Shakespeare's oracle is virtually identical. Far from being original, Apollo's decree is one of the most derived moments in the play.

Yet more important than the derivation from Greene and its comment on the unprotected status of authorship is the fact that whereas Apollo's oracle in *Pandosto* circumscribes the entire novel—the tale somberly closes with Pandosto's suicide once an heir is found—*The Winter's Tale* moves beyond the Apollonian decree, and beyond Robert Greene.[69] The ministrations of Paulina, a character not in *Pandosto*, and the resurrection of Hermione elude both Greene, the author on whom Shakespeare depends for his source, and the authorial Apollo/James, on whom Shakespeare depends for protection.

What, finally, are we to make of this addendum that is supplemental to and hidden from its authors? Needless to say, *The Winter's Tale* was hardly the first work in which Shakespeare took liberty with his sources. Virtually every play he wrote might have earned for the playwright the epithet of an upstart crow. But in this symbol of addenda and supplementarity, the proverbially unruly wife who challenges the authority of husbands and kings, one might conjecture that Shakespeare saw an image of himself. Insofar as Paulina challenges the claim that women are the property of men, she creates a space for her language as both unpropertied and unproprietary.[70] As James's servant, the playwright was in what Constance Jordan has called "a functionally feminized role" vis-à-vis the monarch.[71] Although critics such as C. L. Barber argue that Shakespeare finally recognizes the validity of "female experience" in *The Winter's Tale*,[72] it may be more appropriate to interpret the gender distinctions in the play as culturally embedded and to see Shakespeare as the unruly actor whose subject position regarding his royal patron and his society was far from stable. It is certainly the case that the criticisms leveled against the unruly wife, who infuriates superiors, threatens to undo decorum, and cannot be silenced, were leveled against the actor as well.[73] Like wives, actors were supposed to be mere servants, chaste subscribers to the feudal bonds that called for their obedience. They were frequently taken to task for transgressing and defiling those bonds. Acceptance of the validity of their work, and thus of their independence, was to be long in coming.[74]

It is the play's critique of authorship that most powerfully suggests that one might read the unruly wife and physician, witch and desecrator of graves, as a useful figure for the actor and playwright. Such a critique forces one to be attentive to Natalie Davis's rhetorical question of some years ago: "How could one [in the seventeenth century] separate the idea of subordination from the existence of the sexes?"[75] This is not to claim that Shakespeare was immune from the powerful temptations of authorship.[76] Indeed, in his next and perhaps penultimate play, the playwright might be said to have recognized the bad faith implicit in a figure who consorts with the dead, and whose denials of authorship are intricately bound up with the subjugation of those who implement his commands. But in *The Tempest*, Shakespeare's ghost writer is also a royal figure, a maker of masques, and a fetishizer of books, characteristics that might as easily allude to England's Apollonian king as to the playwright. *The Winter's Tale* clearly distinguishes victims and actors from those who try to control the conditions of performance, dutifully staging Leontes' fantasies only to ensure that they will return to him in the repeatability of the theatrical occasion itself.[77] This repeatability is guaranteed not only by the constant onstage presence of Paulina, but by the offstage presence of the "dead," as well as by a paying audience of remembering witnesses. With its potentially subversive insistence on remembrance, on the dead, on a community of witnesses that royalty tries to annihilate in its quest to create a posture of purity and masculine integrity, *The Winter's Tale* is a carefully crafted challenge to the cultural poetics of the Jacobean court.

But if Shakespeare's tragicomedy refuses to close its great gaps, the next play to be encountered severely curtails the realm of speaking shades. Written by a playwright who was not himself an actor and who was anxious to assert absolute control over the volatile conditions of performance, Pierre Corneille's *Le Cid* champions the posture of authorship that Shakespeare so clearly unsettles. The final chapter turns to a play that does not preserve the past—a potentially dangerous move, as we have seen—but emphatically closes it down, albeit in the interests not of patrons and kings, but of transgressive heroes and dramatists.

7 ·

Imagining the Cid: The Example of Corneille

At first glance, the career of Pierre Corneille seems strikingly insulated from the dynamic of vulnerability discussed throughout this study. Son of a wealthy bourgeois and state administrator in Rouen, trained as a lawyer and possessed of the means to be virtually self-sufficient, Corneille exerted considerable influence over the production of his works at a time when most writers were subject to the whims of patrons and princes. Unlike Shakespeare and most of his contemporaries in France, Corneille generated his own capital for his plays, and he took advantage of his strong financial position to elicit other forms of control over his productions. As early as 1636, he was demanding that actors pay him on a pro-rata basis rather than buy his plays from him outright, and in 1643 he asked the king for the privilege of selecting the companies that would perform his works (the request was granted). Fiercely proprietary of his literary rights, Corneille rushed his controversial *Cid* into publication only six weeks after the play's first performance in January 1637. He thereby deprived the actors who had first presented *Le Cid* at the Hotel de Marais of the usual privilege of exclusively producing it themselves.[1] Moreover, in 1643 he took the unprecedented step of licensing one of his plays (*Cinna*) in his own name rather than that of the bookseller. Finally, Corneille was one of the first practicing playwrights to produce a significant body of theoretical work. His three *Discours* on dramatic poetry and the *Examens* that precede each of the 22 plays in the 1660 edition of his *Oeuvres* constitute an extensive critical and theoretical output virtually unique for its time.[2]

Yet according to Corneille's critics, nowhere did the playwright more overwhelmingly defy the operative norms of cultural production than in the play—and the circumstances surrounding it—that caused the greatest literary scandal of the seventeenth century: *Le Cid*. Modeled on the 1618 Spanish play by Guillen de Castro, *Las Mocedades del Cid*, Corneille's drama centers on the hero or *grande âme* Rodrigue, who exists above and outside of royal law.[3] He invokes for himself a different law instead: the desire of an admiring public. What emerges as an almost inevitable process of legitimation, supported by the vox populi as well as the aristocratic characters within *Le Cid*, was uncannily mirrored in Paris in 1637 by the public that came in droves to applaud Corneille's work.[4] As the following pages will argue, the plot of *Le Cid* foreshadows the historical narrative in which Corneille implicated his audience,[5] enlisting its complicity in his "transgressions" as arriviste from Rouen.

It was the apparent boldness of this appeal that not only infuriated Corneille's fellow dramatists, understandably jealous of their younger colleague's sudden fame, but provoked the interest of the most powerful patron in Paris: Cardinal Richelieu.[6] Just a year prior to the publication of *Le Cid*, Richelieu had supported the creation of the Académie française, designed, as one recent critic has put it, to be "a permanent, institutional instrument . . . with which to maintain royal dominance over the political culture."[7] It was the dramatist Georges de Scudéry, largely responsible for initiating the exchange of some 35 pamphlets written for and against *Le Cid* in almost as many weeks, who first petitioned the newly formed Academy to preside over the quarrel—"It is for me to attack, Corneille to defend, but for you to judge" (Gasté, p. 215). But Richelieu proceeded to advise the apparently reluctant group to comply with Scudéry's request and judge the merits and failings of Corneille's immensely popular play. Under the capable guidance of Jean Chapelain, the members of the Academy dutifully went on to furnish the first real test of Richelieu's cultural preeminence by virtually condemning *Le Cid*.[8] The condemnation looked ahead to the programmatic remarks of the consummate neoclassicist François Hédelin, the abbé d'Aubignac, who advocated a drama that would teach "those things that will enhance public society and reconcile the people to their public duty."[9] The Academy's albeit reluctant responsiveness to official pressure was also indicative of the extent to which France's cultural *officiers* served and would continue to serve as mouthpieces for the ideology of the court.[10]

In light of this attempt to bring Parisian culture within the domain of Richelieu, Corneille's preface to his comedy *La Suivante*, published while *Le Cid* was still in the hands of the Academy, is a direct attack on the official negotiations that were under way. In his dedicatory letter to an anonymous reader, he announces that he is "abandoning [his] work to the public" whom he has always sought to please.[11] The appeal to a public voice, which Corneille distinguishes from that of *les doctes* (the learned), might seem conventional, and indeed on one level it looks back to Erasmus's claim that he was abandoning his incomplete *Adagia* to his readers. Yet the manipulativeness inherent in the *avocat*'s profession of abandonment attests to the striking novelty of Corneille's formulation. As an outsider from the provinces, Corneille was in an unenviable position vis-à-vis his more established colleagues, who in many cases outclassed him.[12] His claim to abandon his play will be seen in the following pages as part of a complex strategy designed to place his spectators and readers in a posture of responsibility, and hence vulnerability. In this light, Corneille may be said to have more in common with Cellini than with Erasmus. Despite the fact that his turn to the *voix publique* sharply distinguishes him from the Florentine goldsmith, he nonetheless shares with Cellini the aggressiveness of a subject trying to situate himself beyond traditional spheres of rivalry and legitimation: the marketplace for Cellini; the salons and courtly circles of Paris for Corneille.

But Corneille's appeal to a broadly defined public had its cost. As the end of this chapter will suggest, that cost was reflected not only in Corneille's three-year silence following the Academy's negative verdict, but in his substantial revisions of *Le Cid* and his critical writings of 1660. Corneille's career, to be sure, is a testament to the growing independence of the writer in early modern society. This independence was considerably mediated, however, by the new bureaucratization of culture, marked as it was by an incipient paternalism that will be the focus of discussion in the course of this chapter. Thus Corneille's career also attests to the continuing need for and interference of institutions of official protection in the seventeenth century. The defensive image of self-possession articulated in the critical writings of 1660 is, as we shall see, far different from that found in the confident *Cid* of 1637, the play that won Corneille a level of popularity unprecedented in the history of French theater and the equally unprecedented hostility of France's academicians. It is to that play and to the "étrange monstre"[13] that immediately preceded it, *L'Illusion comique*, that the following pages turn.[14]

I

"Eres sombra? Eres visión?"
(Are you a shade? are you an apparition?)
Ximena to Rodrigo, in Castro's
Las Mocedades del Cid

At the close of *L'Illusion comique*, produced in early 1636, Corneille launches into a revealing glorification of the early-seventeenth-century stage. To be sure, the play as a whole constitutes Corneille's glowing praise of theater. Most of *L'Illusion comique* is a play within a play, the performance of "spectres parlants" (speaking ghosts)[15] called into a desolate grotto by the powerful magician Alcandre to enact for a desperate father the whereabouts of his long-lost son. But this praise becomes explicit only in the last scene. Dismayed to find out that his son Clindor has become an actor, the spectator Pridamant has his despair put to rest as the magus Alcandre replies:

Cessez de vous en plaindre. A présent le théâtre
Est en un point si haut que chacun l'idolâtre,
Et ce que votre temps voyait avec mépris
Est aujourd'hui l'amour de tous les bons esprits,
L'entretien de Paris, le souhait des provinces,
Le divertissement le plus doux de nos princes,
Les délices du peuple, et le plaisir des grands:
Il tient le premier rang parmi leurs passe-temps.
(1645–52)

(Stop your complaints. The theater has now reached such heights that everyone worships it. That which in your day you viewed with scorn is today the passion of all witty people: the talk of Paris, the fancy of the provinces, the sweetest entertainment of our princes, the delight of the people, and the pleasure of the great: among all of their pastimes, it occupies first place.)

Silenced by Alcandre's persuasive argument and grateful for the magician's having reconciled him to Clindor via the magic art of illusion, Pridamant asks how he might repay the man earlier described to him as omniscient ("Rien n'est secret pour lui dans tout cet univers") (59). To this request, Alcandre generously responds that his services are not for sale. "Servir les gens d'honneur est mon plus grand désir, / J'ai pris ma récompense en vous faisant plaisir" (To serve men of honor is my greatest desire; my recompense is to be found in your pleasure) (1683–84).

In the figure of Alcandre, the audience encounters a strikingly original version of the wise hermit called upon to undo the labyrinthine knots of many a misguided romance of noble heroes and heroines on the European stage.[16] Corneille's unconventional magician has for a foil not the trials of aristocratic love but the urbane setting of Paris in which the rocky career of Pridamant's prodigal son unfolds. It is only the mediating presence of this magician that enables the suspicious Pridamant to accept his son's acting career—a career that follows Clindor's engagement in, and is but little different from, the socially dubious occupations of mountebank, broadsider, and quack.

But the means whereby Alcandre reconciles the bourgeois to Clindor's new role, magnanimous though the gesture might be, reveals a careful understanding of the father's concealed designs. The subject of Alcandre's play within a play is the "sujet" of Pridamant's hidden sorrow—his son;[17] the "commerce des ombres" in which Alcandre engages is the projection of his solitary audience's "traits les plus cachés" (most hidden features) (64), of which the most hidden of all is gnawing guilt: "N'est-il pas vrai que son éloignement / Par un juste remords te gêne incessamment?" (Is it not true that his estrangement harrows you incessantly with just remorse?) (103–4). Playing on the guilt of an overly harsh father who has needlessly disowned his son, the magician feigns Clindor's death in order to evoke from Pridamant a cry of grief, and he resurrects his son to enable a joyful reconciliation, penetrating behind the curtain ("ici on relève la toile") (1610) lowered after Clindor's "death" to reveal that Clindor has been but an actor in a play.[18] But Alcandre penetrates behind another veil as well. Before the play of Clindor's life begins, Alcandre prematurely draws the curtain of his little stage to display a group of nobles, among which is Pridamant's son: "Jugez de votre fils par un tel équipage. / Eh bien, celui d'un Prince a-t-il plus de splendeur?" (Judge your son by his dress: is he not more glamorous than a Prince?) (134–35). As Pridamant discovers in act 5, the noble garment worn by Clindor is merely the garb of an actor. But Alcandre discerns and manipulates Pridamant's desires for social elevation by catering knowingly to his fantasies of becoming a member of the *noblesse*. It is *as* a noble that Clindor first appears, and it is virtually as a noble that he leaves the stage. Once Alcandre impresses upon the still-resistant father the fact that "the theater is a fiefdom where rents are good, and your son's *métier* is so sweet that he gains more goods and more honor than had he stayed at home with you,"[19] Pridamant no longer needs encouragement to accept Clindor's new trade: "I no longer dare complain."[20]

While the magician benevolently refuses payment for his efforts, there is something more underhanded at work in the grotto than his professed liberality suggests, and it hinges on precisely those guilty secrets of Pridamant's heart that are known to no one but Alcandre. In this play, which in many ways is an important prologue to *Le Cid*, one quickly becomes aware of what Bernard Dort has called the discomfiting coexistence of innocence and power in Corneille's drama:[21] of the manner in which Alcandre's vulnerable spectator, chastened by remorse and desirous of transcending his social station, is forced to be complicitous in a social institution that both validates and exploits his secrets "les plus cachés." The dark grotto from which Alcandre warns Pridamant not to step for fear of death ("De ma grotte surtout ne sortez qu'après moi: / Sinon, vous êtes mort") (216–17) becomes both prison and relentlessly private theater over whose "fantômes vains" (empty ghosts) (218) Alcandre exerts control—a control rendered possible by his invasion of the "phantasms" of his audience, revealed to all in "ces lieux sombres" with their uncertain light.

Le Cid also launches a defense of a figure who exists for a substantial part of the play in "lieux sombres"—shadowy realms perhaps best described as the audience's imaginations, where the consummate actor and hero Rodrigue triumphs long before he sets foot on the stage. And just as Clindor is granted immunity by a guilty and forgiving father whose social aspirations are ironically fulfilled by his son, so is the daring Rodrigue absolved by the various parties he has offended in the course of the play. But Rodrigue's immunity from punishment would not as quickly become the immunity of Corneille. A play about a hero who violates a king's authority by engaging in forbidden duels and leading his own army, and a heroine who violates decorum by agreeing to marry her father's murderer, was bound to spark popular sentiment as well as critical hostility in the Paris of the 1630's. This was a period, after all, when Richelieu was attempting to curb the power of the seigneurs, to contain the ambitions of bourgeois such as Corneille, and to forge a cultural ethos that would make France preeminent in Europe. And *Le Cid*, moreover, not only had as its chief protagonist the legendary hero of the nation with which France was currently at war, but virtually plagiarized a Spanish play, according to Corneille's critics.

But it took more than *Le Cid*, which echoes *L'Illusion comique* in its buoyancy and what one critic has called its "confident youth,"[22] to inspire the wrath of Corneille's colleagues and ultimately of Richelieu. In the "Excuse à Ariste," a letter in verse published anonymously (but undoubtedly by Corneille) only weeks after *Le Cid* was first performed, the playwright dared to boast of his recent success—a success he claimed to owe to no one but himself. "Mon travail sans appui monte sur le théâtre / . . . . Je ne dois qu'à moi seul toute ma renommée" (My work is staged in the theater without support . . . . I owe only to myself all my renown) (Gasté, p. 64): so boasted the author of the "Excuse" in a line that became one of the cornerstones of the imminent quarrel.[23] Attacking the inefficacious and corrupt system of patronage, the author declares that he has made his own name "sans brigue"—without the underhanded maneuvers of poets desperate to enter the contaminated circles of high society and courtly patronage. Unlike those servile others, he will execute his own "loix" (laws), the word that tellingly ends the poem. His fellow playwrights might wish to embrace the subservient status of artists who go "de réduit en réduit" (from salon to salon) (Gasté, p. 64) to ensure their reputations and success, but he asks only to live in liberty and to have the right to refuse writing verses at another's command—the pretext for the poem being the request by an ecclesiastic to compose lines for music. In "cette scandaleuse lettre," to quote one of Corneille's more rancorous critics, the playwright Jean Mairet (Gasté, p. 291), Corneille does not merely profess to be outside of the network of patronage and what in a pithy response to Mairet he satirizes as "le petit commerce" in which Mairet engages.[24] Rather, he openly solicits the public to support his independence, a public whose favorable reception of his plays has putatively sanctioned his departure from the official means of dramatic production.

It is with a critique of the "Excuse" that Georges de Scudéry launches his attack on *Le Cid* in his *Observations*. After calling attention to his usual tendency for restraint, Scudéry goes on to declare that Corneille's flagrant defiance of "la cause commune" has left him no choice other than to expose the play's—and by extension, the playwright's—defects:

> When I saw that [the author] was deifying himself by his own hand, that he was speaking of himself as we normally speak of others, that he was even committing his self-praise to print, that he seems to believe that he is conferring too great an honor on the greatest minds of the age to offer them his left hand, I realized that it would be unjust and cowardly of me not to act on the public behalf, and that it would be proper to impel him to read that serviceable inscription that the ancients could find carved above the door of one of the Greek temples: Know thyself.[25]

But given this strident beginning, it is intriguing that Scudéry does not find in the figure of Rodrigue an apt parallel for the brash Corneille who claims in his preface to *Le Cid* that his work has met with universal acclaim. The connection between the writer of "Je ne dois qu'à moi seul toute ma renommée" and the hero Rodrigue who, when asked by the captured Moorish princes for the leader of the Spanish troops, simply responds, "Je me nomme" (I name myself), has seemed to some readers virtually transparent.[26] The playwright brashly announces his independence from the very systems of patronage on which Scudéry has built his entire career; Rodrigue attacks the Moors without his king's authority and with his private army of five hundred companions, handily upsetting the invasion. The playwright, despite his avowed independence from France's powerful elite, goes on to win the praise of the people and the court; Rodrigue obtains not only his king's pardon for murdering Spain's champion in a forbidden duel but the praise and love of the Spanish public and the champion's daughter as well. Much has been made of the fact that the "Excuse" was composed several years before *Le Cid* was even performed.[27] But this hypothetically early date of composition would only confirm an early interest on Corneille's part in distancing himself from official networks of authentication. It would, moreover, argue for the existence of a strategy of self-protection evident both in Corneille's career and, as will be seen, in *Le Cid*: one grounded in the paradoxically assertive rhetoric of vulnerability. Finally, if the "Excuse" was indeed written earlier than *Le Cid*, its belated publication would echo a strategy that we will see at work in *Le Cid* itself: Corneille publishes his scandalous letter only *after* his play has met with untold success.

Scudéry's oversight of a parallel between author of the letter and hero of the play might in part be explained by his insistence, following his brief preamble, that "J'atacque *le Cid*, et non pas son Autheur" (I attack the *Cid*, and not its author) (Gasté, p. 72)—a claim somewhat difficult to believe, given the virulence with which Scudéry begins his pamphlet. Yet in fact his critique of *Le Cid* scarcely addresses the warrior whose "portraict vivant" (living portrait) Corneille's play purports to sketch for the audience. Rather, Scudéry's critique is an unrelenting diatribe against a much different character: the noblewoman Chimène, who renounces her pursuit to avenge her father's death when she confesses her love for her father's murderer. To Scudéry, Chimène becomes nothing less than a "monstre," a "fille désnaturée," and finally a "parricide"—an interpretation that effectively preempts Rodrigue's role in the duel and brings the entire play to bear on Chimène alone.

Although Jean Chapelain is not quite as harsh on Chimène in his *Sentimens de l'Academie françoise*, he nonetheless concurs in condemning a noblewoman unable to resist her passion. Chimène is a "fille trop desnaturée" (Gasté, p. 372) who betrays the duty she owes her father, and who expresses her love so vehemently that she is capable of making a powerless audience forget "the rules" and itself (Gasté, p. 375). "Bad examples are contagious, especially on the stage," intones Chapelain at the beginning of his treatise (Gasté, p. 360), thereby invoking the sentiment of an antitheatrical polemic that flourished throughout the seventeenth century in the writings of the Jansenist Pierre Nicole and the ecclesiastic Bossuet. Just as Nicole would accuse theater (and particularly Corneille's theater) of consisting of "ombres des ombres" that subvert Christian vigilance,[28] so does Chapelain, the ardent defender of the "utilité publique," suggest that Corneille creates a theater of *éclat*[29] that renders its audience not only sympathetic but captive to Chimène's passion. In the accounts of both Chapelain and Scudéry, it is Chimène, not Rodrigue, who is responsible for the atrocities of a play that offends against law and order. It is Chimène who becomes, in effect, the creator of the Cid—and *Le Cid*—and never more blatantly than when she agrees to marry Rodrigue only hours after her father's death.

Such attentiveness to the role of Chimène no doubt stems from a pervasive misogyny alien to neither Scudéry nor Chapelain. Yet a careful reading of the play suggests that in fact Corneille's critics responded to an element of the work half-playfully addressed in *L'Illusion comique*: the extent to which Corneille seeks to implicate his audience in the shadowy projections of figures on the stage and thereby render them complicitous in the creation of a hero far more sympathetic and grandiose than Pridamant's prodigal son.[30] This is not to go so far as to say that Scudéry read *Le Cid* the way Corneille wished it to be read. But it is to suggest that in making Chimène responsible for the play's scandalous denouement, in ascribing to her actions that Rodrigue alone commits, Scudéry only exaggerates, rather than wildly imagines, the rhetorical strategy at work in *Le Cid*. It is a strategy that displaces guilt from Rodrigue onto the admiring spectator, making his crime appear not only willed by others but virtually inevitable.[31]

For to a large extent, Corneille craftily shapes Rodrigue as a product of others' imaginings, as a "spectre parlant." Corneille alludes to the ghostly nature of Rodrigue before the play even begins, in his preface. Praising his hero, who continues to live "six hundred years" after his first appearance in Spanish history, Corneille calls to mind one of the legendary events associated with Rodrigo in the *Romancero*, a collection of verses on el Cid published in the early seventeenth century: "His body, carried about by his army, won battles after his death" (Preface, 4–5). The *Romancero* elaborates in more detail on Rodrigue's ghostly presence. When King Bucar of the Moors attacked Valencia, the embalmed body of the Cid, complete with sword and livery, was placed on a horse and directed into the attacking troops. Frightened by the image that descended upon them, the Moors fled, and the Christians won the day.[32]

Just as Rodrigo is a phantasm who renders his enemy defenseless in the fragment from the *Romancero*, so is Rodrigue an essentially spectral figure in *Le Cid*. Whereas in Corneille's Spanish source, *Las Mocedades del Cid*, Rodrigo appears in the first scene and utters his first words only 30 lines into the play, Corneille's Rodrigue does not appear until the end of act 1. While Corneille may be simply following a dramatic convention, he calls attention to this convention and its ramifications by using Rodrigue's absence to force the other characters to create him. Yet the characters' initial efforts at such creation are significantly tainted with an almost pathological guilt, and as a result those efforts must be painstakingly concealed. The process of imagining the Cid is thus a process of careful and titillating revelation, starting with the first scene. In his attempt to learn who his daughter Chimène wishes to marry, the Comte de Gormas instructs Chimène's confidante, Elvire, to "va l'en entretenir, mais dans cet entretien / Cache mon sentiment et descouvre le sien" (go, converse with her about this, but while conversing hide my feelings and discover her own) (25–26). In the course of this conversation with the confidante, the Comte paints his own "portraict vivant" of Rodrigue for us: "sur tout n'a trait en son visage / Qui d'un homme de coeur ne soit la haute image" (above all, every feature of the man bears the worthy image of a noble spirit) (15–16). Two scenes later, it is the Infante who portrays for the audience and *her* horrified confidante, Léonor, the young man with whom she is in love, despite the fact that she is a princess and Rodrigue but a knight. The Infante will embark on a much more elaborate sequence after she hears that Rodrigue and the Comte have gone off to duel:

> J'ose m'imaginer qu'à ses moindres exploits
> Les Royaumes entiers tomberont sous ses loix,
> Et mon amour flatteur desja ma persuade
> Que je le vois assis au trosne de Grenade,
> Les Mores subjuguez trembler en l'adorant,
> L'Arragon recevoir ce nouveau conquerant,
> Le Portugal se rendre, et ses nobles journées
> Porter delà les mers ses hautes destinées,
> Au milieu de l'Afrique arborer ses lauriers:
> En fin tout ce qu'on dit des plus fameux guerriers,
> Je l'attends de Rodrigue apres cette victoire,
> Et fais de son amour un sujet de ma gloire.
>
> (537–48)

(I dare to imagine that with the least of his exploits, entire realms will fall beneath his laws. My flattering love already persuades me that I see him seated on the throne of Granada, the beaten Moors trembling as they worship him, Aragon greeting this new conqueror, Portugal surrendering itself, and his noble deeds carrying his destinies beyond the sea: to Africa, where he will be crowned with laurels. Finally, all that is said of the most famous warriors I expect to be said of Rodrigue after this victory, and I make his love a subject of my glory.)

The parallel passage in Castro is considerably less evocative; more importantly, it is uttered only *after* the Infanta has seen Rodrigo display his dazzling talents in a tournament.[33] But Corneille's Infante "dares to imagine" Rodrigue as conqueror long before anyone in the play, the unfortunate Comte included, has even seen him with "sword in hand" ("Toy qu'on n'a jamais veu les armes à la main") (410). The pedestrian Léonor instantly tries to disabuse the princess of her fantasy—"Mais Madame, voyez où portez son bras, / En suite d'un combat qui peut-estre n'est pas" (But Madame, look where you carry his arm, in the midst of a combat that may not take place)—but this attempt at deflation is short-lived. The next scene reports of Rodrigue's victory ("Sire, le Comte est mort") (638), and in rapid succession other characters extend and endorse the fantasy of the princess about Rodrigue's ability to fashion his own domain of shade beneath which his victims will adore him. Before the Moors attack Seville, Rodrigue's father Don Diègue urges him to use his "vaillantes mains" in spilling the "sang des Africains" (1093–94), and the king echoes the Infante's lines when he says of the newly defeated Moors, "A ce seul nom de Cid ils trembleront d'effroy, / Ils t'ont nommé [Rodrigue] Seigneur, et te voudront pour Roy" (The name alone of the Cid will make them tremble with terror. Such have they named you, and they will want you for their King) (1853–54). With his *récit* in act 4 of his nocturnal battle, Rodrigue fulfills all of the characters' dreams as he announces that two Moorish princes have fallen into his hands and called him their "Seyid."

This *récit*, in fact, demands close attention, because like the sequence of events just outlined, it demonstrates a constant occurrence in Corneille's play: Rodrigue only reveals himself when others have already revealed their imaginings of him.[34] This lengthy description, performed for the court shortly after Rodrigue's victory, begins with a meticulous account of his furtive plan to conceal himself and his warriors along the river and wait for the Moors to disembark. Surprised by Rodrigue and "five hundred men," whom he has audaciously gathered in the name of the king—"je feins hardiment d'avoir receu de vous / L'ordre qu'on me voit suivre" (I boldly feign to have received from you the order that they see me follow) (1281–82)—the Moors at first panic and retreat. Temporarily bolstered by the presence of their princes, they renew what was to have been their unforeseen invasion. In describing the battles that ensue when the Moors redouble their effort, Corneille gives his hero lines appropriate for the play as a whole:

> O combien d'actions, combien d'exploits celebres
> Furent ensevelis dans l'horreur des tenebres,
> Où chacun seul témoin des grands coups qu'il donnoit,
> Ne pouvoit discerner où le sort inclinoit!
> J'allois de tous costez encourager les nostres,
> Faire avancer les uns, et soustenir les autres,
> Ranger ceux qui venoient, les pousser à leur tour,
> Et n'en pus rien scavoir jusques au point du jour.
> Mais en fin sa clarté monstra nostre advantage,
> Le More vit sa perte et perdit le courage,

> Et voyant un renfort qui nous vint secourir
> Changea l'ardeur de vaincre à la peur de mourir.
>
> (1311–22)

(O how many acts, how many wondrous exploits were shrouded in the horror of the shadows, where each man, sole witness to the great blows that he gave, was unable to tell where fate was leading us! I ran everywhere to encourage our men, to make some advance forward, to restrain others, to marshal the new arrivals, pushing them forward in their turn; and I could know nothing of them until the dawn. But finally the light of day showed us that we won: the disheartened Moors knew they were defeated, and when they saw the reinforcements coming to help us, their ardor to win was vanquished by their fear of death.)

In the relentlessly solitary combats of a dark night each man alone is witness to his victory or defeat, a deadening isolation that can be ended, and its significance grasped, only when daylight reveals the Spaniards' triumph. What Corneille earlier described as "l'obscure clarté" of the stars yields to the precise clarity of daylight and the Moors' recognition of their defeat. Ignorance gives way to knowledge as the Moorish princes, "voiant à leurs pieds tomber tous leurs soldats" (seeing all their soldiers fall at their feet) (1334), ask for the commander of the Spanish troops. Rodrigue steps forward to name himself, and the Moors immediately surrender. In a line already cited in connection with the "Excuse à Ariste," "ils demandent le Chef, je me nomme, ils se rendent" (They ask for the commander, I name myself, they surrender) (1336).

Particularly striking in this passage is its conflation of two contradictory vocabularies of force and of "natural" phenomena, its juxtaposition of a language of "strategèmes" and war with images of a daybreak that peacefully reveals what has transpired. It is notable that the king is complicit in the neutralization of this violence in the same way that Rodrigue elides the forcefulness and deception implicit in his *récit* by insisting that the dispersal of shadows simply obeys the natural cycle of time: "en fin sa clarté monstra nostre advantage." In greeting the man who only hours before was little more than a common criminal, Don Fernand characterizes Rodrigue as the "généreux hérétier d'une illustre famille / Qui fut toujours la gloire et l'appui de Castile" (courageous heir of an illustrious family that has always been the glory and stronghold of Castile) (1219–20). The latent inheritance literally comes to light as dawn touches the shore of Seville and overwhelms what might have been Rodrigue's death sentence. The ensuing rewriting of Rodrigue's identity becomes the inevitable confirmation of the military supremacy of his family—a rewriting that effaces his tarnished past as the murderer of Chimène's father as well as the life story of that father, who was the former champion of Don Fernand's kingdom. But it also neutralizes the violence inherent in Rodrigue's military victory, making the flight of the Moorish soldiers and the capture of their kings less the result of a surprise attack grounded in Rodrigue's act of deception ("je feins hardiment . . .") than the product of a benign, almost apocalyptic process.[35]

The effect of such a collapse of temporality is to absorb the arriviste and potentially dangerous subject Rodrigue into a story that has already been written, that not only sanctions but demands his presence in its unfolding. The great solitary figure who is loyal to nothing but Chimène and his own glory—Rodrigue dreams of little else in his soliloquies than how he will be remembered when he is dead—becomes the product of a script he did not write. For Rodrigue, this emergence into daylight follows two acts of concealment in the shadows that have pursued him since he killed the "sole support" of Spain and the father of his lover. After slaying the Comte, the young criminal moves from one realm of darkness to another in an effort to escape certain retribution at the hands of his king: from his hiding place in the house of mourning where, Elvire accuses him, he has come to brave the shadow of the Comte (755); to "l'ombre de la nuit" in which he masks his departure from Chimène's house (985); to the "sombre" passageways of dark Seville where his father desperately searches for his outlawed son and finds himself embracing "only a shadow" (1024). In each case, Rodrigue only appears when the other who will become his conquered rival reveals his or her own vulnerability. He spends an entire scene concealed behind the curtain while a weeping Chimène admits to her confidante that she still loves Rodrigue despite his horrific act; his father imagines himself near death in the event that he cannot find his son; and the Moors are exposed beneath pale moonlight as they furtively enter

Seville. The sudden emergence of daylight becomes the moment of anagnorisis when the young man recognizes and is recognized in his new role as Spain's champion. The mere act of "voiant" (seeing), performed by the Moors as though they were spectators in a theater, is enough to convince them of their defeat.

But just as the shadowy realm of others' hidden secrets procures for Alcandre his power and mystique in *L'Illusion comique*, so does this realm define the world in which Rodrigue labors, as he conceals himself in order to obtain an advantage over those who will become his subjects. Rodrigue's pretense of having been ordered by the king to gather forces; the carefully orchestrated stratagem designed to deceive its victims; his role during the battle as "life-force and living example, an ubiquitous presence who inspires and sustains":[36] all of these are symptomatic of the deceptive darkness in which Rodrigue spends much of the play. Once those "shadows" are dispersed, however, his criminality is effaced. Or in the lines Don Fernand utters when he instructs Chimène to marry her father's murderer: "Le temps assez souvent a rendu legitime / Ce qui sembloit d'abord ne se pouvoir sans crime" (Time has often sanctioned what at first seemed impossible without crime) (1839–40). But this inevitable process of legitimation is unimaginable without the dynamics of violence and displaced vulnerability that attend it. If it is indeed the Moorish princes who first acknowledge Rodrigue as king, it is likewise true that they do so only when they are in a posture of surrender, abandoned by their men and overwhelmed by the "mille cris éclatans" (thousand startling cries) of Rodrigue's warriors.[37]

It is not incidental that Chimène bursts into the midst of Rodrigue's *récit*, in effect taking over the status of the newly conquered Moors as she invades the courtroom with what Don Fernand disparagingly labels as bothersome news ("fascheuse nouvelle") (1341). Until act 4, it was the Moors who endangered the fragile Castilian state and onto whom Rodrigue's outlawry was displaced. After the battle, however, Chimène becomes the new threat to Castile, as she appeals to Don Fernand to seek the death of the man who has just saved Spain. Soon to be branded a "rebelle" by her king (1797), Chimène must be forced to reveal her concealed passion in the public space of the court. There she becomes, like the Moors, the unknowing participant in a theatrical stratagem as the king seeks to "discover" her secret love by proposing a miniature play within a play. "Contrefaites le triste" (Pretend to be sad), he instructs his court before Chimène's entrance, seeking their complicity in his plan to inform Chimène that the valiant Rodrigue has died of wounds in battle—news that predictably causes Chimène to faint and Don Diègue to observe, "Mais voyez qu'elle pasme, et d'un amour parfait / Dans cette pasmoison, Sire, admirez l'effet" (But see how she faints; Sire, admire the effect of a perfect love in her swoon) (1353–54). Vulnerable not to Don Fernand, who orders her to marry the victor of a duel between Rodrigue and Don Sanche, but to the "secrets de son ame" (secrets of her soul) (1355), Chimène is instructed by her king, "Consulte bien ton coeur, Rodrigue en est le maistre, / Et ta flame en secret rend graces à ton Roy / Dont la faveur conserve un tel amant pour toy" (Consult your heart: Rodrigue is its master, and your love secretly thanks your king, whose favor has conserved such a suitor for you) (1400–1402).[38]

Yet this benign process of theatrical legitimation is only slightly less invasive and manipulative than the encounter that takes place shortly before Rodrigue fights the Moors. In a midnight duel that foreshadows the violence to come, Rodrigue makes a sensational appearance from behind (one presumes) a curtain in Chimène's bedroom to offer her his sword, still stained with her father's blood, in the hope that she will use it to kill him.[39] The encounter occurs only moments after Rodrigue has heard Chimène utter her love for him in what she supposes is the privacy of her boudoir: to her confidante's horrified "Il vous prive d'un père, et vous l'aimez encore!" she replies, "C'est peu de dire aimer, Elvire, je l'adore" (He kills your father, and you still love him!—It is not enough to say that I love him, Elvire: I adore him) (819–20). But what forces the warrior-to-be from his hiding place is Chimène's proposal to concoct what Elvire calls "un dessein . . . tragique": to seek vengeance against Rodrigue and then to kill herself. It is at this moment that Rodrigue, brandishing the gruesome sword, announces that he is offering himself up to his avenger and thus to his death. It is at this moment, too, that Corneille subtly rephrases the lines of Castro's Ximena, as Ximena's interrogation of a "sombra" and "visión" becomes "Elvire, où sommes nous? et qu'est que je voy? / Rodrigue en ma maison! Rodrigue devant moy!" (Elvire, where are we? and what is it I see? Rodrigue in my house! Rodrigue in front of me!) (861–62).[40] Incredibly enough, Corneille repeats this scenario in act 5 when, in an episode completely new to the "legend" of el Cid, Rodrigue seeks Chimène out "en plein jour" (in broad daylight) to announce that he will let Don Sanche kill him in the duel to which the king has reluctantly conceded. Moreover, in both cases, the startled Chimène, her "sombra" taking on a powerfully physical presence before her, refuses to let Rodrigue die. "Go: I am your adversary, not your hangman," she persuades him in her chamber; "If ever love burned within you, be the victor in a combat of which Chimène is the prize," she instructs him when he confronts her before the duel.[41]

What appears to emerge from darkness into light under a king's benign shadow is nothing less than Chimène's (and the audience's) desire—a desire heretofore admitted only in the secret places of the stage. Mimicking the trajectory of *L'Illusion comique*, Corneille strives to protect himself and his marginal figure by implicating the desires of a discerning but captive subject on his behalf.[42] It was precisely this captivity that concerned not so much Scudéry, wary of the extent to which *Le Cid* served as a vehicle for Corneille's deification, but Jean Chapelain, sensitive to the implications that Corneille's play and its unprecedented success had for the institution of theater in France.

Far more cognizant than Scudéry of the patterns of displaced desire in *Le Cid*, Chapelain begins his *Sentimens de l'Academie françoise* by declaring that "those who, driven by some desire for Glory, give their works to the Public, ought not to find it strange that the Public should make itself their Judge" (Gasté, p. 355) (perhaps an allusion to Corneille's profession of abandonment in *La Suivante*). He sets out to reclaim for the "public" that of which Corneille has deprived them: their "liberté" to accept or to reject what is performed before them.[43] Invoking the humanists' conception of a "respublique des lettres" (republic of letters), Chapelain argues that the dazzled public can only be restored to its proper role of judge if the "self-love" that blinds Corneille is tempered by "criticism that does not trespass the bounds of equity." Often such a critique can "open the eyes of a man blinded by self-love, enabling him to see just how far he has strayed from his goal (du bout de la carriere) and encouraging him to redouble his efforts so that he can achieve it" (Gasté, p. 356). "Le bout de la carrière" is a colloquial expression for "goal." But "carriere" literally means a race track, and the word alerts the reader to Chapelain's central metaphor in the *Sentimens*: that of a common ground of competition that should be supervised by the Academy itself. Like Scudéry, Chapelain finds Corneille to be a victim of self-deception. Hence the necessity of undeceiving him ("dessille les yeux"). But whereas Scudéry is content with revealing the deception, Chapelain earnestly seeks a program of reform whereby the chastened Corneille might reenter the "respublique" from which he has deliberately exiled himself, and whereby the republic itself will not fall captive to the clever strategies of the dramatist.

Chapelain's *Sentimens* is written in the official language of the bureaucrat whose project is to create a superficially benevolent paternalism that legislates careers and determines in the interest of the public body when self-love has blinded one to the common cause. It is in the interest of this body that the poet should "correct the evil customs found in history and render them benign through his Poetry for the good of the Public" (Gasté, p. 369), Chapelain says, apropos of Corneille's refusal to transform the evil Chimène of history into a dutiful daughter. Chapelain offers several corrective emendations—not only does he suggest that Corneille give us a "chaste" Chimène who resists love and kills herself, but at one point he recommends that Chimène discover at the end of the play that the Comte was *not*, in fact, her father! Far from protecting Chimène from "les mauvaises moeurs" (the evil customs) of Spain and the sword that so consistently turns against her, Corneille ungallantly subjects his female protagonist to the reputation of "une femme impudique" (a shameless woman). He thus both perpetuates and subjects himself to a tradition that France, the new guardian of manners and culture, should ideally transform. "Just as the historian must defer to the truth, so must the Poet defer to propriety (bien-seance)" (Gasté, p. 416): a "bien-seance" that involves the purgation of history's contaminations in the name of protecting a vulnerable public.[44]

That this doctrine of protection had political resonances can hardly be doubted. Scudéry's accusations against the arriviste Corneille merely set the stage for the verdict of the Academy, which, acting in the interest of its powerful "protecteur," cautioned against the improprieties committed by subjects and monarch alike in Corneille's play. The paradigm of protection advocated by Chapelain and his references to a "republic of letters" constitute an attempt to relocate the gaze of influence in the play. In Corneille's *Cid*, the sanctioning gaze is that of the desiring audience, dazzled by the play's hero and the sword he so powerfully and duplicitously wields. Chapelain's would-be emendations attempt to isolate that gaze and locate its point of origin elsewhere. That "elsewhere" is *beyond* the stage and its dynamics of transgression and desire; it is to be found either in a happy providence who directs the characters toward a decorous tragicomic close, or in a social duty that drives protagonists like Chimène toward tragedy.[45]

Shortly after the Academy reached its verdict, one of several sequels to *Le Cid* appeared. *L'Ombre de Comte Gormas*—a mediocre play by one Beaucaire, judge of Chillac—put the social deviants of Corneille's drama in their place. Dedicated to Richelieu, this "tragédie," as its title suggests, locates the characters of Corneille's *Cid* within the gaze of the dead father, who, like Shakespeare's elder Hamlet, stalks the drama seeking vengeance for his death. Just as Chapelain had advised that it was the dramatist's responsibility to refashion the past in order to render theater and society safe, so does Beaucaire undertake to rewrite the scandalous dynamics of Corneille's play. Rodrigue is killed in a duel by the Comte's son (a completely new character); Chimène retreats to a convent; and the phantom of the dead Comte invades his daughter's dreams to berate her for considering marriage to his murderer.[46] Such a rewriting undoes the numerous legitimations that take place in *Le Cid*. Rodrigue is relegated to the role of murderer and Chimène to that of chaste and obedient daughter whose erotic desires, far from being permitted, as Scudéry puts it, "to bask in royal favor" (Gasté, p. 80), are sublimated in the religiosity so pervasive in Castro's militantly Counter-Reformation play. As the title of his play suggests, Beaucaire willfully restores to medieval Castile, and, more relevantly, to seventeenth-century France, the shadows of obscurity and death by which the scandals revealed by Corneille should have remained shrouded.[47] In dedicating his sequel to Richelieu, he places the subject of *Le Cid* beneath the royal shroud where it belongs: a shroud associated with a paternalism designed to protect its audiences from witnessing and licensing the atrocities sanctioned by Corneille's king.

Corneille's play and his bold "Excuse" challenged an emerging ideology that purported to protect the public against itself and its more overweening members. *Le Cid* refused to sanction a doctrine of theater as safe, as easily legislated, as defensive against potentially disruptive desires and the sovereignty of the private individual. It thereby refused to be a guardian of collective values and high moral standards at a moment when France's powerful prime minister was trying to ennoble his country's literary institutions in the name of nationalism. In staging this refusal, Corneille countered the tragicomic universes endorsed by his most vocal opponents—Mairet, Chapelain, Scudéry—universes that engineered visions of poetic justice and ensured that providential sleights of hand might save characters and audience alike from moral and social transgression.[48] Moreover, Corneille refused to fashion a drama that concealed what Chapelain called "des vérités monstrueuses" ("There are certain monstrous truths which one must suppress for the good of society") (Gasté, p. 366), choosing instead to implicate his audience in the production of those very monstrosities.

Perhaps one of the most extraordinary results of the debate was Corneille's silence. His initial response to Scudéry is notable for his refusal to be drawn into the criticism offered—an indication, as he notes in a letter to Boisrobert, Richelieu's influential secretary, of his own scorn or "mépris." But following the Academy's verdict he was pressured by Boisrobert himself into remaining silent so as not to offend the cardinal and other powerful figures. In his response to Boisrobert, Corneille notes that he had originally intended to reply immediately to "Son Eminence" Cardinal Richelieu regarding the virtual condemnation of his play by the Academy, which had proceeded against him, he observes, "with such violence, and an authority so sovereign, as to stun me into silence."[49] He goes on to claim, however, that he is prepared to obey Boisrobert's cautious suggestion to say nothing, "since I belong to this world a little more than did Heliodorus, who preferred to lose his bishopric rather than his book, and since I long for the good graces of my master [Richelieu] more than for the greatest reputation in the world. I will be silent then, and not out of scorn but respect."[50]

That this silence lasted three years and produced a theatrical corpus strikingly different from the work that preceded it, and that it led to Corneille's eventual reassessment of the role of resistance in *Le Cid*, indicates a significant departure from an earlier, confident dynamic designed to fashion an audience vulnerable to his dramaturgy. Corneille's plays following *Le Cid* as well as his later theoretical writings articulate a strategy of resistance to intervention, as the dramatist moves from the realm of tragicomedy into that of tragedy. As the last part of this chapter will argue, rather than repeat the formula of the transgressive and celebrated subject that was so successful in *Le Cid*, Corneille develops a drama that attempts to preserve an innocent subject from manipulation. If *Le Cid* forcibly implicates the political society of Seville (and the audiences of Paris) in the rise of its self-possessed hero, Corneille's revision of *Le Cid* argues for a new integrity of the dramatic subject who tries to escape the invasiveness of the stage. Chapelain's comments about an audience deprived of its liberty to judge and a Chimène who should resist the "injuste ordonnance" of a king who caters to her desires are curiously echoed in Corneille's revisions and *Examen*, although in a manner at which Chapelain himself could hardly have guessed.

II

Immediately following the quarrel over *Le Cid*, Corneille appeared to capitulate to Richelieu and his Academy by composing several tragedies that correspond to "the rules."[51] More importantly, they violently restrain the desiring feminine figure. Chimène's counterpart is sacrificed to her brother in *Horace*, forced to abandon her plan to murder an emperor by the gracious demeanor of Augustus himself in *Cinna*, and turned from erotic to Christian love in *Polyeucte*. In each case, the "femme impudique" is either silenced or made to divert her desiring gaze onto a powerful and morally respectable authority.[52] Yet it is not altogether clear whether Corneille fashions this new role for the feminine protagonist out of respect for the Academy's verdict—and one should not rule out the significance of his acceptance into the Academy in 1647—or whether, as the following remarks on the revised *Cid* will suggest, that role registers what Corneille would come to define as his protest against the interference of France's cultural authorities.

It was, in fact, only in 1648 that Corneille turned again to *Le Cid*, labeling it a "tragédie" rather than a tragicomedy. (A more thoroughgoing revision was soon to come, the 1660 edition, to which I will turn momentarily.) Critical to Corneille's 1648 text is the addition of an "Avertissement" in which the playwright finally answers the charges of the French Academy. The "Avertissement" begins as an explicit defense of "cette heroine," who, Corneille announces, would consider him an ingrate if, "after having made her known in France, and having won my own reputation through her, I did not attempt to remove that shame which others have cast upon her" (Couton, 1: 693). Corneille proceeds to offer several Spanish texts in Chimène's defense, two of them passages from the *Romancero* defending Ximena's choice of "un marido honrado" (an honorable husband). But one verse passage that Corneille cites, from a comedy by Guillen de Castro entitled *Engañarse engañado*, is unrelated to the Spanish Ximena and seemingly unrelated to *Le Cid* as well. It is spoken by a princess: "Yasi, la que el desear / Con el resistir apunta, / Vence dos vezes, si junta / Con el resistir el callar" (Thus the woman who equally desires and who equally resists her desire conquers twice, if joined to her resistance is her silence) (Couton, 1: 694).

Corneille offers this verse to justify why Chimène withholds her secret from Don Fernand for so long: "This, if I don't fool myself, is how Chimène acts in my work when in the presence of the king and the Infante"; whereas in the presence of her confidante Elvire and Rodrigue, such resistance is unnecessary. One sees here the beginnings of what will become in 1660 an explicit dichotomy between Chimène and the character whom she will "resist" with more weapons than just her silence: the king. But in Corneille's apparently frivolous interest in an unrelated passage from Castro there is another rationale at work. Tied to Corneille's belatedly gallant efforts to secure for Chimène the honor of which his enemies have attempted to deprive her (and his play) is a concern with his own protracted silence following the Academy's verdict. The verbs "el resistir" and "el callar," which Corneille so arbitrarily picks from a Castro play unrelated to *Le Cid*, also speak of the playwright, who was gradually intuiting a profound connection between himself and his heroine.

For as will be recalled, Corneille's remarks to Boisrobert in his letter of acquiescence oscillate between his anger over the "violence" of an Academy that forces him to "fermer la bouche" (keep his mouth shut), and his *decision* to remain silent "not out of scorn but respect." It is thus not incidental that in the next paragraph in the "Avertissement," Corneille shifts abruptly from defending Chimène to protecting himself. "As for the rest, I find myself obliged to disabuse the public of two errors which have circulated concerning my tragedy, and which seem to have been authorized by my silence" (Couton, 1: 694): first, that he ever consented to being judged by an Academy that should have no authority over things dealing with "ni l'Etat ni la religion" (neither the state nor religion)—such as *Le Cid*;[53] and second, that his play deviated from "the rules" invoked by Scudéry and Chapelain and first codified by Aristotle. In his retort to this second misinterpretation "authorized by [his] silence," Corneille promptly returns to the character for whom silence is both punishment and weapon. Suggesting that Chimène is at the center of a play that conforms to Aristotle's demands that the "tragic hero" fall through human weakness into an unhappiness which s/he does not deserve and at the hands of someone who should love him/her (Couton, 1: 696), Corneille anticipates his extensively revised 1660 edition of the play. For if the 1637 *Cid* had centered on "un héros" whose "nom, au bout de six cents ans, vient encor de triompher en France" (name, after six hundred years, comes to triumph again in France), as Corneille boasts in his dedication to Richelieu's niece, Madame de Combalet, the "Avertissement" begins to shift that center to the woman who serves as the vehicle for *Le Cid*'s unequivocally tragic dimension and for Corneille's personal defense.

The revised *Cid* was published twelve years later—minus the preface to Madame—as part of Corneille's three-volume *Oeuvres*, complete with new prefaces to his plays and his *Trois Discours sur le poème dramatique*. In the second of his three discourses, Corneille announces the triumph, "in our century," of a new form of tragedy condemned by Aristotle but practiced with great success by Corneille himself in *Le Cid* (Couton, 3: 154). Once again, Chimène occupies the center of Corneille's musings on tragic form, as he defines this new, "modern" tragedy as a drama of "ceux qui connaissent, entreprennent et n'achèvent pas" (Couton, 3: 152)—characters who fully comprehend the catastrophes that loom before them and whose passionate and articulate struggles win for them the audience's pity.[54] Chimène's doomed struggle inspires far more passion than does that of an Oedipus, whose actions turn on what Corneille calls the improbable "embellishment" of *agnition* (anagnorisis) (Couton, 3: 154). Thus Corneille refutes the process of recognition that characterizes the original *Cid* as he delineates the nature of the tragedy suffered by Chimène and others. Such characters

> font de leur côté tout ce qu'ils peuvent et qu'ils sont empêchés d'en venir à l'effet par quelque puissance supérieure, ou par quelque changement de fortune qui les fait périr eux-mêmes, ou les réduit sous le pouvoir de ceux qu'ils voulaient perdre, il est hors de doute que cela fait une tragédie d'un genre peut-être plus sublime que les trois qu'Aristote avoue. (Couton, 3: 153)
>
> do as much as they can, but are prevented from reaching their goal by some superior power, or by a sudden change in fortune that either makes them perish or brings them within the sway of those they wanted to defeat[.] It is beyond doubt that this produces a tragedy of a kind perhaps more sublime than the three kinds discussed by Aristotle.

With these lines, Corneille transforms the "tragicomédie" of Rodrigue into the tragedy of Chimène's silencing. At the same time, however, he makes Chimène the agent of a new power: the sublime, produced when her plans are thwarted by "quelque puissance supérieure" and by her own recognition from the start of the play of her inevitable dilemma. As H. T. Barnwell has noted, Corneille's interest in the sublime may well have been sparked by his reading of the newly translated Longinian text.[55] The "sublime" act of self-recognition, in the face of dangers that threaten to undermine what Corneille attempts to stabilize *as* the notion of a "self," constitutes a radical shift of focus in the playwright's theorizing. If identity had once been possible only in display and others' complicity, it is now possible only insofar as it *resists* display.[56]

With this new notion of a selfhood articulated only in Chimène's tragic self-configuration rather than through the dazzling dramaturgy of Rodrigue, Corneille goes on to define the sublime *not* as a result of victimization but as a process of active resistance to the invasiveness and *éclat* of others. This reading is particularly apparent in the 1660 *Examen* to *Le Cid*, in which Corneille reflects on Don Fernand's final command that Chimène marry her father's murderer within the year. In a passage that directly touches on his earlier remarks regarding his own misconstrued silence, Corneille writes:

> Je sais bien que le silence passe d'ordinaire pour une marque de consentement; mais quand les rois parlent, c'en est une de contradiction: on ne manque jamais à leur applaudir quand on entre dans leurs sentiments; et le seul moyen de leur contredire avec le respect qui leur est dû, c'est de se taire, quand leurs ordres ne sont pas si pressants qu'on ne puisse remettre à s'excuser de leur obéir lorsque le temps en sera venu, et conserver cependant une espérance légitime d'un empêchement qu'on ne peut encore déterminément prévoir. (Couton, 1: 701)

> I know that silence usually is seen as a mark of consent; but when kings speak, it functions as a sign of contradiction. One never fails to applaud when one agrees with their judgments; and the only way to contradict them with the respect that is owed them is to remain silent, when their orders are not so pressing that one is not able to excuse oneself from obeying them when the time will come, while still conserving some legitimate hope of an obstacle as of yet unforeseen.

Thus does Corneille underline retrospectively what Mitchell Greenberg has called "the enigma of *Le Cid*, its scandal . . . its ultimate stillness."[57] Granted, this "scandal" had been present *in potentia* from the play's first performance in 1637; in response to the king's lines Chimène says nothing—nor does anyone else. But it is only long after *Le Cid* has first appeared onstage and in print, and only after the lengthy quarrel has ended, that Corneille chooses to highlight this scandalous lack of conclusiveness, both by altering the play's genre and by explicitly suggesting that Chimène's silence should be interpreted not as obedience but as protest. If the reading of *Le Cid* in the second *Discours* propels us toward a view of the play's tragic dimension as founded on Chimène's character alone, the *Examen* recovers for that tragic character a positive force. It opens the play up to uncertainty and prompts the audience to read Chimène's silence as only temporary, even strategic.

The emendations Corneille made to *Le Cid* in his 1660 edition directly address these concerns. Given Corneille's repeated emphasis on Chimène's resistance to a "puissance supérieure," it is telling that his revisions tend to displace the play's vehicle of mastery from Rodrigue onto Don Fernand, who becomes a much more formidable monarch than before. If in 1637 Rodrigue's deeds won him his status as the Cid, in 1660 it is the king who legitimizes Rodrigue as hero. The Infante tells Chimène in the early text that "ses faicts nous ont rendu ce qu'ils nous ont osté, / Et ton pere en luy seul se voit ressucité" (his deeds have given us that of which they deprived us, and your father sees himself revived in Rodrigue alone) (1189–90); in 1660 she remarks that "le Roy mesme est d'accord de cette verité / Que ton pere en luy seul se voit ressucité" (the King himself agrees with this truth that your father in him alone sees himself revived) (1179–80). It is now, moreover, the king for whom Rodrigue fights rather than for Spain: while he is eager to "defendre l'Estat" in the early text (1262), in the revision he declares to Don Fernand that he would have been happy risking his life "en combatant pour vous" (1252).[58]

In making the king the new vehicle of justice and legitimation, as well as of an absolute power that Rodrigue's father will ardently defend in lines new to the 1660 text,[59] Corneille inaugurates a new *institution* of monarchy, one in which the king has become virtually interchangeable with his state. But in becoming newly responsible for the production of Rodrigue's *gloire*, Don Fernand also emerges as Chimène's primary antagonist. In 1637, Chimène blames herself for the "shame and scandal" of her union with Rodrigue—she accuses herself of having "trop d'intelligence" (too much complicity) in the Comte's death, and notes in her final line of the play that she will suffer "un reproche eternel, / D'avoir trempé mes mains dans le sang paternal" (an eternal reproach for having dipped my hands in paternal blood) (1835–38). In the revision, however, "she turns against Don Fernand himself the reproach that she had run the risk of receiving."[60] Is it possible, she demands to know from the king, that he will ever be able to behold her married to her father's killer? Is it possible that he should violate his sense of justice in ordering her to forego her duty to her father? Finally, is it possible that Rodrigue can be so necessary to the monarchy that she should become a mere prize or "salaire"?[61] The Chimène of 1637 was concerned with little more than the haste with which the king ordered her to move from funeral meats to marriage ceremony when he said, "Et ne sois point rebelle à mon commandement / Qui te donne un espoux aimé si cherement" (And no longer rebel against my command, that gives you a spouse so dearly loved) (1797–98). She now, however, frames her response in a series of questions, and therefore she gives the king no answer. Her interrogation of Don Fernand rather protests her manipulation by a king who is prepared to violate justice in order to protect his newest hero. In short, she refuses to honor the political imperative that demands her acquiescence.

To an extent, this refusal is in keeping with a subtle but striking reformulation of Chimène's integrity throughout the play as a whole. When revising *Le Cid* in 1660, Corneille struck the entire first scene, in which the Comte attempts to "descouvre" and thus control Chimène's as yet unknown passion. The revised *Cid* opens instead with a conversation between *Chimène* and her confidante—a change suggestive of Corneille's insistence on his heroine's relative independence from the overbearing father figures of the play. That Chimène is now "permitted" to articulate her identity without the shadow of that father is apparent in one telling line from the scene in which Chimène and Elvire converse in the bedroom shortly before Rodrigue's spectacular appearance. The climactic "Je scay que je suis fille, et que mon pere est mort" (I know that I am a daughter, and that my father is dead) (834), at the end of a lengthy passage in which Chimène defends her *honneur*, now becomes the enigmatic "Je scay ce que je suis" (I know what I am),[62] the ambiguity of which calls attention to a new integrity unavailable to representation.[63] No longer does Chimène "abandon" herself immediately prior to the play's final scene: "Va, va," she had instructed Don Sanche after he had allowed her to believe that he had defeated and killed Rodrigue; "Je mourray bien sans ce cruel secours, / Abandonne mon ame au mal qui la possede, / Pour vange mon amant je ne veux point qu'on m'aide" (Go, go, I will certainly die without this cruel help, abandoning my soul to the evil that possesses it; to avenge my lover, I desire that no one assist me) (1746–48). In removing these lines from his final version, Corneille gives us a Chimène who refuses self-abandonment, withholding from the merciless knight the sign of her "possession."

But if those in authority—particularly a Don Fernand from whom Chimène's even tacit consent is purposefully withheld—become the newly invasive figures of the play, Corneille is no less attentive to the dynamics that surrounded Rodrigue in his earlier version of *Le Cid*. He in fact calls attention to the bad faith inherent in a Rodrigue guided only by fantasies of mastery. In the 1660 *Examen*, he observes that the horrifying moment when Rodrigue displays the sword still tainted with the Comte's blood "no longer pleases me" ("Pour ne déguiser rien, cette offre que fait Rodrigue de son épée à Chimène . . . ne me plair[ait] pas maintenant") (Couton, 1: 702). Nor does he approve of the second time that Rodrigue indecorously declares that he is seeking death, forcing from a startled Chimène the "mot lâché" (shameful word) that urges him to vanquish Don Sanche in combat. The muted fashion in which Corneille expresses his displeasure should not conceal the extent to which these scenes represent a dramaturgy he can no longer condone. Not only does he undermine the performative authority sought by Rodrigue in the earlier *Cid* (and arguably possessed by Alcandre in *L'Illusion comique*), but he creates a subject resistant to that authority, thereby destroying a theater that located its origins and source of protection in the desires of the subject for a transgressive and charismatic "master."

Thus while Corneille's new focus on Chimène's integrity reflects the playwright's bitterness regarding the quarrel, it also illustrates his reevaluation of an earlier posture that sought to escape accountability. His reassessment of Chimène becomes in large part his reassessment of the influence of his early theater on his public: a theater that, as a worried Chapelain observed toward the end of the *Sentimens*, made the audience "forget" its social duty. But the revisions to the 1637 *Cid* also suggest that Corneille might have looked back on his play and a vociferous quarrel that continued to haunt him (and, indeed, French literary criticism) as a blueprint for the burgeoning new state. The manner in which monarchy might contain its potentially transgressive subjects is to make them grateful, to deprive them of their public voices, to marginalize them while enabling them to believe that they are content in that marginalization—precisely as Don Fernand does to Chimène when he instructs her to follow her heart's "desires." The king's wresting from a silent and ashamed Chimène her "secret" in the crowded courtroom, his command that she marry the victor of the duel between Rodrigue and Don Sanche, can be interpreted in the 1637 *Cid* as the means by which Don Fernand consolidates and protects his newly created monarchy. In this scenario, Chimène's protests about her public duty are undermined, even infantilized. But in 1660, her protests and resistant silence, now explicitly marked as such by the playwright, take on the status of a viable challenge to an unjust command. As Michel Prigent has noted, other plays of the 1660's similarly enact the disappearance and flight of the hero from a stage increasingly associated with a contaminated and corrupt authority.[64] This is a flight, for the most part, into subjectivity and silence, a tacit acknowledgment that the space of visualization is also a space of danger. But it is also a flight from Corneille's earlier theatrical dynamics, and one that recognizes the potential that those dynamics might have for a tyranny all their own.

It is against both the tyranny of Corneille's earlier dramaturgy and the newly defined tyranny of Don Fernand that Chimène's silence militates at the close of the new *Cid*. If Chimène originally doubled for an audience incapable of protecting itself against a transgressive hero who wins even monarchs to his cause, she now becomes a metaphor for the playwright himself: the new "hero" whose angry silence is purchased for the sake of his/her monarch's defense. Corneille goes from eliciting and manipulating his audience's secret "plaisir" to renouncing that aim by protesting against the penetration of Chimène's "traits les plus cachés"—or, alternately, by perceiving that penetration as the essence of tragic sublimity. From a theater of *éclat*, Corneille moves to a theater that registers the problematic nature of *éclat*. He thus initiates a theater that turns against itself by undermining the dynamic of power that had functioned unilaterally to disclose the vulnerabilities of others.

In the aftermath of the quarrel, defending Chimène's integrity provides Corneille with a means of defending his *own* integrity as playwright—an integrity grounded not in exposure but in a refusal to speak and the attendant ambiguities of that refusal. In its new designation as a tragedy, *Le Cid* becomes the tragedy of feminine silence, a silence that Corneille's stage takes care to protect and to preserve. Insofar as that silence can also be claimed to function as the silence of the playwright—more and more obsessed, as the pages of the *Discours* attest, with sanctifying the theater as a realm where secrets might be withheld from "la puissance supérieure"—the stage of the new *Cid* is a far cry from the stage presided over by the "benevolent" Alcandre. Alcandre sought absolute if removed control over the means of production in a fashion not entirely unlike that once sought by Corneille himself. The original *Cid* ironically formulated a dramaturgy that might easily be appropriated by the French Academy or a monarch such as Louis XIV,[65] making Corneille, like the later Rousseau, an unwitting agent in the elaboration of the technology of power.[66] In his wish to preserve his independence from networks of cultural authority increasingly co-opted by the state, he created a vocabulary of astonishment that would eventually be appropriated by the monarch himself. But with his 1660 *Cid*, Corneille articulates a new opposition to the regnant power, which he had not earlier been able to resist.[67] It is such an opposition that might be said to characterize the modern subject, aware at once of its own fragility vis-à-vis the state and of its construction of a hidden space "elsewhere" that the state might not penetrate. Moreover, the canonization of Corneille's revised *Cid* as one of the central *tragedies*—rather than tragicomedies—of French theater attests to the extent to which that opposition would be valorized by Corneille's successors, including the greatest tragedian of the seventeenth century, Jean Racine.

Epilogue

> The great tragic sites [in Racine's theater] are arid lands, squeezed between the sea and the desert, shade and sun raised to the absolute state. One need merely visit Greece today to understand the violence of limitation, and how much Racinian tragedy, by its "constrained" nature, corresponds to these sites Racine had never seen: Thebes, Buthrotum, Troezen—these capitals of tragedy are villages. Troezen, where Phaedra dies, is a scorched knoll fortified by rubble. The sun produces a landscape that is pure, distinct, depopulated; life is without shade, which is simultaneously repose, secrecy, exchange, and flaw.[1]

If in early Corneille theater betokens acceptance and glory, in late Racine theater promises only danger and exposure, a process of disclosure that leads inexorably to death. Particularly in *Phèdre*, Racine's last secular play, theater is dominated by one gaze in particular, that of the father: of Thésée; of Minos; of Racine's spiritual father, the Jansenist Pierre Nicole; of Louis XIV. This is a gaze from which, as Phèdre herself claims, one can never escape. Yet Phèdre alone possesses such tragic certainty, while the play's other characters constantly attempt futile acts of flight. The hapless Hippolyte announces in his opening lines his intention "to flee the pleasant lands" of Troezen; Aricie, in the briefest of pastoral interludes, cries, "How dear to me will such an exile be . . . I will live forgotten by all mortals"; and Thésée, once he realizes that he has cursed his son without reason, pleads, "Let me flee far from you . . . Would I were in another universe!"[2] In this realm without shade, the father who once furnished solace in a mythical past is paradoxically present. But his ominous presence serves only to inflict the pain of a dazzling light that prohibits "repose, secrecy, [and] exchange"—precisely those qualities which the late Renaissance writers focused on in this book sought, and which they tended to find in the shelter of various communities.

Yet Racine's demystifying of Corneille's belatedly protective dramaturgy suggests that with Corneille we have already begun to witness the failure of those communities. We have seen how Corneille manipulated the theater audiences who attended his play in record numbers; we have seen, too, how he sought control over acting companies in a way that would never have occurred to Shakespeare. Finally, of course, Corneille resisted the ideology of power he had earlier prescribed in what might be called a chastened appeal to a group composed of like-minded men and women opposed to the intrusiveness of the state. And yet this group had none of the concreteness that the other communities discussed in this work possessed. In a way, Corneille's appeal in the 1648 "Avertissement" and in Chimène's protest at the close of the 1660 *Cid* was grounded in a notion of personal integrity that may be shared by others but that originates with the individual convinced of his or her self-righteousness. Such a conviction, I would argue, earlier figures discussed in this book did not have. Their certainties depended on validation from without. It is, moreover, because of such individual conviction that Racine is able to compose a theater that preys upon the now-isolated Phèdre, Hippolyte, Aricie, and Thésée—all torn from their respective families and communities and forced into the unforgiving glare of the one father who is ubiquitous.

Obviously there were other options to what Corneille tentatively registered as the failure or refusal to privilege communal over individual validation, and obviously that privileging continued in isolated cases; Molière comes to mind as one example in France. But overall, along with embittered contemporaries such as Milton, Racine represents the deathblow to what had been a vital and distinctive literature. This literature was historically unable to defend itself by recourse either to principles such as genius and the aesthetic or to a protective paternal deity, whose demise Cellini painstakingly charted. In their unwillingness to take the final step into the stark tragedy delineated by Racine, the writers of this strategic literature composed alternatives to the scenario of disenabling exposure imagined so vividly by the late-seventeenth-century French dramatist. With the tragic exception of Tasso, who realized as early as the *Aminta* his inability to separate himself from the powerful institutions that provided such ambivalent protection, these authors all constituted oppositional communities within and beyond their texts, defending themselves from becoming vulnerable solitaries who inhabited the margins of power and had no identity other than that conferred upon them by that power. It is in part for this reason that the potentially autobiographical figures of these texts acquire such highly mediated and mediating roles, from Cellini of the *Trattati*, content to pose as artisan rather than genius, to Chimène of the revised *Cid*, newly imbued with the rhetoric of protest. At the same time, in affirming their allegiance to an ethos different from the dominant political or religious order, these writers also precluded the regnant power from constituting itself as ubiquitous and invulnerable, the sole maker of meanings. As this book has shown, this was a period in which the exercise of power was hardly univocal, and it is important to bear in mind that theory and practice are two very different things. The often profound gap between the two is one that the writers in this book were able to exploit with varying degrees of success.

Clearly there were writers of the late Renaissance whose careers suggest other patterns of response to the pressures of the era—those who willingly became spokespersons for their patrons, such as Giraldi Cinzio and Samuel Daniel, and those who claimed for their work a space of cultural immunity divorced from the market and politics, such as Corneille's contemporaries Pierre Le Moyne and Guez de Balzac.[3] At moments in their careers, to be sure, the six figures encountered in these pages might be said to have flirted with either sycophantism or Philip Sidney's claim that poetry never lies because it never professes to tell the truth. On the whole, however, Cellini, Teresa, Tasso, Spenser, Shakespeare, and Corneille resisted the easy temptations of conformity and cynicism, instead producing literature that challenged the invulnerability not only of early modern institutions but of the constitutive act of writing itself. In striving again and again to make that act of writing an act of resistance, in attempting to preserve for themselves a space of repose, secrecy, and especially exchange—and sometimes, admittedly, of flaw—these writers shielded themselves from the tragic stage created by and perhaps for Jean Racine. They thus bequeathed to their future readers strategies whereby the psychic and historical vulnerabilities of those who write can be displaced onto their theoretically invulnerable protectors, and they revealed to their contemporaries the paradoxically insidious nature of protection.

Reference Matter

Notes

For complete references to works cited in short form in these notes, see Works Cited, pp. 275–99.

Chapter 1

1. From Epistle 82, line 24: "You recall the fierce serpent in Africa, more frightful to the Roman legions than the war itself, and assailed in vain by arrows and slings; it could not be wounded even by 'Pythius' (ne Pythio quidem vulnerabilis erat), since its huge size, and the toughness which matched its bulk, made spears, or any weapon hurled by the hand of man, glance off." *Seneca ad Lucilium Epistulae Morales*, 3: 256–59. In a footnote, Gummere observes that "Pythius" refers to "an especially large machine for assaulting walls."
2. *De constantia* (On firmness), in *Moral Essays*, 1: 54–58.
3. Epistle 9, lines 2–3, in *Seneca ad Lucilium Epistulae Morales*, 1:42–45. The passage discussing the condition of *apatheian* reads, "For [this word] may be understood [to refer to] a soul that cannot be harmed (invulnerabilem animum) or a soul entirely beyond the realm of suffering."
4. *The Riverside Shakespeare*. All further citations to Shakespeare are also from this edition. Citations are to act, scene, and line.
5. Macbeth's preceding lines nicely echo Marcellus's address to the dead King Hamlet: "As easy mayst thou the intrenchant air / With thy keen sword impress as make me bleed." *Macbeth*, 5.8.9–10.
6. V. G. Kiernan, in *Society and Change 1550–1650*, argues that this one-hundred-year period was crucial in shaping the transition from the medieval state to the early modern state; see, in particular, his concluding comments. For a recent study that argues against the largely artificial gap

between Renaissance and Baroque, sixteenth and seventeenth centuries—a gap the present work also hopes to bridge—see Snyder, *Writing the Scene of Speaking*. Other treatments of a distinctively "new" phase of the Renaissance that began in the second half of the sixteenth century and was characterized by a largely pessimistic view of earlier humanistic achievements and a new defensiveness vis-à-vis authority include a number of the essays collected in Aston, ed., *Crisis in Europe 1560–1660*; Cochrane, "A Case in Point"; Bouwsma, "Venice, Spain, and the Papacy"; Gundersheimer, "The Crisis of the Late French Renaissance"; Patterson, *Censorship and Interpretation*; Maravall, *Culture of the Baroque*; and the essays in Desan, ed., *Humanism in Crisis*.

7. Much work has been done on the renewed importance of Seneca for the late sixteenth century; two examples are Braden, *Anger's Privilege*, and Fumaroli, *L'Age de l'eloquence*.

8. As only a few examples from a massive bibliography that counters and/or refines Burckhardt's claims, one might cite the work of Hans Baron, particularly "The Limits of the Notion of 'Renaissance Individualism' "; the writings on Florentine civic life by Francis William Kent, *Household and Lineage in Renaissance Florence*; and the challenging work on the French sixteenth century by Natalie Davis, *The Return of Martin Guerre* and "Boundaries and the Sense of Self." For appraisals of Burckhardt related specifically to questions of literary production, see David Quint's fine introduction to Parker and Quint, eds., *Literary Theory / Renaissance Texts*, and Kerrigan and Braden, *The Idea of the Renaissance*, pp. 3–54.

9. Greene, *The Vulnerable Text* and *The Light in Troy*; Greenblatt, *Renaissance Self-Fashioning* and *Shakespearean Negotiations*; Ferguson, *Trials of Desire*; Davis, *Society and Culture in Early Modern France* and *The Return of Martin Guerre*; Crewe, *Trials of Authorship*.

10. This concept is essentially Freudian, although Freudian psychoanalysis continually demystifies it. See Freud's characterization of "the true heroic feeling, which one of our best writers has expressed in the inimitable phrase, 'Nothing can happen to me!' It seems, however, that through this revealing characteristic of invulnerability we can immediately recognise His Majesty the Ego, the hero of every day-dream and every story." "Creative Writers and Day Dreaming," p. 150.

11. Dependency "was the condition of most people, of wage laborers as well as serfs and slaves, of most men as well as of most women. 'Dependence,' therefore, was a normal, as opposed to a deviant, condition; and it did not carry any moral opprobrium." Fraser and Gordon, "Decoding 'Dependency.' " (The citation is from page 6 of the manuscript; my thanks to Nancy Fraser for making this material available to me prior to publication.) Yet while Fraser and Gordon may argue that dependency carried no stigma

in the early modern period, it is possible to see a gradual shift in attitudes precisely because of the historical conditions noted below: the new pursuit of invulnerability by church and state and the discomfort of "dependents" as a result.

12. See Arenal, "The Convent as Catalyst for Autonomy," regarding the often supportive and semi-autonomous atmosphere of the convent.

13. As Michael D. Bristol has suggested, Greenblatt's concept of the "social" is "a disembodied and abstract conception . . . in which collective experience is apprehended only through secondary refractions, codes, conventions, ideological formations and images of power. These have a tenuous, alien and sometimes baleful relation to the self, which is consistently presented in the condition of isolation. . . . *Renaissance Self-Fashioning* thus vividly depicts the pathos of individual opposition by meditating on the shifts in power itself and on such choices as conformity, impotent rebellion or 'subversive submission.'" *Carnival and Theatre*, p. 15.

14. Authorship here is meant not in terms of relation to past literary communities, but in terms of autonomy from contemporary and competing authors. In this manner, this study significantly differs from the sensitive and important work of scholars such as David Quint, Jacqueline Miller, and, as will become more apparent in the following pages, Thomas Greene.

15. *Works*, Eclogue I, lines 83–84. Further references to the *Eclogues* will be cited parenthetically in the text.

16. *The Light in Troy*, p. 141.

17. Greene says of Petrarch's interlinear gloss that it was based "on a mechanical and reductive interpretation inspired by Donatus but spelled out now with a relentlessly heavy hand." He chides Petrarch for "misreading" Virgil and muses that this "misreading" might be the result of Petrarch's "historical isolation." *The Light in Troy*, pp. 35–36.

18. My translation. The eclogue and Petrarch's Latin gloss are in de Nolhac, *Petrarque et l'Humanisme*, 1:146. De Nolhac also finds Petrarch's gloss a "bizarre document" that nonetheless takes on greater significance if one sees Petrarch applying to Virgil the allegorical explication necessary for understanding his *own* eclogues (p. 147).

19. Bk. 24, letter 12, in *Rerum familiarium libri*, 3: 340.

20. See Nancy Struever's stimulating chapter, "Petrarchan Ethics," in *Theory as Practice*.

21. These poems, of course, emulate Virgil's pastoral and epic phases. Petrarch's "Coronation Oration" is studded with passages from Virgil's *Georgics* and might be said to represent Petrarch's attempt to emulate Virgil's laboring poet—an attempt carried out in much different fashion by Spenser, as will be seen in Chapter 5.

22. For the compelling argument that the "romance of early Humanism"

was a condition of Petrarch's exile, see Giamatti, "Hippolytus Among the Exiles," particularly pp. 18–19, in *Exile and Change.*

23. Eclogue I, lines 47–48. The text is from Thomas Bergin's edition of the *Bucolicum carmen.* The reference to deserts and mountain peaks is made in lines 8–10 of the poem, pp. 2–3, when Monicus asks Silvius, "Quis vel inaccessum tanto sudore cacumen / Montis adire iubet, vel per deserta vagari / Muscososque situ scopulos fontesque sonantes," translated by Bergin as "Who, pray, bids you ascend with so much painful exertion / Lofty, unscaled mountain peaks, or to wander through desert wastelands, / Over moss-covered crags or where lonely cataracts thunder?"

24. "The tree of patronage [is subject] to forces that the ruler does not control; while the tree itself is transferred from the territory of idyll to that of elegy." Patterson, *Pastoral and Ideology*, p. 52.

25. One might, of course, see in Petrarch's Virgilian attempts an acute desire for, and even envy regarding, Virgil's posture of safety, and it is worth recalling Petrarch's sporadic engagement with the dynamics of empire-making throughout his career. Yet while Petrarch—like the other writers presently to be discussed in detail—no doubt yearned for political stability and a position of influence vis-à-vis Europe's most powerful leaders, he was also dissatisfied and even impatient with the overly fetishized integrity of Virgil's life and work. As Frances Yates and others have pointed out, after the embarrassing failure of Cola di Rienzi, Petrarch turned without hesitation to the Holy Roman Emperor Charles IV, seeking to persuade him to restore the imperium to Rome and unify Italy. See Yates, *Astraea*, pp. 13–18. The work of Rodolfo de Mattei is also important in assessing Petrarch's vacillations between Italian nationalism and his appeals to the Holy Roman Emperor; see *Aspetti di storia del pensiero politico*, vol. 1.

26. "The literary text is that organization of verbal signifiers perennially subject to interpretation and misinterpretation, historical erosion, exposure, inversion, decentering, ingurgitation by the aporetic abyss—that organization that perennially regains a provisional, still questionable, uncanny gathering of force. This recovery is precarious; its very assertion is vulnerable, since a hermeneutic of faith will always appear less rigorous than its opposite." *The Vulnerable Text*, p. xvi.

27. See Victoria Kahn's persuasive analysis of the humanist concept of reading as eminently practical, designed to make readers more effective *actors.* Reading for a Petrarch or a quattrocento humanist such as Bruni or Lorenzo Valla becomes "a series of discriminations analogous to kinds of discriminations we make in acting in the social and political spheres." Kahn, *Rhetoric, Prudence, and Skepticism in the Renaissance*, pp. 44–45.

28. Petrarch saw his own project as involving a movement "ab umbris ad lumina"—from shadows to the light. A. Bartlett Giamatti suggests that this

passage, from *Aeneid*, bk. VII, lines 770–71 in which Virgil describes the death of Hippolytus and his resurrection through the intervention of the physician Aesculapius, was crucial to the formation of Petrarch's humanist project. See "Hippolytus Among the Exiles," pp. 18–19, in *Exile and Change*.

29. When in the dark wood of the first canto of the *Inferno* Dante asks the Roman poet whether he is "od ombra od omo certo" (a shadow or a man), Virgil responds, "Non omo, omo già fui" (Not a man; a man I once was) (canto 1, lines 66–67), anticipating Dante's later interpretation (in the *Purgatorio*) of his poetry as a shadow from which others might both learn and ultimately emerge. *La Divina Commedia*, ed. C. H. Grandgent, rev. Charles S. Singleton (Cambridge, Mass.: Harvard Univ. Press, 1972).

30. See *The Vulnerable Text*, pp. xii–xviii.

31. For this list of sixteenth- and seventeenth-century figures who engage in the "carnival imagery" of a Rabelais, see Bakhtin, *Rabelais and His World*, p. 11.

32. For a succinct historical trajectory of the transition from medieval to Renaissance writing, see Bakhtin's brief discussion in *The Dialogic Imagination*, pp. 71–83.

33. The differences between the two critics are most apparent in an essay by Greene that explicitly criticizes Bakhtin. While Bakhtin finds festivity and plenitude in Rabelais, Greene argues for an "indigence" of "economic or existential or metaphysical" cast. In contrast to Bakhtin's emphasis on the totally accessible nature of the Rabelaisian text, Greene questions the possibility of "restorative communication" in Rabelais. See "The Hair of the Dog That Bit You: Rabelais' Thirst," in *The Vulnerable Text*, pp. 84, 90.

34. I am indebted to Professor Ronald Witt for this qualification. It is of interest, however, that when quattrocento figures such as Nicholas of Cusa, who denied original sin, and Lorenzo Valla, who exposed fabrications such as the Donation of Constantine, were forced to recant their theological and scientific writings, they were permitted to live "as free and respected men." Cusa even retained his ecclesiastical post. "The Renaissance popes themselves [prior to the sixteenth century] regarded the retractions as a formality," comments Agnes Heller. But with the Reformation and increased suspicion on the part of the church regarding speculative discourse, ecclesiastical authorities began to seek recantations in order to pursue "an ideological victory over the opponent." See Agnes Heller, *Renaissance Man*, p. 33.

35. For the analogy between writing and giving birth, see Bakhtin's passage in *Problems in Dostoyevsky's Poetics*, p. 51: "If the umbilical cord uniting the hero to his creator is not cut, then what we have is not a work of art but a personal document."

36. "The *Canzoniere* was produced by a consciousness as firmly cut off

from external alterity as any we know, a consciousness responsive only to its own memories and phantasms, dreams and torments." Hence Petrarch's "genuine fear of exposure" and his defenses against it. See "Petrarch *Viator*," in *The Vulnerable Text*, pp. 36–37.

37. Bakhtin's comments about words "set free" are closely related to his theory, expressed succinctly in the first essay in *The Dialogic Imagination* (particularly pp. 39–48), that no one's words are ever his or her own. This is a theory Bakhtin refined throughout his long career, culminating in the essays in *Speech Genres and Other Late Essays*.

38. *Rabelais and His World*, p. 269.

39. Ibid.

40. Quoted in *The Dialogic Imagination*, p. 163.

41. Ibid., p. 134. For a "Bakhtinian" reading of *The Praise of Folly*, see Bristol, *Carnival and Theatre*, pp. 130–33. Interestingly (and perhaps ironically), Martin Luther also adopted the mouthpiece of the fool in some of his writings around 1520 as a means of projecting into his text what Robert Weimann has called "an intellectual station of precarious independence of at least some of the dominant secular and clerical forms of institutional power." Weimann calls attention to the "element of vulnerability" inherent in this act of daring "self-representation." "History and the Issue of Authority in Representation," p. 456. Perhaps the central difference between Luther and Erasmus consists in what Weimann notes as the former's "desperate" use of the motley as opposed to Erasmus's playful use of the fool. For a Luther associated with dogmatic assertion, taking refuge in the figure of Folly must have been a desperate strategy indeed, whereas Folly seems to have embodied for Erasmus precisely the resistance to dogma that shaped his writings.

42. The suggestive phrase is that of Joel Altman, in *The Tudor Play of Mind*, p. 54. Altman footnotes Walter Kaiser's *Praisers of Folly* (Cambridge, Mass.: Harvard Univ. Press, 1963), p. 36, which notes that there is no precedent for such a speaker in encomiastic literature. Erasmus complains about Dorp's "pick[ing] out a couple of words and tak[ing] them out of context" in "Letter to Martin Dorp," in Radice's edition of *The Praise of Folly*, p. 232.

43. See, for example, Wayne Rebhorn's "Erasmus's Learned Joking" and Victoria Kahn's *Rhetoric, Prudence, and Skepticism*, pp. 102–14, for recent efforts to discern a "unifying plot" in *The Praise of Folly*. Kahn suggestively concludes that Erasmus *refuses* such unification, a point she develops in "Humanism and the Resistance to Theory."

44. *The Praise of Folly*, p. 208. Further references to Erasmus's work are cited parenthetically in the text. References to *The Praise of Folly* and the "Letter to Martin Dorp" are to Radice's edition.

45. The Latin text is from *Opus Epistolarum Des. Erasmi Roterodami*, 1:105.

46. *The Antibarbarians*, in *Collected Works of Erasmus*, 23:64. All citations in the text to *The Antibarbarians* are to this volume.

47. Cited in *Erasmus on His Times*, p. 29.

48. It is precisely this defiance of "location," as well as the capaciousness and accommodation of the Erasmian text, that is at the heart of Terence Cave's chapters on Erasmus in *The Cornucopian Text* and, indeed, of *The Cornucopian Text* as a whole. Relying heavily on deconstructive premises, Cave suggests that sixteenth-century texts anticipate the indeterminacy and sensuality of what Roland Barthes calls "the pleasurable text." For a critique of Cave's use of post-structuralism—as well as for the recognition that the works of Erasmus and some of his contemporaries are vulnerable to a deconstructive reading precisely because they do not make the author's "moral doctrines" available to the reader—see Jardine and Grafton, eds., *From Humanism to the Humanities*, pp. 140n–41n.

49. Apparently first composed as an oration in 1492–93, *The Antibarbarians* was rewritten as a dialogue in 1495, heavily revised over the next 25 years, and finally published in 1520. Margaret Mann Phillips finds the revised edition greatly influenced by the controversies surrounding the publication of Erasmus's New Testament and Luther's appearance on the European scene. She makes the telling point that Erasmus's earlier hostility to monasticism is revamped in the later edition as hostility to the faculty at Louvain. See her introduction to *The Antibarbarians*, in *Collected Works of Erasmus*, 23:11. For a somewhat different appraisal of the revisions to the text, see Hyma, *The Youth of Erasmus*, pp. 182–204.

50. See Batt's observation in *The Antibarbarians*, pp. 119–20, that Bernard was only "speaking figuratively" of the woods: "In this he was . . . imitating the ways of the poets; when they are going to write a song they usually seek after woods and streams." "These [theologians] are the people who want no changes in a text, for fear of exposing their own ignorance," Erasmus complains in his letter to Martin Dorp, subtly implicating his young reader as well.

51. For this aspect of university education, see Altman, *The Tudor Play of Mind*.

52. The letter to Dorp is also a response to Dorp's complaint about the imminent publication of Erasmus's Greek New Testament. The threat Erasmus's translation posed to the integrity of the Latin Vulgate—and, by extension, of the church in a period of intense criticism and change—cannot be overestimated. See the passage in the letter in which Erasmus responds to the attack on his New Testament and the theologians' desire for an invulnerable church: "You say that in their time the Greek texts were more

accurate than the Latin, but that today the situation is reversed, and we should not trust the writings of those who disagreed with the teaching of the Roman Church" (p. 245). Dorp's position anticipates that of the Counter-Reformation church regarding the creation of a church invulnerable to history, a position that the chapter on Tasso will develop.

53. *Erasmus-Luther*, p. 7.

54. See most recently Richard M. Berrong's study, *Rabelais and Bakhtin*, chap. 3, for a critique of Bakhtin's work. Other recent studies that challenge Bakhtin's view of the folk and call attention to the darker aspects of carnival include Hayman, "Toward a Mechanics of Mode"; Bernstein, "When the Carnival Turns Bitter"; and the introduction to Bauer, *Feminist Dialogics*.

55. See *Erasmo in Italia 1520–1580*, esp. pp. 320–21: "One must conclude that the man of letters, who gave free rein to the imagination 'by invoking [his works] as poetic fictions,' found himself exposed to the persecutions of the Inquisition, and his artistic creativity in great danger. . . . It was around the name of Erasmus that the dissent and protest against an intellectual and moral way of life were polarized, as is evident in the prohibition of Erasmus's books." My translation; the phrase in quotation marks is from an Inquisitor's report.

56. On the process of pardoning in France, see Davis, *Fiction in the Archives*.

57. See Thornley, "The Destruction of Sanctuary." On the restricted powers of the medieval English king, see Lander, *The Limitations of English Monarchy*.

58. On feudal immunities, see especially Bloch, *Feudal Society*, 2: 361–68, which defines immunity as the combination of two privileges: "exemption from certain fiscal burdens; and the immunity of a territory from visitation by the royal officials, for any reason whatsoever." On the changing status of immunities in Renaissance Europe, see Anderson, *Lineages of the Absolutist State*.

59. Regarding these developments in France, see Davis, "The Reasons of Misrule," in *Society and Culture in Early Modern France*, pp. 121–23; regarding England, see Marcus, *The Politics of Mirth*. Davis's remarks both engage and criticize Bakhtin and have been very suggestive for this study; see "The Reasons of Misrule," pp. 119, 122–23. On issues of censorship, see Patterson, *Censorship and Interpretation*.

60. See Lane's essays, gathered under the rubric of "The Cost of Protection," in *Venice and History*, pp. 373–428. For a general discussion of the evolution of European government in the late sixteenth and seventeenth centuries, see Steensgaard, "The Seventeenth-Century Crisis."

61. On Cinzio, who invoked the Estense prince as a *tutor* who protected his peoples, and who wrote a number of plays for the Ferrarese court, see Lebatteux, "Idéologie monarchique." On Bodin, see Bossy, *Christianity in*

the West, chap. 6; on Machiavelli, see the writings of Federico Chabod, including *Scritti sul Rinascimento*. On Lipsius and other Counter-Reformation apologists, Marc Fumaroli's *L'Age de l'eloquence* is a useful introduction.

62. *Erasmus on His Times*, p. 44.

63. For a study of the role of negation in More and ensuing attempts—such as that of Budé—to "theologize" and thus "place" Utopia, see Helgerson, "Inventing Noplace."

64. See the essays in Berger's recent collection of writings from 1962 through 1985, *Second World and Green World*, particularly "Naive Consciousness and Cultural Change," pp. 63–107. In this article, Berger creates a distinction between two modes of thought, indicative of what he calls traditional and modern forms of reasoning: the empirical and the hypothetical. The former "begins and ends with the world as experienced in naive consciousness" (p. 88); it depends on an Aristotelian-Thomistic epistemology and aims to "produce knowledge of the object as it truly is" (p. 89). The hypothetical mode, characteristic of the Renaissance and early modern era, is "*counter-factual*—unquestionably fictional, imaginary, or make-believe" (p. 88) and dependent on "construct formation." Once thought has disengaged itself from naive consciousness, it tends to "organize its life situation into a set of *heterocosms*" (p. 90) that become the basis not only for speculation but for action.

Berger's account of the "mental shift" in the Renaissance is an important antidote to accounts of Renaissance literature, such as that of Stephen Greenblatt, which rely on anthropological analyses. It provides the rationale for why, at a certain period in the late Renaissance, traditional authorities in the name of the church or absolutist state attempted not only to suppress technological innovation but to control the imaginative and technological powers of a new historical elite. It was only in the context of this intellectual shift—clearly exacerbated by social and religious changes—that the late Renaissance suspicion and control of declarations of "immunity" became necessary. Whereas earlier historical elites had "maintained and exercised their power primarily by their ability to appeal to the traditional order and to draw sanction from criteria, beliefs, ideals, etc.," the new elite "receives its power and legitimacy from its control of the new counterperceptual environment, the new technology, developed by the radical abstraction of postmedieval thought and culture" (p. 94).

65. See Richard Strier's similarly constructed formulation in his essay, "Faithful Servants." In discussing the theories of resistance of Marian exile John Ponet and James I's tutor George Buchanan, Strier calls attention to the late sixteenth century as a moment "when resistance to legally constituted authority becomes a moral necessity and neutrality not a viable possibility" (p. 104).

66. This is not, of course, to suggest that Erasmus succeeded in doing

without the protection of patronage altogether. His letters are full of praises of William Mountejoy, Leo X, and other European luminaries of the period. But by the same token, Erasmus's situation was not yet that of the six figures whom the rest of this book is devoted to exploring. For some brief remarks on Erasmus and his patrons—and for a good introduction to the dynamics of Renaissance patronage and its changing status between the time of Erasmus and that of Shakespeare—see Gundersheimer, "Patronage in the Renaissance," pp. 3–23. As Gundersheimer tellingly notes, "Erasmus lived on patronage . . . but he always appreciated its dangers." p. 5.

67. "The Formation of Intellectuals," in *The Modern Prince and Other Writings*, p. 120.

68. This study both builds on and departs from the cogent and suggestive analysis of Margaret Ferguson, who identifies the "defenses" at work in texts by Joachim du Bellay, Tasso, and Philip Sidney in order to insist on the extent to which at least the first two writers find themselves trapped by what Ferguson calls "the predicament of relations," which she diagnoses in primarily Lacanian terms. Sidney emerges from this stifling predicament largely unscathed, perhaps because of his relative independence from the dynamics of patronage and subservience. See Ferguson, *Trials of Desire*, particularly the introduction.

69. In *De clementia*, bk. 1, chap. 1, passage 5, p. 219, Seneca notes of his "pupil" Nero, "Rarissimam laudem et nulli adhuc principum concessam concupisti innocentiam" (You desire a very rare praise, and one never granted to an emperor, innocence).

70. The idea of a French monarchy that recaptures the expansiveness of the Roman imperium desired by Petrarch and grounded in generosity and protection has been explored in detail by Frances Yates. See *Astraea* as well as the musings at the end of "Bruno and Campanella on the French Monarchy," in *Renaissance and Reform*, 2:138, in which she suggests that Italian artists at Francis I's court saw themselves as working "in the service of a monarchy which could stand in Europe for a universal idea."

71. See *Lineages of the Absolutist State*, chap. 2, "Class and State: Problems of Periodization."

72. One need only think here of the last book of Petrarch's letters, in which he addresses dead poets and philosophers of the past, or—in a somewhat less remote context—Erasmus's appeals to the readers of his *Adages* to take up the pen where he has left off.

Chapter 2

1. The Italian text of the *Vita* is from Cellini, *Opere*, ed. Bruno Maier, I. lxxix. All further citations to the *Vita* will be from this edition. References

are to book and chapter. Where indicated, the English translation is from Cellini, *Autobiography*, trans. George Bull; otherwise, it is my own. This passage is from Bull, p. 144.

2. Cited in Wittkower and Wittkower, *Born Under Saturn*, p. 188.

3. See Dino S. Cervigni's brief account of the *Vita*'s eighteenth-century reception in *The 'Vita' of Benvenuto Cellini*, pp. 12–13.

4. Burckhardt's treatment of Cellini is brief and to the point. In his chapter on biography, Burckhardt writes, "By [Cellini's] side Northern autobiographers, though their tendency and moral character may stand much higher, appear incomplete beings. He is a man who can do all and dares do all, and who carries his measure in himself. Whether we like him or not, he lives, such as he was, as a significant type of the modern spirit." *Civilization of the Renaissance in Italy*, 2: 330.

5. This view is also implicit in Burckhardt, who speaks of Cellini's surviving artwork as "perfect only in [its] little decorative specialty." *Civilization of the Renaissance in Italy*, 2: 330. For a recent assessment of Cellini's artwork and its relationship to the style of the *Vita*, see Mirollo, *Mannerism and Renaissance Poetry*, chap. 2.

6. These documents, now in the Biblioteca Laurenziana in Florence, have been examined and discussed by several Cellini scholars, including Francesco Tassi in *Ricordi, prose e poesie di Benvenuto Cellini* and, most recently, Dario Trento in *Benvenuto Cellini*.

7. *Cellini*, p. 165. Pope-Henessy notes elsewhere in this magisterial study that Cosimo was praised by his contemporaries as thrifty and hostile to ostentatious display; he was said to have valued the "antica parsimonia" of the ancient Florentine republic, banning in 1546 the "excessive and superfluous expenditure on clothes and ornaments of men as well as women."

8. Greenblatt, "Fiction and Friction," p. 36.

9. For an intriguing reading of the sexual politics of the Medusa myth, see Hertz, "Medusa's Head."

10. Renza, "The Veto of the Imagination," esp. pp. 290–95.

11. Cited in Pope-Henessy, *Cellini*, pp. 174–75. Pope-Henessy speculates that the phrases here and elsewhere on the base of the *Perseus* were probably written with the help of Cellini's friend Varchi, and comments that "in a very real sense the base is the key to the *Perseus*."

12. See the comments of Ettore Camesasca in his edition of Cellini's *Vita*, p. 13. On Cosimo's principate in its early years, see Spini, *Cosimo I e l'independenza del principato mediceo*, esp. chap. 2.3, "La costruzione del poter assoluto," and Guarini, *Lo stato mediceo di Cosimo I*.

13. See Pope-Henessy, p. 173, noting that Cellini *did* at some point need permission to carry out the additional work.

14. See Nancy Vickers's somewhat analogous analysis of the statue of

Jupiter that Cellini created for Francis's fountain at Fontainebleau: "For Cellini, Francis's 'fathering of the arts' was literal; Jupiterlike, he inseminated them with a shower of gold. Through them he took his pleasure; through them he left his mark on French culture." "The Mistress in the Masterpiece," p. 38.

15. On the dynamics of this patronage system, see the remarks of Wittkower and Wittkower, *Born Under Saturn*, chap. 2, "Artists and Patrons."

16. For the classic work on Florence's "demise," see Cochrane, *Florence in the Forgotten Centuries*.

17. For this characterization of the *Vita*, see Mirollo, *Mannerism and Renaissance Poetry*, p. 83.

18. On the shift from "the medieval to the modern understanding of artistic poesis," which mirrors the larger change from a devolutionary to an evolutionary world model, see Hans Robert Jauss's suggestive comments in "Poesis."

19. The sentiment is echoed in the *Trattato dell'Oreficeria*, in which Cellini notes that Francis's remark that he surpasses the ancients is the best remuneration possible for his labors: "A questo il re disse: 'Ringraziato sia Iddio che alli dì nostri è nato anche degli uomini, i quali le opere loro ci piacceno molto più che quelle delli antichi.'" *Opere*, p. 728.

20. For others' praises of Francis I as patron, see Ranum, *Artisans of Glory*, pp. 29–49. Ranum notes that the writings of contemporaries such as Guillaume Budé were sufficiently influential to allow "seventeenth-century men of letters [to look] back upon Francis I's reign as the beginning of a golden age of learning, eloquence, and patronage" (p. 29).

21. See his 1554 letter to Iacopo Guidi, in which Cellini refers to himself as the "divoto ed amorevole vassallo e servo di sua illustrissima Eccellenza [Cosimo]" while pleading that Guidi urge his master to reward him for the *Perseus* ("dico che umilmente io priego sua Eccellenza, che mi doni delle mie fatiche di nove anni tutto quello che al santissimo e discretissimo giudizio pare e piace"). *Opere*, pp. 1005–6.

22. For the use of this phrase regarding economies within which gift-giving establishes the primary cycle of exchange, see Marcel Mauss's classic work, *The Gift*, and Pierre Bourdieu's *Outline of a Theory of Practice*. Both Mauss and Bourdieu go on to insist that gift-giving establishes its own forms of domination and coercion, an element explored more fully apropos of Cellini in the discussion of the marvelous in the final section of this chapter.

23. See *The Trew Law of Free Monarchies* (1597), in which James argues that "as the Father of his fatherly duty is bound to care for the nourishing, education, and vertuous government of his children, even so is the king bound to care for all his subjects." *The Political Works of James I*, p. 55. The quotation in the text from the *Basilikon Doron* is on p. 24 of the *Political*

Works. On James as "nourish-father" in various portraits of the period, see Goldberg, "Fatherly Authority."

24. See Coppélia Kahn's reading of Shakespeare's *Timon of Athens* in " 'Magic of bounty.' "

25. *The Masque of Queens* (perf. 1609), in *The Works of Ben Jonson*, 7: 315. In his marginalia, Jonson notes, "The Antients expressed a brave, and masculine *virtue*, in three figures (Of *Hercules*, *Perseus*, and *Bellerophon*) of which I chose that of *Perseus*, armed, as I have him describ'd out of *Hesiod*" (p. 302n). In his comments on the masque in *Ben Jonson's Plays and Masques*, Robert M. Adams notes that "all these identifying emblems [of Jonson's Perseus, such as his sandals, wallet, shield, and sword] are to be seen on Cellini's famous statue of Perseus in Florence, which Inigo Jones had seen and Jonson surely heard about" (p. 330n).

26. In a Lacanian reading of the *Vita*, Francoise Duranton-Mallet suggests that Cellini almost never speaks of his mother, transferring her maternal qualities to his father. The insoluble conflict of the text is that between law and desire, embodied in the same figures (Cellini's real father and numerous patrons): "The father thus doubles as the good father, who even assumes the role of the mother, and the bad father, who represents the law in opposition to desire." "Propositions pour une lecture analytique de *La Vita* de Benvenuto Cellini," p. 226.

27. Commenting on the merchant Bindo Altoviti, who had apparently cheated Cellini out of some money he had invested and for whom Cellini had been asked to design a bronze bust, Cellini bitterly comments, "Da poi che così male io avevo fatto la mia faccenda con Bindo Altoviti, col perdere la mia testa di bronzo e 'l dargli li mia danari a vita mia, io fui chiaro di che sorte si è la fede dei mercatanti" (I had conducted my affairs so badly with Bindo Altoviti, what with losing my bronze bust and giving him my money for life, that I was left without any illusions as to what the faith of a merchant was worth) (II.lxxxii; Bull, p. 352).

28. Kerrigan and Braden, *The Idea of the Renaissance*, p. 45, describing the expansion of the capitalist marketplace in the sixteenth century. Such expansion "touches society as a whole, and on a deep level, with a new sense of the awesomely abstract power of money: *Pecuniae obediunt omnia* (Money controls everything) (Erasmus, *Adages* I.3.87)" (pp. 43–44).

29. That Cosimo should have asked Cellini's enemy Bandinelli to arrive at the "giusto prezzo" of the *Perseus* only adds insult to injury in Cellini's account—particularly given that earlier *capitoli* of the *Vita* had been entirely focused on Bandinelli's lack of good judgment; see, for example, I.xlv, II.liv.

30. As recorded in Pliny, since antiquity artists had been at the bottom of the social scale because they earned money with their hands; see Pliny, *Natural History*, XXXV.85.

31. Barocchi, ed., *Trattati d'arte del cinquecento*, 1:66. Bronzino is drawing on a tradition that places painting above the other fine arts. That tradition goes back at least to Leon Battista Alberti, who in his 1436 treatise, *On Painting*, insisted that painting contains a "divine force." Also relevant to the discussion is Alberti's observation, almost a hundred years before Castiglione's book of manners, that "polite manners and easy bearing will do more to earn goodwill and hard cash than mere skill and industry." Cited in Wittkower and Wittkower, *Born Under Saturn*, pp. 15–16.

32. *Vite*, proem to pt. 3, vol. 4, p. 13; cited in Biagi, "La *Vita* del Cellini," p. 133. While Biagi finds in Vasari a "Cellinian" perspective on the relationship between "fatiche" and *difficoltà*, she fails to call attention to Vasari's sublimation of the physical in his use of "ingegno."

33. *Le vite dei più eccellenti pittori, scultori e architetti*, 7: 623.

34. See Wittkower and Wittkower, *Born Under Saturn*, p. 231; the citation is from Bandinelli's *Il Memoriale di Baccio Bandinelli*.

35. Varchi collected the numerous letters and treatises that formed part of the debate in his *Due lezioni* of 1547. Not surprisingly, Michelangelo (whom Cellini notes as one of his greatest influences) also argues for sculpture's supremacy as a representational rather than a mimetic art. But Michelangelo emphasizes the extent to which sculpture is capable of eliciting a hidden or Platonic essence, whereas Cellini's preference for sculpture is founded in his argument for the artist's godlike ability to be a *homo faber*. On Michelangelo's aesthetics, see Clements, *Michelangelo's Theory of Art*.

36. Other poems in the collection also play on the deceptiveness of the "ombre" of *disegno*. See, for example, the close of "Il boschereccio contro il Lasco," in *Opere*, p. 883: "Sculpì natura 'l mondo e gli animali / e pose all'ombre lor nome disegnio" (Nature sculpted the world and the animals, and gave to their shadows the name *disegnio*), and the seventh poem in *Opere*, p. 888: "Quella [scultura] merita onor, perché 'l disegno / vien sol da lei; sol quella eterna dura; / e l'altra è l'ombra sol d'ogni figura: / persa la luce, torna al ceco regno" (Sculpture merits honor, because *disegno* comes only from her; she alone endures, and the other is only the shadow of every figure: once the light is lost, she returns to the blind kingdom).

37. The first fourteen sonnets in Bruno Maier's collection all revolve around "la sacra santa scultura" and its superiority to *disegno*. Even in the "Sonnetti spirituali," Cellini characterizes "Dio" almost exclusively as *deus faber*; see particularly Sonnets 32, 46, 47, and 49.

38. For the Neoplatonic and alchemical interests of Cosimo I and his son Francesco, see Orlandi, *Cosimo e Francesco de'Medici Alchimisti*, and Berti, *Il Principe del studiolo*.

39. See Alfred Sohn-Rethel's analysis of the exploitation of the artisan

in *Intellectual and Manual Labor*, pp. 111–17, "The Forms of Transition from Artisanry to Science."

40. In his recent edition of Cellini's *Vita*, Ettore Camesasca suggests that the autobiography demonstrates more the artisan at work than the artist who, thanks to Vasari's (and Cosimo's) Accademia del Disegno and the efforts of figures such as Albrecht Dürer to bring mathematics and artisanal creation together, was beginning to become versed in theoretical as well as practical pursuits. "The *Trattati* of Cellini are much closer to the remote 'recipe book' of C. Cennini [ca. 1390] than they are to the celebrated *Vite* of his rival [Vasari]." *Vita*, p. 23. Cellini's return to the "recipe" books of guildsworkers, which discussed in minute detail the various crafts at which they had gradually become experts, thus becomes a refutation of the more theoretical treatises that were beginning to appear in the mid-sixteenth century.

41. Tellingly, one of the lengthiest chapters in either *Trattato* is Cellini's detailed explanation to Francis in the *Trattato dell'Oreficeria* of the making of a beautiful drinking bowl in the king's collection, prompting Francis's usual excessive praise. *Opere*, p. 648.

42. " 'Benvenuto, questa figura non ti può venire così di bronzo, perché l'arte non te lo promette' " (II.lxxiii).

43. See Pope-Henessy, *Cellini*, p. 186, citing and translating several of the verses that Cellini had printed in an appendix to his *Trattato della Scultura*. *Cellini*, p. 186.

44. See Nancy Vickers's remarks apropos of Petrarch, who, like the mythical hero Perseus, "works through fragmentation and reification to neutralize and appropriate the threat [of the feminine]." " 'The Blazon of Sweet Beauty's Best,' " p. 112.

45. *The Forge and the Crucible*, pp. 56–57.

46. For the argument that not only patrons but Cellini's other "protector" as well—God—withdraw their power in the second half of the *Vita*, see Marziano Guglielminetti's chapter on Cellini in *Memoria e scrittura*.

47. *The Passions of the Soul* (1648), in *Descartes: Selections*, p. 380.

48. "The rich and powerful take pleasure in 'being forced' (essere sforzato) by the artist." Biagi, "La *Vita* del Cellini," p. 94. Nancy Vickers's discussion of the rivalry between Francis I and Cellini in "The Mistress in the Masterpiece" tellingly reveals the extent to which Cellini's protestations of "equality" disguise competitiveness and violence. Her persuasive reading argues that this rivalry is in fact displaced onto Francis's mistress and the women Cellini so violently abuses throughout the *Vita*.

49. For this characterization of the economy of gift-giving, in which participants are bound together rather than alienated by the mediation of

money, see Jean-Christophe Agnew's insightful first chapter of *Worlds Apart*, esp. pp. 19–27. The pioneering work of Marcel Mauss, of course, uncovered the interest inherent in the supposedly altruistic nature of gift-giving; see *The Gift*.

50. See particularly Baudrillard's preface, in which he invokes Lacan's description of the mirror stage to create an analogy with the mirror of production: "At the level of all political economy there is something of what Lacan describes in the mirror stage: through this scheme of production, this *mirror* of production, the human species comes to consciousness *in the imaginary*. Production, labor, value, everything through which an objective world emerges and through which man recognizes himself objectively—this is imaginary." *The Mirror of Production*, p. 19. See too Baudrillard's acute chapter on Marxist anthropology, in which he argues that "everything that speaks in terms of totality (and or 'alienation') under the sign of a Nature or a recovered essence speaks in terms of repression and separation" (pp. 55–56).

51. To this extent, Cellini's strategies of legitimation differ from those of other roughly contemporary painters, such as one Giulio Mancini, who, as Francis Haskell describes in *Patrons and Painters*, insisted on correlating his commission with the amount of time he spent on a work; see pp. 130–31. A rich collection of documents dealing with painters and their patrons can be found in D. S. Chambers, *Patrons and Artists in the Italian Renaissance*.

52. Bonino, *Lo Scittore, il potere, la maschera*, p. 50. Bonino links Cellini's production of "narcisismo" to his social predicament of alienation. Such alienation ultimately triumphs over the compensatory narcissism of the text, as the unfinished nature of the *Vita* bears witness.

53. See Ettore Camesasca's suggestion in his edition of the *Vita*, p. 19: "In effect, Cellini's autobiography is a dialogue between Benvenuto and Cosimo I, the interlocutor to be convinced."

54. "Io promessi inel principio del mio libro di dire parte della causa che movea a scrivere questo volume, la qual causa io dissi che moverebbe gli uomini a grande sdegno del caso e compassione di me." *Opere*, p. 713.

55. For a discussion of the "cultural self-sufficiency" of workers in eighteenth-century France and the manner in which the dominant culture perceived them as potentially disruptive, see Koepp, "The Alphabetical Order."

56. Cited in Heinzelman, *The Economics of the Imagination*, p. 154.

57. On the interest of patrons in learning the process of *il fare* in the sixteenth century, see Goldthwaite, "The Economic and Social World of Italian Renaissance Maiolica."

Chapter 3

1. The Spanish text of *Las Moradas* is from Tomás's edition, p. 171; the English translation, with occasional revisions of my own, is from Peers, *The Interior Castle*, pp. 168–69. All further citations to *Las Moradas* will be from these editions. Page numbers will be cited parenthetically in the text, with pagination for the Spanish edition preceding that for the English.

2. For a comparison of the autobiographies of Cellini and Teresa, see Mirollo, "The Lives of Saints Teresa of Avila and Benvenuto of Florence."

3. Teresa had already faced difficulties for the manuscript of her *Vida*, and her name first appears on Inquisition trial records in 1575. See Lincoln, *Teresa: A Woman*, p. 122.

4. On the Spanish context of the Counter-Reformation see Kamen, *Inquisition and Society in Spain*, and Perez, "Cultura y sociedad en tiempos de Santa Teresa."

5. See A. D. Wright's comment in "The Borromean Ideal" that "while Italian pastors concentrated on practice, Spanish Inquisitors concentrated on mental attitudes and expressions of belief, even more than on practice." *San Carlo Borromeo*, p. 201. On the extent to which women's interiority in particular was "devalued," see Guilhem, "L'Inquisition et la dévaluation des discours feminins."

6. On the *alumbrados*, see Menendez y Pelayo, *Historia de los heterodoxos españoles*, 2: 187–97. In *Espiritualidad y literatura en el siglo XVI*, Francisco Márquez Villanueva observes that many *alumbrados* tended (like Teresa) to be *conversos* (converts). His intriguing essay, "Santa Teresa y el linaje," identifies the various strategies Teresa employed to keep her *conversa* status concealed.

7. See Ottavia Niccoli, "La fine delle profezie."

8. See Alison Weber's brief description of Magdalena's life and its dangers for a figure such as Teresa—accused during her lifetime of being "another Magdalena de la Cruz"—in her chapter on the *Vida* in *Teresa of Avila*, pp. 44–45.

9. Bell, *Holy Anorexia*, p. 171.

10. For the continuation into the Renaissance of the attitudes expressed toward women in the *Malleus maleficarum*, written by two German Dominicans, see Ian MacLean's succinct discussion of fifteenth- and sixteenth-century attitudes toward women's physiology and their propensity for possession and melancholy. *The Renaissance Notion of Woman*, pp. 28–46.

11. Cited in Jensen, "Anna O.," p. 289. Pappenheim's remark, which anticipates the more recent attempts by scholars such as Foucault to derive the secular confessional from the spiritual one, hardly disguises Anna O.'s own near-tragic involvement with the burgeoning science of psychoanalysis.

The advocate of such a science may be far from objective, and Dr. Breuer's critical blindness (of which Freud made much) to his own involvement in Anna's "case" is symptomatic of the dangers posed by the psychoanalyst's ignorance and assumption of objectivity. The mediation of authorities whose lack of self-knowledge perpetrates an attack on the knowledge of supposedly inferior others thus has the potential of becoming the "two-edged sword" of which Pappenheim spoke. It is a sword that can injure not only the "patient" but the doctor himself, as shown by Breuer's panicked refusal to bring the talking cure to a close—following Anna O.'s insistence that she was about to bear his child, he quickly abandoned the case.

12. Cited in Jacobus, *Reading Women*, p. 203.

13. Indeed, throughout her life Teresa was concerned with the very real problems of melancholy within the cloistered community. Alison Weber addresses Teresa's passages on melancholy in the sixth chapter of *Las Fundaciones* in *Teresa of Avila*, pp. 139–47.

14. See Peers's description of the palamito, *The Interior Castle*, p. 37n.

15. Michel de Certeau has argued that a command inaugurates and informs all mystical writing. See his chapter, "Mystic Speech," in *Heterologies*, pp. 80–100, as well as his chapter on Teresa in *La Fable mystique*, pp. 257–79. Although de Certeau's valuable analyses have been useful for this study, they largely neglect to take into account the presence of the mediating *institution* that desired to control the privacy of the woman mystic. His consideration of woman as a "collective subject," which owes much to the work of French feminists Hélène Cixous and Luce Irigaray, is suggestive and will be developed later in this chapter. Like Cixous and Irigaray, de Certeau conflates the collective subject with the feminine hysteric who experiences pleasure (*jouissance*) in the multiple zones of her body: "The body becomes the organ of all these spiritual 'favors' and 'graces.' It is played by these caresses, it becomes their means of speaking." *La Fable mystique*, p. 271. This account of *jouissance* ignores the necessary defenses that Teresa must elaborately construct in the pages of her text—defenses that a critic such as Irigaray would discount as unnecessary in her vision of the feminine: "Let it be known that the faculty of laughter in man is only a fourth-degree characteristic, just as, and in a quite other way, the body is not essentially defined by touch and impenetrability, but instead by extension." *Speculum of the Other Woman*, p. 190.

16. E. Allison Peers calls attention to the emendations in his notes. *The Interior Castle*, p. 101n. Not only did Gracián and Yanguas display a marked uneasiness with Teresa's concept of certainty, so did Luis de León when he published Teresa's works posthumously. In one passage in the *Vida*, for example, he substituted the word "trust" ("confiar") for Teresa's "certainty"

("estar cierta"); see Peers's note in *The Life of the Holy Mother Teresa of Jesus*, in *The Complete Works of Saint Teresa of Jesus*, 1: 236n.

17. Another pertinent example of the confessors' emendations is their deletion of the sentence, "As I write this, the noises in my head are so loud that I am beginning to wonder what is going on in it"—noises that interfere with Teresa's desire to "obey those who commanded me to write." Seeing Teresa as potentially disobedient had to be disallowed, a disallowing with which Teresa apparently concurred. See *The Interior Castle*, p. 77n.

18. *The Life of the Holy Mother Teresa of Jesus*, in *Complete Works*, p. 15. Unless otherwise noted, further references to the *Life* will be from this translation and will be cited in the text. Regarding Teresa's depiction of her father in the *Life*, see Gari Laguardia's essay, "Santa Teresa and the Problem of Desire," especially the following comment: "Teresa characterizes her father as a bad 'reader' of her discourse: in final measure, he cannot penetrate and decipher her code. Unable to 'read' her discourse, don Alonso is consequently barred from participating in the intimate dialogue that Teresa so insistently desires" (p. 524).

19. Lefkowitz, *Heroines and Hysterics*, pp. 54–55.

20. Musurillo, ed., "The Martyrdom of Perpetua and Felicitas," p. 111.

21. When her father came once again to appeal to Perpetua, he said, "Miserere, filia, canis meis"—"Have pity on my grey head, my daughter." Several lines later Perpetua did express her sympathy for her father "since he alone of all my kind would be unhappy to see me suffer." Ibid., pp. 112–13.

22. Ibid., p. 120. On the "feminization" of the early Christian God, see Pagels, "What Became of God the Mother?"

23. Teresa frequently calls attention throughout the text to her stylistic infelicities and to her inability to reflect on what she has already written. See, for example, "Oh, Sisters! How shall I ever be able to tell you of the riches and the treasures and the delights of the fifth Mansion? I think it would be better if I were to say nothing of the Mansions I have not yet treated, for no one can describe them" (96), and "Almost five months have passed since I began this book, and, as my head is not in a fit state for me to read it through again, it must all be very confused and I may possibly say a few things twice over" (118). Most scholars of Teresa's prose have tended to interpret her style as indicating haste in writing or a putative lack of forethought. One of the first critics to posit Teresa's language as consciously revolutionary was Juan Augusto Marichal, in "Santa Teresa en el ensayismo hispánico."

24. On the importance of the "spark" or synteresis for the mystical discourse of medieval and early Renaissance writers, see Steven E. Ozment's valuable introduction to *Mysticism and Dissent*, particularly pp. 3–8.

25. This posture of absolute submission is particularly apparent in the work's opening pages. After acknowledging that she has been "commanded" to write by Gracián and cannot, out of fear of disobedience, refuse, Teresa insists that she has no knowledge in advance as to the content of her writing. "Estando hoy suplicando a Nuestro Señor hablase por mí, porque yo no atinaba a cosa que decir ni como comenzar a cumplir esta obediencia, se me ofreció lo que ahora diré" (While I was beseeching Our Lord today that He would speak through me, since I could find nothing to say and had no idea how to begin to carry out the obligation laid upon me by obedience, something occurred to me which I will now set down) (5; 28). The moment of the present ("hoy") exists only between the two gerunds "estando" and "suplicando"; time and, by extension, Teresa herself come into being only through the constant act of prayer. In turn, "something" is offered to her ("se me ofreció") that she will proceed to say ("diré") with, it would appear, impunity.

26. See the enlightening discussion of Rosa Rossi, *Esperienza interiore e storia nell'autobiografia di Teresa d'Avila*, especially p. 65, where Rossi notes that "the memory and knowledge" that Teresa has of mystical experience are the "true reference points" of the narration.

27. The Spanish text makes the unity of subject and object much more apparent than the English translation is capable of doing: "Eramos *tan una cosa ella* y *yo*, que no pasaba cosa por su alma que yo estuviese inorante de ella, y ansí puedo ser buen testigo." (186–87; my italics).

28. One might find an analogy between Teresa's subtle undertaking of the confessor's mediating role and that of Gertrude of Helfta, a late-thirteenth-century German mystic. As Caroline Walker Bynum notes in *Jesus as Mother*, p. 203, "In a number of visions, [Gertrude] herself serves as a direct channel of grace to the sisters, acting with authority reserved to the priesthood and explicitly identified as priestly." Like Teresa's late sixteenth century in Spain, the thirteenth century was a period of suppression of women's religiosity and of their active role in the church; see ibid., pp. 250–51.

29. "Autobiography and Narrative," p. 18. For several recent theories of woman's autobiography, see Mason, "The Other Voice," particularly p. 235, where Mason concludes that the four women autobiographers she addresses "record and dramatize self-realization and self-transcendence through the recognition of another," and Stanton, "Autogynography," which likewise pursues the persistent alterity of women's autobiographies. That Teresa defined her life in relation to the "other" that is God has often been recognized; that her later writings defined her life in relation to the female community for which she wrote and in which she found her own authority has not

been as frequently acknowledged, but will be demonstrated in the remaining pages of this chapter.

30. For a reading of Teresa's construction of an exclusively feminine space, see Boudot, *La Jouissance de Dieu ou le roman courtois de Thérèse d'Avila*; for an alternative view closer to my own, see Paul Julian Smith's recent article, "Writing Women in Golden Age Spain." Yet while seeing Teresa as "trapped in the mirror of a man-made language," Smith offers as an "escape" only the "womanly space . . . of maternal, bodily enclosure" (p. 233). Like de Certeau's analysis, Smith's ultimately fails to take account of Teresa's *real* community of *hermanas*; it also ignores the fact that there is little maternal imagery in either the *Vida* or Teresa's other works.

31. *Teresa of Avila*, pp. 45–46.

32. As a glance at E. Allison Peers's index of scriptural references in Teresa's *Obras* attests, *Las Moradas* incorporates more biblical language than any of Teresa's other works; see *Complete Works*, 3: 398–99.

33. For this useful opposition between "makers" of meaning and "bearers" of meaning, see Laura Mulvey's influential article, "Visual Pleasure and Narrative Cinema." At the same time, Mulvey's construction does not allow for the potential subversiveness of both Perpetua's and Teresa's antisocial roles as "bearers" of God's meaning.

34. Paul primarily challenges the Jewish patriarchy of which he was an active part before his sudden conversion to Christianity; but for a reading that suggests he is more influenced than is commonly realized by the feminine dynamics of the Christian communities to which he preaches, see Parvey, "The Theology and Leadership of Women in the New Testament." Magdalene's challenge to patriarchy will be discussed in the following section.

35. Once again, Teresa's fascination with God's "inscriptions" on the soul is evident. See the *Libro de la Vida*, pp. 298–99 ("Parecíame en todas las partes di mi alma [Cristo] veía claro como en un espejo"); for the poem, see *Complete Works*, 3: 287–88.

36. "Full of Life Now," p. 69.

37. For the conversion scene, see Augustine, *Confessions*, bk. 8, chap. 12, p. 177: "I was asking myself these questions, weeping all the while with the most bitter sorrow in my heart, when all at once I heard the singsong voice of a child in a nearby house. Whether it was the voice of a boy or a girl I cannot say, but again and again it repeated the refrain, 'Take it and read, take it and read.' . . . I stemmed my flood of tears and stood up, telling myself that this could only be a divine command to open my book of Scripture and read the first passage on which my eyes should fall."

38. For a suggestive reading of an Augustine whose "project of narrating

his own life is doomed to a dead end and must be redeemed by his reading of the sacred texts"—a "redemption" unnecessary for Teresa, who does not undertake such a project without the sacred texts in the first place—see Lionnet, *Autobiographical Voices*, p. 39.

39. For a fascinating exploration of one Italian miller's "misuse" of texts such as Boccaccio's *Decameron*, see Carlo Ginzburg's *The Cheese and the Worms*.

40. Chanu, *Eglise, culture, et société*, p. 346.

41. See Peers, *Studies of the Spanish Mystics*, 1: 293–94.

42. See Peers, *Studies of the Spanish Mystics*, 1: 295n, on the adverse criticism surrounding the publication of Teresa's works because of her use of the vernacular.

43. Teresa also mentions events in the New Testament, then professes ignorance as to where those events might be found: "Thus, one day, when Jesus Christ was praying for His Apostles (I do not know where this occurs)" ("no sé dónde es") (230; 216).

44. For Mary Magdalene's prominence in Catholic tradition as "the penitent whore" brought "into existence by the powerful undertow of misogyny in Christianity, which associates women with the dangers and degradation of the flesh," see Warner, *Alone of All Her Sex*, pp. 224–35.

45. Teresa thus brings together Luke 7, in which "a woman of the city, who was a sinner . . . brought an alabaster flask of ointment . . . and began to wet his feet with her tears," and Luke 10, in which Jesus was received into the home of Mary and Martha. Such a conflation is hardly original with Teresa; as Warner notes, while the Greek church always distinguished three separate women—Mary of Bethany, Lazarus's sister; Mary Magdalene, the witness of the Resurrection; and the "sinner" above—the Western church, beginning at the time of Gregory the Great, combined all three figures under the name Mary Magdalene. *Alone of All Her Sex*, p. 228. On the extensive cult of Mary Magdalene in the Middle Ages and its "definitive decadence" in the fifteenth and sixteenth centuries, see Saxer, *Le Culte de Marie Madeleine en Occident*, 2: chap. 3. As Saxer's book makes clear, Teresa was hardly alone in embracing Magdalene as a patron saint. See, for example, Richard Kieckhefer's brief discussion of Catherine of Siena's adoption of Mary Magdalene as her mother when her own mother died. *Unquiet Souls*, pp. 133–34.

46. On the passage in Luke, see Ruether, *Sexism and God-Talk*, p. 67; on Magdalene's prominence in the Gnostic Gospels, see Fiorenza, "Word, Spirit and Power," pp. 51–57. Ruether provides a sustained discussion of Luke's "Mariology" and the expanded role his Gospel offers to women in *Sexism and God-Talk*, pp. 153–54. For Luke's social and economic revisionism, see Esler, *Community and Gospel in Luke-Acts*.

For another view of Magdalene as a woman whose speech has "auctoryte" and whose centrality in the moment of the Resurrection redeems the supposedly fallen nature of woman, see the remarks of Christine de Pisan, *The Boke of the Cyte of Ladyes*, sigs. Ee2, Ee3v; cited in Jordan, *Renaissance Feminism*, p. 110.

47. See the comment of Guido Mancini that Osuna was much more reserved and abstract, while Teresa made her own life the model for her spiritual guidebooks (*Teresa de Avila*, p. 97), and Roland Barthes's discussion of Loyola's intense drive to achieve a homogeneity and purification of discourse that might serve him in his attempt to control his readers (*Sade/Fourier/Loyola*).

48. See Alison Weber's comments on melancholy in *Teresa of Avila*, pp. 144–45. Weber's reading differs from mine in suggesting that Teresa's late work actually embraces Counter-Reformation doctrine, although she allows for the possibility that Teresa's apparent capitulations can be seen as strategic retreats.

49. "Psychoanalysis and Renaissance Culture," p. 214.

50. Perhaps the two most influential readings of the statue have been those of Georges Bataille and Jacques Lacan. Not incidentally, Bernini's depiction of Teresa can be found on the covers of, respectively, *Eroticism: Death and Sensuality* and *Le Séminaire XX*.

51. Indicative of one final irony in Teresa's "afterlife," as José Antonio Maravall notes in *Culture of the Baroque*, is the fact that her canonization in 1622, along with that of other Spanish saints such as Ignatius and Francis Xavier, was "celebrated and extolled in support of a social system, for the glory and protection of the monarchy whose charisma [these saints] strengthened. The poems singing the praises of their canonizations were also taken advantage of for glorifying the monarchy and its order, which henceforth would have yet another guardian in heaven" (p. 144). Thus is Teresa's female community denied yet once more, as she becomes a vehicle for that other model of patriarchy in early modern Spain, the Spanish monarchy.

Chapter 4

1. Lanfranco Caretti uses this term regarding the blend of lyric and epic strands in Tasso's writing; see *Ariosto e Tasso*, esp. p. 73.

2. On the pastoral play as a supposed reflection of the court's hidden desires, see Radcliff-Umstead, "Love in Tasso's *Aminta*." Yet whereas Radcliff-Umstead argues that Tasso's play fulfills those desires—he concludes that "the urbane members of the Ferrarese court found in the *Aminta* a projection of their dream to reconcile the demands of refined Culture with those

of primitive Nature" (p. 83)—I will argue that the *Aminta* frustrates those very desires. Louise George Clubb's article from the same volume, "The Pastoral Play," offers a more flexible theory of the pastoral genre, noting that "theatrical representation in the regular pastoral play was not a *speculum*, and the purely literary nature of its milieu made it a theatrical instrument of great range" (p. 68). See her most recent contribution to the study of pastoral in *Italian Drama in Shakespeare's Time*, chap. 6.

3. Cody, *The Landscape of the Mind*, p. 60.

4. For a recent and provocative reading of the *Conquistata*, see Godard, "Du 'Capitano' au 'Cavalier Sovrano.'"

5. *Gerusalemme Liberata*, ed. Fredi Chiappelli, VII. 15. All citations from the *Gerusalemme Liberata* will be from this edition. References are to canto and stanza. Translations of Tasso's poetry are my own.

6. "[Sono lieto] quanto che io sono stato il primo à destare ne gli animi degli huomini desiderio di questo vertuosissimo Soggetto, meritevole di ogni gran fortuna, tutto che egli si goda la quiete con tali fermezza di animo che pare, che non invidij lo stato à gran Prencipi." *Aminta di Torquato Tasso*, p. 3. It is on page 2 that Manuzio expresses his regrets for Tasso's present condition and notes that the *Aminta* came into his possession "from the hands [of Tasso] during his better days" and that the play "could no longer remain concealed by me without doing grave injury to the glory of its Author." Angelo Ingegneri virtually echoes Manuzio in his enthusiastic 1598 treatise, devoted almost exclusively to pastoral, entitled "La rappresentazione delle favole sceniche." On the productive period between 1572 and 1588, when Guarini's tremendously influential *Pastor Fido* was completed, see Clubb, "The Making of the Pastoral Play." On the fortunes of the *Aminta* in France and elsewhere, see Cremona, *L'Influence de l'Aminta*; for a briefer discussion of the *Aminta* and its European fortune, see Herrick, *Tragicomedy*, chap. 5.

7. On this earlier Ferrarese tradition, see Pieri, *La scena boschereccia nel rinascimento italiano*, pp. 151–210.

8. For the setting and scenography of the play, see Cavicchi, "La scenografia dell'*Aminta*."

9. On the difficulty of keeping the rural Campagna to the west of Ferrara in control, see Ariosto's fourth Satire, written when the writer was appointed commissioner of Garfagnana by the Este during the 1520's.

10. *The Prince*, pp. 50–51; my italics. On Machiavelli's advocacy of a "golden age" that would break all continuity with the past, see Federico Chabod's comment: "In Machiavelli the prince had appeared as an isolated individual, without any link to the past, without the halo of venerable tradition." *Giovanni Botero*, in *Scritti sul Rinascimento*, p. 323.

11. There is a striking similarity between the use of pastoral by Renaissance princes and its use by modern ethnographers. Renato Rosaldo suggests that anthropologists occasionally invoke pastoral for an ultimately self-

serving function when he notes that the shepherd with which both Edward Evans-Pritchard and LeRoy Ladurie identify themselves symbolizes a point *beyond* domination where "neutral ethnographic 'truth' can collect itself." See "From the Door of His Tent," esp. pp. 96–97.

12. For a description of the Belvedere as a place that "demonstrated in an intimate way the ruler's dominion over the environment of the court," see Yoch, "The Limits of Sensuality," pp. 65–67; on the gardens of the Belvedere and elsewhere around Ferrara, see Solerti, *Ferrara e la corte Estense*, and Venturi, *Le scene dell'Eden*, pp. 35–52. More generally, see Comito, *The Idea of the Garden in the Renaissance*, and the articles collected in Ragionieri, *Il Giardino Storico Italiano*.

13. The remainder of this section will counter the interpretation of critics who believe that the *Aminta* enacts an unhesitating tribute to the Este court; see, most recently, Walter Cohen, who reads the *Aminta*'s happy ending as an expression of "the impact of absolutism and the Counter-Reformation [which] led to a movement from satiric to providentially romantic comedy." *Drama of a Nation*, p. 100. While Cohen's observation on romantic comedy reflects the change in climate discussed in my last chapter, his generalization regarding the *Aminta* seems only partially accurate. Tasso's generic choice indeed conforms to the d'Este's wishes for "tragicomedia," evident as early as the 1550's when Giraldi Cinzio began to write his *tragedie di lieto fine* (tragedies with a happy ending). But the *Aminta* is by no means an unthinking acceptance of the rationale for that choice, as Cohen's perfunctory remark would appear to imply. In discussing the *Aminta*'s "genre," Gabriele Niccoli's brief article "Teoria e prassi" is particularly suggestive in arguing that the play has an essentially *tragic* structure, in contrast to the tragicomic basis of Guarini's *Pastor Fido*.

14. For the relationship between Tasso's youthful lyrics and the *Aminta*, see Claudio Varese's brief but informed discussion in *Torquato Tasso*, pp. 171–74; for a discussion of the "specular" poetics of Tasso's lyrics, see Daniele, *Capitoli Tassiani*, chap. 3, "Le meliche del Tasso."

15. *Aminta e Rime*, 1: 95–96. All citations from the *Aminta* and lyrics will be from this edition of his selected works; translations are my own. References to the *Aminta* are to act, scene, and line number. The line numbers are continuous through each act.

16. For the argument that the "mirror" has functioned in a large number of texts by women as a means through which women characters have been able to create their "conscious will"—much to the unease of men—see La Belle, *Herself Beheld*. On the use of the mirror in Tasso (primarily in the *Gerusalemme Liberata*), see Rima, "La metafora dello specchio dal Tasso al Marino." For an intriguing discussion of the possibilities of a "feminine pastoral" in which "woman's verbs—predicates of becoming—are disguised as states of being," see Nancy K. Miller, "Writing (from) the Feminine."

17. *Aminta e Rime*, 1: 168.

18. *Aminta e Rime*, 2: 215.

19. This view is in direct contrast to that of Gianni Venturi, who maintains in *Le scene dell'Eden*, p. 115, that the "idyll" of Silvia and Aminta occurs in a space that "is not the court but that is in view of the court." But given the numerous "messages" that dominate the play—we hear of, but do not see, Silvia's rescue by Aminta, his plunge from the cliff, and their final reunion—the point would seem to be precisely the opposite of that which Venturi makes: the "idyll" is, in fact, *never* seen by the court, which is prohibited from witnessing the most pastoral scene of the play. Two readings of the play more in line with my own are those of Alain Godard, "La Première Répresentation de l'*Aminta*," and Giulio Ferroni, *Il Testo e la scena*, noting convincingly that "the world of Silvia and Aminta is completely 'other' with respect to that of Dafne and Tirsi" (p. 35).

20. On the rationale for the addition of this passage—given that it includes a sustained criticism of one of Tasso's more virulent opponents, Speroni Sperone, it was not considered decorous to include it in the original presentation—see B. T. Sozzi's edition of the *Aminta* and his lengthy commentary on the scene.

21. Riccardo Scrivano points to this absence of catharsis in *La Norma e lo scarto*, p. 226, although for entirely different reasons; for him the *Aminta* only threatens catastrophes that are never realized.

22. See Claudio Varese's remark on Rayssiguier in *Torquato Tasso*, p. 184: "[Rayssiguier] manhandled the text and betrayed Tasso" in his failure to realize the extent to which the *Aminta* depends on the play and exchange of two completely different levels of representation.

23. Pope to William Walsh, July 2, 1706, in *Correspondence*. My thanks to Nancy Struever for this reference. On Pope's reading of Guarini's *Pastor Fido*, to which he alludes in this letter, see Perella, "Pope and the *Pastor Fido*."

24. "Ac velut effusa si quando grandine nimbi / praecipitant, omnis campis diffugit arator / omnis et agricola, et tuta latet arce viator / aut amnis ripis aut alti fornice saxi, / dum pluit in terris, ut possint sole reducto / exercere diem: sic obrutus undique telis / Aeneas nubem belli." (And as when at times storm-clouds pour down in showers of hail, every ploughman, every husbandman flees the fields, and the wayfarer cowers in safe stronghold, be it river's bank or vault of lofty rock, while the rain falls upon the lands, that so, when the sun returns, they may pursue the day's task: even thus, o'erwhelmed by javelins on all sides, Aeneas endures the war-cloud. . . .) *Aeneid* X.803–9.

25. "Non cedo io, no; fia con memoria eterna / de le mie offese eterno anco il mio sdegno. / Risorgerò nemico ognor più crudo, / cenere anco

sepolto e spirto ignudo" (IX.99). The lines are strikingly similar to those uttered by Dido on her funeral pyre: "Exoriare, aliquis nostris ex ossibus ultor, / qui face Dardanios ferroque sequare colonos, / nunc, olim, quocumque dabunt se tempore vires" (Arise from my ashes, unknown avenger! to chase with fire and sword the Dardan settlers, to-day, hereafter, whenever strength be given!). *Aeneid* IV.625–27.

26. See Sidney Painter's brief discussion of the battle in *A History of the Middle Ages 284–1500*, pp. 213–14.

27. See H. Jedin's magisterial *History of the Council of Trent* for historical background. For a substantial revisionist argument *against* the Council's restrictive influence on Italian culture, see Cochrane, "Counter Reformation or Tridentine Reformation?"

28. A Holy League was formed—briefly—in 1572 to keep the Turks away from Venice; but it was dissolved in 1573 when Venice withdrew from it. See Setton, *The Papacy and the Levant, 1204–1571*.

29. See Riley-Smith, *The First Crusade*, p. 150.

30. On Erasmus, see his letter to Paul Volz as well as his 1516 *Paraclesis*, in *Christian Humanism and the Reformation*. On Luther, see *Luther's Works: Lectures on Genesis*, 2: 215: "The Church in our day has two deadly enemies, the Turk and the pope. But both make a display of the name of God, and they suppose that there is nothing they cannot get by means of this title."

31. For Tasso's "sacramental theology," see Stephens, "Saint Paul Among the Amazons."

32. Migiel, "Tasso's Erminia," p. 62. Migiel goes on to suggest that the extensive narrative privileges Erminia is granted make her a "second narrator" of the *Gerusalemme*: "[Erminia's ability] to recognize the Christian soldiers [in canto III] and to recount their virtues and defects in a potentially ambiguous way make her a character with attributes and functions remarkably similar to those of the narrator" (pp. 63–64).

33. "È esso stesso il poeta, nel motivo a lui prediletto dell'amante ignorato, e fantastico e infelice. . . . Ed è, di tutte le figure del poema, quella in cui il poeta ha più pienamente narrato se stesso: o meglio, più eloquentemente espresse le voci elegiache e dolenti dell'anima sua." Donadoni, *Torquato Tasso*, p. 232.

34. Armida, of course, also bears a resemblance to Ariosto's *femme fatale*; like Angelica, she is introduced among the Christians to provoke disorder. Yet Armida's regal and calculated departure to her enchanted castle in the *Gerusalemme*'s fifth canto has little in common with Angelica's frantic escape in canto I of the *Furioso* from a Christian world within which she refuses to be defined. Angelica, moreover, departs not for an enchanted palace to which she may lure an enemy army, but for her homeland.

35. See Peter Wiggins's reading of Angelica as a figure who makes herself

invulnerable through her possession of the magic ring and yet is apparently unaware of her newfound independence: "With the magic ring she is perfectly free to do without a companion, and yet this alternative never enters her mind." *Figures in Ariosto's Tapestry*, p. 15.

36. *Orlando Furioso*, ed. Cesare Segre, XXIV.3. Further references to the *Furioso* are from this edition and are cited parenthetically in the text; references are to canto and stanza.

37. See Murtaugh, "Erminia Delivered," for an insightful reading of the parallels between the *Aminta* and the scene in canto XIX of the *Gerusalemme*.

38. "[Tancredi e Argante] ritrovano ombrosa angusta valle / tra più colli giacer, non altrimenti / che se fosse un teatro" (Tancredi and Argante find a shaded, narrow valley lying among a few hills, not any different than if it was a theater) (XIX.8).

39. See Beatrice Corrigan's claim that Erminia's entry into Jerusalem is similar to that of Goffredo, made in the "full light of day." What Corrigan does not mention are the starkly different pretexts under which the two figures enter. See "Erminia and Tancredi."

40. The provisionality of Erminia's *albergo* also betokens a larger sense of provisionality in the poem: Jerusalem would only be a temporary resting place for its faithful "peregrini," for it was, as discussed above, reconquered by the Turks, in whose hands it remained in Tasso's own time. The failure of a permanent center and the suggestion that not only Erminia but the others who have entered Jerusalem will once again become "peregrini" provide powerful counterpoints to a poem—and more importantly, as will be seen, to an "Allegoria"—that implies an apocalyptic triumph.

41. *The Book of the Courtier*, bk. 4, chap. 10, p. 294.

42. Javitch, *Poetry and Courtliness in the English Renaissance*, pp. 94–95.

43. *Stanze per la giostra*, bk. I, stanza 4. For a translation and an introduction to Poliziano and his relationship to the Medici, see the excellent edition by David Quint, *The Stanze of Angelo Poliziano*.

44. Lorenzo was widely acknowledged both within and outside of Florence as a poet; see, for example, "La ninfa fiesolana," his songs for carnival, and his sonnets with their ample Neoplatonic commentary, collected in *Scritti scelti*.

45. On Poliziano's relationship to the Medici, see Maier, *Ange Politien*, and more recently, Annabel Patterson's succinct pages in *Pastoral and Ideology*, pp. 81–85. Necessarily, Ariosto's narrator's notorious "errancies" and his demystification of all patrons in moments such as St. John's lunar revelations to Astolfo become the inheritance of Tasso's poem as well. Without the apocalyptic "certainty" granted by the attainment of Jerusalem, without the heavens' unification of the "Christian people," the poet is unwilling to

acknowledge the inspirational protection of a patron—or, for that matter, to sanction Alfonso's own short-lived attempts to engage in a crusade. The vision Goffredo receives during his own Astolfo-like journey to the heavens checks the imperial urges of his future student Alfonso, as lines are given to the Christian *capitano* worthy of an Ariosto or an Armida who lures Alfonso's ancestor Rinaldo to her fortunate island one canto later. Looking down to earth, Goffredo gazes at the vision of human folly that shines up at him through the smoke and clouds ("[Goffredo] ammirò che pur a l'ombre, a i fumi, / la nostra folle umanità s'affise, / servo imperio cercando e muta fama, / ne' miri il ciel ch'a sé n'invita e chiama") (Goffredo marveled that our human folly attaches itself to shadows and vapors, seeking servile empire and silent fame, and does not turn to heaven, that invites and calls us to itself) (XIV. 11). The captain is disabused of such *contemptus mundi* when the dead warrior Ugone informs him, in lines that return to the opening of the *Gerusalemme*, that "al fin tutti i tuoi compagni erranti / ridurrà il Ciel sotto i tuoi segni santi" (at the end, Heaven will bring back all of your errant companions beneath your sacred signs) (XIV. 18). But Alfonso, safe within his Ferrarese harbor, has presumably received no such signs of heaven's wishes.

46. Tasso's frequent appeals to shade and his tendency to conceive shade in negative terms in the poem should be noted here. Shade, of course, characterizes the noxious forest surrounding Jerusalem as well as the island where the truant Rinaldo lies in "ozio" with the temptress Armida. But it is also used to designate the protective device surrounding pagans such as Solimano in canto X and the Egyptian troops in canto XX, as well as the moral degeneracy of the Christian heroes.

47. Tasso to Scipione Gonzaga, October 4, 1575, in *Lettere di Torquato Tasso*, 1: 117.

48. Scholars are divided on the significance of the allegory added to the *Gerusalemme* when it was first published in 1581. Some, such as Sergio Zatti, see the allegory as a capitulation to the censors that Tasso could easily have avoided (*L'Uniforme cristiano*, p. 102), while others, such as Michael Murrin, read the belatedly furnished interpretation as the key to the epic's hidden unity (*The Allegorical Epic*, pp. 88–107). Still others, most recently Lawrence Rhu and William Kennedy, observe the tensions and constraints that "an overall ideological framework like the 'Allegoria' forces upon [Tasso]." See Rhu, "From Aristotle to Allegory," p. 128, and Kennedy, "The Problem of Allegory in Tasso's *Gerusalemme Liberata*." But given that most of the *Gerusalemme* was apparently completed by the time Tasso penned his allegory and that the allegory represents a paring down of the poem that is more fully registered in the heavily revised *Conquistata*, a discussion of what the "Allegoria" *suppresses* would seem to be critical. For

an exacting reading of the changes made in the *Conquistata*, particularly those that suppress the poem's historicity and create "an absolute space" paralleling that of a church invulnerable to historical change, see Godard, "Du 'Capitano' au 'Cavalier Sovrano,'" pp. 205–64. For readings of the "Allegoria" in light of the *Gerusalemme*'s evolution into the *Conquistata*, see Derla, "Sull'allegoria della *Gerusalemme Liberata*," and Olini, "Dalle direzioni di lettura alla revisione del testo." My own analysis owes a great deal to Walter Stephens's intriguing discussion in his unpublished paper, "Tasso's Allegory," of the allegory's attempt to suppress the *Gerusalemme*'s putatively dangerous "Pauline theology." Part of this chapter was generated as a response to Stephens's work.

49. On the tendency of Counter-Reformation art to stress a psychomachia that subordinates the individual to an abstract and ahistorical struggle of "essences," see Dempsey, "Mythic Inventions in Counter-Reformation Painting," p. 72. Dempsey suggestively brings the *Gerusalemme* into his discussion.

50. For the text of the "Allegoria," see Angelo Solerti's nineteenth-century edition of the *Gerusalemme*, 2: 27. Further references in the text to the "Allegoria" are to this edition.

51. For a reading suggesting that in the *Conquistata*, Tasso no longer emphasizes "the horizontal dimension of history" connecting the earthly Jerusalem and the heavenly Jerusalem, see the insightful argument in Quint, *Origin and Originality in Renaissance Literature*, p. 121.

52. See Bouwsma, "Three Types of Historiography in Post-Renaissance Italy," p. 308, which speaks of the extent to which Counter-Reformation historiography is premised on "the essential invulnerability of the visible church . . . to historical change."

53. The refusal to translate the Latin Mass into the vulgar, like the withholding of the chalice from the people—an issue that preoccupied several Tridentine sessions—betrays a defensiveness regarding the newly and rigorously defined class of sacerdotes. See Chanu, *Eglise, culture et société*, esp. pp. 355–80. Apropos of the *Gerusalemme*'s perhaps most blatantly "religious" moment, the Mass offered at the top of the Mount of Olives in canto XI, the narrator notes that the "primieri" (first-ranked) *heard* the "alti misteri" (high mysteries) of the Mass, whereas those farthest from the altar merely *saw* them. See Giovanni Getto's critique of the *Gerusalemme* as a work whose Counter-Reformation consciousness is betrayed by Tasso's melancholia, and his comment on the liturgy in canto XI as symptomatic of Tasso's own "indifference" regarding church ceremony. *Malinconia di Torquato Tasso*, pp. 56–58.

54. Fredi Chiappelli has so designated him; see his note on the *Gerusalemme*, XII.87–88 in his edition.

55. In the letter to Gonzaga expressing his misgivings about Antoniano's interventions, Tasso notes his doubts about the use of allegory per se. In a guarded acknowledgment that the recourse to allegory would jeopardize the poetic and thus the imaginative portion of his work, Tasso remarks, "I do not judge allegory necessary to the poem, as even Aristotle never made mention of it in this sense; and while I value those who profess to use it, it does not readily suit the poet. Nevertheless, I wanted to go through the labor to introduce it, even if I won't say, as did Dante, 'Sharpen here, reader, your eyes to the truth; / Because here the veil is so fine / That it is simple to pass within it.' It does not displease me to speak in this manner . . . [while I will] leave it to your judgment if this type of speaking is harmful to one's art, or not." *Lettere*, 1: 118. Calling attention to the "veil" of the poem—to its penetrable if opaque corporeality—is not, apparently, "displeasing" to Tasso. But the Dantesque invitation to the reader to penetrate the veil would seem to manifest a want of art. Or as Tasso suggests a few lines later, "Since it can supply only an accidental perfection, allegory is not able to cancel the defects of imitation." Given allegory's only accidental perfection, it can scarcely outweigh the imitative principle that is integral to the creation of the poem itself. The attempt to impose allegory amounts to nothing less than a betrayal of what Tasso considered to be the strikingly corporeal body of the poem. His early critical writings defend the claim that the integrity of epic should be derived from *within* rather than imposed from without. "Opera della natura è la bellezza, la qual consist[e] in certa proporzion di membra" (Beauty is the work of nature, which consists of a certain proportion among its members), Tasso had written in a *Discorso* of 1567, in which he also claimed that the poet should make his matter visible to his readers' senses so that they would believe that what they were reading was vividly, corporeally present before them. *Discorsi dell'arte poetica*, in *Scritti sull'arte poetica*, p. 37. Once that corporeality is construed only as a "velo," however, beneath which lurks a naked *essere intrinseco*, the body merely invites an interpretative violence that mimics the violence exacted on the pastoral setting of the *Aminta*.

56. For the verdict of the Crusca and the debates that surrounded Tasso's poem, see Weinberg, *A History of Literary Criticism in the Italian Renaissance*, 2: 954–1073.

57. See especially *Conquistata* I.6: "Tu [Cintio] l'altrui lingue piú famose, e l'arti / piú belle, e i sacri studi in pregio torni; / e pria che d'ostro il crin, l'interne parti / di virtù vera e vera luce adorni" (You [Cinthio] hold in esteem the most famous tongues of others, and the most beautiful arts and the sacred studies; and before you deck your locks with purple, you adorn your inner life with true virtue and true light). See also Robert Durling's comment apropos of the new dedication: "There is no longer any mention

of *errore*, either of the poet or of his heroes. The emphasis is instead exclusively public; Tasso praises the Cardinal and the Pope for their revivification of the papacy and for their patronage of the arts." *Figure of the Poet*, p. 265n. Durling's discussion of the poet's struggle "against the massive institutionalization and formulation of doctrine that was then taking place in Italy" (p. 195) has been central to this discussion.

58. "[Ferrara], con la ressidenza dei Duchi sempre aggrandiva, ma quando da essi fosse abbandonata sotto il dominio di preti, li quali indubitamente non voriano spender con gran beneficio dei vicini, impaludirà e si renderia in solittudine." *Delle Historie Venitiane*, cited in Salmons, "An Unpublished Account of the End of Este Rule in Ferrara," pp. 140–41.

Chapter 5

1. For two brief discussions of Spenser's borrowings from Tasso, see Cheney, *Spenser's Image of Nature*, and Lindenbaum, *Changing Landscapes*, pp. 184–87.

2. *The Faerie Queene*, ed. Thomas P. Roche, 3.5.42. All further references will be from this edition and will be cited parenthetically in the text. References are to book, canto, and stanza.

3. In the episode with Timias, Spenser might be said to point to a paradox present in Virgil's *Eclogues*: that the shade of pastoral is also the shade of death, a death Spenser conceives of as that of masculinity. On the double meaning of "umbra" in Virgil's poetry, see Peter L. Smith, "Lentus in Umbra." For the dynamics of the Spenserian bower, see Patricia Parker's suggestive "Suspended Instruments: Lyric and Power in the Bower of Bliss," in *Literary Fat Ladies*, pp. 54–66.

4. "Ne let his fairest *Cynthia* refuse, / In mirrours more then one her selfe to see, / But either *Gloriana* let her chuse, / Or in *Belphoebe* fashioned to bee: / In th'one her rule, in th'other her rare chastitee." 3.proem.5.

5. See Heisch, "Queen Elizabeth I," for a discussion of Elizabeth's use of the "mother-father" metaphor, particularly in the early stages of her reign.

6. On this see the comments of Louis Montrose in "The Elizabethan Subject and the Spenserian Text." For a more general discussion of Elizabeth's body as the body of the state, see Stallybrass, "Patriarchal Territories." Marie Axton's *The Queen's Two Bodies* is a fascinating discussion of Elizabeth's attempts to use the body politic / body natural metaphor to her advantage.

7. David Lee Miller, *The Poem's Two Bodies*, p. 235.

8. *King James His Welcome to London*, sig. C.

9. See Merritt Hughes's comment on Spenser's "assertions of the rights of one of Virgil's heirs to the patronage of the heirs of Augustus" and—a point that will become increasingly important in the pages to come—

on Spenser's being "only too conscious that the laborer was worthy of his hire." *Virgil and Spenser*, p. 320. For a lively discussion of the meaning of the Virgilian career for Spenser and other poets, see Lipking, *The Life of the Poet*. On the competitive climate in which Spenser wrote, see Whigham, *Ambition and Privilege*.

10. See the opening lines of the *Aeneid*: "Arms I sing and the man who first from the coasts of Troy, exiled by fate, came to Italy and Lavinian shores; much buffeted on sea and land by violence from above, through cruel Juno's unforgiving wrath." I.1–4. The Spenser citation is from *Spenser's Minor Poems*, ed. Ernest de Sélincourt, p. 61. All subsequent references to Spenser's poetry will be from this edition and will be cited parenthetically in the text. References are to line number.

11. Berger, "The Aging Boy," p. 25. David Lee Miller speaks of Colin's pathetic inability "to master his own nature in the season of labor and growth." "Authorship, Anonymity, and *The Shepheardes Calender*," p. 235.

12. *Le Calendrier des Bergers* was first published in 1497 and was translated into English in 1503; the work went through many subsequent editions and revisions. See Capp, *English Almanacs 1500–1800*, for an illuminating study of the genre to which the French calendar—and perhaps, indirectly, Spenser's calendar—belonged. My thanks to Andrew Weiner for loaning me his personal copy of the prints to *Le Calendrier des Bergers*. For discussions of the labors of the months, see Rosemond Tuve's *Seasons and Months* and Mary Parmenter's "Spenser's 12 Aeglogues Proportionable to the 12 Monthes." On georgic overtones in *The Shepheardes Calender*, see Patrick Cullen's *Spenser, Marvell, and Renaissance Pastoral*. Three valuable essays in Barbara Lewalski's *Renaissance Genres* suggest a new interest in English georgic as a genre that does *not* entirely rely on the Virgilian tradition: Alastair Fowler's "Beginnings of English Georgic," Annabel Patterson's "Pastoral vs. Georgic," and John King's "Spenser's *Shepheardes Calender*." King's essay is especially helpful for its excellent account of a native tradition of "georgic" satire, on which see also his *English Reformation Literature*.

13. MacCaffrey, "Allegory and Pastoral in *The Shepheardes Calender*"; Montrose, "Of Gentlemen and Shepherds." Ten years of emphasis on cultural poetics and determination *not* to idealize the artistic product have played down MacCaffrey's observations; as David Lee Miller's "Authorship, Anonymity, and *The Shepheardes Calender*" attests, there is a tendency to see Colin from the standpoint of limits, to view him as a victim of an all-encompassing process that his pathetic art cannot withstand. The status of Colin's art and the "life" of the calendar have thus been subtly rearranged. Yet such rearranging overlooks the calendar as a necessarily limited—because human—artifact; as Pierre Bourdieu has demonstrated, the calendar externalizes man's labors rather than a universal "nature." *Outline of a Theory*

of Practice, esp. pp. 172–76. While I do not wish to advocate a full-scale return to MacCaffrey's argument for the "power of imagination," her emphasis on the limitations of Spenser's calendar should be reexamined. If the calendar is not exactly transcended by the artist, it *is* interrupted by the poet impatient with the process it exemplifies.

Recent attention to the now almost canonical *Arte of English Poesie* by George Puttenham has led to a rather systematic avoidance of Spenser's vocabulary of labor in his early poetry and an insistence instead on his production of and participation in a courtly norm that, according to Louis Montrose's impressive argument, was created by suppressing the "intimate connection" between "herding and farming that was in fact typical of the Elizabethan countryside." "Of Gentlemen and Shepherds," p. 425. Montrose's other essays on pastoral ("Gifts and Reasons" and " 'Eliza, Queene of Shepheardes' ") focus on the genre's courtly dimension—a focus that tends to restrict his otherwise scintillating approach to pastoral.

14. In *Tottel's Miscellany*, p. 59. It might also be noted that *Tottel's Miscellany* contains numerous allusions to the sterility of the Petrarchan lover, bearing out Carol Thomas Neely's claims in "The Structure of English Sonnet Sequences" for the essential sterility of the sonnet sequence—a genre that has its roots in the fundamentally feudal structure between the knight and his lady.

15. See Greenblatt, *Renaissance Self-Fashioning*, p. 144.

16. E. H. Miller's chapter on patronage in *The Professional Writer in Elizabethan England* contains several examples of dedications that rely on metaphors of husbandry, including those of Churchyard and Barnabe Barnes.

17. For this characterization of georgic as a "potent" genre, see Heinzelman, *The Economics of the Imagination*, p. 145.

18. These are precisely the terms with which a number of critics have recently defined Spenser's relationship to Virgil's poem of labor. For the most part, their readings have focused on *The Faerie Queene* and on Spenser as the benevolent, almost self-effacing poet who trains his readers in the labors necessary for the creation of English empire. See Sessions, "Spenser's Georgics," and Low, *The Georgic Revolution*, chap. 2. Richard Neuse, in "Milton and Spenser," does not argue for *The Faerie Queene* as georgic, but sees the *Epithalamion* as a "georgic" act of self-effacement: the poet steps "into a larger plane of existence where he is no more than one among many centers of consciousness" (p. 617). On the general importance of georgic in the period, see M. J. O'Loughlin, *The Garlands of Repose*, and L. P. Wilkinson, *The "Georgics" of Virgil*, pp. 274–96. James Turner's *Politics of Landscape* provides a valuable discussion of the conflation of a religious poetic and a vocabulary of labor in seventeenth-century England.

19. The phrase is David Lee Miller's, from "Authorship, Anonymity, and *The Shepheardes Calender*," p. 219.

20. Vives, "In Georgica Vergilii," 1: 552. Erasmus also goes to the *Georgics* for examples of copious discourse. See *On Copia of Words and Ideas*, esp. bk. I, chap. ii, "By Whom Copia Was Developed and by Whom Practiced."

21. See Peter Sacks's argument that Spenser's early work is predominantly elegiac in *The English Elegy*, esp. p. 46: "If Spenser is above [Colin's] melancholy withdrawal, it is curious how reticent he is about asserting his superiority. Nowhere within the poem is there an adequate answer to Colin."

22. *Georgics* IV. 563–66. The final line is a near-repetition of the opening line of the first Eclogue ("Tityre, tu patulae recubans sub tegmine fagi").

23. For recent discussions of the role of Orpheus in Spenser's poetry, see Thomas Cain, *Praise in "The Faerie Queene"*; Berger, "Spenser's Critique of Pastoral Love and Art"; Goldberg, *Voice/Terminal/Echo*, pp. 43–48; and Loewenstein, "Echo's Ring."

24. On anxiety about misinterpretation, see Louis Montrose's comment in "The Elizabethan Subject and the Spenserian Text," p. 329, that Spenser tries to "direct and delimit the interpretative activity of that elite community of readers by whom he himself is authorized to write." Joseph Loewenstein hints suggestively of a Spenser who "came to find print imperiled, not liberating; print exposes him to a censorious state, and then provides him with a sphere of self-defense." "The Script in the Marketplace," p. 273. On the question of premature publication, see Richard Helgerson's comment that in correspondence with Gabriel Harvey during the period of *The Shepheardes Calender*, Spenser worries about "whether he should publish at all." *Self-Crowned Laureates*, pp. 78–79. It would appear that Spenser, like Milton, whose "Lycidas" opens with "I come to pluck your Berries harsh and crude, / And with forc'd fingers rude, / Shatter your leaves before the mellowing year," is articulating a fear intimately associated with pastoral as a genre of beginnings: that one is disseminating or publishing too soon.

25. See Paul Alpers's comments about the authority that print confers on Spenser's pastoral in "Pastoral and the Domain of Lyric in Spenser's *Shepheardes Calender*," pp. 174–75.

26. Williams, *The Country and the City*, p. 32. For a corrective to Williams's argument for Jonson's blind acceptance of Jacobean ideology, see William Cain, "The Place of the Poet." I thank Jonathan Goldberg for this reference.

27. From "To Penshurst," in *Poems*, p. 89.

28. As Marcel Detienne observes in *Crise agraire et attitude religieuse chez Hésiode*, p. 49: "Prosperity and the general profits that the peasant draws

from his work are not 'givens' separable from a personal relationship with the gods and the earth." Elsewhere Detienne comments on the "innumerable rules" that the peasant of Hesiod's day was expected to follow. See also Mary Douglas's *Purity and Danger* for an exploration of the rigorous obedience of taboos in archaic cultures.

29. Whether Jonson was invoking this Virgilian dynamic when writing his poems to potential patrons is difficult to tell; at the very least, the numerous references to the *Georgics* in "To Sir Robert Wroth" should alert us to the possibility that he was engaged in exposing the subtleties of Virgil's poem, instead of simply falling prey to the insidious demands of protocapitalism. Referring explicitly to Ian Donaldson's edition of Jonson's *Poems*, Alastair Fowler calls attention to these georgic references in "Beginnings of English Georgic," p. 122n.

30. John Heywood, *Of Gentylnes and Nobylyte*, p. 10.

31. Bourdieu, *Outline of a Theory of Practice*, pp. 172–73, discusses the transition from an archaic, artificially maintained economy based on "good faith" to one that explicitly acknowledges self-interest.

32. Putnam, *Virgil's Poem of the Earth*, p. 149.

33. For a careful reading of the second Georgic, see Muecke, "Poetic Self-Consciousness in *Georgics* II."

34. Michael Putnam discusses Virgil's relationship to Lucretius in *Virgil's Poem of the Earth*, pp. 146–48.

35. "The Ciconian dames . . . tore the youth limb from limb and strewed him broadcast over the field" (IV.520–22). In Latin, the final phrase is "sparsere per agros." This ghastly phrase is the last reference in the *Georgics* to the fields of which it has been Virgil's principal concern to sing.

36. When Aristaeus first calls upon his mother, Cyrene, he defines himself as the "complete" husbandman: "Lay the hostile flame to my stalls, destroy my crops, burn my seedling, and swing the stout axe against my vines, if such loathing for my honor hath seized thee" (IV.330–32). In three brief lines, he mentions three of the four "arts" Virgil summarized at the beginning of the first Georgic: farming, oenology, and breeding; that Aristaeus is also a bee-keeper—a fact central to the fourth Georgic—is, of course, already known.

37. As David Lee Miller has observed apropos of the poem's dedicatory sonnet to Leicester, *Virgils Gnat* intimates that Spenser's own "season" has been "insecure." *The Poem's Two Bodies*, p. 63. Richard Helgerson calls attention to Spenser's "lack of financial support" during the period. *Self-Crowned Laureate*, p. 75. To this extent, the poem itself constitutes an interruption of the process of "fruitfulness," an outcry *against* the cycle within which the poet is supposedly the conscientious laborer passively awaiting his reward for not transgressing his boundaries.

38. *P. Ovidius, Metamorphosis* II.61–66, trans. Arthur Golding, p. 140v.

39. See the *Culex*: "Vos sede piorum, / vos manet heroum contra manus. hic et uterque / Aeacides." (For you, O heroines, over against you in the house of the righteous, there waits a band of heroes. Here are the two sons of Aeacus) (lines 295–97).

40. See, for example, interpretations such as that of W. L. Renwick, who in his commentary to Spenser's *Complaints*, p. 218, remarks that "it would appear that [Spenser] had been checked by Leicester for some well-meant indiscretion."

41. Indeed, as Paul E. McLane has suggested, Spenser tended if anything to idealize Leicester and his relationship to him; see *Spenser's Shepheardes Calender*, pp. 136–37.

42. David Lee Miller, *The Poem's Two Bodies*, p. 66.

43. As Patrick Cullen and others have demonstrated, Mantuan consistently opposes "hard" pastoral to "soft" pastoral, thereby demystifying the desire for the idyllic found in Theocritus and Virgil. Central to the formulation of hard pastoral is a vision of poetry as work—as well as the failure of others to acknowledge the poet's claims to meaningful labor, with a resulting alienation from a world of productivity. One can see how central this dynamic is to Mantuan by briefly considering Eclogue 5, in which the wealthy landowner Silvanus greets a slumbering Candidus with a request for a song. Silvanus's portrait of the easeful shepherd returns us to the bucolic idealism found in Virgil's first Eclogue, where the singing Tityrus is greeted by the exile Meliboeus. But Mantuan inverts the Virgilian dynamic by silencing "Tityrus" and transforming Meliboeus from an exile bereft of his lands into a selfish and wealthy man. The latter's desire to hear a song without offering anything in return devalues poetry as work by insisting on its spontaneous, timeless, and therefore nondisruptive status. By refusing to acknowledge Candidus's insistence that "A Verse it is a stately thing, and craves a cruell paines"—the line is from George Turberville's 1567 translation of Mantuan, sig. G.iiv—Silvanus forces the starving Candidus to use against him the only weapon he has left: a curse that will inflict on Silvanus the sterility Candidus already experiences. Candidus utters the final lines in the poem, and he employs them to memorable effect by associating Silvanus with Midas, the mythological figure who was both a notoriously bad judge of song and an avaricious miser who turned everything he touched to a sterile and "unnatural" gold. If the poet cannot be part of a cycle of georgic fertility, then his only defense is to translate Silvanus's "fruits" into sterility.

We have seen a similar desire before, in the *Vita* of Cellini. But just as Cellini's narrative of hypermasculinity is doomed to fail, so is Candidus's plea for self-validation. Craftsman and shepherd alike have recourse only to a parable of sterility: their own, and, in the cycle of revenge they wish to inflict on their ignorant and dangerous patrons, that of powerful others. Spenser's departure from this sterility of pastoral patronage is notable; he transforms the stingy Silvanus into the sympathetic and generous Piers, and while Cuddie is busy blaming the great, failed Augustus and Maecenas beyond the world of the eclogue, he in no way implicates Piers in his criticisms. For two sensitive recent readings of Spenser's debt to Mantuan, see Hoffman, *Spenser's Pastorals*, and Shore, *Spenser and the Poetics of Pastoral.*

44. "Quid petis ergo / carmen et *invadis partes, Silvane, alienas*" (lines 47–48; my italics). The lines are from Wilfred P. Mustard's edition of *Eclogues of Baptista Mantuanus*.

45. The phrase is from the beginning of the sixth and final book of Ovid's incomplete *Fasti*, in which Ovid portrays himself meditating on the origins of the word "June." Declaring in a defiant vein that he will "sing the truth" about the month's name—"[though] some will say I lied, and think that no deities were ever seen by mortals"—he invokes the isolated grove familiar to readers of the *Metamorphoses*. This is the "nemus arboribus densum" where he is visited by three goddesses: "but not those whom the teacher of ploughing beheld when he followed his Ascraean sheep; nor those whom Priam's son compared in watery Ida's dells." Having differentiated himself from Hesiod, who was visited by the Muses at the beginning of his epic *Theogony*, and Paris, whose choice of Venus as the most beautiful goddess launched another Greek epic, Ovid sanctions *his* new epic by claiming that Juno addressed him as "vates, Romani conditor anni" (poet, minstrel of the Roman year) who has "dared to chronicle great things in slender couplets." See *Fasti* VI.5–19, trans. James Frazer, p. 319.

46. Peter Sacks discusses the elegiac creation of "a fiction whereby nature and its changes, the occasions of [man's] grief, are made to depend on [man]." *The English Elegy*, p. 20. Elegy thus becomes the vehicle with which man attempts to master nature. Virgil, of course, has featured the potency of elegy before, most prominently in his fifth Eclogue, where it has the ability to transform Julius Caesar into a god. In the *Georgics*, however, Virgil's narrator attempts to contain the elegiac, in a manner that suggests it has no place in his new poem. Indeed, it is possible to say that Virgil's entire career was devoted to suppressing the elegiac; the fourth Eclogue, for example, radically turns the nostalgic pastoral vision toward the future, not the past, in an obsessive move to endorse the powers of Roman empire. Such efforts, of course, are not always successful; the most forward-looking moment of the *Aeneid*, Anchises' presentation of future worthies of Rome to Aeneas, is muted by grief over the younger Marcellus's death. The effect of such moments on Virgil's corpus as a whole lies outside the scope of this book, but what is clear is the extent to which elegy reveals the fragility of the sup-

posedly "organic" myths of empire and patronage, myths that are as much a part of "Aprill" as they are of the *Georgics*. And at least in Virgil, the elegiac alternative becomes a force that must be reckoned with (and dispersed) when it threatens the cyclic vitality of the georgic calendar. Orpheus's celibate, elegiac posture following Eurydice's second death clearly presents such a threat; the participants in Virgil's mythical cycle *must* attempt to disperse Orpheus's "labors" in order to defend the existence of that cycle.

47. E. K. offers the paraphrase "overlaboured and sunneburnt" (312) as a commentary on Colin's line, "Shee is my goddesse plaine, / And I her shepherds swayne, / Albee forswonck and forswatt I am" (97–99).

48. Schenck, *Mourning and Panegyric*, pp. 48–49. Also see Goldberg, *Voice/Terminal/Echo*, p. 53, noting that in "Aprill," "praise is founded on elegiac strains." John King has alerted me to the connection between funereal and coronation imagery in the London pageants for Margaret of Anjou in 1445. See Kipling, "The Funeral Coronations for Margaret of Anjou."

49. See Jonathan Goldberg's comment on the "presentation of flowers required of an elegy" in "Aprill." *Voice/Terminal/Echo*, p. 53.

50. See Nancy Vickers's seminal articles on the blazon, including "Diana Described" and " 'The Blazon of Sweet Beauty's Best.' "

51. "The Elizabethan Subject and the Spenserian Text," p. 322. I disagree, however, with Montrose's assertion—based on a point made by Robert Weimann—that laboring over something virtually makes it one's own (p. 337n). As the following remarks elaborate, Colin's Orphism is considerably mediated and enabled by his ever-watchful community of fellow shepherds.

52. On Crowley, see King, *English Reformation Literature*, esp. p. 432. On Spenser's Protestantism, see Hume, *Edmund Spenser*; King, "Spenser's *Shepheardes Calender* and Protestant Pastoral Satire"; and Weiner, "Spenser and the Myth of Pastoral."

53. See Anthony Low's argument about the centrality of work in Spenser's pastorals in *The Georgic Revolution*, chap. 2, and Patrick Cullen's discussion of Mantuan's influence on Spenserian pastoral in *Spenser, Marvell, and Renaissance Pastoral.*

54. See the useful comments of Theresa Krier apropos of the delicacy with which Spenser had to treat the "challenge" of a female patron. *Gazing on Secret Sights*, pp. 74–75.

55. See the observation of David Lee Miller to this effect in "Spenser's Vocation, Spenser's Career," p. 218.

56. For one influential interpretation suggesting that Spenser is registering complete disillusion with the court in book 6, see Javitch, *Poetry and Courtliness in the English Renaissance*.

57. I thus take issue with John Guillory's comment that the Graces'

disappearance is a sign of the poet's mastery of loss; see *Poetic Authority*, p. 44.

Chapter 6

1. "Patronage in the Renaissance," p. 23.

2. For the social and economic history of the actor in sixteenth-century England, see Bradbrook, *The Rise of the Common Player*. References to the organization of the players' companies are on pp. 62–63.

3. *Reformation to Industrial Revolution*, vol. 2, 1530–1780, p. 89; cited in Kernan, *The Playwright as Magician*, p. 56.

4. Or as the antitheatrical writer "I.G." noted, Roman laws "ordayned that for no pastime shewed, or another thing spoken, [the Players] should be so bould to take any mony." *A Refutation of the Apology for Actors*, p. 51 (published with Thomas Heywood's *An Apology for Actors*). This attack was echoed in a somewhat different vein by the writers of *Histrio-Mastix* and *The Parnassus Plays*, who saw the actor's and playwright's trade as a sordid money-making venture that would contaminate their own literary efforts. The hero of *Histrio-Mastix* prefers sacred "poverty" and the sheltered cloisters of academe to the potentially lucrative business of the stage. See *Histrio-Mastix* sig. Ev; for a brief discussion of the play, see Edwards, *Threshold of a Nation*, pp. 19–25. Given these fears that the commercialism of theater would taint the "pure" efforts of would-be humanists and the newly won respectability of the trades by parodying all that was sacred to the very concept of *work*, it seems possible to argue that it was not the liminality of the actor that made him liable to attack, but his emergence from liminality. Thus one must be careful to avoid making the claims of Steven Mullaney in his argument for theater's "liberty" in Elizabethan England (*The Place of the Stage*). Borrowing Louis Althusser's vocabulary of "internal distanciation," Mullaney attempts to locate theater's power as critical institution in its privileged geographical distance from affairs of the city and the realm. Yet Althusser's remarks rest on the utopian image of the artwork as an entity uncontaminated by the material—a recourse to the aesthetic challenged by Pierre Bourdieu in his essay, "Symbolic Anthropology."

5. *The Rise of the Common Player*, p. 39.

6. James's action may well have been motivated by the realization that he could employ the successful institution of the theater for his own ends, as well as prevent it from falling into the hands of members of the nobility for theirs. See Burt, "Licensed by Authority," arguing that royal licensing was "one index of the court's unwillingness to restrain market forces that gave rise to resistance within the aristocracy and in Puritans of different social ranks" (p. 556n), and Thomson, "Playhouses and Players in the Time

of Shakespeare," p. 71, observing that James's concern about the power of the English barons led him to restrict patronage of theater companies to members of the royal family.

7. See Bristol, *Carnival and Theatre*, pp. 122–23, and Leah Marcus's chapter on *Measure for Measure* in *Puzzling Shakespeare*, pp. 165–202.

8. Shade and its cognate, shadow, rarely reflect the positive aspects of nurturance and protection in Shakespeare's corpus. Tellingly, it is only rulers sick of kingship and longing for lives they will never have—Henry VI, Imogen—who invoke restful images of a shade traditionally associated with shepherds. In a noted passage spoken in the midst of battle, Henry incongruously meditates on the shade offered by the hawthorn bush "to shepherds looking on their silly sheep" and beneath which the herdsman takes his "wonted sleep" (3 *Henry VI*, 2.5.42–49). But Henry's musings are an isolated case. For the most part, "shade" and "shadow" are used in conjunction with death or associations of death. Even in Shakespeare's most pastoral of plays, *As You Like It*, shade is invoked only in the context of the melancholy boughs beneath which a duke ponders his exile and the deadly site where a lioness waits for the sleeping Oliver to awaken (2.7.111, 4.3.113). Thus, too, the pathetic Thisby in the mechanicks' play in *A Midsummer Night's Dream* "dr[aws] his dagger and die[s]" beneath the "mulberry shade" (5.1.149), the exiled Suffolk alludes to the "sweetest shade" of cypresses in 2 *Henry VI* (3.2.323), and Malcolm searches for "some desolate shade" beneath which he and Macduff can "weep our sad bosoms empty" (*Macbeth*, 4.3.1–2).

9. See Shakespeare's use of the word "shroud" elsewhere, as in Romeo's "Hide me with a dead man in his shroud" (*Romeo and Juliet*, 4.1.85). Thidias's ominous invitation is perhaps inspired by the eighth book of Virgil's *Aeneid*, in which the dying Cleopatra is depicted on Aeneas's shield as being drawn into the "mourning Nile, of mighty frame, opening wide his folds and with all his raiment welcoming the vanquished to his azure lap and sheltering streams" (contra autem magno maerentem corpore Nilum / pandentemque sinus et tota veste vocantem / caeruleum in gremium latebrosaque flumina victos) (VIII.711–13). Appropriately, the next lines of the *Aeneid* turn immediately to Caesar "entering the walls of Rome in triple triumph." No lovingly paternal Nile, Octavius is a much different father figure, whose request is spurned by the Cleopatra who seeks "liberty" rather than the insidious protectiveness of Octavius's mantle.

10. Shortly before her suicide, Cleopatra fears what will happen not only when she is "hoist[ed] up / And show[n] . . . to the shouting varletry / Of censuring Rome" (5.2.55–57) but when "some squeaking Cleopatra [will] boy [her] greatness / I'th'posture of a whore" (5.2.220–21). Behind this nightmare is the assumption that those who act beneath Octavius's royal

shroud must carry out their emperor's wishes, enacting only the script he wants them to perform.

11. Thus *The Winter's Tale* refuses to work within the framework of a dramatic economy that recognizes "the unacknowledged presence of authority and hierarchy and . . . the harmonizing language of unity and homogeneity"—an economy found in forms such as the masque and the "Tragicomedie," in which James saw a divine dispensation for himself and his subjects. For this description of "the classical version of mimesis," see Weimann, "Mimesis in *Hamlet*," p. 276. Leah Marcus notes that both the masque and the "Tragicomedie" (at least as James used the term) "celebrate a[n] . . . overriding destiny which grows out of the royal will and the king's special prescience." *Puzzling Shakespeare*, p. 142.

12. See Goldberg, *James I and the Politics of Literature*, pp. 43–51.

13. On James's anxieties vis-à-vis both his paternal and his maternal sources of legitimation, see Orgel, "Prospero's Wife."

14. See James's frequent appeals to the first book of Samuel in *The Trew Law of Free Monarchies*, in *The Political Works of James I*, esp. pp. 55–61. While the emphasis on divine right looks back to the thaumaturgical legacy of the Middle Ages, James invested that doctrine with a new insistence on fatherhood as the obligatory form in which sovereignty was embodied. For general background, see Bossy, *Christianity in the West: 1400–1700*, pp. 153–61.

15. In *Workes of the Most High and Mightie Prince, James I*, p. 245.

16. Glynn Wickham is the most ardent champion of the view that the tragicomedies did confirm that vision. See, in particular, "King Lear as Prologue." Jonathan Goldberg sees in *Cymbeline* a frank celebration of "Augustan and Christian peace": "the Solomonic reign of James joins justice, peace, unity, and plenty into an overwhelming image of reconciliation." *James I and the Politics of Literature*, p. 240.

17. For the dynamics of the Jacobean masque, see Orgel, *The Illusion of Power*.

18. See *Ben Jonson: The Complete Masques*, ed. Stephen Orgel, p. 530. Further references to the masque will be from this edition; line numbers will be cited parenthetically in the text.

19. This is Stephen Orgel's characterization of the royal spectator of *The Masque of Queens*. "Jonson and the Amazons," p. 133.

20. See Barish's discussion of Jonson's antitheatricality in "Jonson and the Loathèd Stage," and the final chapter in Greene's *The Light in Troy*.

21. As Stephen Orgel has noted in his commentary on the disappearance of the antimasque in *Queens*, "no confrontation between [the worlds of the antimasque and the revels] is possible. The moral victory, the triumph of virtue, is therefore achieved not through drama, the ordinary means of the

poet and playwright, but through Inigo Jones's machinery." *Ben Jonson: The Complete Masques*, p. 8. See the recent comment by A. Lynn Magnusson that "the impotence of evil in Jonson's masque . . . is mere cleverness, a toy of thought aimed at flattering the monarch and his court. . . . The superior perspective from which evil is illusion is itself merely an expensive—and potentially dangerous—illusion." "Interruption in the *Tempest*," p. 64. Magnusson's argument that *The Tempest* fails to cater to such an illusion has been important for the following discussion of *The Winter's Tale*.

22. *Worlds Apart*, p. 147.

23. Speaking of the Stuart masque in its final phase under Charles I as nothing less than an expression of autocracy, Stephen Orgel comments: "We tend to see in such productions only elegant compliments offered to the monarch. In fact they are offered not to him but by him, and they are direct political assertions." *The Illusion of Power*, p. 52.

24. See Thomas Greene's remarks on the vulnerability of the masque form: "Perhaps court spectacle can best be regarded as a vulnerable institution, vulnerable always to the suspicion of manipulation but struggling intermittently to *earn* its idealizations, to transcend a vulgarity of motive it can never permanently exorcise." "Magic and Festivity at the Renaissance Court," p. 657.

25. Writing against "SCOT an Englishman, [who] is not ashamed in publike print to deny, that ther can be such a thing as Witchcraft," James ardently defends the reality of "spirits, & Spectres that appeares & trobles persones." *Daemonologie*, pp. xi–xii.

26. This failure "proves" that the king is "the child & servant of God, and they but servants to the devil," and that he is "the Lords annointed, and they but vesselles of Gods wrath," as the writer of *Newes from Scotland* concluded in 1591. *Newes from Scotland*, p. 29. For Stuart Clark's argument that James wrote *Daemonologie* to satisfy political and religious pretensions at a time when they could not be expressed in other ways, see "King James's *Daemonologie*," p. 164.

27. The "writer" of *A Discourse on the Maner of the Discoverie of the Powder Treason* describes the king as the gifted interpreter of a secret message that warns him of the plot against his life. And as is claimed in *Newes from Scotland*, written by a source close to the court in the early 1590's after James and Anne were almost drowned, the king "hazarde[d] himselfe in the presence of such notorious witches" (p. 29) to learn the means by which they sought his demise. But since James alone can confirm "the verye woordes which passed between the Kings Maiestie and his Queene at Upslo in Norway the first night of their mariage," reported to him by one Agnis Sampson when she "tak[es] his Maiestie a little aside" (p. 15), he alone can verify her confession that she indeed conspired to kill him at the instigations of

the devil and can thus convict her as a witch. The plot's failure attests not so much to the impotence of demons, possessed of an uncanny ability to re-present the most intimate secrets of kings, as to the sanctity of James as God's "annointed." Even in *Newes from Scotland*, devoted, like the later *Daemonologie*, to proving the actual existence of witches, there is a fine line between what James alone might authorize and what is "objectively" true.

28. For the argument that Jonson's early masques were *not* simple exercises in "purgation," see Loewenstein, *Responsive Readings*, pp. 100–102.

29. Thus we have the banquet scenes and wedding masque in *The Tempest*, the thunderous descent of Jupiter in *Cymbeline*, and the royal pageant at the end of *Henry VIII*. *The Winter's Tale* arguably has the briefest of masques—the dance of shepherds and shepherdesses, performed by both rustics and princes, followed shortly thereafter by the antics of satyrs. In each case, however, the masque form is qualified, challenged, or interrupted by events beyond it. See, for example, Frye, "Romance as Masque"; Leech, "Masking and Unmasking in the Late Plays"; and Magnusson, "Interruption in *The Tempest*."

30. For Goldberg, the "spectacle of state" that the playwright and king are meant to control is in fact in "other hands." See "*Macbeth* and Source," pp. 259–60.

31. For the affinities between *Macbeth* and *The Winter's Tale*, see Knight, *The Crown of Life*, p. 82. After citing a series of parallels between the two plays—including the "dallyings" of the "unreal" and real, the "horrible imaginings" of both kings' "fantastical" crimes, the orchestration of evil as "essential 'nothing,' unreality, a delirium, which yet most violently acts on the real"—the critic concludes, "We are nearer *Macbeth* than *Othello*."

32. See Carol Thomas Neely's remark that *The Winter's Tale* refuses to allow for male parthenogenesis. *Broken Nuptials in Shakespeare's Plays*, p. 194.

33. 1.1.45. All citations of *The Winter's Tale* are to J. H. P. Pafford's edition. Greene's novel, *Pandosto, The Triumph of Time*, appears in an appendix to that edition. The passage in the text is from page 185; further page references will be cited in the text.

34. See Nevil Coghill's cogent analysis of the scene and Hermione's "*visibly pregnant*"—and hence visibly threatening—state. "Six Points of Stage-Craft in *The Winter's Tale*," p. 33. Polixenes' lines return in the words of Hermione's waiting-women in act 2: their queen is "spread of late into a goodly bulk" and is "round[ing] apace" (2.1.19–20, 16).

35. See Muriel Bradbrook's remarks on the masquelike structure of *The Winter's Tale* in *The Living Monument*, pp. 208–9.

36. He thus would seem to strive to become the omniscient author of Greene's novel, who *does* construct a narrative of suspicion in his obser-

vation that the queen "used [Egistus] so familiarly that her countenance bewrayed how her mind was affected towards him, oftentimes coming herself into his bed chamber to see that nothing should be amiss to mislike him. This honest familiarity increased daily more and more betwixt them . . . [and] there grew such a secret uniting of their affections, that the one could not well be without the company of the other." *Pandosto*, pp. 185–86.

37. Such an attempt, in Crewe's reading of *The Rape of Lucrece*, "could be only an act of folly or abomination" for Shakespeare. *Trials of Authorship*, p. 159.

38. As David Underdown has emphasized, the charivari that were targeted at adulterous couples and families with "scolding" wives during the sixteenth and seventeenth centuries frequently featured one man, dressed in drag, beating another man: "The husband was as much the subject of disapproval—for tolerating the offence—as the wife." See "The Taming of the Scold," p. 129. On the rituals of shaming related to scolding and adultery—two "crimes" often related, as we shall see—see Ingram, "Ridings, Rough Music and Mocking Rhymes in Early Modern England." Also see Boose, "Scolding Brides and Bridling Scolds," and Parker, *Literary Fat Ladies*, pp. 8–35, although neither critic calls attention to the shaming rituals to which husbands were exposed.

39. There is, of course, another policy of preemption at work in Leontes' accusations of Hermione that characterizes the misogynistic treatises and satires of seventeenth-century England in general, as one contemporary woman writer recognized. Esther Sowernam's 1618 treatise against the popular antifeminist Swetnam is, as Ann Rosalind Jones has argued, a diagnosis of "the defense mechanisms through which men project their sexual desires onto women"—a projection that prevents them from being associated with the very lust from which they would disassociate themselves. See "Counterattacks on 'the Bayter of Women,'" pp. 53–57. For Swetnam's views of the "shrew," see Woodbridge, *Women and the English Renaissance*, pp. 86–87.

40. I thus take issue with Andrew Gurr, who argues that the bear's entrance onstage breaks the illusion of realism in the play. "The Bear, the Statue, and Hysteria in *The Winter's Tale*."

41. Thus she furnishes, as Mary L. Livingston has observed, a "distanced comment" on "the disastrous abuse of art in Leontes' court sixteen years earlier." "The Natural Art of *The Winter's Tale*," p. 342. Elsewhere in this article, Livingston talks about the "extravagant language of court compliment" and the "tragic overdevelopment of courtly arts" in the first three acts of the play (pp. 342, 345). Her comments are suggestive for a discussion of the masque as an exaggerated form of the "courtly arts."

42. But see Walter Cohen's comment that "although Perdita's noble

birth renders her lines unintentionally ironic, the egalitarianism of her statements does not suffer on that account. Perdita says 'our cottage,' not 'my cottage,' and thus looks ahead to the end of the play." *Drama of a Nation*, p. 394.

43. See *The Politics of Mirth*, p. 19.

44. For the reading of Polixenes as satyr, see Garner, "Time and Presence in *The Winter's Tale*," p. 360. As Marilyn Williamson has argued, the pastoral insets of *Cymbeline* and *The Winter's Tale* disrupt rather than uphold patriarchal structures. See *The Patriarchy of Shakespeare's Comedies*.

45. The phrase is that of Joan Hartwig, in "Cloten, Autolycus, and Caliban." Also see Cox, "The Role of Autolycus in *The Winter's Tale*," p. 285, and Carol Thomas Neely's reflections on Autolycus as a comic and ultimately harmless version of Leontes (*Broken Nuptials*, p. 204). One might augment the above studies by suggesting that Autolycus's first song, full of references to daffodils, sweet birds, and the lark, corrupts this pastoral vocabulary by tossing in the "doxy over the dale" and transforming the "white sheet bleaching on the hedge" to the bed where he and his "aunts" will tumble in the hay (4.3.1–12). We are recalled to Leontes' allusion to his "sully[ing] / The purity and whiteness of [his] sheets" (1.2.327). Like Autolycus, Leontes attempts to transform innocent landscapes into tainted ones. Like Autolycus, he invests a language innocent of double entendre with sexual overtones, such as when he turns Camillo's use of the word "satisfy" regarding his royal mistress into something quite different (1.2.231–33).

46. In an attack that seems to look back to Mopsa's response, one writer at the end of the seventeenth century laments those who are "apt to believe idle Romances, and Poetical Fictions, for Historical Varieties . . . and for this only reason, *Because they are Printed*." Quoted in McKeon, *The Origins of the English Novel 1600–1740*, p. 46. McKeon goes on to place the naive responses of Autolycus's "readers" in the context of the development of romance as a genre that separates learned readers from the unlearned.

47. See Natalie Davis's musings on printing and social control in "Printing and the People," in *Society and Culture in Early Modern France*, pp. 220–25. But as Davis also suggests, while print might have served as a vehicle for ideological control, it also led to a widening circle of authors in the city if not in the countryside, enabling "those without the ordinary attributes expected of an author in the later Middle Ages" to get their books printed and to find an audience.

48. Ironically, such legitimacy is sought regarding ballads that have a remote connection to the goings on in Sicily, demonstrating how far the "news" of a husband's monstrous issue has traveled in sixteen years, and how distorted the tale has become once separated from its author and spread among the populace. See Roy Battenhouse's comments in "Theme and

Structure in *The Winter's Tale*," p. 132. In Battenhouse's reading, the fish that beaches itself on the sand in one song by Autolycus becomes kings stranding themselves in "prideful isolation"; the usurer's wife delivering herself of twenty moneybags becomes a grotesque displacement of Leontes' obsessions projected onto the innocent but fertile body of the female.

49. Dolan continues: "Heywood employs the figure of the murderous wife as a representative of the social disorder that the theatre can suppress by exposing." " 'Home-rebels and house-traitors,' " p. 2. My thanks to Professor Dolan for making this material available to me prior to its publication.

50. It is telling that in the first of his two examples, the murderous wife has also been sexually "wanton"; it was "to be possest of such a Gentleman (meaning him)" that she "had poysoned her husband" seven years earlier (sig. G1v).

51. Gosson spends most of *Plays Confuted* protesting the mutability of players, the means by which boys "put on the attyre, the gesture, the passions of a woman," and mean citizens "take upon [them] the title of a Prince with counterfeit porte and traine" (*Plays Confuted*, sig. C5; cited in Agnew, *Worlds Apart*, p. 126). On theater as a locus for insubordination, see the recent articles by Jean E. Howard, "Renaissance Antitheatricality," pp. 163–88, and "Crossdressing, the Theatre, and Gender Struggle in Early Modern England." Muriel Bradbrook, in *The Rise of the Common Player*, pp. 17–95, and Margot Heinemann, in *Puritanism and Theatre*, pp. 35–47, provide splendid discussions of the social legislation and prejudices against actors in the seventeenth century.

52. There is a hidden agenda to this particular defense, as a brief epilogue suggests. In his reference to "some abuse lately crept into" theater—"an inveighing against the State, the Court, the Law, the Citty, and their governements"—Heywood alludes to the children's companies that jeopardize "the Royall and Princely services" extended to actors. Protesting against those writers who commit "their bitternesse, and liberall invectives against all estates, to the mouthes of Children, supposing their iuniority to be a priviledge for any rayling," Heywood ends his pamphlet urging his censors not to confuse the public stage with the unruly children's companies: "But wise and iuditial Censurers . . . wil not (I hope) impute these abuses to any transgression in us, who have ever been carefull and provident to shun the like" (sig. G3v).

53. Writing 35 years before Heywood, Lodge presses for theatrical reforms that would produce the following results: "Then should the wicked bee poynted out from the good, a harlot woulde seeke no harbor at stage plais, lest she shold here her owne name growe in question: and the discourse of her honesty cause her to bee hated of the godly." *A Reply to Stephen Gosson's Schoole of Abuse*, p. 25.

54. Leontes first invokes the tragic ghost that would haunt him should he remarry: "One worse, / And better us'd, would make her sainted spirit / Again possess her corpse, and on this stage / (Were we offenders now) appear soul-vex'd, / And begin, 'Why to me?'" (5.1.56–60).

55. See, for example, Howard, "Renaissance Antitheatricality"; Greenblatt, *Shakespearean Negotiations*; Goldberg, "*Macbeth* and Source"; Tennenhouse, *Power on Display*; and Erickson, *Patriarchal Structures in Shakespeare's Drama*. One reading that departs from the work of the above critics is that of Peter Stallybrass, who at the end of "Patriarchal Territories," p. 142, argues that the unruly Emilia in *Othello* is privileged as an "agent of truth" who "interrogate[s] class and gender hierarchies alike." Stallybrass's remarks on unruly women are in turn based on Natalie Davis's classic essay, "Women on Top," in *Society and Culture in Early Modern France*.

56. This interpretation, which is that of Peter Erickson (*Patriarchal Structures*, p. 163), may or may not be correct; we can hardly know Paulina's response to Leontes' offer of marriage.

57. Paulina *is* called a midwife once in the play: by Leontes, who uses the term as one of disparagement (2.3.159). On women and medicine, see Muriel Joy Hughes, *Women Healers in Medieval Life and Literature*.

58. Shakespeare deliberately avoids using the conventional literary tropes of the doctor who sweetens medicine to encourage its imbibing. For a discussion of these tropes, see Olson, *Literature as Recreation in the Later Middle Ages*. Olson discusses theater's connection with "physick" on pp. 64–75. A different formulation of the connection between medicine and literature, and one that seems closer to Paulina's role in the play, can be found in Fish, *Self-Consuming Artifacts*, p. 3. Discussing the theological and philosophical roots of the "good physician," Fish suggests that the good doctor "tells his patients what they *don't* want to hear in the hope that by forcing them to see themselves clearly, they may be moved to change the selves they see." Richard Strier discusses Shakespeare's "good physicians" in "Faithful Servants"; he alludes to Paulina on pp. 124–25.

59. See what G. Wilson Knight has called Paulina's resentment of the "past slipping away" in the scene in which the court poet depicts Perdita as "the most peerless piece of earth, I think, / That e'er the sun shone bright on" (5.1.94–95). *The Crown of Life*, p. 120.

60. "Sir, royal sir, forgive a foolish woman: / The love I bore your queen —lo, fool again! / I'll speak of her no more, nor of your children: / I'll not remember you of my own lord / (Who is lost too): take your patience to you, / And I'll say nothing" (3.2.227–32).

61. For the role of conscience in the late plays, see Strier, "Faithful Servants," and Slights, "The Politics of Conscience in *All is True*." Jonathan Goldberg's comments in *James I and the Politics of Literature*, p. 118, about

a James who dreaded the extension of conscience to his audience—in the *Basilikon Doron*, James's "appeals to the reader's conscience turn into demands of ownership"—are suggestive. Finally, in "Proud Majesty Made a Subject," pp. 460–61, David Kastan argues that "in setting English kings before an audience of commoners, the theatre nourished the cultural conditions that eventually permitted the nation to bring its King to trial, not because the theatre approvingly represented subversive acts, but rather because representation became itself subversive." Given that conscience is "a faculty common to all," as Camille Slights observes ("The Politics of Conscience," p. 65), the exercise of individual conscience can prompt the potentially subversive phenomenon of which Kastan speaks.

62. Paulina identifies the statue as a shade brought back from the dead: "Come! / I'll fill your grave up" (5.3.100–101), and her spectators clearly see her as a conjurer (see, e.g., Leontes' "My evils conjur'd to remembrance") (5.3.40).

63. See *The Fountaine of Ancient Fiction*, pp. 112–13, in which Cartari "concludes with these descriptions of the Inferni" by describing Charon, assumed by Boccaccio and others to be a symbol of Time. Just as the ancient Charon presides over the "transportation and passing over of the soules of mortall men," so does the elderly figure of Time. It is also of interest that Queen Proserpine is said to rule over and be "attended with many furies and ugly spirits" (p. 107), among whom are the "*Harpiae*, employed by the gods in punishing the sinnes of mortall men, who are said also to remaine and inhabite in the infernall kingdome" (pp. 108–9). Paulina's role as Harpy is not significantly different from that of Ariel, who disrupts the banquet attended by Alonso and Sebastian dressed "like a Harpy" (*Tempest*, 3.3). Thomas Kyd makes Proserpine the goddess who authorizes Don Andrea's departure from the underworld to join Vengeance as the privileged spectators of *The Spanish Tragedy*.

64. "Impute it not a crime / To me, or my swift passage, that I slide / O'er sixteen years, and leave the growth untried / Of that wide gap" (4.1.4–7).

65. The image or *simulacra* that Pygmalion caresses after visiting Venus's temple is, as Ovid suggests, *his* young girl; hence the prefix *suae* (*Metamorphosis* X.280). Despite Venus's intervention, the unnamed girl represents Pygmalion's artistic ideal, and her beauty is therefore a credit to his powers as craftsman. But Leontes' petulance upon seeing an aged Hermione—"But yet, Paulina, / Hermione was not so much wrinkled, nothing / So aged as this seems" (5.3.27–29)—intimates that the statue who stands before him is *not* his and has never been. On the rhetoric of possession in the play, see Cavell, *Disowning Knowledge in Six Plays of Shakespeare*, p. 218, and Blum, "'Strike all that look upon with mar[b]le.'" On the statue scene and the references to "that rare Italian master" Julio Romano, see Barkan, *The Gods*

Made Flesh. Barkan discusses a Latin verse from Vasari's *Lives* that refers to Romano as a Prometheus-like figure whom Jupiter seeks to kill because he makes "sculpted and painted bodies breathe and the homes of mortals . . . equal to those in heaven" (p. 285). Barkan's discussion suggests that Shakespeare's supposedly arcane reference to the sixteenth-century sculptor hints at a vision of the artist as violator of the decorous boundaries between divinity and mortality—the boundaries Paulina challenges in moving between the living and the dead.

66. In some suggestive but incomplete remarks on *The Winter's Tale* in his fifth chapter in *Shakespearean Negotiations*, Stephen Greenblatt comments that Leontes believes that Hermione "is defiled beyond redemption," when in fact it is he who "is horribly staining himself." The play's "last act movingly depicts a ceremony conducted by a woman, Paulina, to cleanse the king," thereby reintegrating him into a renewed community (p. 132). But one could also argue that the king is *never* cleansed: for the wrinkled Hermione who withholds from Leontes her speech is also the Hermione who presents a daily, living image of what Leontes had thought he had murdered. If earlier it was Paulina who wounded with her torrents of words, it is now Hermione who has the potential to inflict pain with her silence. It is telling that Greenblatt truncates his discussion of *The Winter's Tale* with the above observation about "a ceremony conducted by a woman." Is this because so much of his work depends on demonstrating Shakespeare's allegiance to "masculine self-differentiation" and to an ideological discourse that "coded" the "passage from male to female . . . as a descent from superior to inferior and hence as an unnatural act or a social disgrace" (p. 92)?

67. "We have a new departure in the 'invisible masque,' all the more impressive through being invisible, just as later Apollo's power is made transcendent through his continuing invisibility." Leech, "Masking and Unmasking in the Late Plays," p. 53.

68. The phrase is from Greene's 1592 *Groatsworth of Wit*. Schoenbaum suggests that Greene might have been drawing on two distinct, but not mutually exclusive, classical traditions for his epithet. In one, found in Aesop and Martial, the crow is a bird who flagrantly imitates and rivals his social betters; in the other, found in Horace, the crow plunders and thus plagiarizes his luster. "Is Greene then maliciously suggesting that Shakespeare has appropriated the flowers of *his* wit?" Schoenbaum muses. *William Shakespeare*, pp. 152–53.

69. This shows the inadequacy of Northrop Frye's point that "the power of human desire that revives Hermione . . . is identical, first, with the power of nature to bring new life out of death, and second, with the will of Apollo, whose oracle is being fulfilled." The oracle has *already* been fulfilled, and the

"power" that revives Hermione is beyond Apollo's bounds. See *A Natural Perspective*, p. 116.

70. One might argue that Paulina divorces what the seventeenth century largely assumed to be inseparable: the unchastity of the female tongue and the unchastity of the female body. Paulina's interruptive efforts empower the tongue as a vehicle that can defend women's chastity and prove that husbands' attempts to legislate control of both tongue and body are misguided efforts of absolutism. Powerful female speech thus is *not* associated with the idea of sexual sin by the end of *The Winter's Tale*. For discussions of the correlation between unchaste body and unchaste speech, see Parker, *Literary Fat Ladies*, p. 26; Jardine, "Cultural Confusion and Shakespeare's Learned Heroines"; and Ferguson, "A Room Not Their Own."

71. "Seeing through Jane Eyre."

72. Barber argues that the playwright was secure enough in his masculine identity to experiment toward the end of his career with the validity and nourishing aspects of a so-called female experience; see Barber and Wheeler, *The Whole Journey*, p. 334. Others are more cynical about Shakespeare's supposed validation of women in *The Winter's Tale*; see the remarks of Peter Erickson, *Patriarchal Structures*, pp. 167–68. *Shakespeare Out of Court*, by Holderness, Potter, and Turner, came to my attention after I completed this chapter; by and large, their analysis of *The Winter's Tale* and comments on Paulina's importance in the play's finale (pp. 195–235) agree with my own.

73. *The Stage-Players Complaint* is a dialogue between two actors who defend themselves as masters of the tongue. Says "Quick" to "Reed," "Me think you're very eloquent: Prithee tell me, Don't *Suada*, and the Jove-begotten-brain *Minerva* lodge in your facundious tongue: You have without doubt some great cause of alacrity, that you produce such eloquent speeches now." In *The Old Book Collector's Miscellany*, 3:1. A more serious defense of actors was launched two years later, in *The Actors Remonstrance or Complaint*, whose writer argues that through actors' "tongues," "the most exact and natural eloquence of our English language [is] expressed and daily amplified." In *The Old Book Collector's Miscellany*, 3: 5. As noted earlier, Stephen Gosson argued that players "infected" the commonwealth with their indecorous actions and speech.

74. In a passage from *The Compleat Gentleman* (1622), Henry Peacham links players with painters and tradesmen, thus saving them "from the stigma of Idleness" while removing them from gentility. See Muriel Bradbrook's comments in *The Rise of the Common Player*, p. 66.

75. *Society and Culture in Early Modern France*, p. 128.

76. See Steven Mullaney's chapter on *Pericles*—"an experiment [in authorship] never repeated"—in *The Place of the Stage*, p. 147, and Marjorie

Garber's suggestive comments about Shakespeare's fashioning of himself as a ghostly author in *Shakespeare's Ghost Writers*.

77. See Alexander Leggatt's observation on Cleopatra: "If Antony's dream of immortality is a wistful fantasy, Cleopatra's, being rooted in the repeatability of the theatrical occasion itself, has greater substance." *Shakespeare's Political Drama*, p. 185.

Chapter 7

1. See the remarks of Milorad R. Margitić in his edition of *Le Cid*, p. xviii, on the "astonishing haste" with which Corneille published his play, in complete violation of the usual waiting period of at least six months between performance and publication.

2. For much of this biographical information, see Dort, *Corneille*. Only Ben Jonson preceded Corneille as a playwright of stature who produced a significant body of reflection on poetics. There are striking similarities between the English playwright and Corneille. See Stanley Fish's suggestive article, "Authors-Readers," which argues that Jonson sought to reverse the relationship between himself and his reader.

3. This characterization of the play is that of Paul Bénichou. See *Man and Ethics*, esp. pp. 46–51.

4. As Maurice Déscôtes has noted, *Le Cid* was one of the first plays in Paris to "pack the house" with aristocrats and bourgeois alike. *Le Public de théâtre et son histoire*, p. 95. Even one of Corneille's sharpest critics, Georges de Scudéry, would be forced to confess that everyone had been dazzled by the play: "la Cour aussi bien que le Bourgeois" (the court as well as the bourgeois) had been conquered by "un fantasme" called *Le Cid*. *Observations sur "le Cid,"* in Gasté, ed., *La Querelle du Cid*, p. 71. All further references to pamphlets from the quarrel will be to Gasté's edition; page numbers will be given in the text. Translations here and throughout the chapter are my own, unless otherwise noted. My thanks to Mary Ann Frese Witt for checking my translations from the French.

5. Several critics have remarked on the "consent and vigilant complicity of crowds of onlookers" in the process of heroic formation. Those critics include Jean Starobinski in *L'Oeil vivant*, from which the above phrase is taken (see Arthur Goldhammer's partial translation of *L'Oeil vivant* as *The Living Eye*, p. 7), and Hans Verhoeff in "Le Don chez Corneille." Verhoeff, however, assumes that in *Le Cid*, the "ratification" of the spectator is a matter of the spectator's free consent rather than the product of subtle manipulation; see pp. 31–32.

6. Richelieu had nonetheless recruited Corneille in 1635 to become one of *les grands poètes* to compose dramas for "toute la France" (all of France)—

a phrase that disguises Richelieu's pretensions to stage dramas for an elite, courtly audience rather than for a broader "public" which, he believed, should have no part in French cultural life. For the phrase "toute la France," see the letter by Jean Chapelain regarding the *Comédie des Tuilleries* produced by "les cinq poètes"; cited in Searle, "L'Académie française et *Le Cid*," pp. 350–51. Evidence suggests that Corneille collaborated in just one of his patron's projects, and in that only with reluctance.

7. Ranum, *Artisans of Glory*, p. 152. Just as he had stabilized political situations in France's provinces by removing power from the traditional aristocracy and placing it in the hands of a loyal bureaucracy, so did Richelieu set out in the early 1630's to stabilize cultural production. This was apparent not only in the creation of the French Academy but in Richelieu's streamlining of the acting profession. In authorizing three bands of *comédiens* to establish permanent theaters in Paris (the Bourgogne, the Marais, and the St. Germain), Richelieu brought these errant troupes under the gaze of the state—or more precisely, himself. This gaze was concretized in the Salle de la Comédie, built for theatrical productions in the Hotel Richelieu. As Timothy Murray has noted, this theater did away with "the unruly *parterre*" of the public theater, employing a hierarchical seating plan organized according to social status: "The higher one's rank, the closer one sat to the cardinal, who enjoyed the place of honor." *Theatrical Legitimation*, pp. 118–19. Regarding the relationship of Richelieu to the Academy, see Church, *Richelieu and Reason of State*, pp. 341–50. On Richelieu's Machiavellian tactics, see Thuau, *Raison d'état et pensée politique à l'époque de Richelieu*, esp. pp. 33–102.

8. Antonin Fabre's study of Jean Chapelain, *Etudes littéraires sur le XVIIe siècle*, makes him a virtual victim of Richelieu. See also Colbert Searle's comment that "without a doubt, the Academy would have abandoned the affair [of *Le Cid*] without the intervention of the Cardinal." "L'Académie française et *Le Cid*," p. 359. Other critics have hastened to minimize Richelieu's role in the Academy's verdict; see, for one example, Batiffol, *Richelieu et Corneille*, chap. 5 (appropriately entitled "Richelieu est resté dehors de la querelle du *Cid*"), pp. 125–47. The first historian of the Academy, Paul Pellisson-Fontanier, had the embarrassing task of acknowledging that Corneille was by far its most renowned member (he was initiated in 1647) while attempting to account for Chapelain's aversion to *Le Cid*; see his *Relation contenant l'histoire de l'Académie française* (published anonymously in 1652). See Orest Ranum's comments on the *Relation* in *Artisans of Glory*, pp. 240–44.

Corneille's views on Richelieu are perhaps nowhere more tellingly expressed than in the sonnet "Sur la mort du Roi Louis XIII," published posthumously. In this biting little poem, Corneille suggests that the king was an "esclave dans sa cour" (slave in his court) and that thanks to the tyranny of his prime minister, "son règne fut pourtant celui de l'injustice" (his reign was one of injustice). In *Oeuvres complètes*, ed. Georges Couton, 1: 1062.

9. "Des choses qui maintiennent la société publique, qui servent à retenir les peuples dans le devoir." *Troisième dissertation concernant le Poème dramatique*, cited in Couton, *Corneille et la fronde*, p. 11. Couton notes that although d'Aubignac's work was not published until long after Richelieu's death, it was written much earlier and is indicative of "the authoritarian generation" that achieved prominence under Richelieu's tutelage. It is noteworthy that most of d'Aubignac's work on theater (including *La Pratique du théâtre* and *Dissertation sur la condemnation des théâtres*), much of it vehemently critical of Corneille's early work, was published just several years before Corneille chose to publish his own defensive *Discours* and *Examens* in 1660. For a reading that departs from this traditional interpretation of d'Aubignac's commitment to the ethic of neoclassicism, see Murray, *Theatrical Legitimation.*

On the relationship between classicism and absolutism, see Immanuel Wallerstein's succinct formulation: "Classicism, like absolutism, was not a description of reality, but a program . . . of returning the political and cultural initiatives to the upper strata, the better to digest the fundamental social change that was represented by the genesis of a capitalist world-economy." *The Modern World-System*, 2: 33.

10. See Marc Fumaroli's remarks on the transformation of the court between 1604 and 1642 from "an aggregate of petty feudal courts" to one court "of the King and his Minister." He goes on to observe that the Academy was entrusted with the mission of forging an official "langage de Cour" and that the only *Hotel* flourishing by the end of this period was the Rambouillet, presided over by Chapelain. *L'Age de l'eloquence*, p. 683.

11. "Et après y avoir corrigé ce qu'on m'y fait connaître d'inexcusable, je l'abandonne au public." *Oeuvres complètes*, 1: 385. He goes on to add, "Puisque nous faisons des Poèmes pour être représentés, notre premier but doit être de plaire à la Cour et au Peuple, et d'attirer un grand monde à leurs représentations. Il faut, s'il se peut, y ajouter les règles, afin de ne déplaire pas aux Savants . . . mais surtout gaignons la voix publique" (Since we write poems so that they can be staged, our first aim ought to be the Court and the People, so that we can attract the whole world to our plays. If possible, it is also necessary to observe the rules, so that the *Savants* are not displeased . . . but above all, let us gain the acclaim of the public). Ibid., 1: 387.

12. As Colbert Searle notes, when Corneille came to Paris from Rouen in the early 1630's, his fame rested on his works alone. "L'Académie française et *Le Cid*," p. 336. This was not a position from which one could hope to gain much credibility in early seventeenth-century Paris. See André Stegmann's convincing argument in *L'Héroisme Cornélien*, 1: 41–49.

13. This is Corneille's own characterization of his play, from his preface to *L'Illusion comique*, first published in 1639.

14. It is misleading to argue, as some critics have, that Corneille represents the viewpoint of the enlightened bourgeoisie—misleading largely because before the eighteenth century, members of the bourgeoisie were primarily interested not in articulating their class solidarity but in gaining for themselves the *lettres de noblesse* sought by and granted to Corneille's father in 1637. See Rohou, "The Articulation of Social, Ideological and Literary Practices in France," pp. 139–65, and Dort, *Corneille*. Both critics see Corneille exploiting for his own purposes the tensions between king and aristocracy so pronounced during Richelieu's reign as prime minister. On the other hand, critics such as Jean Apostolides and Mitchell Greenberg find in Corneille an early apologist for absolute monarchy—another view I will take up in the following pages. See Apostolides' *Le Prince sacrifié* and his brief "Commentaire" in Demorest and Leibacher-Ouvrard, eds., *Pascal / Corneille*, pp. 123–27; also see Greenberg, *Corneille, Classicism, and the Ruses of Symmetry*. Colette Scherer offers the most sensible critique of the views noted above when she suggests that Corneille's opinions regarding class are "the convictions of an *officier* and a writer who believes himself equal to a nobleman." *Comédie et société sous Louis XIII*, p. 134. For a reading of *Le Cid* that argues against seeing Rodrigue and Chimène as "bourgeois" characters, see Burger, "*Le Cid* de Corneille," pp. 427–45.

15. Line 212. All line references to *L'Illusion comique* are from Marc Fumaroli's edition.

16. Alcandre nonetheless plays a recognizably conventional role in a genre frequently used to defend "the craftsmanship of theatre itself" as well as the autonomy of modern drama from antiquity. On the use of tragicomedy as a defense of the métier of theater, see Soare, "Parodie et catharsis tragi-comique."

17. When Pridamant's friend Dorante explains to Alcandre why he has brought Pridamant to the magician's grotto, Alcandre brusquely interrupts: "Je sais ce qui l'amène: / Ce fils est aujourd'hui le sujet de sa peine" (I know what brings him here: his son is today the cause of his suffering) (101–2).

18. See Jean Rousset's comments on the "power of the playwright" as revealed in Alcandre's ability to make Pridamant believe that the fiction is genuine and to disabuse him of that belief. "Le Destinataire de l'illusion théâtrale."

19. "Le Théâtre est un fief dont les rentes sont bonnes, / Et votre fils rencontre en un métier si doux / Plus de biens et d'honneur qu'il n'eût trouvé chez vous" (1802–4).

20. "Je n'ose plus m'en plaindre" (1671). For a discussion of Clindor's reintegration into the social order—from which Alcandre stands aloof—see Albanese, "Motifs de théatralité dans *L'Illusion comique*." For a description

of the seventeenth-century bourgeois as "the town dweller who lives nobly off his *rentes* without carrying on any craft or trade," see Mousnier, *Social Hierarchies*, p. 86.

21. See Bernard Dort's comments in "Les Deux Ages de Corneille," p. 25.

22. Georges Couton finds in *Le Cid* "an optimistic confidence in life and youth." *Corneille*, p. 51.

23. The first diatribe against Corneille, a bad poem by Jean Mairet, was entitled "L'Autheur du vray cid espagnol a son traducteur francois, sur une Lettre en vers, qu'il a faict imprimer Intitulée (*Excuse à Ariste*) ou apres cens traits de vanité, il dit parlant de soymesme. *Je ne doy qu'a moy seul toute ma Renommée.*" Gasté, p. 67. See M. Guizot's comment on this line and what he judges to have been Richelieu's reaction: "Astonished that any one should consider himself independent, and indignant that he should venture to declare it, Richelieu believed himself set at defiance." *Corneille and His Times*, p. 154.

24. "On scait le petit commerce que vous pratiquez, et vous n'avez point d'applaudissements que vous ne gaigniez à force de sonnets et de reverences." The language is from Corneille's "Advertissement au Besançonnois Mairet," in Milorad Margitić's edition of *Le Cid*, p. 201. Elsewhere Corneille accuses Mairet of using connections to pass "pour honneste homme d'origine," which Mairet is *not*; ibid., p. 197.

25. *Observations sur le Cid*; Gasté, p. 72. Portions of the *Observations* have been translated by Townsend Brewster and published in Dukore, ed., *Dramatic Theory and Criticism*. The passage in the text is from Brewster's translation; other translations are my own.

26. Line 1336. All passages from the 1637 *Cid* are from Margitić's edition; line numbers will be noted in the text. As in Margitić's edition, the seventeenth-century orthography will be respected. All passages from and comments by Corneille on later versions of *Le Cid* are from Georges Couton's edition of Corneille's *Oeuvres complètes*; page numbers will be given in the text for the prose works, line numbers for the 1660 *Cid*. On the parallel between Rodrigue and the author of the "Excuse," see Georges Couton's observation that "not enough has been made of this document" in terms of elaborating Corneille's creation of a "self-portrait" in his early plays. *Corneille*, p. 18. Other contemporaries of Corneille *do* make the connection that Scudéry fails to make. Jean Mairet sarcastically links Corneille with his "Heros" in his "Epistre familiere" (Gasté, p. 291), and the noted epistolary writer and critic Guez de Balzac intentionally blurs author and character in his biting response to Scudéry, writing: "Si le Cid est coupable, c'est d'un crime qui a eu recompense: s'il est puni, ce sera apres avoir triomphé: s'il faut que Platon le bannisse de sa Republique, il faut qu'il le couronne de fleurs en

le bannissant" (If the Cid is to blame, it is for a crime which had a reward; if he is punished, it will be after having triumphed; if Plato must banish him from his Republic, he must crown him with flowers when banishing him). "Lettre de Monsieur de Balzac," Gasté, p. 455.

27. See Margitić's comments in his edition of *Le Cid*, pp. 174–75n.

28. "Car si toutes les choses temporelles ne sont que des figures & des ombres, en quel rang doit-on mettre les Comedies qui ne sont que les ombres des ombres, puis que ce ne sont que de vaines images des choses temporelles, & souvent de choses fausses?" (Because if all temporal things are only appearances and shadows, then in what class should one put plays, which are only the shadows of shadows, seeing that they are only the empty images of temporal things, and often of deceptive things?) This hypothetical question comes at the close (p. 72) of Nicole's *Traité de la comédie*, much of which consists of an attack on Corneille. Jean Rousset suggests that Nicole's principal fear is that "les sentiments" of the actor will "ricochet onto the spectator, the 'secret actor' on the stage." *L'Intérieur et l'extérieur*, pp. 161–62.

29. Toward the end of his treatise, Chapelain speaks of the "charmes esclatans" of which Corneille is "maistre"; Gasté, p. 414. It is useful to note that *éclat*—generally defined as dazzling brightness—also came to mean *scandal* in the seventeenth century. The first such use cited in *Le grand Robert* is that by Molière in *Tartuffe*, act 4, scene 5: "Et le mal n'est jamais que dans l'éclat qu'on fait."

30. This argument is in keeping with what Gordon Pocock has observed to be Corneille's tendency to "withdraw responsibility" for his message by displacing it onto the audience instead. See *Corneille and Racine*, esp. p. 21. Pocock adds, "Th[is] attitude is now familiar, but it does not fit very well the moral rules of French classicism."

31. This line of approach differs from the readings of both Mitchell Greenberg and Timothy Murray. On the one hand, Greenberg uses a Lacanian model to discuss the "politically dangerous aspects of theatrical pleasure," which must always be controlled. Corneille both exploits this pleasure and contains it within "the law of the Father." See his introduction to *Corneille, Classicism, and the Ruses of Symmetry*, esp. pp. 5–15. On the other hand, Murray adopts Lyotard's critique of libidinal pleasure to argue that French neoclassicism ironically works *against* this law in order to endorse the spectator's pleasure and make him/her the producer of the play in a manner that displaces authorial control. See *Theatrical Legitimation*, pp. 188–206. While Murray does not discuss Corneille at length, his few remarks on the playwright suggest that he sees Corneille engaging in an attempt to "authorize" his powerful patron Richelieu at the same time that he seeks legitimation from Richelieu; see pp. 115–25. My argument in the following pages borrows from Greenberg's and Murray's careful discussions while

refusing to accept their conclusions about either Corneille's subscription to the "law" of the monarch or his authorization of a powerful spectator. It departs rather more sharply from those interpretations that focus on the preeminence of reason in Corneille. For a recent critique that nicely suggests that "*raison* in Corneille is indeed almost a synonym for volonté," see Braden, *Renaissance Tragedy and the Senecan Tradition*, p. 137.

32. *Romancero général, ou recueil des chants populaires de l'Espagne*, ed. Damas Hinard; cited in Margitić's edition of *Le Cid*, p. 3.

33. "Será un bravo Cavallero, / Galán, bizarro y valiente" (He will be a worthy knight, gallant, brave, and valiant). *Las Mocedades del Cid*, lines 590–91.

34. As several critics have observed, Rodrigue's elaborate description of his success in battle is almost completely superfluous to the main action, since the scene opens with Don Fernand congratulating Rodrigue on his victory and bestowing on him the title that the Moors have already given him, the Cid. But this welcoming of Rodrigue to his new role as Spain's hero *before* we have heard the narrative from Rodrigue himself merely confirms the effect that the play as a whole strives to create: the suggestion that Rodrigue's heroism is legitimized by its onstage spectators even before it is witnessed or narrated. See Reiss, *Toward Dramatic Illusion*, p. 166.

35. One recent discussion of the scene observes that the victory against the Moors is presented as virtually a "miracle." Margitić, *Essai sur la mythologie du Cid*, pp. 78–79.

36. The characterization is that of Serge Doubrovsky. *Corneille et la dialectique du héros*, p. 124.

37. To be sure, Corneille cleverly arranges the occasion of the *récit* so that it appears to be the product not of the surrendered Moors but of the newly freed people of Seville. Act 4, scene 1 abruptly opens with Chimène's question to her confidante Elvire: "N'est-ce point un faux bruit? le scais-tu bien, Elvire?" (Is this not a rumor? can you tell for sure, Elvire?) (1111). The "faux bruit" to which Chimène alludes is the "commune voix" that sings in the streets of Seville and raises "les glorieux exploits" of the dazzling "jeune Heros" Rodrigue to the heavens. When asked where she has heard "ces nouvelles estranges," Elvire responds, "Du peuple qui par tout fait sonner ses louanges, / Le nomme de sa joye, et l'objet, et l'autheur, / Son Ange tutelaire, et son liberateur" (Everywhere the people are singing his praises, calling him the cause and object of their joy, their guardian angel and liberator) (1124–26).

38. Chimène will again participate unknowingly in a moment of "tromperie" (deception) when she believes that Don Sanche's appearance at her house in act 5 signals his defeat of Rodrigue in the duel they have fought to avenge her father's honor. After she defends her love for Rodrigue

before the entire court, Don Fernand gently informs her, "Ton amant n'est pas mort" (Your lover is not dead) (1769), and Don Sanche steps forward to explain, "Cet objet l'a trompée" (This object deceived her) (1780), proffering to Don Fernand the sword that led Chimène to confess her love for the Rodrigue she erroneously believed to be dead.

39. On the role of the sword as a virtual protagonist in the play, see Georges Couton's remarks in his edition of Corneille's *Oeuvres complètes*, 1: 1453, and Doubrovsky, "Corneille: Masculin / Feminin," p. 97.

40. Over twenty years ago, Serge Doubrovsky wrote in an influential study on the Hegelian nature of Corneille's tragedy that Chimène's refusal to kill Rodrigue is symptomatic of her fatal weakness to conquer herself ("Chimène wants to follow his example, but she cannot . . . she remains trapped in her passion, arrested at the stage of desire"). *Corneille et la dialectique du héros*, p. 110. Rodrigue becomes for Doubrovsky the representative of an aristocratic superiority that constitutes the essence of heroism in Corneille. Tellingly, Doubrovsky has recently revised his reading of this critical encounter between lovers by suggesting that the law of gender overrides the law of genre in this scene: "I now realize that it is no longer a confrontation between two men but one between a man and a woman. . . . Despite the chivalric code or the doctrine of the *précieux*, the woman can never be the double or the alter ego of the man." "Corneille: Masculin / Feminin," p. 98. Given this essential inequality, moreover, Doubrovsky finds that Rodrigue acts not from a selflessness that demonstrates the absolute superiority of the conqueror, but out of bad faith. Thus this scene of virtual rape reveals not Rodrigue's self-abnegation but his desire *not* to die (p. 99). André Stegmann anticipates Doubrovsky's self-criticism when he notes that *Le Cid* differs sharply from Corneille's other tragedies precisely because "the hero is completely preoccupied with himself. It is both his strength and his weakness." *L'Héroisme Cornélien*, 2: 579.

41. "Va, je suis ta partie, et non pas ton bourreau" (950); "si jamais l'amour eschauffa tes esprits, / Sors vainqueur d'un combat dont Chimene est le prix" (1565–66).

42. Particularly striking in the published text of *Le Cid* is that such fatal submission is staged a *third* time, in the remarks made by Corneille in his preface. Dedicated to Richelieu's niece, Madame de Combalet, the preface is a provocative mirror for the events of the play as well as a telling example of Corneille's daring manipulation of the rhetoric of patronage. A munificent patron of the arts and frequent guest at the Rambouillet, Madame de Combalet was a lady-in-waiting to the queen and would shortly become duchess of Aiguillon. Corneille's dedication of *Le Cid* to Madame seems a particularly bold move, given that his play, with its permutations of the conventions of the popular stage (quid pro quos, duels, swoons, the con-

stant threat of scandal), catered to the very public whom Richelieu and "les grandes" had been protesting against.

Yet the dedication was composed only *after* Richelieu's niece had guaranteed the play's worth by giving it her blessing: "One can hardly doubt the value of something which has the good fortune of pleasing you: the judgment that you have given my play is the assured mark of its price, and as you always so liberally give to what is truly beautiful the esteem that it merits, false beauty will never have the power to deceive you" (On ne peut douter avec raison de ce que vaut une chose qui a le bonheur de vous plaire: le jugement que vous en faites est la marque asseurée de son prix; et comme vous donnez tousjours liberalement aux veritables beautez l'estime qu'elles meritent, les fausses n'ont jamais le pouvoir de vous esblouir). *Le Cid*, ed. Margitić, p. 4. Although the dramatist seems to attest to Madame's freedom of judgment, this latter phrase cleverly implies that while Madame can't be fooled by false beauty, she *can* be dazzled by the "*veritables* beautez" of *Le Cid*. The dedicatory letter strives to maintain a delicate balance between vindicating Madame de Combalet's free "jugement" and insinuating that Corneille's play has overpowered her. But there is another complicating element at work in the preface as well. Madame de Combalet was apparently instrumental in obtaining for Corneille's father in 1637 the *lettres de noblesse* that conferred upon the playwright's family the aristocratic status it had long sought. Thus Corneille discreetly alludes to "des effets qui me sont trop advantageux pour m'en taire" (consequences which are too advantageous to me to keep silent about)—a silence he nonetheless maintains. The allusion neatly recapitulates the process at work in *Le Cid* itself, as do the references earlier in the preface to the body of Spain's champion, which won such surprising *éclat* for its nation long after the Cid's death. Madame's desire to assist Corneille and her confirmation of the play's worth have initiated the dramatist into the social echelon with which he elsewhere professes himself unconcerned. But she has also succeeded in convincing Corneille that he ought not to be "astonished" by either his play's reception or his family's undeserved honor.

43. "The passions, powerfully expressed . . . take away [from those who see them] all the freedom of the understanding." Gasté, p. 414.

44. See Ranum, *Artisans of Glory*, pp. 169–96, on Chapelain's role in advising Colbert on the production of royal historiography in the 1640's.

45. Corneille's earlier plays dramatized a fairly conventional sequence from shadows to light and the revelation of a providential "truth" associated with the tragicomic; see, in particular, his tragicomedy *Clitandre*. As its 1637 subtitle announces, *Le Cid* appears to follow faithfully in the genre of the tragicomic. But it is finally unclear whether it is Rodrigue or the audience's desire for him that is validated. Nor is it clear whether the play ever

emerges fully from the shadowy projections of its spectators. Antoine Soare has suggested that *Le Cid* put an "end to the tragicomic season in Paris," since it parodies the "paradise of illusions" that tragicomedy preserved. See "Parodie et catharsis tragicomique," pp. 279–83. On Mairet and the reformulation of tragicomedy's moral purpose in the early 1630's, see Gethner, "Jean de Mairet and Poetic Justice." On dramatic criticism in general in the 1630's, see Henry Phillips's useful book, *The Theatre and Its Critics in Seventeenth-Century France.* Micheline Sakharoff makes some interesting comments regarding the similar pursuits of Descartes and Richelieu in their writings: both wish to "dissipate the veils of darkness and confusion" and to attain a clarity similar to that generally obtained at the close of tragicomedy. For her discussion of Descartes's movement out of the "forest of tragicomedy" and Richelieu's "lucid gaze," see *Le Héros, sa liberté et son efficacité de Garnier à Rotrou,* pp. 85–94.

46. For a brief summary of Beaucaire's play, see André Stegmann, *L'Héroisme Cornélien,* 1: 68.

47. Numerous pamphlets in early-seventeenth-century France purported to be written by the "shadows" of dead kings and counts, and Beaucaire may well have borrowed his title in an attempt to locate his play within the genre of princely "advice." See, for example, *L'Ombre de Henri le Grand* (1615), *L'Ombre de Monseigneur le duc de Mayenne* (1622), and *L'Ombre de Sandricourt* (1631).

48. See the sources in note 45. Also relevant is the observation by Marie-Hélène Huet that the essence of neoclassicism is the fear that the "passive and alienated gaze" of the spectator will become "an active and total participation." *Rehearsing the Revolution,* p. 44.

49. This 1637 letter to Boisrobert is cited in Margitić's edition of *Le Cid,* p. 205.

50. Cited in Margitić's edition of *Le Cid,* p. 207. As Margitić notes, Heliodorus, bishop in Thessalia during late antiquity, resigned his ecclesiastical office when he refused to disown a novel he had written in his youth, *The Ethiopians, or the Loves of Theogenes and Chariclea.*

51. For one recent argument regarding this compliance, see Koch, "*Horace.*"

52. For two recent arguments to this effect, see the chapters on *Horace, Cinna,* and *Polyeucte* in Greenberg, *Corneille, Classicism, and the Ruses of Symmetry*; also see Lagarde, "Le sacrifice de la femme chez Corneille."

53. "On . . . peut décider [le mérite du drame] par les règles de la prudence humaine" (One can judge the play's merit by the rules of prudence), not by "politics" (Couton, 1: 695). Corneille protests making drama the property of the state rather than of "tout le monde" (the whole world), which has the freedom to judge if not the power to force its judgment. He

thus returns to his rhetoric of abandonment, although with a slight difference. It is now directed against the efforts of political authorities to "force" the public to believe in particular interpretations.

Corneille thereby echoes the sentiments of an anonymous supporter who angrily wrote in 1638 that the members of the Academy were exercising "une espece d'inquisition sur les Lettres" (a kind of inquisition into literature) (Gasté, p. 418) and argued that poetry inhabits a "jurisdiction donc particuliere, extraordinaire, absolue et non sujette aux loix des autres disciplines" (special and extraordinary jurisdiction, absolute and not subject to the laws of other disciplines). *Observations sur les Sentimens de l'Academie francoise*, Gasté, p. 451.

54. "Les grandes et fortes émotions qui renouvellent à tous moments et redoublent la commisération" (Couton, 3: 153)—a pity that Corneille defends as being more in keeping with the taste of his era than the *horreur* Aristotle had believed critical to tragic catharsis. For Corneille's dismissive views of catharsis, see his remarks in the second *Discours*, in Couton, 3: 145–49. His comments on Chimène as a character who fails to achieve her designs are on p. 147.

55. See Barnwell's brief discussion of Corneille's reliance on Longinus in his edition of *Pierre Corneille: Writings on the Theatre*, pp. 226–27n. For a more general discussion of the sublime in French drama, see Barnwell's *The Tragic Drama of Corneille and Racine*, pp. 229–30.

56. These observations are indebted to Timothy Reiss's point that Corneille moves in his late plays from focusing on admiration to focusing on the sublime, a shift in emphasis that corresponds to what Reiss sees as a "decreased emphasis on theatricality." *Toward Dramatic Illusion*, p. 170.

57. *Corneille, Classicism, and the Ruses of Symmetry*, p. 65. Greenberg suggestively comments later in his study about silence's "indiscretion," its "refusal to mirror the desire of the Sovereign" (pp. 163–64).

58. Interestingly, in her 1660 lines to Don Fernand arguing that justice should be served and her father avenged, Chimène insists that Rodrigue is a threat not to Castile—her point in the 1637 text—but to the *king*: "Immolez, non à moy, mais à vostre couronne, / Mais à vostre grandeur, mais à vostre personne, / Immolez dis-je, Sire, au bien de tout l'Estat / Tout ce qu'enorgueillit un si haut attentat" (Sacrifice, not to me, but to your crown, to your grandeur, to your person: I say sacrifice, Sire, for the good of all the State, all that such a great outrage swells with pride) (693–96).

59. See the much-altered fourth scene of act 1, in which Rodrigue's father, Don Diègue, is insulted by the Comte. In defending the king's choice of himself as the prince's tutor, Don Diègue had claimed in 1637, "Mais le Roy m'a trouvé plus propre à son desir" (But the king found me more suited

to his desire) (158); he now argues, "Mais on doit ce respect au pouvoir absolu / De n'examiner rien quand un Roy l'a voulu" (But one owes this respect to absolute power, not to examine anything when a king has wished it) (163). As will be seen, Corneille's commentary on Chimène's response to the king's desire challenges this platitude.

60. Pintard, "De la tragicomédie à la tragédie," p. 465.

61. "Pourrez-vous à vos yeux souffrir cet Hymenée? / Et quand de mon devoir vous voulez cet effort, / Toute vostre justice en est-elle d'accord? / Si Rodrigue à l'Estat devient si necessaire, / De ce qu'il fait pour vous dois-je estre le salaire, / Et me livrer moy-mesme au reproche eternel / D'avoir trempé mes mains dans le sang paternel?" (1806–12). Only the last line of this closing passage was in the 1637 text, and it is now rephrased significantly as a question, almost a dare.

62. For a suggestive study that notes that the use of "je suis" in the late plays is indicative of a rupture between hero(ine) and world, see Ubersfeld, " 'Je suis' ou l'identité héroïque chez Corneille."

63. Another example of Chimène's subtly defined integrity can be found in the change Corneille made to line 1203: what had been "Quoy que mon coeur pour luy contre moy s'interesse" (Although my heart takes his side against myself) becomes "Quoy que pour ce vainqueur mon amour s'interesse" (Although my love takes the side of this conqueror) (1193). The minor change suggests Corneille's attempt to create a Chimène less divided—and therefore less vulnerable—than before.

64. Prigent, *Le Héros et l'état dans la tragédie de Pierre Corneille*, p. 29. Also see Prigent's programmatic article, "L'Exercise du pouvoir dans les tragédies de Corneille," pp. 593–95. Other plays from this period include *Oedipe* (1659), *Sophonisbe* (1663), and *Othon* (1664). For a study that closely approximates Prigent's, see Ubersfeld, "Corneille."

65. Louis Marin has subtly analyzed the mechanics of "force" in formulations of seventeenth-century sovereignty. See his chapter entitled "Le roi ou la force justifiée," in *Le Portrait du roi*, pp. 23–46. While my reading ultimately bears out those of Greenberg and Apostolides, as discussed in notes 14 and 31, these critics insist that Corneille *knowingly* shapes a monarchical discourse in *Le Cid*. I suggest that *Le Cid* only accidentally participates in the fashioning of such a discourse of power. For the discourse of invulnerability embraced by Louis XIV, see Joan deJean's suggestive study, *Literary Fortifications*, particularly her introduction.

66. For this characterization of Rousseau, see Gutman, "Rousseau's *Confessions*," pp. 116–17. One might say that Corneille most fully recognizes the appropriateness of his dramaturgy for monarchical purposes in *Cinna*, a play that makes the hero and the monarch the same person. And yet even

in *Cinna*, written in 1643 and generally held to be one of Corneille's most unambiguous paeans to "empire," it is clear that the playwright is already reformulating his theater of *éclat*.

It is striking that Jean Chapelain came to view himself and his Academy as unwitting agents in the creation of a powerful monarchy. See his bitter comment, written after the quarrel of the *Cid* was long over, that in his day, poets are ruled "par le goût de la Cour" (by the taste of the Court)—and not, as in the golden age of Ronsard and Francis I, "la Cour par le goût des Poètes" (the Court by the taste of the Poets). Quoted in Borgerhoff, *The Freedom of French Classicism*, p. 59.

67. Gutman also makes this point about Rousseau: "Just as the creation and celebration of his own self contained the imperative that led to that self's annihilation, so the creation of a public self subject to the microphysics of power gave rise to a counterforce that would oppose all regnant power." "Rousseau's *Confessions*," p. 117.

Epilogue

1. Roland Barthes, *On Racine*, p. 3.

2. "Le dessein en est pris: je pars, cher Théramène, / Et quitte le séjour de l'aimable Trézène" (1.1); "Hélas! qu'un tel exil, Seigneur, me serait cher! / Dans quels ravissements, à votre sort liée, / Du reste des mortels je vivrais oubliée!" (5.1); "Laissez-moi, loin de vous, et loin de ce rivage, / . . . Confus, persécuté d'un mortel souvenir, / De l'univers entier je voudrais me bannir" (5.7). All citations are from *Oeuvres complètes de Racine*, ed. Raymond Picard. References are to act and scene.

3. Thus Pierre Le Moyne suggested that "la Sorbonne n'a point de juridiction sur le Parnasse"; "les erreurs de ce pays-là ne sont sujettes ni qux Censures ni à l'Inquisition" (the Sorbonne has no jurisdiction over Parnassus; the errors of this country are subject neither to Censors nor to the Inquisition). One of Corneille's most ardent supporters, Guez de Balzac, also refused to "confondre les critères du beau et du vrai, laissait à la littérature la liberté d'user, sans scrupule excessif, de la fiction, des images. . . . La littérature est un jeu, et ce jeu est innocent" (conflate the criteria of the good and the true, leaving to literature the freedom of using, without excessive scruple, [anything] from fiction, and from painting. . . . Literature is a game, and this game is innocent). Opposed to this view were Pascal and Racine's "father" Pierre Nicole, who claimed that the source of beauty is the truth. All of these statements are cited in Lafond, "Littérature et morale au XVIIe siècle," p. 400.

Works Cited

Agnew, Jean-Christophe. *Worlds Apart: The Market and the Theater in Anglo-American Thought, 1550–1750*. Cambridge: Cambridge Univ. Press, 1986.

Albanese, Ralph, Jr. "Motifs de théâtralité dans *L'Illusion comique*." In Margitić, ed., *Corneille comique*, pp. 129–49.

Alpers, Paul. "Pastoral and the Domain of Lyric in Spenser's *Shepheardes Calender*." In Greenblatt, ed., *Representing the English Renaissance*, pp. 163–80.

Altman, Joel. *The Tudor Play of Mind*. Berkeley: Univ. of California Press, 1978.

Anderson, Perry. *Lineages of the Absolutist State*. London: NLB, 1974.

Apostolides, Jean. "Commentaire." In Demorest and Leibacher-Ouvrard, eds., *Pascal/Corneille: Desert, retraite, engagement*, pp. 123–27.

———. *Le Prince sacrifié: Théâtre et politique au temps de Louis XIV*. Paris: Minuit, 1985.

Arenal, Electa. "The Convent as Catalyst for Autonomy: Two Hispanic Nuns of the Seventeenth Century." In Beth Miller, ed., *Women in Hispanic Literature*, pp. 147–83.

Ariosto, Ludovico. *Orlando Furioso*. Ed. Cesare Segre. 2 vols. Milan: Mondadori, 1976.

Aston, Trevor, ed. *Crisis in Europe 1560–1660*. London: Routledge and Kegan Paul, 1965.

Augustine. *Confessions*. Trans. R. S. Pine-Coffin. Harmondsworth, Eng.: Penguin, 1961.

Axton, Marie. *The Queen's Two Bodies: Drama and the Elizabethan Succession*. London: Royal Historical Society, 1977.

Bakhtin, Mikhail. *The Dialogic Imagination*. Trans. Caryl Emerson and Michael Holquist. Austin: Univ. of Texas Press, 1983.

———. *Problems in Dostoyevsky's Poetics*. Trans. and ed. Caryl Emerson. Minneapolis: Univ. of Minnesota Press, 1984.

———. *Rabelais and His World*. Trans. Hélène Iswolsky. Bloomington: Indiana Univ. Press, 1984.

———. *Speech Genres and Other Late Essays*. Trans. Vern W. McGee. Ed. Caryl Emerson and Michael Holquist. Austin: Univ. of Texas Press, 1986.

Barber, C. L., and Richard P. Wheeler. *The Whole Journey*. Berkeley: Univ. of California Press, 1986.

Barish, Jonas. "Jonson and the Loathèd Stage." In W. Blisset, J. Patrick, and R. Van Fossen, eds., *A Celebration of Ben Jonson*, pp. 27–53. Toronto: Univ. of Toronto Press, 1973.

Barkan, Leonard. *The Gods Made Flesh: Metamorphosis and the Pursuit of Paganism*. New Haven, Conn.: Yale Univ. Press, 1986.

Barnwell, H. T. *The Tragic Drama of Corneille and Racine: An Old Parallel Revisited*. Oxford: Clarendon Press, 1982.

Barocchi, Paola, ed. *Trattati d'arte del cinquecento*. Milan: Rizzoli, 1960.

Baron, Hans. "The Limits of the Notion of 'Renaissance Individualism': Burckhardt After a Century." In *In Search of Florentine Civic Humanism*, vol. 2, pp. 155–81. Princeton, N.J.: Princeton Univ. Press, 1988.

Barthes, Roland. *On Racine*. Trans. Richard Howard. New York: Performing Arts Journal Publications, 1983.

———. *Sade/Fourier/Loyola*. Paris: Seuil, 1972.

Batiffol, Louis. *Richelieu et Corneille*. Paris: Calmann-Lévy, 1936.

Battenhouse, Roy. "Theme and Structure in *The Winter's Tale*." *Shakespeare Survey* 33 (1980): 123–38.

Baudrillard, Jean. *The Mirror of Production*. Trans. Mark Poster. St. Louis: Telos Press, 1975.

Bauer, Dale. *Feminist Dialogics: A Theory of Failed Community*. Albany: State Univ. of New York Press, 1988.

Bell, Rudolph. *Holy Anorexia*. Chicago: Univ. of Chicago Press, 1985.

Bénichou, Paul. *Man and Ethics: Studies in French Classicism*. Trans. Elizabeth Hughes. Garden City, N.Y.: Anchor Books, 1971.

Bennassar, Bartolomé, ed. *L'Inquisition espagnole XVe–XIXe siècle*. Paris: Hachette, 1979.

Berger, Harry, Jr. "The Aging Boy: Paradise and Parricide in Spenser's *Shepheardes Calender*." In Maynard Mack and George deForest Lord, eds., *Poetic Traditions of the English Renaissance*, pp. 25–46. New Haven, Conn.: Yale Univ. Press, 1982.

———. *Revisionary Play: Studies in the Spenserian Dynamics*. Berkeley: Univ. of California Press, 1988.

———. *Second World and Green World: Studies in Renaissance Fiction-Making*. Berkeley: Univ. of California Press, 1988.

———. "Spenser's Critique of Pastoral Love and Art." *English Literary History* 50 (1985): 27–60.

Bernstein, Michael André. "When the Carnival Turns Bitter: Preliminary Reflections upon the Abject Hero." *Critical Inquiry* 10 (1983): 283–305.

Berrong, Richard M. *Rabelais and Bakhtin: Popular Culture in "Gargantua and Pantagruel."* Lincoln: Univ. of Nebraska Press, 1986.

Berti, Luciano. *Il Principe del studiolo: Francesco I de'Medici e la fine del rinascimento fiorentino*. Florence: Edam, 1967.

Biagi, M. L. Altieri. "La *Vita* del Cellini: Temi, termini, sintagmi." In *Benvenuto Cellini artista e scrittore, Quaderni dell'Accademia Nazionale dei Lincei* 177 (1972): 61–163.

Bloch, Marc. *Feudal Society*. Trans. L. A. Manyon. 2 vols. Chicago: Univ. of Chicago Press, 1961.

Blum, Abbe. "'Strike all that look upon with mar[b]le': Monumentalizing Women in Shakespeare's Plays." In Haselkorn and Travitsky, eds., *The Renaissance Englishwoman in Print*, pp. 99–118.

Bonino, Guido D. *Lo Scrittore, il potere, la maschera*. Padua: Liviana, 1979.

Boose, Lynda E. "Scolding Brides and Bridling Scolds: Taming the Woman's Unruly Member." *Shakespeare Quarterly* 42, no. 2 (1991): 179–213.

Borgerhoff, E. B. O. *The Freedom of French Classicism*. Princeton, N.J.: Princeton Univ. Press, 1950.

Bossy, John. *Christianity in the West: 1400–1700*. Oxford: Oxford Univ. Press, 1985.

Boudot, Pierre. *La Jouissance de Dieu ou le roman courtois de Thérèse d'Avila*. Paris: Hallier, 1979.

Bourdieu, Pierre. *Outline of a Theory of Practice*. Trans. R. Nice. Cambridge: Cambridge Univ. Press, 1977.

———. "Symbolic Anthropology." *Critique of Anthropology* 4 (1979): 77–85.

Bouwsma, William. "Three Types of Historiography in Post-Renaissance Italy." *History and Theory* 4 (1965): 303–14.

———. "Venice, Spain, and the Papacy: Paolo Sarpi and the Renaissance Tradition." In Cochrane, ed., *The Late Italian Renaissance*, pp. 353–76.

Bradbrook, Muriel. *The Living Monument: Shakespeare and the Theatre of His Time*. Cambridge: Cambridge Univ. Press, 1976.

———. *The Rise of the Common Player*. London: Chatto and Windus, 1962.

Braden, Gordon. *Renaissance Tragedy and the Senecan Tradition: Anger's Privilege*. New Haven, Conn.: Yale Univ. Press, 1985.

Bristol, Michael D. *Carnival and Theatre*. New York: Methuen, 1985.

Burckhardt, Jacob. *Civilization of the Renaissance in Italy*. Trans. S. G. C. Middlemore. 2 vols. New York: Harper and Row, 1958.

Burger, Peter. "*Le Cid* de Corneille et le matériau de la tragicomédie." *Papers on French Seventeenth Century Literature* 21 (1987): 427–45.
Burt, Richard A. "Licensed by Authority." *English Literary History* 54 (1987): 529–60.
Bynum, Caroline Walker. *Jesus as Mother*. Berkeley: Univ. of California Press, 1982.
Cain, Thomas. *Praise in "The Faerie Queene."* Lincoln: Univ. of Nebraska Press, 1978.
Cain, William. "The Place of the Poet in Jonson's 'To Penshurst' and 'To my Muse.'" *Criticism* 21 (1979): 34–48.
Capp, Bernard. *English Almanacs 1500–1800*. Ithaca, N.Y.: Cornell Univ. Press, 1979.
Caretti, Lanfranco. *Ariosto e Tasso*. 2d ed. Turin: Einaudi, 1967.
Cartari, Vincenzo. *The Fountaine of Ancient Fiction*. Trans. Richard Linche. London, 1599.
Castiglione, Baldesar. *The Book of the Courtier*. Trans. Charles S. Singleton. Garden City, N.Y.: Anchor Books, 1959.
Castro, Guillen de. *Las Mocedades del Cid*. Ed. Victor Said Armesto. Madrid: Espas-Calpe, 1945.
Cave, Terence. *The Cornucopian Text: Problems of Writing in the French Renaissance*. Oxford: Oxford Univ. Press, 1979.
Cavell, Stanley. *Disowning Knowledge in Six Plays of Shakespeare*. Cambridge: Cambridge Univ. Press, 1987.
Cavicchi, Adriano. "La Scenografia dell'*Aminta* nella tradizione scenografica pastorale ferrarese del secolo XVI." In Maria Teresa Muraro, ed., *Studi sul teatro veneto fra rinascimento ed età barocca*, pp. 53–72. Florence: Leo S. Olschki, 1971.
Cellini, Benvenuto. *Autobiography*. Trans. George Bull. Harmondsworth, Eng.: Penguin, 1961.
———. *Opere*. Ed. Bruno Maier. Milan: Rizzoli, 1968.
———. *Vita*. Ed. Ettore Camesasca. Milan: Rizzoli, 1985.
Cervigni, Dino S. *The "Vita" of Benvenuto Cellini: Literary Tradition and Genre*. Ravenna: Longo, n.d.
Chabod, Federico. *Scritti sul rinascimento*. Turin: Einaudi, 1967.
Chambers, D. S. *Patrons and Artists in the Italian Renaissance*. London: Macmillan, 1970.
Chanu, Pierre. *Eglise, culture, et société: Essais sur réforme et contre-réforme*. Paris: Société d'edition d'enseignement superieur, 1981.
Cheney, Donald. *Spenser's Image of Nature: Wild Man and Shepherd in "The Faerie Queene."* New Haven, Conn.: Yale Univ. Press, 1966.
Church, William F. *Richelieu and Reason of State*. Princeton, N.J.: Princeton Univ. Press, 1972.

Clark, Stuart. "King James's *Daemonologie*: Witchcraft and Kingship." In Sydney Anglo, ed., *The Damned Art: Essays in the Literature of Witchcraft*, pp. 156–81. London: Routledge and Kegan Paul, 1977.
Clements, Robert J. *Michelangelo's Theory of Art*. New York: New York Univ. Press, 1961.
Clubb, Louise George. *Italian Drama in Shakespeare's Time*. New Haven, Conn.: Yale Univ. Press, 1989.
———. "The Making of the Pastoral Play." In J. A. Molinaro, ed., *Petrarch to Pirandello*, pp. 45–71. Toronto: Univ. of Toronto Press, 1973.
———. "The Pastoral Play: Conflations of Country, Court and City." In Lorch, ed., *Il Teatro italiano del Rinascimento*, pp. 65–73.
Cochrane, Eric. "A Case in Point: The End of the Renaissance in Florence." In Cochrane, ed., *The Late Italian Renaissance*, pp. 43–73.
———. "Counter Reformation or Tridentine Reformation? Italy in the Age of S. Carlo Borromeo." In Headley and Tomaro, eds., *San Carlo Borromeo*, pp. 31–46.
———. *Florence in the Forgotten Centuries: 1527–1800*. Chicago: Univ. of Chicago Press, 1973.
———, ed. *The Late Italian Renaissance*. New York: Harper and Row, 1970.
Cody, Richard. *The Landscape of the Mind*. Oxford: Clarendon Press, 1967.
Coghill, Nevil. "Six Points of Stage-Craft in *The Winter's Tale*." *Shakespeare Survey* 11 (1958): 31–41.
Cohen, Walter. *Drama of a Nation*. Ithaca, N.Y.: Cornell Univ. Press, 1985.
Comito, Terry. *The Idea of the Garden in the Renaissance*. New Brunswick, N.J.: Rutgers Univ. Press, 1978.
Corneille, Pierre. *Le Cid, tragi-comédie. Texte de la première édition*. Ed. Milorad R. Margitić. Amsterdam: John Benjamins, 1989.
———. *L'Illusion comique*. Ed. Marc Fumaroli. Paris: Larousse, 1970.
———. *Oeuvres complètes*. Ed. Georges Couton. 3 vols. Paris: Gallimard, 1980–87.
———. *Pierre Corneille: Writings on the Theatre*. Ed. H. T. Barnwell. Oxford: Blackwell, 1965.
Corrigan, Beatrice. "Erminia and Tancredi: The Happy Ending." *Italica* 40 (1963): 325–33.
Couton, Georges. *Corneille*. Paris: Hatier, 1958.
———. *Corneille et la Fronde: Théâtre et politique il y a trois siècles*. Clermont: Bussac, 1951.
Cox, Lee Sheridan. "The Role of Autolycus in *The Winter's Tale*." *Studies in English Literature* 9, no. 2 (1969): 283–301.
Cremona, Isida. *L'Influence de l'Aminta sur la pastorale dramatique française*. Paris: Librairie Philosophique J. Vrin, 1977.
Crewe, Jonathan. *Trials of Authorship: Anterior Forms and Poetic Reconstruc-*

tion from Wyatt to Shakespeare. Berkeley: Univ. of California Press, 1990.

Cullen, Patrick. *Spenser, Marvell, and Renaissance Pastoral*. Cambridge, Mass.: Harvard Univ. Press, 1970.

Daniele, Antonio. *Capitoli Tassiani*. Padua: Antenore, 1983.

Davis, Natalie Zemon. "Boundaries and the Sense of Self in Sixteenth-Century France." In Thomas C. Heller, ed., *Reconstructing Individualism*, pp. 53–63.

———. *Fiction in the Archives: Pardon Tales and Their Tellers in Sixteenth-Century France*. Stanford, Calif.: Stanford Univ. Press, 1987.

———. *The Return of Martin Guerre*. Cambridge, Mass.: Harvard Univ. Press, 1983.

———. *Society and Culture in Early Modern France*. Stanford, Calif.: Stanford Univ. Press, 1976.

De Certeau, Michel. *La Fable mystique*. Paris: Gallimard, 1982.

———. *Heterologies: Discourse on the Other*. Trans. Brian Massumi. Minneapolis: Univ. of Minnesota Press, 1986.

DeJean, Joan. *Literary Fortifications: Rousseau, Laclos, Sade*. Princeton, N.J.: Princeton Univ. Press, 1984.

De Mattei, Rodolfo. *Aspetti di storia del pensiero politico*. 2 vols. Rome: Giuffré, 1980.

Demorest, Jean-Jacques, and Lise Leibacher-Ouvrard, eds. *Pascal / Corneille: Desert, retraite, engagement*. Paris: Papers on French Seventeenth Century Literature, 1984.

Dempsey, Charles. "Mythic Inventions in Counter-Reformation Painting." In P. A. Ramsey, ed., *Rome in the Renaissance: The City and the Myth*, pp. 55–76. Binghamton, N.Y.: Center for Medieval and Early Renaissance Studies, 1982.

De Nolhac, Pierre. *Petrarque et l'humanisme*. 2 vols. Paris: Champion, 1907.

Derla, Luigi. "Sull'allegoria della *Gerusalemme Liberata*." *Italianistica* 7 (1978): 473–88.

Desan, Philippe, ed. *Humanism In Crisis: The Decline of the French Renaissance*. Ann Arbor: Univ. of Michigan Press, 1991.

Descartes, René. *Descartes: Selections*. Ed. Ralph M. Eaton. New York: Scribners, 1955.

Déscôtes, Maurice. *Le Public de théâtre et son histoire*. Paris: Presses Universitaires de France, 1964.

Detienne, Marcel. *Crise agraire et attitude religieuse chez Hésiode*. *Collection Latomus* 68 (1963): 9–64.

Dolan, Frances E. "'Home-rebels and house-traitors': Murderous Wives in Early Modern England." *Yale Journal of Law and the Humanities* 4 (1992): 1–31.

Donadoni, Eugenio. *Torquato Tasso*. Florence: La Nuova Italia, 1920.

Dort, Bernard. *Corneille*. Paris: l'Arche, 1957.

———. "Les Deux Ages de Corneille." In Richter, ed., *Convegno di studi su Pierre Corneille*, pp. 19–26.

Doubrovsky, Serge. *Corneille et la dialectique du héros*. Paris: Gallimard, 1964.

———. "Corneille: Masculin / Feminin. Reflexions sur la structure tragique." In Demorest and Leibacher-Ouvrard, eds., *Pascal / Corneille*, pp. 89–127.

Douglas, Mary. *Purity and Danger*. London: Ark, 1984.

Dukore, Bernard, ed. *Dramatic Theory and Criticism*. New York: Holt, Rinehart and Winston, 1974.

Duranton-Mallet, Françoise. "Propositions pour une lecture analytique de *La Vita* de Benvenuto Cellini." *Revue des Etudes Italiennes* 29, no. 4 (1983): 223–31.

Durling, Robert. *The Figure of the Poet in Renaissance Epic*. Cambridge, Mass.: Harvard Univ. Press, 1965.

Edwards, Philip. *Threshold of a Nation*. Cambridge: Cambridge Univ. Press, 1979.

Eliade, Mircea. *The Forge and the Crucible*. Trans. Stephen Corrin. Chicago: Univ. of Chicago Press, 1978.

Erasmus, Desiderius. *The Antibarbarians*. Trans. Margaret Mann Phillips. In *Collected Works of Erasmus*, vol. 23. Toronto: Univ. of Toronto Press, 1978.

———. *Christian Humanism and the Reformation: Selected Writings of Erasmus*. Ed. John Olin. New York: Fordham Univ. Press, 1975.

———. *Erasmus-Luther: Discourse on Free Will*. Trans. Ernst F. Winter. New York: Frederick Ungar, 1961.

———. *Erasmus on His Times: A Shortened Version of the Adages of Erasmus*. Trans. and ed. Margaret Mann Phillips. Cambridge: Cambridge Univ. Press, 1967.

———. *On Copia of Words and Ideas*. Trans. Donald King and H. D. Rix. Milwaukee: Marquette Univ. Press, 1963.

———. *Opus Epistolarum Des. Erasmi Roterodami*. Ed. P. S. Allen. Oxford: Clarendon Press, 1910.

———. *The Praise of Folly*. Trans. Betty Radice. Harmondsworth, Eng.: Penguin, 1971.

Erickson, Peter B. *Patriarchal Structures in Shakespeare's Drama*. Berkeley: Univ. of California Press, 1985.

Esler, Philip Francis. *Community and Gospel in Luke-Acts*. Cambridge: Cambridge Univ. Press, 1987.

Fabre, Antonin. *Etudes littéraires sur le XVIIe siècle: Chapelain et nos deux premières académies*. Paris: Perrin, 1890.

Fenton, John. *King James His Welcome to London. With Elizaes Tomb and Epitaph*. London, 1603.

Ferguson, Margaret W. "A Room Not Their Own: Renaissance Women as

Readers and Writers." In Clayton Koelb and Susan Noakes, eds., *The Comparative Perspective on Literature*, pp. 93–116. Ithaca, N.Y.: Cornell Univ. Press, 1988.

———. *Trials of Desire: Renaissance Defenses of Poetry*. New Haven, Conn.: Yale Univ. Press, 1983.

Ferguson, Margaret W., Maureen Quilligan, and Nancy J. Vickers, eds. *Rewriting the Renaissance*. Chicago: Univ. of Chicago Press, 1986.

Ferroni, Giulio. *Il Testo e la scena: Saggi sul teatro del cinquecento*. Rome: Bulzoni, 1980.

Fiorenza, Elisabeth Schussler. "Word, Spirit and Power: Women in Early Christian Communities." In Ruether and McLaughlin, eds., *Women of Spirit*, pp. 29–70.

Fish, Stanley. "Authors-Readers: Jonson and the Community of the Same." In Greenblatt, ed., *Representing the English Renaissance*, pp. 231–64.

———. *Self-Consuming Artifacts: The Experience of Seventeenth-Century Literature*. Berkeley: Univ. of California Press, 1972.

Fowler, Alastair. "Beginnings of English Georgic." In Lewalski, ed., *Renaissance Genres*, pp. 105–25.

Fraser, Nancy, and Linda Gordon. "Decoding 'Dependency': Inscriptions of Power in a Keyword of the Welfare State." Unpublished manuscript, 1991.

Freccero, John. "Autobiography and Narrative." In Thomas C. Heller, ed., *Reconstructing Individualism*, pp. 16–29.

Freud, Sigmund. "Creative Writers and Day Dreaming." In *Standard Edition*, vol. 9, pp. 144–53. London: Hogarth Press, 1964.

Frye, Northrop. *A Natural Perspective*. New York: Columbia Univ. Press, 1965.

———. "Romance as Masque." In Kay and Jacobs, eds., *Shakespeare's Romances Reconsidered*, pp. 11–39.

Fumaroli, Marc. *L'Age de l'eloquence*. Geneva: Droz, 1980.

Garber, Marjorie. *Shakespeare's Ghost Writers*. New York: Methuen, 1987.

Garner, Stanton B., Jr. "Time and Presence in *The Winter's Tale*." *Modern Language Quarterly* 46, no. 4 (1985): 347–67.

Gasté, Armand, ed. *La Querelle du Cid*. Paris: Welter, 1898.

Gethner, Perry. "Jean de Mairet and Poetic Justice: A Definition of Tragicomedy?" *Renaissance Drama* 11 (1980): 171–87.

Getto, Giovanni. *Malinconia di Torquato Tasso*. Naples: Ligouri, 1979.

Giamatti, A. Bartlett. *Exile and Change in Renaissance Literature*. New Haven, Conn.: Yale Univ. Press, 1984.

Ginzburg, Carlo. *The Cheese and the Worms: The Cosmos of a Sixteenth-Century Miller*. Trans. John Tedeschi and Anne Tedeschi. Baltimore, Md.: Johns Hopkins Univ. Press, 1980.

Godard, Alain. "Du 'Capitano' au 'Cavalier Sovrano': Godefroi de Bouillon dans la *Jérusalem conquise*." In *Réécritures 3: Commentaires, parodies, variations dans la littérature italienne de la Renaissance*, vol. 3, pp. 205–64. Paris: Univ. de la Sorbonne Nouvelle, 1987.

———. "La Première Représentation de l'*Aminta*: La Cour de Ferrare et son double." In André Rochon, ed., *Ville et campagne dans la littérature italienne de la Renaissance*, vol. 2, pp. 197–285. Paris: Sorbonne, 1977.

Goldberg, Jonathan. "Fatherly Authority: The Politics of Stuart Family Images." In Ferguson, Quilligan, and Vickers, eds., *Rewriting the Renaissance*, pp. 3–32.

———. *James I and the Politics of Literature*. Baltimore, Md.: Johns Hopkins Univ. Press, 1983.

———. "*Macbeth* and Source." In Howard and O'Connor, eds., *Shakespeare Reproduced*, pp. 242–64.

———. *Voice / Terminal / Echo*. New York: Methuen, 1986.

Goldthwaite, Richard A. "The Economic and Social World of Italian Renaissance Maiolica." *Renaissance Quarterly* 42, no. 1 (1989): 1–33.

Gramsci, Antonio. *The Modern Prince and Other Writings*. Trans. Louis Marks. New York: International Publishers, 1983.

Greenberg, Mitchell. *Corneille, Classicism, and the Ruses of Symmetry*. Cambridge: Cambridge Univ. Press, 1986.

Greenblatt, Stephen. "Fiction and Friction." In Thomas C. Heller, ed., *Reconstructing Individualism*, pp. 30–52.

———. "Psychoanalysis and Renaissance Culture." In Parker and Quint, eds., *Literary Theory / Renaissance Texts*, pp. 210–24.

———. *Renaissance Self-Fashioning*. Chicago: Univ. of Chicago Press, 1980.

———. *Shakespearean Negotiations*. Berkeley: Univ. of California Press, 1988.

———, ed. *Representing the English Renaissance*. Berkeley: Univ. of California Press, 1988.

Greene, Thomas. *The Light in Troy*. New Haven, Conn.: Yale Univ. Press, 1982.

———. "Magic and Festivity at the Renaissance Court." *Renaissance Quarterly* 40, no. 4 (1987): 636–59.

———. *The Vulnerable Text: Essays in Renaissance Literature*. New York: Columbia Univ. Press, 1986.

Guarini, Elena Fasano. *Lo stato mediceo di Cosimo I*. Florence: Sansoni, 1973.

Guglielminetti, Marziano. *Memoria e scrittura: L'autobiografia da Dante a Cellini*. Turin: Einaudi, 1977.

Guilhem, Claire. "L'Inquisition et la dévaluation des discours feminins." In Bennassar, ed., *L'Inquisition espagnole*, pp. 197–240.

Guillory, John. *Poetic Authority: Spenser, Milton, and Literary History*. New York: Columbia Univ. Press, 1983.
Guizot, M. *Corneille and His Times*. London: R. Bentley, 1852.
Gundersheimer, Werner L. "The Crisis of the Late French Renaissance." In Molho and Tedeschi, eds., *Renaissance Studies in Honor of Hans Baron*, pp. 791–808.
———. "Patronage in the Renaissance: An Exploratory Approach." In Lytle and Orgel, eds., *Patronage in the Renaissance*, pp. 3–23. Princeton, N.J.: Princeton Univ. Press, 1981.
Gurr, Andrew. "The Bear, the Statue, and Hysteria in *The Winter's Tale*." *Shakespeare Quarterly* 34, no. 4 (1983): 420–25.
Gutman, Huck. "Rousseau's *Confessions*: A Technology of the Self." In Luther H. Martin et al., eds., *Technologies of the Self*, pp. 99–120. Amherst: Univ. of Massachusetts Press, 1988.
Hartwig, Joan. "Cloten, Autolycus, and Caliban: Bearers of Parodic Burdens." In Kay and Jacobs, eds., *Shakespeare's Romances Reconsidered*, pp. 91–103.
Haselkorn, Anne M., and Betty S. Travitsky, eds. *The Renaissance Englishwoman in Print*. Amherst: Univ. of Massachusetts Press, 1990.
Haskell, Francis. *Patrons and Painters: A Study in the Relations Between Italian Art and Society in the Age of the Baroque*. New York: Knopf, 1963.
Hayman, David. "Toward a Mechanics of Mode: Beyond Bakhtin." *Novel* 16, no. 2 (1983): 101–20.
Headley, John M., and John B. Tomaro, eds. *San Carlo Borromeo: Catholic Reform and Ecclesiastical Politics in the Second Half of the Sixteenth Century*. Washington, D.C.: Folger Books, 1988.
Heinemann, Margot. *Puritanism and Theatre*. Cambridge: Cambridge Univ. Press, 1980.
Heinzelman, Kurt. *The Economics of the Imagination*. Amherst: Univ. of Massachusetts Press, 1978.
Heisch, Allison. "Queen Elizabeth I: Parliamentary Rhetoric and the Exercise of Power." *Signs* 1 (1975): 31–55.
Helgerson, Richard. "Inventing Noplace, or the Power of Negative Thinking." In Stephen Greenblatt, ed., *The Power of Forms in the English Renaissance*, pp. 101–22. Norman, Okla.: Pilgrim, 1981.
———. *Self-Crowned Laureates*. Berkeley: Univ. of California Press, 1983.
Heller, Agnes. *Renaissance Man*. Trans. Richard E. Allen. New York: Schocken Books, 1981.
Heller, Thomas C., ed. *Reconstructing Individualism: Autonomy, Individuality, and the Self in Western Thought*. Stanford, Calif.: Stanford Univ. Press, 1986.
Herrick, Martin. *Tragicomedy*. Urbana: Univ. of Illinois Press, 1962.

Hertz, Neil. "Medusa's Head: Male Hysteria Under Political Pressure." *Representations* 1, no. 4 (1983): 40–50.
Heywood, John. *Of Gentylnes and Nobylyte*. Ed. K. W. Cameron. Raleigh, N.C.: Thistle Press, 1941 [1522–23].
Heywood, Thomas. *An Apology for Actors*. Ed. Richard H. Perkinson. New York: Scholars' Facsimiles and Reprints, 1941 [1612].
Histrio-Mastix, or The Player Whipt. Ed. John S. Farmer. London: Tudor Facsimile Texts, 1912 [1610].
Hoffman, Nancy Jo. *Spenser's Pastorals*. Baltimore, Md.: Johns Hopkins Univ. Press, 1977.
Holderness, Graham, Nick Potter, and John Turner. *Shakespeare Out of Court: Dramatizations of Court Society*. London: Macmillan, 1990.
Howard, Jean E. "Crossdressing, the Theatre, and Gender Struggle in Early Modern England." *Shakespeare Quarterly* 39, no. 4 (1988): 418–40.
———. "Renaissance Antitheatricality and the Politics of Gender and Rank in *Much Ado About Nothing*." In Howard and O'Connor, eds., *Shakespeare Reproduced*, pp. 163–88.
Howard, Jean E., and Marion F. O'Connor, eds. *Shakespeare Reproduced*. New York: Methuen, 1987.
Huet, Marie-Hélène. *Rehearsing the Revolution: The Staging of Marat's Death, 1793–97*. Trans. Robert Hurley. Berkeley: Univ. of California Press, 1982.
Hughes, Merritt Y. *Virgil and Spenser*. 2d ed. New York: AMS Press, 1971.
Hughes, Muriel Joy. *Women Healers in Medieval Life and Literature*. New York: King's Crown Press, 1943.
Hume, Althea. *Edmund Spenser: Protestant Poet*. Cambridge: Cambridge Univ. Press, 1984.
Hyma, Albert. *The Youth of Erasmus*. Ann Arbor: Univ. of Michigan Press, 1930.
I.G. *A Refutation of the Apology for Actors*. Ed. Richard H. Perkinson. New York: Scholars' Facsimiles and Reprints, 1941 [1615].
Ingegneri, Angelo. "La Rappresentazione delle favole sceniche." In Ferruccio Marotti, ed., *Lo Spettacolo dall'umanesimo al manierismo*, pp. 271–308. Milan: Feltrinelli, 1974 [1598].
Ingram, Martin. "Ridings, Rough Music and Mocking Rhymes in Early Modern England." In Barry Reay, ed., *Popular Culture in Seventeenth-Century England*, pp. 166–97. London: Croom Helm, 1985.
Irigaray, Luce. *Speculum of the Other Woman*. Trans. Gillian C. Gill. Ithaca, N.Y.: Cornell Univ. Press, 1985.
Jacobus, Mary. *Reading Women: Essays in Feminist Criticism*. New York: Columbia Univ. Press, 1986.

James I. *Daemonologie*. Ed. G. B. Harrison. London: Bodley Head, 1924 [1597].

———. *The Political Works of James I*. Ed. Charles Howard McIlwain. New York: Russell and Russell, 1965.

———. *Workes of the Most High and Mightie Prince, James I*. London, 1616.

Jardine, Lisa. "Cultural Confusion and Shakespeare's Learned Heroines." *Shakespeare Quarterly* 38, no. 1 (1987): 1–18.

Jardine, Lisa, and Anthony Grafton, eds. *From Humanism to the Humanities*. Cambridge, Mass.: Harvard Univ. Press, 1986.

Jauss, Hans Robert. "Poesis." *Critical Inquiry* 9 (1982): 591–608.

Javitch, Daniel. *Poetry and Courtliness in the English Renaissance*. Princeton, N.J.: Princeton Univ. Press, 1978.

Jedin, H. *History of the Council of Trent*. 2 vols. St. Louis: B. Herder, 1957.

Jensen, Ellen M. "Anna O.—A Study of Her Later Life." *Psychoanalytic Quarterly* 39, no. 2 (1970): 269–93.

Jones, Ann Rosalind. "Counterattacks on 'the Bayter of Women': Three Pamphleteers of the Early Seventeenth Century." In Haselkorn and Travitsky, eds., *The Renaissance Englishwoman in Print*, pp. 53–57.

Jonson, Ben. *Ben Jonson: The Complete Masques*. Ed. Stephen Orgel. New Haven, Conn.: Yale Univ. Press, 1969.

———. *Ben Jonson's Plays and Masques*. Ed. Robert M. Adams. New York: Norton, 1979.

———. *Poems*. Ed. Ian Donaldson. London: Oxford Univ. Press, 1975.

———. *The Works of Ben Jonson*. Ed. C. H. Herford, Percy Simpson, and Evelyn Simpson. 11 vols. Oxford: Clarendon Press, 1925–52.

Jordan, Constance. *Renaissance Feminism: Literary Texts and Political Models*. Ithaca, N.Y.: Cornell Univ. Press, 1990.

———. "Seeing through Jane Eyre: Interpreting the Female Subject and Female Authority in Renaissance Europe." Paper presented at the Newberry Library Conference on Women and Gender in the Middle Ages and the Renaissance, Chicago, Ill., May 5, 1991.

Kahn, Coppélia. "'Magic of bounty': *Timon of Athens*, Jacobean Patronage, and Maternal Power." *Shakespeare Quarterly* 38, no. 1 (1987): 34–57.

Kahn, Victoria. "Humanism and the Resistance to Theory." In Parker and Quint, eds., *Literary Theory / Renaissance Texts*, pp. 373–96.

———. *Rhetoric, Prudence, and Skepticism in the Renaissance*. Ithaca, N.Y.: Cornell Univ. Press, 1985.

Kamen, Henry. *Inquisition and Society in Spain in the Sixteenth and Seventeenth Centuries*. Bloomington: Indiana Univ. Press, 1985.

Kastan, David. "Proud Majesty Made a Subject: Shakespeare and the Spectacle of Rule." *Shakespeare Quarterly* 37, no. 4 (1986): 459–75.

Kay, Carol McGinnis, and Henry E. Jacobs, eds. *Shakespeare's Romances Reconsidered*. Lincoln: Univ. of Nebraska Press, 1978.

Kennedy, William. "The Problem of Allegory in Tasso's *Gerusalemme Liberata*." *Italian Quarterly* 60, no. 1 (1972): 27–51.

Kent, Francis William. *Household and Lineage in Renaissance Florence*. Princeton, N.J.: Princeton Univ. Press, 1977.

Kernan, Alvin B. *The Playwright as Magician*. New Haven, Conn.: Yale Univ. Press, 1979.

Kerrigan, William, and Gordon Braden. *The Idea of the Renaissance*. Baltimore, Md.: Johns Hopkins Univ. Press, 1989.

Kieckhefer, Richard. *Unquiet Souls: Fourteenth-Century Saints and Their Religious Milieu*. Chicago: Univ. of Chicago Press, 1984.

Kiernan, V. G. *Society and Change 1550–1650*. New York: St. Martin's Press, 1980.

King, John. *English Reformation Literature: The Tudor Origins of the Protestant Tradition*. Princeton, N.J.: Princeton Univ. Press, 1982.

———. "Spenser's *Shepheardes Calender* and Protestant Pastoral Satire." In Lewalski, ed., *Renaissance Genres*, pp. 369–98.

Kipling, Gordon. "The Funeral Coronations for Margaret of Anjou." *Medieval Theatre* 4 (1982): 5–27.

Knight, G. Wilson. *The Crown of Life*. London: Oxford Univ. Press, 1947.

Koch, Philip. "*Horace*: Reponse Cornelienne à la querelle du *Cid*." *Romanic Review* 76 (1985): 148–61.

Koepp, Cynthia J. "The Alphabetical Order: Work in Diderot's *Encyclopédie*." In Steven Laurence Kaplan and Cynthia J. Koepp, eds., *Work in France: Representations, Meaning, Organization, and Practice*, pp. 229–57. Ithaca, N.Y.: Cornell Univ. Press, 1986.

Krier, Theresa M. *Gazing on Secret Sights: Spenser, Classical Imitation, and the Decorums of Vision*. Ithaca, N.Y.: Cornell Univ. Press, 1990.

La Belle, Jenijoy. *Herself Beheld: The Literature of the Looking Glass*. Ithaca, N.Y.: Cornell Univ. Press, 1988.

Lafond, Jean. "Littérature et morale au XVIIe siècle." In Marc Fumaroli, ed., *Critique et création littéraires en France au XVIIe siècle*, pp. 395–406. Paris: Editions du centre national de la recherche scientifique, 1977.

Lagarde, François. "Le sacrifice de la femme chez Corneille." *Stanford French Review* 12 (1988): 187–204.

Laguardia, Gari. "Santa Teresa and the Problem of Desire." *Hispania* 63 (1980): 523–31.

Lander, J. R. *The Limitations of English Monarchy in the Later Middle Ages*. Toronto: Univ. of Toronto Press, 1989.

Lane, Frederic. *Venice and History: The Collected Papers of Frederic C. Lane*. Baltimore, Md.: Johns Hopkins Univ. Press, 1966.

Lebatteux, Guy. "Idéologie monarchique et propagande dynastique dans l'oeuvre de Gimbattista Giraldi Cinthio." In André Rochon, ed., *Les Ecrivains et le pouvoir en Italie à l'époque de la Renaissance*, pp. 244–312. Paris: Univ. de la Sorbonne Nouvelle, 1974.

Leech, Clifford. "Masking and Unmasking in the Late Plays." In Kay and Jacobs, eds., *Shakespeare's Romances Reconsidered*, pp. 40–59.

Lefkowitz, Mary R. *Heroines and Hysterics*. New York: St. Martin's Press, 1981.

Leggatt, Alexander. *Shakespeare's Political Drama*. London: Routledge, 1988.

Lewalski, Barbara, ed. *Renaissance Genres: Essays on Theory, History, and Interpretation*. Cambridge, Mass.: Harvard Univ. Press, 1986.

Lincoln, Victoria. *Teresa: A Woman: A Biography of Teresa of Avila*. Albany: State Univ. of New York Press, 1984.

Lindenbaum, Peter. *Changing Landscapes: Anti-Pastoral Sentiment in the English Renaissance*. Athens: Univ. of Georgia Press, 1986.

Lionnet, Françoise. *Autobiographical Voices: Race, Gender, Self-Portraiture*. Ithaca, N.Y.: Cornell Univ. Press, 1989.

Lipking, Lawrence. *The Life of the Poet*. Chicago: Univ. of Chicago Press, 1981.

Livingston, Mary L. "The Natural Art of *The Winter's Tale*." *Modern Language Quarterly* 30, no. 3 (1969): 340–55.

Lodge, Thomas. *A Reply to Stephen Gosson's Schoole of Abuse, In Defence of Poetry, Music and Stage-Plays*. London: Shakespeare Society, 1853 [1577].

Loewenstein, Joseph. "Echo's Ring: Orpheus and Spenser's Career." *English Literary Renaissance* 16 (1986): 287–302.

———. *Responsive Readings: Versions of Echo in Pastoral, Epic, and the Jonsonian Masque*. New Haven, Conn.: Yale Univ. Press, 1984.

———. "The Script in the Marketplace." In Greenblatt, ed., *Representing the English Renaissance*, pp. 265–87.

Lorch, Maristella de Panizza, ed. *Il Teatro italiano del Rinascimento*. Milan: Edizioni di Communità, 1980.

Low, Anthony. *The Georgic Revolution*. Princeton, N.J.: Princeton Univ. Press, 1985.

Luther, Martin. *Luther's Works. Vol. 2, Lectures on Genesis*. Ed. J. Pelikan. St. Louis: Concordia Publishing House, 1960.

MacCaffrey, Isabel G. "Allegory and Pastoral in *The Shepheardes Calender*." *English Literary History* 36 (1969): 88–109.

Machiavelli, Niccolò. *The Prince*. Trans. and ed. Richard Adams. New York: Norton, 1968.

MacLean, Ian. *The Renaissance Notion of Woman*. Cambridge: Cambridge Univ. Press, 1980.

Magnusson, A. Lynn. "Interruption in *The Tempest*." *Shakespeare Quarterly* 37, no. 1 (1986): 52–65.
Maier, Ida. *Ange Politien: La formation d'un poète humaniste 1469–1480*. Geneva: Droz, 1966.
Mancini, Guido. *Teresa de Avila: La libertà del sublime*. Pisa: Giardini, 1981.
Mandel, Barrett J. "Full of Life Now." In Olney, ed., *Autobiography: Essays Theoretical and Critical*, pp. 49–72.
Mantuan, Baptista. *Eclogues of Baptista Mantuanus*. Ed. Wilfred P. Mustard. Baltimore, Md.: Johns Hopkins Univ. Press, 1911.
———. *The Eclogues of Mantuan*. Trans. George Turberville. Ed. Douglas Bush. New York: Scholars' Facsimiles and Reprints, 1937 [1567].
Maravall, Juan Antonio. *Culture of the Baroque*. Trans. Terry Cochran. Minneapolis: Univ. of Minnesota Press, 1986.
Marcus, Leah. *The Politics of Mirth: Jonson, Herrick, Milton, Marvell, and the Defense of Old Holiday Pastimes*. Chicago: Univ. of Chicago Press, 1986.
———. *Puzzling Shakespeare*. Berkeley: Univ. of California Press, 1988.
Margitić, Milorad R. *Essai sur la mythologie du Cid*. University, Mississippi: Romance Monographs, 1976.
———, ed. *Corneille comique*. Paris: Papers on Seventeenth Century French Literature, 1982.
Marichal, Juan Augusto. "Santa Teresa en el ensayismo hispánico." In *La Voluntad de estilo*. Barcelona: Seix Barral, 1957.
Marin, Louis. *Le Portrait du roi*. Paris: Minuit, 1981.
Mason, Mary G. "The Other Voice: Autobiographies of Women Writers." In Olney, ed., *Autobiography: Essays Theoretical and Critical*, pp. 207–35.
Mauss, Marcel. *The Gift*. Trans. I. Cunningham. New York: Norton, 1976.
McKeon, Michael. *The Origins of the English Novel 1600–1740*. Baltimore, Md.: Johns Hopkins Univ. Press, 1987.
McLane, Paul E. *Spenser's Shepheardes Calender: A Study in Elizabethan Allegory*. Notre Dame, Ind.: Univ. of Notre Dame Press, 1961.
Medici, Lorenzo de'. *Scritti scelti*. Ed. Emilio Bigi. Turin: Unione editrice torinese, 1955.
Menchi, Silvana Seidel. *Erasmo in Italia 1520–1580*. Turin: Bollati Boringhieri, 1987.
Menendez y Pelayo, Marcelino. *Historia de los heterodoxos españoles*. 2 vols. Madrid: Biblioteca de Autores Cristianos, 1956.
Migiel, Marilyn. "Tasso's Erminia: Telling an Alternate Story." *Italica* 64 (1987): 62–75.
Miller, Beth, ed. *Women in Hispanic Literature: Icons and Fallen Idols*. Berkeley: Univ. of California Press, 1983.
Miller, David Lee. "Authorship, Anonymity, and *The Shepheardes Calender*." *Modern Language Quarterly* 40, no. 3 (1979): 219–36.

———. *The Poem's Two Bodies: The Poetics of the 1590 "Faerie Queene."* Princeton, N.J.: Princeton Univ. Press, 1988.

———. "Spenser's Vocation, Spenser's Career." *English Literary History* 50 (1983): 197–231.

Miller, E. H. *The Professional Writer in Elizabethan England.* Cambridge, Mass.: Harvard Univ. Press, 1959.

Miller, Jacqueline T. *Poetic License: Authority and Authorship in Medieval and Renaissance Contexts.* New York: Oxford Univ. Press, 1986.

Miller, Nancy K. "Writing (from) the Feminine: George Sand and the Novel of Female Pastoral." In Carolyn G. Heilbrun and Margaret R. Higonnet, eds., *The Representation of Women in Fiction*, pp. 124–51. Baltimore, Md.: Johns Hopkins Univ. Press, 1983.

Mirollo, James V. "The Lives of Saints Teresa of Avila and Benvenuto of Florence." *Texas Studies in Literature and Language* 29 (1987): 54–73.

———. *Mannerism and Renaissance Poetry.* New Haven, Conn.: Yale Univ. Press, 1984.

Molho, Anthony, and John A. Tedeschi. *Renaissance Studies in Honor of Hans Baron.* Dekalb: Northern Illinois Univ. Press, 1971.

Montrose, Louis Adrian. "'Eliza, Queene of shepheardes,' and the Pastoral of Power." *English Literary Renaissance* 10 (1980): 153–82.

———. "The Elizabethan Subject and the Spenserian Text." In Parker and Quint, eds., *Literary Theory / Renaissance Texts*, pp. 303–40.

———. "Gifts and Reasons: The Contexts of Peele's *Arraignement of Paris.*" *English Literary History* 47 (1980): 433–61.

———. "Of Gentlemen and Shepherds: The Politics of Elizabethan Pastoral Form." *English Literary History* 50 (1983): 415–59.

Mousnier, Roland. *Social Hierarchies: 1450 to the Present.* Trans. Peter Evans. London: Croom Helm, 1973.

Muecke, Frances. "Poetic Self-Consciousness in *Georgics* II." In A. J. Boyle, ed., *Virgil's Ascraean Song*, pp. 86–102. Berwick, Victoria: Aureal Publications, 1979.

Mullaney, Steven. *The Place of the Stage.* Chicago: Univ. of Chicago Press, 1988.

Mulvey, Laura. "Visual Pleasure and Narrative Cinema." In *Visual and Other Pleasures*, pp. 14–26. Bloomington: Indiana Univ. Press, 1989.

Murray, Timothy. *Theatrical Legitimation: Allegories of Genius in Seventeenth-Century England and France.* Oxford: Oxford Univ. Press, 1987.

Murrin, Michael. *The Allegorical Epic: Essays in Its Rise and Decline.* Chicago: Univ. of Chicago Press, 1980.

Murtaugh, Kristen Olson. "Erminia Delivered: Notes on Tasso and Romance." *Quaderni d'italianistica* 3, no. 1 (1982): 12–25.

Musurillo, Herbert, ed. and trans. "The Martyrdom of Perpetua and Felicitas." In *Acts of the Christian Martyrs*. Oxford: Clarendon Press, 1972.

Neely, Carol Thomas. *Broken Nuptials in Shakespeare's Plays*. New Haven, Conn.: Yale Univ. Press, 1985.

———. "The Structure of English Sonnet Sequences." *English Literary History* 45 (1978): 359–89.

Neuse, Richard. "Milton and Spenser: The Virgilian Triad Revisited." *English Literary History* 45 (1978): 606–39.

Newes from Scotland. Ed. G. B. Harrison. London: Bodley Head, 1924 [1591].

Niccoli, Gabriele. "Teoria e prassi: Note sulla questione della tragicommedia pastorale in Italia e in Francia." *Quaderni d'italianistica* 8, no. 2 (1987): 227–36.

Niccoli, Ottavia. "La Fine delle profezie." Paper distributed at the Newberry Library Conference in Honor of Eric Cochrane, Chicago, Ill., May 1988.

Nicole, Pierre. *Traité de la comédie*. Ed. Georges Couton. Paris: Les Belles Lettres, 1961 [1653].

Niderst, Alain, ed. *Pierre Corneille*. Paris: Presses Universitaires de France, 1985.

Olini, Lucia. "Dalle direzioni di lettura alla revisione del testo: Tasso tra 'Allegoria del poema' e *Giudizio*." *Rassegna della Letteratura Italiana* 7 (1985): 53–68.

Olney, James, ed. *Autobiography: Essays Theoretical and Critical*. Princeton, N.J.: Princeton Univ. Press, 1980.

O'Loughlin, M. J. *The Garlands of Repose*. Chicago: Univ. of Chicago Press, 1978.

Olson, Glending. *Literature as Recreation in the Later Middle Ages*. Ithaca, N.Y.: Cornell Univ. Press, 1982.

Orgel, Stephen. *The Illusion of Power*. Berkeley: Univ. of California Press, 1975.

———. "Jonson and the Amazons." In Elizabeth D. Harvey and Katharine Eisaman Maus, eds., *Soliciting Interpretation: Literary Theory and Seventeenth-Century English Poetry*, pp. 119–39. Chicago: Univ. of Chicago Press, 1990.

———. "Prospero's Wife." In Ferguson, Quilligan, and Vickers, eds., *Rewriting the Renaissance*, pp. 50–64.

Orlandi, Giulio Lensi. *Cosimo e Francesco de'Medici alchimisti*. Florence: Nardini, 1978.

Ovidius, Naso. *Fasti*. Trans. James Frazer. Cambridge, Mass.: Loeb, 1976.

———. *The XV Bookes of P. Ovidius Naso, Entytuled "Metamorphosis."* Trans. Arthur Golding. London, 1584.

Ozment, Steven E. *Mysticism and Dissent: Religious Ideology and Social Protest in the Sixteenth Century*. New Haven, Conn.: Yale Univ. Press, 1973.

Pagels, Elaine H. "What Became of God the Mother?: Conflicting Images of God in Early Christianity." In Elizabeth Abel and Emily K. Abel, eds., *The Signs Reader: Women, Gender, and Scholarship*, pp. 97–107. Chicago: Univ. of Chicago Press, 1983.

Painter, Sidney. *A History of the Middle Ages 284–1500*. New York: Knopf, 1953.

Parker, Patricia. *Literary Fat Ladies*. New York: Methuen, 1987.

Parker, Patricia, and Geoffrey Hartman, eds. *Shakespeare and the Question of Theory*. New York: Methuen, 1985.

Parker, Patricia, and David Quint, eds. *Literary Theory / Renaissance Texts*. Baltimore, Md.: Johns Hopkins Univ. Press, 1986.

Parmenter, Mary. "Spenser's 12 Aeglogues Proportionable to the 12 Monthes." *English Literary History* 3 (1936): 190–217.

Parvey, Constance F. "The Theology and Leadership of Women in the New Testament." In Ruether, ed., *Religion and Sexism*, pp. 117–49.

Patterson, Annabel. *Censorship and Interpretation: The Conditions of Writing and Reading in Early Modern Europe*. Madison: Univ. of Wisconsin Press, 1984.

———. *Pastoral and Ideology*. Berkeley: Univ. of California Press, 1987.

———. "Pastoral vs. Georgic: The Politics of Virgilian Quotation." In Lewalski, ed., *Renaissance Genres*, pp. 241–67.

Peers, E. Allison. *Studies of the Spanish Mystics*. 3 vols. London: Sheldon Press, 1927.

Pellisson-Fontanier, Paul. *Relation contenant l'histoire de l'Académie française*. Paris, 1652.

Perella, Nicholas. "Pope and the *Pastor Fido*." *Philological Quarterly* 40, no. 3 (1961): 444–48.

Perez, Joseph. "Cultura y sociedad en tiempos de Santa Teresa." In Teofanes Egido Martinez, Victor Garcia de la Concha, and Olgario Gonzalez de Cardenal, eds., *Actas del Congreso Internacional Teresiano*, vol. 1, pp. 31–40. Salamanca: Univ. of Salamanca, 1983.

Petrarch, Francis. *Bucolicum carmen*. Trans. Thomas Bergin. New Haven, Conn.: Yale Univ. Press, 1974.

———. "Coronation Oration." Trans. E. H. Wilkins. In *Studies in the Life and Works of Petrarch*, pp. 300–313. Chicago: Univ. of Chicago Press, 1960.

———. *Rerum familiarium libri*. Trans. Aldo S. Bernardo. 3 vols. Albany: State Univ. of New York Press, 1975–82.

Phillips, Henry. *The Theatre and Its Critics in Seventeenth-Century France*. Oxford: Oxford Univ. Press, 1980.

Pieri, Marzia. *La Scena boschereccia nel Rinascimento italiano*. Padua: Liviana, 1983.

Pintard, René. "De la tragicomédie à la tragédie: L'Exemple du *Cid*." In *Missions et démarches de la critique. Mélanges offerts au Professeur J. A. Vier*, pp. 455–66. Paris: Klincksieck, 1973.

Pliny, the Elder. *Natural History*. Trans. H. Rackman. 10 vols. Cambridge, Mass.: Harvard Univ. Press, 1949–83.

Pocock, Gordon. *Corneille and Racine: Problems of Tragic Form*. Cambridge: Cambridge Univ. Press, 1973.

Poliziano, Angelo. *The Stanze of Angelo Poliziano*. Trans. David Quint. Amherst: Univ. of Massachusetts Press, 1979.

Pope, Alexander. *Correspondence*. Ed. G. Sherburn. 5 vols. Oxford: Oxford Univ. Press, 1956.

Pope-Henessy, John. *Cellini*. New York: Abbeville Press, 1985.

Prigent, Michel. *Le Héros et l'état dans la tragédie de Pierre Corneille*. Paris: Presses universitaires de France, 1986.

———. "L'Exercise du pouvoir dans les tragédies de Corneille." In Niderst, ed., *Pierre Corneille*, pp. 593–604.

Putnam, Michael. *Virgil's Poem of the Earth*. Princeton, N.J.: Princeton Univ. Press, 1979.

Quint, David. *Origin and Originality in Renaissance Literature: Versions of the Source*. New Haven, Conn.: Yale Univ. Press, 1983.

Racine, Jean. *Oeuvres complètes de Racine*. Ed. Raymond Picard. 2 vols. Paris: Gallimard, 1950.

Radcliff-Umstead, Dennis. "Love in Tasso's *Aminta*: A Reflection of the Este Court." In Lorch, ed., *Il Teatro italiano del Rinascimento*, pp. 75–84.

Ragionieri, Giovanna. *Il Giardino storico italiano*. Florence: Leo S. Olschki, 1981.

Ranum, Orest. *Artisans of Glory: Writers and Historical Thought in Seventeenth-Century France*. Chapel Hill: Univ. of North Carolina Press, 1980.

Rebhorn, Wayne. "Erasmus's Learned Joking: The Ironic Use of Classical Wisdom in *The Praise of Folly*." *Texas Studies in Literature and Language* 19 (1977): 246–67.

Reiss, Timothy. *Toward Dramatic Illusion*. New Haven, Conn.: Yale Univ. Press, 1971.

Renza, Louis A. "The Veto of the Imagination: A Theory of Autobiography." In Olney, ed., *Autobiography: Essays Theoretical and Critical*, pp. 268–95.

Rhu, Lawrence. "From Aristotle to Allegory: Young Tasso's Evolving Vision of the *Gerusalemme Liberata*." *Italica* 65 (1988): 111–30.

Richter, Mario, ed. *Convegno di studi su Pierre Corneille*. Vicenza: Accademia Olimpica, 1984.

Riley-Smith, Jonathan. *The First Crusade and the Idea of Crusading*. Philadelphia: Univ. of Pennsylvania Press, 1986.

Rima, Beatrice. "La Metafora dello specchio dal Tasso al Marino." *Lingua e Stile* 18 (1983): 75–92.

Rohou, Jean. "The Articulation of Social, Ideological and Literary Practices in France: The Historical Moment of 1641–43." In Francis Barker, ed., *1642*, pp. 139–65. Essex: Univ. of Essex Press, 1981.

Rosaldo, Renato. "From the Door of His Tent: The Fieldworker and the Inquisitor." In James Clifford and George E. Marcus, eds., *Writing Culture*, pp. 77–97. Berkeley: Univ. of California Press, 1986.

Rossi, Rosa. *Esperienza interiore e storia nell'autobiografia di Teresa d'Avila.* Bari: Adriatica, 1977.

Rousset, Jean. "Le Destinataire de l'illusion théâtrale." In Richter, ed., *Convegno di studi su Pierre Corneille*, pp. 41–48.

———. *L'Intérieur et l'extérieur*. Paris: José Corti, 1968.

Ruether, Rosemary Radford, ed. *Religion and Sexism: Images of Woman in the Jewish and Christian Traditions*. New York: Simon and Schuster, 1974.

———. *Sexism and God-Talk: Toward a Feminist Theology*. Boston: Beacon Press, 1983.

Ruether, Rosemary Radford, and Eleanor McLaughlin, eds. *Women of Spirit: Female Leadership in the Jewish and Christian Traditions*. New York: Simon and Schuster, 1979.

Sacks, Peter. *The English Elegy: Studies in the Genre from Spenser to Yeats*. Baltimore, Md.: Johns Hopkins Univ. Press, 1985.

Sakharoff, Micheline. *Le Héros, sa liberté et son efficacité de Garnier à Rotrou*. Paris: Nizet, 1967.

Salmons, June. "An Unpublished Account of the End of Este Rule in Ferrara: Niccolo Contarini's *Istorie Veneziane* and Events in Ferrara, 1597–98." In June Salmons and Walter Moretti, eds., *The Renaissance in Ferrara and Its European Horizons*, pp. 123–44. Cardiff: Univ. of Wales Press, 1984.

Saxer, Victor. *Le Culte de Marie Madeleine en Occident*. 2 vols. Paris: Clavrenil, 1959.

Schenck, Celeste Marguerite. *Mourning and Panegyric: The Poetics of Pastoral Ceremony*. University Park: Pennsylvania State Univ. Press, 1988.

Scherer, Colette. *Comédie et société sous Louis XIII*. Paris: Nizet, 1983.

Schoenbaum, Samuel. *William Shakespeare: A Compact Documentary Life*. New York: Oxford Univ. Press, 1977.

Scrivano, Riccardo. *La Norma e lo scarto*. Rome: Bonacci, 1980.

Searle, Colbert. "L'Académie française et *Le Cid*." *Revue d'histoire littéraire de la France* 21 (1914): 331–74.

Seneca. *De clementia*. Ed. Carolus Hosius. Leipzig: B. G. Teubneri, 1900.

———. *Moral Essays*. Trans. John W. Basore. 3 vols. London: Heinemann, 1928.

———. *Seneca ad Lucilium Epistulae Morales*. Trans. Richard M. Gummere. 3 vols. London: Heinemann, 1917.

Sessions, William. "Spenser's Georgics." *English Literary Renaissance* 10 (1980): 202–37.

Setton, Kenneth M. *The Papacy and the Levant, 1204–1571*. Philadelphia: American Philosophical Society, 1976.

Shakespeare, William. *First Folio: A Facsimile Edition*. Ed. Helge Kökeritz. New Haven, Conn.: Yale Univ. Press, 1954.

———. *The Riverside Shakespeare*. Ed. G. Blakemore Evans. Boston: Houghton Mifflin, 1974.

———. *The Winter's Tale*. Ed. J. H. P. Pafford. London: Methuen, 1963. Reprint. London: Routledge, 1988.

Shore, David. *Spenser and the Poetics of Pastoral: A Study of the World of Colin Clout*. Montreal: McGill-Queens, 1985.

Slights, Camille Wells. "The Politics of Conscience in *All is True* (or *Henry VIII*)." *Shakespeare Survey* 43 (1990): 59–68.

Smith, Paul Julian. "Writing Women in Golden Age Spain: Saint Teresa and María de Zayas." *Modern Language Notes* 102 (1987): 220–40.

Smith, Peter L. "Lentus in Umbra." *Phoenix* 19 (1965): 298–304.

Snyder, Jon. *Writing the Scene of Speaking: Theories of Dialogue in the Late Italian Renaissance*. Stanford, Calif.: Stanford Univ. Press, 1989.

Soare, Antoine. "Parodie et catharsis tragi-comique." *French Forum* 9 (1984): 276–89.

Sohn-Rethel, Alfred. *Intellectual and Manual Labor: A Critique of Epistemology*. Atlantic Highlands, N.J.: Humanities Press, 1978.

Solerti, Angelo. *Ferrara e la corte Estense*. Città di Castello: S. Lapi, 1900.

Spenser, Edmund. *Complaints*. Ed. W. L. Renwick. London: Scholartis Press, 1928.

———. *The Faerie Queene*. Ed. Thomas P. Roche. New Haven, Conn.: Yale Univ. Press, 1981.

———. *Spenser's Minor Poems*. Ed. Ernest de Sélincourt. Oxford: Clarendon Press, 1910.

Spini, Giorgio. *Cosimo I e l'independenza del principato mediceo*. Florence: Valecchi, 1980.

The Stage-Players Complaint (1641) and *The Actors Remonstrance or Complaint* (1643). In Charles Hindley, ed., *The Old Book Collector's Miscellany*, vol. 3. London: Reeves and Turner, 1873.

Stallybrass, Peter. "Patriarchal Territories: The Body Enclosed." In Ferguson, Quilligan, and Vickers, eds., *Rewriting the Renaissance*, pp. 123–42.

Stanton, Domna C. "Autogynography: Is the Subject Different?" In Domna Stanton, ed., *The Female Autograph*, pp. 3–20. Chicago: Univ. of Chicago Press, 1987.

Starobinski, Jean. *The Living Eye*. Trans. Arthur Goldhammer. Cambridge, Mass.: Harvard Univ. Press, 1989.

———. *L'Oeil vivant*. Paris: Gallimard, 1961.

Steensgaard, Niels. "The Seventeenth-Century Crisis." In Geoffrey Parker and Lesley M. Smith, eds., *The General Crisis of the Seventeenth Century*, pp. 26–51. London: Routledge and Kegan Paul, 1978.

Stegmann, André. *L'Héroisme Cornélien: Genèse et signification*. 2 vols. Paris: Armand Colin, 1968.

Stephens, Walter. "Saint Paul Among the Amazons: Gender and Authority in *Gerusalemme Liberata*." In Kevin Brownlee and Walter Stephens, eds., *Discourses of Authority in Medieval and Renaissance Literature*, pp. 169–200. Hanover, N.H.: Univ. Press of New England, 1989.

———. "Tasso's Allegory." Paper presented at the Villa Spelman in Florence, Italy, July 1989.

Strier, Richard. "Faithful Servants: Shakespeare's Praise of Disobedience." In Heather Dubrow and Richard Strier, eds., *The Historical Renaissance*, pp. 104–33. Chicago: Univ. of Chicago Press, 1988.

Struever, Nancy S. *Theory as Practice: Ethical Inquiry in the Renaissance*. Chicago: Univ. of Chicago Press, 1992.

Tassi, Francesco. *Ricordi, prose e poesie di Benvenuto Cellini con documenti la maggior parte inediti in seguito e ad illustrazione dellà 'Vita' del medesimo*. Florence, 1829.

Tasso, Torquato. *Aminta*. Ed. B. T. Sozzi. Padua: Sansoni, 1957.

———. *Aminta di Torquato Tasso*. Paris, 1584.

———. *Aminta e Rime*. Ed. Francesco Flora. 2 vols. Turin: Ricciardi, 1976.

———. *Discorsi dell'arte poetica e in particolare sopra il poema eroico*. In Ettore Mazzali, ed., *Scritti sull'arte poetica*, vol. 1, pp. 3–64. Turin: Einaudi, 1977.

———. *Gerusalemme Conquistata*. Ed. Luigi Bonfigli. 2 vols. Bari: Laterza e figli, 1934.

———. *Gerusalemme Liberata*. Ed. Fredi Chiappelli. Milan: Rusconi, 1982.

———. *Gerusalemme Liberata, Edizione Critica*. Ed. Angelo Solerti et al. 3 vols. Florence, 1895.

———. *Lettere di Torquato Tasso*. Ed. Cesare Guasti. 5 vols. Florence: Le Monnier, 1901.

Tennenhouse, Leonard. *Power on Display: The Politics of Shakespeare's Genres*. New York: Methuen, 1986.

Teresa of Avila. *The Complete Works of Saint Teresa of Jesus*. Trans. E. Allison Peers. 3 vols. New York: Sheed and Ward, 1946.

———. *The Interior Castle*. Trans. E. Allison Peers. New York: Image Books, 1961.

———. *Libro de la Vida*. Ed. Guido Mancini. Madrid: Taurus, 1982.

———. *Las Moradas*. Ed. Tomás Navarro Tomás. Madrid: Espasa-Calpe, 1962.

Thomson, Peter. "Playhouses and Players in the Time of Shakespeare." In Stanley Wells, ed., *The Cambridge Companion to Shakespeare Studies*. Cambridge: Cambridge Univ. Press, 1986.

Thornley, I. "The Destruction of Sanctuary." In R. W. Seton-Watson, ed., *Tudor Studies*, pp. 182–207. London: Longmans, 1924.

Thuau, Etienne. *Raison d'état et pensée politique à l'époque de Richelieu*. Paris: Armand Colin, 1966.

Tottel's Miscellany. Ed. Hyder E. Rollins. Cambridge, Mass.: Harvard Univ. Press, 1966 [1557].

Trento, Dario. *Benvenuto Cellini: Opere non esposte e documenti notarili*. Florence: Museo Nazionale del Bargello, 1984.

Turner, James. *The Politics of Landscape*. Oxford: Oxford Univ. Press, 1979.

Tuve, Rosemond. *Seasons and Months: Studies in a Tradition of Middle English Poetry*. Paris: Libraire universitaire, 1933.

Ubersfeld, Anne. "Corneille: Du roi au tyran, un itinéraire." In Milorad R. Margitić, ed., *L'Image du souverain dans le théâtre de 1600 à 1650*, pp. 11–44. Paris: Papers on French Seventeenth Century Literature, 1987.

———. "'Je suis' ou l'identité héroïque chez Corneille." In Niderst, ed., *Pierre Corneille*, pp. 641–50.

Underdown, David. "The Taming of the Scold: The Enforcement of Patriarchal Authority in Early Modern England." In Anthony Fletcher and John Stevenson, eds., *Order and Disorder in Early Modern England*, pp. 116–36. Cambridge: Cambridge Univ. Press, 1985.

Varese, Claudio. *Torquato Tasso: Epos, parola, scena*. Florence: Messina, 1976.

Vasari, Giorgio. *Le Vite dei più eccellenti pittori, scultori e architetti*. Ed. G. Milanesi. 9 vols. Florence: 1878–85.

Venturi, Gianni. *Le Scene dell'Eden: Teatro, arte, giardini nella letteratura italiana*. Ferrara: Italo Bovolenta, 1979.

Verhoeff, Hans. "Le Don chez Corneille." In Margitić, ed., *Corneille comique*, pp. 15–34.

Vickers, Nancy. "'The Blazon of Sweet Beauty's Best': Shakespeare's *Lucrece*." In Parker and Hartman, eds., *Shakespeare and the Question of Theory*, pp. 95–116.

———. "Diana Described: Scattered Woman and Scattered Rhyme." *Critical Inquiry* 8 (1981): 265–79.

———. "The Mistress in the Masterpiece." In Nancy K. Miller, ed., *The Poetics of Gender*, pp. 19–41. New York: Columbia University Press, 1986.

Villanueva, Francisco Márquez. "Santa Teresa y el linaje." In *Espiritualidad y literatura en el siglo XVI*, pp. 142–205. Madrid: Alfaguara, 1968.

Virgil. *Works*. Trans. H. R. Fairclough. 2 vols. Cambridge, Mass.: Harvard Univ. Press, 1974.

Vives, Juan Luis. "In Georgica Vergilii" [1518]. In *Obras completas*, trans. Lorenzo Riber, vol. 1, pp. 543–52. Madrid: Aguilar, 1948.

Wallerstein, Immanuel. *The Modern World-System*. 2 vols. New York: Academic Press, 1980.

Warner, Marina. *Alone of All Her Sex: The Myth and the Cult of the Virgin Mary*. New York: Knopf, 1976.

Weber, Alison. *Teresa of Avila and the Rhetoric of Femininity*. Princeton, N.J.: Princeton Univ. Press, 1990.

Weimann, Robert. "History and the Issue of Authority in Representation: The Elizabethan Theater and the Reformation." *New Literary History* 17, no. 3 (1986): 449–76.

———. "Mimesis in *Hamlet*." In Parker and Hartman, eds., *Shakespeare and the Question of Theory*, pp. 275–91.

Weinberg, Bernard. *A History of Literary Criticism in the Italian Renaissance*. 2 vols. Chicago: Univ. of Chicago Press, 1961.

Weiner, Andrew. "Spenser and the Myth of Pastoral." *Studies in Philology* 85 (1988): 390–406.

Whigham, Frank. *Ambition and Privilege: The Social Tropes of Elizabethan Courtesy Theory*. Berkeley: Univ. of California Press, 1984.

Wickham, Glynn. "King Lear as Prologue: From Tragedy to Tragicomedy." *Shakespeare Survey* 26 (1973): 33–48.

Wiggins, Peter. *Figures in Ariosto's Tapestry*. Baltimore, Md.: Johns Hopkins Univ. Press, 1986.

Wilkinson, L. P. *The Georgics of Virgil*. Cambridge: Cambridge Univ. Press, 1969.

Williams, Raymond. *The Country and the City*. Oxford: Oxford Univ. Press, 1973.

Williamson, Marilyn. *The Patriarchy of Shakespeare's Comedies*. Detroit: Wayne State Univ. Press, 1986.

Wittkower, Rudolf, and Margot Wittkower. *Born Under Saturn*. New York: Norton, 1963.

Woodbridge, Linda. *Women and the English Renaissance*. Urbana: Univ. of Illinois Press, 1984.

Wright, A. D. "The Borromean Ideal and the Spanish Church." In Headley and Tomaro, eds., *San Carlo Borromeo*, pp. 188–207.

Yates, Frances. *Astraea: The Imperial Theme in the Sixteenth Century*. London: Ark, 1985.

———. *Renaissance and Reform: The Italian Contribution.* 2 vols. London: Routledge and Kegan Paul, 1983.

Yoch, James J. "The Limits of Sensuality: Pastoral Wilderness." *Forum Italicum* 16 (1982): 60–81.

Zatti, Sergio. *L'Uniforme cristiano e il moltiforme pagano: Saggio sulla "Gerusalemme Liberata."* Milan: Saggiatore, 1983.

Index

In this index an "f" after a number indicates a separate reference on the next page, and an "ff" indicates separate references on the next two pages. A continuous discussion over two or more pages is indicated by a span of page numbers, e.g., "57–59." *Passim* is used for a cluster of references in close but not consecutive sequence.

NOTTINGHAM
WITHDRAWN
UNIVERSITY LIBRARY

Library of Congress Cataloging-in-Publication Data

Tylus, Jane, 1956–
Writing and vulnerability in the late Renaissance / Jane Tylus.
p. cm.
Includes bibliographical references and index.
ISBN 0-8047-2138-6
1. European literature—Renaissance, 1450–1600—History and criticism.
2. Subjectivity in literature. 3. Authorship. 4. Dependence (Psychology)
in literature. 5. Autonomy (Psychology) in literature. I. Title.
PN721.T95 1993
809'.894'09031—dc20 92-32209
CIP
REV.

∞ This book is printed on acid-free paper.